TEA PARTY

THE AWAKENING

Foreword by
&
Anthology Compiled by
Brent Morehouse

Copy Editor
John Matthew Fox

TEA PARTY – THE AWAKENING

Copyright © 2010 by Brent Morehouse
All rights reserved.

New Patriot Publishing

www.newpatriotpublishing.com

Hardcover Edition
ISBN – 0-9828885-2-X
ISBN – 978-0-9828885-2-0

Paperback Edition
ISBN – 0-9828885-0-3
ISBN – 978-0-9828885-0-6

Kindle Edition (Ebook)
ISBN – 0-9828885-1-1
ISBN – 978-0-9828885-1-3

LCCN – 2010910822

Printed in the United States of America.

Preface

It was 11:00 PM and my cell phone was ringing…

…I went to the dining room table where I had left my phone, I didn't recognize the area code, I smiled. Before this, I would ignore unrecognized area codes—especially on my cell phone, and at 11:00 at night! However, since I began contacting Grassroots leaders throughout the nation, I looked forward to speaking with another 'stranger,' a stranger who would ultimately transform into a friend—over hundreds or thousands of miles, without face-to-face contact.

I answered the call. It was Randy. When we spoke a week or so ago, he had mentioned that he wasn't very proficient on the keyboard, so he preferred to write down his story for me. He called me at 11:00 PM just to read it to me.

I listened to this man, in his sixties, a veteran, a Purple Heart recipient, I listened to him tell his story, I listened to the sound of the pages rustling as he turned them over, I listened as tears ran down my cheeks. I will never forget that moment.

The emotion I felt was extreme humility that I had the honor of being the first one to hear his story, but also sound confirmation that the fabric of our Country is still woven with Patriots.

TEA PARTY – THE AWAKENING

www.newpatriotpublishing.com

Acknowledgements

Since this book is mostly written by the Grassroots leaders themselves, their stories provide honest and accurate insights about the movement.

While they prefer the term "organizers" over the term "leaders," in my mind they are leaders because they took it upon themselves to lead rallies, often taking the responsibility for all the necessary steps, especially for their first rally. Many told me that they had no idea how many people would show up to their first rally. Their efforts were rewarded with amazing turnouts.

As you read their stories, you will see many acknowledgements made by the Grassroots leaders themselves.

I would also like to acknowledge my wife, Susan, who was not only supportive of this endeavor from the very beginning, but also actively assisting me, my children Ali and Sam, who would always ask about the book daddy was working on. Friends who helped me along the way, supportive with ideas, and honest feedback; James, Ayres, Gaylene and Pam, thank you. Matt, for assisting me in contacting hundreds of Tea Party and 9-12 group leaders.

www.newpatriotpublishing.com

Foreword

I was intrigued when a friend invited me to a Tea Party Rally that was being held in Orange County, California. It was early in 2009, my friend had made a sign, and though I don't recall what it said, I attended empty handed.

I didn't know what to expect. Apparently, neither did the local officials, since they had uniformed police officers everywhere, including a horse-mounted "regiment"! *(ok, it wasn't a regiment, but maybe a company, and they* were *horse-mounted.)*

The attendance was somewhere around 2,000 people, and most of the people attending had signs made up—which told me that they had planned on attending this event for at least the amount of time it took to get a sign made.

The event was very peaceful. I did not hear or see any arguments between attendees and on-lookers, even though lunchtime pedestrian traffic in the County Court Building district was especially heavy.

Although the Tea Party (TEA) is sometimes referred to as an acronym for Taxed Enough Already, that rally (and subsequent rallies I have attended) wasn't focused on paying taxes, at least not as a primary theme. I don't know who created that acronym, but it is not an accurate or all-encompassing definition of the movement.

If I were to classify a "theme" of the rally, I would say that the people attending, and those who spoke (the rally speakers), were venting their frustration about the irresponsibility of our federal government in areas as diverse as immigration, entitlements, freedom of speech, social security, recent healthcare legislation and reckless spending.

The "Like Always" Approach is Not Working

Looking back, I was attracted to the movement because I saw other people who, like me, realized at some level that the system was broken, and that the "like always" approach was not working. If this were not the case, then they, and I, would have stayed home, possibly put a political sign in the yard, a bumper sticker on the car, and maybe even written a check to our favorite candidate (The 'like always' approach). Another way to put it, our 'like always' approach, has resulted in their 'business as usual' approach!

Whether people came to this conclusion consciously or subconsciously, I think this conclusion is the key ingredient of the authentic grassroots movement, and the catalyst for its massive growth.

Unintentional Author

Not long after that first rally, I decided I had to do something for myself. I had to read, I had to research, I couldn't continue to trust that all would just keep operating "like always." I had finally woken up, from apathy to a defensive mode of my country.

I made a decision to educate myself, to get informed. The first thing I did was to read and study the Constitution. Embarrassing as it was at the time, I didn't recall *ever* reading the Constitution or even the Federalist Papers. Then I started researching the major geopolitical topics, deficit spending, the national and public debt, unfunded future liabilities, trade deficits, off-shoring of U.S. jobs, social issues of the day and so on.

I consumed books, I learned about all these topics and more—international banking, currency valuations, currency crisis, debt crisis, balance of payments, the true costs of trade deficits, the relationship between the federal government and the state governments, movements within the state governments aimed at resisting the unbridled growth of the federal government, and so on.

I wrote down what I learned and what I still had questions about. Not long after I started this, maybe two or three months, I decided to turn my notes into a book project. It would be a political book unlike most on the shelves. It would contain research information (like others) that would serve to legitimize our grievances; however, it would also provide a fresh new path, a new approach with specific solutions. This book would not pit Republicans against Democrats, and it would not attempt to classify people as conservatives or liberals. That is how I became an unintentional author of *Bill Of Reform*.

What about *this* book? *Tea Party – The Awakening*?

Working on *Bill of Reform* actually took me down a path of being yet again, an unintentional author. Near the end of my writing and research, I decided to contact Tea Party Leaders (rally organizers).

I asked them if they would give me their personal stories. What specifically motivated them to get involved: what did they hear, what did they see, or what did they experience?

My purpose for doing this was to incorporate "a few" of these stories into the foreword section of my book, since I wrote about attending my first Tea Party, and the path I took after waking up.

Encouragement and Validation

Quite honestly, I minimized this by underestimating the impact it would have on me. Something happened that I did not quite expect, after speaking with a half dozen or so of the rally organizers, and reading the stories that they had sent to me. I knew that I needed to contact as many Tea Party leaders as I could.

These stories were compelling, they were encouraging, funny, each was unique and they validated many of my beliefs and concerns. I absolutely wanted to read more.

Not only did I want to read as many stories as I could get, I also enjoyed speaking to the Tea Party leaders over the phone. Our conversations covered many topics. As I listened, I began to get a uniform picture of the movement—naturally, because it was being told by the rally organizers themselves, both in the stories they submitted to me and during our many, many conversations.

These stories also contain words of wisdom, prudent cautions, and embodied civic courage that was refreshing, and which I think will appeal to others. In my research work, I had read many writings of our founding fathers, who were the original "Tea Partiers." Our founding fathers did not operate in a vacuum—they were deliberate and disciplined about their writings to each other. The letters between Madison and Jefferson alone would fill three volumes the size of phone books.

I decided to collate these stories and give them back to the Tea Party leaders that I had contacted. My hopes were that they would be encouraged and that their efforts would be validated even more after reading these personal stories from other leaders within the movement.

I've had the privilege of contacting hundreds of Tea Party, 9-12 and other group leaders, organizers and speakers, with written correspondence and many very, very long phone calls! I can't tell you how many times I got the "look" from my wife while I was standing over the BBQ grill in our back yard, on the phone. You know the look.

The Establishment

The Tea Party movement has been an enigma for many in the press. Since the press is conditioned to the "like always" approach, they don't know what to think of these movements. The political parties are also confused and threatened by them—they don't know for sure if they are adversaries, or if they represent a momentum that could be harnessed for their own continuous and never ending gains. As such, we have seen the movement treated as both adversary to the status quo and as an opportunity for political advancement.

Bill Clinton recently referred to the Tea Party movement as "confused people who don't know where their place in society is." I don't think Bill Clinton actually believes that, but why would he say it?

Because he is the DH, the Designated Hitter—he has no office to protect, no future political aspirations to guard, and therefore he is the perfect hit-man to try to convince as many people as possible not to join the movement. After all, who would want to be associated with a bunch of confused people?

That is just one example of the establishment's reaction to the Tea Party Movement. Because the Democrats currently hold most of the D.C. power, they feel threatened by a grassroots movement that is fed up with the establishment. On the other side of the coin, since the Republicans are on the "out" right now and desperately want back in, they initially saw this as a movement that they could automatically co-opt.

However, we have seen this co-opt movement from the GOP fizzle in many areas, why? Because the GOP found out that the Tea Party movement isn't quite happy with them either!

Senator Lindsey Graham (R-SC) recently said in an interview that he thought the Tea Party would die out because they don't have a cohesive vision.

The established parties want to make sure of *one thing*—they stay in power. There you have it, the reason the Tea Party and groups like 9-12 and others exist. They are convinced that we need to purge Congress of incumbents within both parties and that we need to elect citizens whose ambitions lie in restoring our country to its historical roots.

Is this Brent just speculating? No, I made it a point to ask every Tea Party leader the following question. "If this were a Presidential election year, and since the Republicans are on the 'outside', if they were to win control of Congress and the White House, would our problems be fixed?"

Everyone I asked couldn't say *"No"* fast enough! There was not one person who even tried to qualify the answer, such as, "well, it depends on how long they have control for" ... or some other type of qualification. Nada, zip. That is why Graham, a Republican Washington insider, is fearful of the Tea Party movement.

Also, every Tea Party leader confirmed the following statement: "The reason you and I, strangers to each other, are talking to each other across this country, is because our federal government has grown unconstitutionally and is out of control."

FOREWORD

An Accurate Depiction

I think Lesley Hollywood, a Tea Party leader, says it best:

> "Pundits would analyze the movement from the out-
> side, rarely able to agree on what was happening on
> the inside. I always found it humorous that no one
> would come inside the movement and talk to those
> who were heavily involved before forming opinions.
> Well, they were all wrong. The Tea Party is the epi-
> tome of an organic grassroots movement, so de-
> centralized some may consider it a fault. It consists of
> people like me, your average moms and dads, busi-
> nessmen and laborers, the unemployed and the
> overworked, the young and trendy, the old and tradi-
> tional."

I went inside the movement, and the story needs to be told.

Then and Now

The name Tea Party refers to the famous Boston Tea Party—most
everyone recalls reading about the angry mob that threw the King's
Tea into Boston Harbor. Also, most probably remember the "no
taxation without representation" principle that was a central theme
of the movement, a movement that turned into a revolution.

Other than the name, is there anything else we should know about
the Tea Party movement of the 1770s? That is a question I asked
myself. I was not prepared for the answers I found.

Taking a closer look, the 1773 Tea Party was not just about taxes. It was about liberty and the acknowledgement of Natural
Law. We'll talk more about Natural Law a little later.

The Tea Act passed by Parliament actually *reduced* the colonies'
cost for tea by 50% , including the tax! The members of the Brit-

ish House of Commons couldn't understand why the "dull moorish mobs" in the colonies were so bent on rebellion. Parliament clearly did not understand Natural Law.

There are amazing similarities between today and the 1770s. I've grouped these similarities into three categories: *Political, Economic, and Subversive Actions.*

1770s Tea Party: Why Did It Exist?

The 1770s Tea Party movement began because of unconstitutional acts, acts perpetuated over decades (most notably starting in 1733 with the Molasses Act) which finally came to a head with the Stamp Act, the Townshend Acts, The Tea Act and the Coercive Acts. *(The English 'Constitution' was an unwritten one, however, like the words 'Just' and 'Unjust', it existed, and is the reason we have a 'written' Constitution today).* The most famous of these was the Tea Act. Over decades, these acts became the millstone around the early Americans' necks. The Boston Tea Party was the most prominent display of unified outrage towards the tyranny of these unconstitutional acts. The Sons & Daughters of Liberty would not be satisfied simply with the repeal of the Tea Act—the tipping point had been reached. It is noteworthy that although the Tea Act of 1773 was the tipping point, there were still other acts including the Coercive Acts that were passed after the Tea Act.

2010 Tea Party: Why Does It Exist?

The 2010 Tea Party exists because unconstitutional acts that have existed for decades finally came to a head with the recent Acts of TARP, the stimulus packages and the Health Care Act. The most famous of these was the Health Care Act. These acts are a millstone around the proverbial necks of Americans today. The Tea Party Rallies are the most prominent displays of unified outrage towards the tyranny that has crept into our government. The Tea Party movement today, will not be satisfied with merely the repeal of the Health Care legislation—the tipping point has been reached. It is noteworthy to point out that although the Health Care Act was the tipping point, there were still other acts such as the Financial Reform Bill that have been passed after the Health Care Act.

1770s Tea Party: Grassroots or Establishment?

Early Tea Partiers had solid grassroots origins. Americans were outraged throughout the colonies, although the Boston Tea Party was the event that gained notoriety, other cities and ports had their own Tea Parties. The "like always" approach of sending petitions to Parliament and King George was not working. Early Americans consumed a lot of tea! Instead of drinking tea, they switched to coffee, a preference that still exists today.

2010 Tea Party: Grassroots or Establishment?

The current Tea Party is unabashedly grassroots. Americans today are angry and frustrated at the modern Parliament, which is not only Congress but the whole federal government. Our "like always" approach of electing over 90% of incumbents as career politicians in both parties, has not worked. With no corporate headquarters and no national committee, millions of Americans are coming out of their daily lives to show that they are angry and frustrated with the irresponsible and arrogant leadership that exists today in our federal government. *In both parties.*

1770s: The Awakening

The common explanation of the time was that people were awakening to the existing tyrannies they had been living with. Patrick Henry's speech in the House of Burgesses was described as a blast that was blown from the "trumpet of sedition," waking Americans from their lethargy.[1]

---

[1] John C. Miller, *Origins of the American Revolution, 122*

"When all this black roll of impositions is view'd together, what a shocking series of partial, tyrannic oppression do they present," exclaimed an American in 1776. [2]

2010: The Awakening

The common explanation from Tea Partiers today is that they "woke up." Ordinary citizens with no political backgrounds *chose* to wake up when they recognized the threat to their liberty. It wasn't just their own liberties that were threatened, though—many Tea Partiers have commited themselves to the movement in order to preserve and restore the same liberties for their children and grandchildren: "I thought about my children and my grandchildren and I wanted them to know that I was part of making a difference for them to live a better life."[3] While not a member of a State Assembly (like Henry), Rick Santelli's famous February 19, 2009 'rant' on the CME trading floor in Chicago was the wake-up call for many snoozing Patriots.

1770s: Called Every Name In The Book

The Tea Partiers of the 1770s era were called the Sons of Liberty, a name given to them during a speech in Parliament by a sympathetic member of the House of Commons. The Daughters of Liberty, a named derived from the Sons of Liberty, was commonly used to describe the Patriotic women of the time: "One prudent matron, by a strict economy at the head of her family, will do more for the good of her country than five hundred noisy Sons of Liberty, with all their mobs and riots."[4]

However, *never* did the establishment in England or in the colonies use "Sons of Liberty" as a description.

[2] John C. Miller, *Origins of the American Revolution,* 22, *Pennsylvania Packet*, May 13, 1776
[3] Joan Sterling, *Tea Party The Awakening*
[4] John Penn to Thomas Penn, Dec. 15, 1765, Penn MSS., Historical Society of Pennsylvania. John C. Miller, *Origins of the American Revolution, 140*

They preferred "radicals," "mongrel breeds," and "madmen." The establishment was riddled with elitists who described the Tea Partiers of the 1770s as "the scum or offscouring of all nations, leavened with convicts and outcasts."[5] They deplored that any "crack-brained zealot for democracy" should be listened to in America.

2010: Called Every Name In The Book

Today, the establishment in Congress and the established media have characterized the Tea Party participants as being confused, angry, frustrated, violent, and the seemingly un-fatigue-able racist (just to name a few). Recently a CNN reporter covering a Tea Party rally (which depicted grandmas in folding chairs!) said, "this is not what I consider family viewing!" as she signed off to her reporting station, after arguing with one of the rally attendees. Fatigueable

1770s: The Political Parties

Within each Colonial House of Assembly (members were elected by Americans), there were Tories and Whigs. These two parties defined the establishment within the American political sphere of influence. The Royal Governor was appointed by the Crown, while the Upper House of Legislature, the Council, was appointed by the Governor. The Tories were considered at the time (by the Tea Partiers of 1770s), as obstacles to independence—they were socialists and imperialists. A well-known Tory of Massachusetts, Thomas Hutchinson, in a confidential letter to a English friend (intercepted by the sticky fingers of Benjamin Franklin!), combated the "loose, false and absurd notion" of independence, and that "an abridgement of what are called English liberties" in America were needed to keep the colonies in subjection.

---

[5] *Morning Post and Daily Advertiser*, Jan. 7, 1775, John C. Miller *Origins of the American Revolution, 203*

The Whigs were viewed by the Tea Partiers as the party more in line with their yearnings for freedom and true independence from England. I think it is fair to say that at this stage in history, the Tories would more likely be viewed as the modern Democrats, and the Whigs would more likely be viewed as the modern Republicans. Trust me, that is not an accolade for the Republican leadership of today!

2010: The Political Parties

We know them, Democrats and Republicans. The Tea Partiers of today view the Democratic leadership as obstacles to freedom, and principles of personal responsibility, they view the Democratic leadership as being taken over by socialists, and elitist rulers (at best). President Obama, currently the top leader of the Democratic Party, recently told Congressional Democrats that he was "amused by the Tea Party protests."[6] The Tea Party movement views the Republican party as more in line with their goals, such as limited government and responsible fiscal policies.

1770s: Whigs Show Their True Colors

The Tea Partiers were more than rioters, although their public rallies often contained effigies of their perceived tyrannical leaders hung by the neck. They also focused their anger and frustration toward creating change. They realized the practical barriers of the aristocracy that existed in the colonial parties, both within the Tories and the Whigs, would be hard to supplant from the outside. So they decided to court the Whigs (the Whigs were more than willing to listen, *at first*).

Two famous Whig families were the DeLanceys and the Livingstons, who constantly vied for control over the New York assembly, *the powers of government.*

---

[6] *www.gatewaypundit.firstthings.com/2010/04*

Oliver DeLancey, at first, openly attended the meetings (rallies) of the Tea Partiers and spoke of his patriotism like the "common people." But DeLancey soon shattered the hopes of this co-opt between the Tea Partiers and the Whigs when he withdrew his support and organized his own group of Tea Partiers! When other Whigs realized that if the revolutionary movement were not stopped it would escape from their control and lead to the rule of the common people, they attempted to halt the tide. *They became Tories!*[7] The Tea Partiers were becoming increasingly intolerant of those "timid or trimming Whigs" who sought safety in the middle of the road. "When a Country is divided," they declared, "*Neutrality* is little better than *Treason!*"[8]

In the end, the Declaration of Independence wasn't just a victory of the Whigs over the Tories, it was the radical faction of the Whigs (The Tea Partiers) that won over the establishment faction of the Whigs. The established Whigs had opposed independence hardly less than the Tories! The difference was also that the Whigs finally checked their consciences and threw in their lot with the Tea Partiers.

2010: The GOP Shows Their True Colors

Today's Tea Partiers are more than rioters, although they can be seen at rallies with signs (probably no hung effigies). They are channeling their anger and frustration toward creating change. Since the Democrats are the current "ruling" party, there has been somewhat of a trial courtship between the Tea Partiers and the GOP.

The GOP is naturally attracted by this wave of energy by millions of *voters*, and of course, since the GOP is on the outside looking in, they see the Tea Party as an opportunity to ride the wave back into power. Again, these are the *natural instincts of a political party.*

[7] John C. Miller, *Origins of the American Revolution, 300, 301*
[8] *Ibid.*, 298, *Boston Gazette*, August 7, 1769

TEA PARTY – THE AWAKENING

The Tea Partiers viewed the GOP as more in line with them for a couple of reasons. First, there are more Republicans in the Tea Party than Democrats. Varying polls put the numbers at around 57% Republicans and 43% Democrats/Independents. So the first natural inclination is to look at not only "your" party, but also, as it turns out in this case, the party that is out of power (receiving less blame) than the party in power. Secondly, nearly all Tea Partiers realize the barriers that exist in creating a third party, hence another reason to a trial courtship with the GOP, (the GOP was more than willing to listen, *at first*).

So what happened? When it became clear that the GOP was more concerned about the GOP than the direction of the country, the Tea Partiers weren't too happy with them. Just like the establishment Whigs in the 1770s, the establishment in the GOP showed their true colors.

But isn't it true that the Tea Partiers are more apt to support Republicans than Democrats? Yes, it is; however, the Tea Partiers of today, just like in the 1770s, are mostly working within the boundaries of a two party system. They realize to affect change, it will be much easier to replace the Republican obstacles (establishment) than to create a third party. The two party system is very entrenched by laws in each State, obviously for protecting the two parties. However, these laws don't provide protection from within! Just like the Democratic Party Leadership has been taken over by Socialists, the Republican Party Leadership will be taken over by Patriots. So although it may be a (R) that is on the ticket, the "R" stands for *Reformer*, rather than Republican.

Remember how the establishment in New York (lead by the Delaneys) spun off and created their own group of protesters in the 1770s? The same thing has happened today.

Fearing the Tea Party movement, a group was created called the Patriot Majority. However, unlike a grassroots movement, this group was created largely by two people: Craig Varoga and George Rakis, both Democratic Party strategists! Patriot Majority funded American Public Policy Center (APPC), which has in turn created a web site called TheTeaPartyIsOver.org.[9] Its only substantial airtime occurred when CBS News (go figure) set up a "Tea Party Conflict" story, which hosted Craig Varoga pitted against Debbie Dooley of the Tea Party Patriots, a coalition of Tea Party groups that represent tens of millions of Americans.

Just like the 1770s, the real grassroots movement cannot be co-opted and it cannot be artificially re-created to serve an opposite agenda. By the way, who funds Patriot Majority? Service Employees International Union, Workers of America, Teamsters Union, United Food & Commercial Workers Union: "But by far the largest donations have come from a collection of unionized government workers, the American Federation of State, County and Municipal Employees (AFSCME)" Contributing millions of dollars.[10] You *really* should read this article.

1770s: More Than Signs and Riots

The Tea Partiers of the 1770s were not only getting their physical exercise at riots (rallies) they were also exercising their brains. The Tea Party movement started in anger and frustration, but quickly added a feverous desire for knowledge. Although Americans in the 1770s were not highly educated, they were very well read. *They didn't pay others to read to them.*

Americans began to consume books at a rate never seen before, especially in the history of colonial peoples and principles of liberty and natural law.

[9] Joseph Abrams, *Anti-Tea Party Web Site Part of Scheme to Funnel Funds Published Feb. 10, 2010 : FoxNews.com www.foxnews.com/politics/2010/02/09/anti-tea-party-web-site-scheme-funnel-funds/* [10] *Ibid.,*

For example, William Molyneaux's *The Cause of Ireland*, published in 1698, became so popular in America that three new editions were published between 1770 and 1776. John Lord Somers' *The Judgment of Whole Kingdoms and Nations*, first published in 1710 but reprinted in cheap editions in Philadelphia in 1773 and Newport in 1774, was even more widely read.[11]

Yet, if any one man can be said to have dominated the philosophy of the American Revolution, it would be John Locke, who authored *Two Treaties of Government* in 1690. John Locke was considered to be the founding father of American principles. Although Natural Law was not original with Locke—it came from Cicero, the famous Roman orator, born in 106 B.C.—Locke retransmitted Cicero's principles of liberty that shaped the modern western world of today.[12] Subsequently, Locke's assertations were further transmitted by *Cato's Letters*, 144 essays by John Trenchard and Thomas Gordon, which further championed Locke's ~Cicero's principles.

2010: More Than Signs and Rallies

Today, Tea Partiers are not only getting their physical exercise by making signs and attending rallies and marches, they are also exercising their brains! The Tea Party movement started with anger and frustration, then immediately morphed into the second phase of education. Today, Patriots have an almost unquenchable thirst for knowledge on our history, founding fathers, government workings and specific legislation (bills).

Many Tea Party groups have a specific committee that deals with the flow and channeling of new information, including suggested reading. Just as early Americans did, today's Tea Partiers are bringing back books that haven't been in print for decades.

---

[11] *Founding Father's Library*: A Bibliographical Essay by Forrest McDonald
[12] John C. Miller, *Origins of the American Revolution, 170*

Today, Patriots are filling their shelves with literary works such as:

The 5000 Year Leap, W. Cleon Skousen (1981)
The Road to Serfdom, F. A. Hayek (1940)
Atlas Shrugged, Ayn Rand (1930)
Origins of the American Revolution, John C. Miller (1943)
Original Intent: The Courts, the Constitution & Religion, David Barton (2000)
The U.S. Constitution, Declaration of Independence, the Federalist Papers and correspondence of our founding fathers (of course).

1770s: New Communication Technology

The revolution may not have even happened if it wasn't for a new communication technology: the colonial post. Americans rarely had occasion to cross provincial lines, let alone become aware of other's existence, but the colonial post allowed for the rapid exchange of colonial newspapers, correspondence between merchants and creation of groups of learned men that would exchange writings.

2010: New Communication Technology

Think about organizing a rally, sending out correspondence to hundreds or thousands of attendees, handling all the logistics—*without the Internet!* Think about collecting political information, videos, speeches, legislation, voting records—*without the Internet!*

As you are reading this book, the Administration and Congress are actively seeking the power to turn off the Internet. The 'Internet Kill-Switch Bill' PCNAA passed by Senate committee in June of 2010, now it's on to the Senate for a vote! Today's Tea Party movement would be extremely difficult without the Internet. Patriot's fears of this are justified.

POLITICAL SIMILARITIES	
Tea Party of the 1770s	Tea Party of 2010
Why? British Unconstitutional Acts	Why? American Unconstitutional Acts
Stamp Act—Townshend Acts	TARP, Stimulus
Tipping Point? Tea Act	Tipping Point? Health Care
Grassroots—Sons of Liberty	Grassroots—Tea Partiers
Described as "Awakening"	Described as "Awakening"
Called every name in the book	Called every name in the book
Tories	Democrats
Whigs	Republicans
Whigs showed true colors	GOP showed true colors
Educational Movement	Educational Movement
Aided by Technology (Post)	Aided by Technology (Internet)

The table above summarizes some of the similarities that we've covered *so far*. I think it is important to reiterate or further expand on the Educational Movement similarity. It is true both then and now, that the first phase of the movements were rooted in anger and frustration. *There is plenty to be angry about.* However, today, the lost story about the Tea Party movement is that it is an Educational Movement. This is what I call phase two of the movement and is the most ignored fact about today's movement.

The next category of similarities; the *Economic Similarities.*

FOREWORD

1770s: Private Debt, Real Estate and Unemployment

The economy was "burthened beyond all possible bearing ... private debts were never so pressing in the memory of man."[13] Rhode Island real estate was selling for half its former value, credit had all but disappeared from the colonies, and unprecedented unemployment plagued the New World. New York land was selling at ruinous prices and foreclosures were happening at an astonishing rate. "It seems as if all our American World must inevitably break," wrote William Livingston of New York. [14]

2010: Private Debt, Real Estate and Unemployment

I know what you're thinking: that all this information is a real downer. But the truth needs to be shown. Today, private debt is at an unprecedented level. Real Estate has lost half or more of its value in many parts of the country and today's unemployment numbers are second only to the Great Depression (a close second).

1770s: Government Pensions

A Pennsylvanian said of Parliament, "The unbounded luxury and profusion of that nation will make money more and more necessary to them, and we may as well think of filling a bottomless pit, as of satisfying their wants, whether £7 or £800 sterling is paid for a coach—thousands given in pensions—£10,000 lavished on a ball."[15]

---

[13] John C. Miller, *Origins of the American Revolution, 116, The Burd Papers,* edited by Lewis Burd Walker, Philadelphia, 1976, 65-67. Extract of a letter from Mr. William Donaldson of New York, 1766, Lee MSS., Harvard University Library. *Boston Gazette*, July 29, September 16, 1765. *South Carolina Gazette*, October 22, 1764.

[14] *Ibid.*, 116, *Diary of John Rowe*, edited by Anne Rowe Cunningham, Boston, 1903, 75.

[15] *Ibid.*, 121, *Pennsylvania Chronicle*, October 10, 1768, Postscript.

2010: Government Pensions

Just like the 1770s, money is more and more necessary to Congress. Unfortunately, it is indeed like filling a bottomless pit. In my upcoming book *Bill of Reform*, (shameless plug), I dedicate a complete chapter to what this government of ours has done regarding pensions! It is unbelievable. *No wonder why Federal Employee Unions are giving money hand over fist to fight the Tea Party movement.*

1770s: Trade Deficits

The colonies imported £500,000 of goods from Great Britain, yet only sold £300,000 in return. In response to this trend, George Washington said that the wealth of Americans would "centre in Great Britain, as certain as the Needle will settle to the Poles."[16] George Washington understood what today's congressmen and governmental economists can't seem to grasp. Actually, some do grasp the concept; however, it's in alignment with their goals of *global equalization.* If they believe that, they're probably riding unicorns on the weekends.

In the 1770s the trade deficit was 66%—meaning they imported 66% more than they exported.

2010: Trade Deficits

The last year we saw a trade surplus was 1975! Initially the trade deficits were rather small—4% in 1976, 4 years later still creeping along at 7% in 1980, then soaring to 45% in 1986! Since then our Trade Deficits have been massive, peaking at 56% in 2005. From 1976 to 2009, we have transferred over $7.5 trillion dollars in wealth to foreign countries. *What would George Washington say?*

---

[16] John C. Miller, *Origins of the American Revolution, 20, The Writings of George Washington,* edited by J. C. Fitzpatrick, Washington, 1931, II, 466.

FOREWORD

1770s: National Debt

Great Britain's national debt was £140,000,000. The population of Great Britain at the time was 8 million.[17] The average national income per capita was £16 per year.[18] What does this mean?

The National Debt was **110%** of the National Annual Income.

2010: National Debt

The United States national debt is $13,300,000,000,000. That's $13.3 trillion dollars, as of August 2010.[19] Note, this does not even include $5.5 trillion in Fannie Mae & Freddie Mac debt that the Government is guaranteeing.[20] The population of the United States is 309 million. The average national income per capita is $39,138.[21] What does this mean?

The National Debt is **110%** of the National Annual Income.

Admit it—that is freaky!

This one similarity prompted me to look deeper into history. I recalled reading about England's debt in John C. Miller's book; however, I didn't think about it until weeks after I had read the book. I decided to look into Great Britain's debt—I wanted to know how it compared to our debt today. Here's why: throughout my reading and research, it became clear that Parliament was getting more and more frantic at extracting more and more revenue from the colonies.

[17] John C. Miller, *Origins of the American Revolution, 120, 121*
[18] Gregory Clark, *The Long march of history: Farm Laborers' wage in England* 1208-1850, Department of Economics UC-Davis, Davis CA
[19] United States Treasury
[20] Lorraine Woellert and John Gittelsohn – *Article in Bloomberg 6/13/10*
[21] Bureau of Business & Economic Research, UNM Last Revised 4/1/10 http://bber.unm.edu/econ/us-pci.htm

In other words, as the National Debt grew, the liberties that the colonists had enjoyed since the early 1600s were being encroached upon more and more. Interestingly familiar, however, I was shocked when I saw the *identical* numbers!

It made me wonder why. Why hadn't the colonists revolted in 1650? 1690? 1730? Because they were doing well enough, and the encroachments (acts) like the Molasses Act in 1733 and the earlier Navigation and Trade Acts were bearable.

Parliament was irresponsible and Britain's merchants (today's Congress and multi-national corporations) were corrupt. This eventually led to the de facto behavior of a powerful government that is not bound by Natural Law. The government dictated the rules, not the collective individuals, (The People).

This one amazing similarity opened my eyes to look at the bigger picture at what was going on, then and now. Granted, Parliament was not as crafty as the U.S. federal government. Parliament simply called a "tax" a "tax," and unlike Congress, which has devised a more clever route of passing Acts … which are "programs" that are meant to "help us."

As National Debt grows, our liberties will shrink—that is the result of our neglect to watch our elected officials and hold them accountable to the sound principles that our country was founded on.

Before we move on, I'd like to share something else with you regarding National Debt. The following quote is from Albrecht Ritschl, *Sustainability of High Public Debt.* Mr. Ritschl wrote this report while he was an Assistant Professor at Universitat Pompeu Fabra, Barcelona, Spain. The report was a study, like the title suggests, of the sustainability of high public (national) debt. His study is historical, spanning over 300 years of national debts from Britain, France and Germany. This is what he had to say about a long-term accumulation of debt during peacetime (which is what we have today, regardless of the wars in the Middle East):

"The implications of these results for present-day politics are twofold. First, as European debt policies of the past were largely induced by major wars ... there is little historical experience with long-term accumulation of national debt in peacetime. This is probably *discomforting*, as it indicates that the debt record of the last few decades may be the result of a *regime change* whose *nature is not yet fully understood. "* Albrecht Ritschl, *Sustainability of High Public Debt.* 1996, pg. 19. *Italics mine.*

Although the recent debt-crisis riots in Europe didn't get much media attention in the U.S., the riots lend some credibility, fourteen years later, to Ritsch's words, "discomforting," and whose "nature is not yet fully understood."

To state it clearly, I simply think it's prudent to look at history—governments that deal with the pressure of a mounting debt *don't behave well!* I write about the details in *Bill of Reform*, and I don't want to get bogged down here, but trust me when I say that the $1 trillion Health Care legislation is about *revenue and power* much more than it's about "helping us."

1770s: Refusal to Develop Natural Resources

Britain refused to allow soil and coal mines to be developed, such as the Louisbourg coal mines. It was contended that the British government made "an abridgement of the common bounties of Heaven, for the water is not allowed to flow, or the earth to produce." These laws helped to establish the conviction that imperial policy was being perverted to the enrichment of the British monopolists.[22]

---

[22] John C. Miller, *Origins of the American Revolution, 23, The Writings of Benjamin Franklin,* edited by A. H. Smyth, New York, 1906, IV, 244-245. *Pennsylvania Gazette*, February 22, 1775. Ramsay, I, 62.

2010: Refusal to Develop Natural Resources

It is said that America is the "Saudi Arabi of Coal." Meaning we have as much coal as the Saudi's have oil. This is actually misleading in terms of our oil resources. America is actually the *"America* of Coal.", in oil terms. Yes, we have more oil than anyone else in the world! In the 1950s we also exported more oil than anyone else in the world. What about peak oil? (The theory that the earth is running out of oil, that demand has exceeded availability.) *Nonsense.*

From December 2009 to May 2010 we imported 1.7 million barrels per day, (b/d) from the Persian Gulf.[23] On an annual basis, that amounts to approximately 620 million barrels of oil imported from the Gulf. The United States has over 2 trillion barrels of shale oil, of the estimated 2.6 trillion barrels in the whole world (77%!). This oil is located in three States: Utah, Colorado and Wyoming. It is not as easy to retrieve as conventional oil; however, more than 700 billion barrels of this U.S. oil shale occurs in concentrations richer than what's currently mined in Alberta, Canada's tar sand.[24]

Speaking of Alberta's tar sand oil, it is reported they are sitting on as much as 300 billion recoverable barrels, and another trillion+ barrels that could be recovered in the future with newer technology.[25]

Just those two areas (3 states, plus Canada's Alberta) represent well over 1,000 years of oil imports from the Gulf. The fact is, we also don't even know how much conventional oil we have, because oil *exploration* is unlawful in most areas! If you care about this topic, it's easy enough to research the truth.

[23] U.S. Energy Information Administration, www.eia.doe.gov
[24] James W. Bunger, Peter M. Crawford, Harry R. Johnson, *Is oil shale America's answer to peak-oil challenge?* , August 9, 2004 edition of Oil & Gas Journal
[25] Brendan I. Koerner, *The Trillion-Barrel Tar Pit,* July 2004

ECONOMIC SIMILARITIES	
Tea Party of the 1770s	Tea Party of 2010
Private Debt all-time high	Private Debt all-time high
High Unemployment	High Unemployment
Real Estate Collapse	Real Estate Collapse
Gross abuse in Gov't Pensions	Gross abuse in Gov't Pensions
Trade Deficits 66%	Trade Deficits peaked to 56%
National Debt 110% of Incomes	National Debt 110% of Incomes
Refusal to develop resources	Refusal to develop resources

The economic similarities of then and now, combined with the political similarities, caused a massive ground swell of grassroots Americans to rise up for reform. That's right, our forefathers did not want a revolution, they simply wanted to reform Parliament, instilling Cicero's/Locke's principles of Natural Law.

Now let's cover the final category of similarities: *Subversive Actions/Similarities*, which may serve to answer Ritschl's riddle … a "regime change whose nature is not yet fully understood."

1770s: Political Pamphlets

The first pamphlet was printed in 1621 in Britain by Thomas Archer. In 1695 the "Liberty of Unlicensed Printing" removed government control from the press (freedom of the press). Well … not exactly.

In 1770, Alexander McDougall printed a political pamphlet that got him thrown in jail. It was titled, *"To the Betrayed Inhabitants of the City and Colony of New York"* and was anonymous until a little pressure was applied to the printer! McDougall spent three months in jail, and never faced sentencing because of the tide of popular opinion forced the State Assembly to release him. *Note*: when the State Assembly threw him in jail, the Tories and Whigs were the entrenched establishment in the colonies.

Other famous pamphlets and pamphleteers included Thomas Paine's *Common Sense* and Benjamin Franklin's *Poor Richard's Almanac*.

2010: Political Pamphlets

Article by Terence P. Jeffery

"Solicitor General Elena Kagan, nominated to the U.S. Supreme Court by President Barack Obama, told that court in September that Congress could constitutionally prohibit corporations from engaging in political speech such as publishing pamphlets that advocate the election or defeat of a candidate for federal office.

"Kagan's argument that the government could prohibit political speech by corporations was rejected by a 5-4 majority of the Supreme Court in the case of Citizens United v. Federal Election Commission. Justice Anthony Kennedy wrote the majority opinion in that case, and in a scathing concurrence Chief Justice John Roberts took direct aim at Kagan's argument that the government could ban political pamphlets.

"The Government urges us in this case to uphold a direct prohibition on political speech. It asks us to embrace a theory of the First Amendment that would allow censorship not only of television and radio broadcasts, but of pamphlets, posters, the Internet, and virtually any other medium that corporations and unions might find useful in expressing their views on matters of public concern," wrote Roberts. "Its theory, if accepted, would empower the Government to prohibit newspapers from running editorials or opinion pieces supporting or opposing candidates for office, so long as the newspapers were owned by corporations—as the major ones are. First Amendment rights could be confined to individuals, subverting the vibrant public discourse that is at the **foundation of our democracy."**

Justice Kennedy described the law Kagan had defended as an illegitimate attempt to use "censorship to control thought."

"When Government seeks to use its full power, including the criminal law, to command where a person may get his or her information or what distrusted source he or she may not hear, it uses censorship to control thought," Kennedy wrote in the majority opinion. "This is unlawful. The First Amendment confirms the freedom to think for ourselves."[26]

CAN YOU BELIEVE THIS!? Please notice! It was only defeated by a 5-4 vote. Obviously when Kagan is on the court, we know what her vote will be. PATRIOTS WAKE UP! Seriously, how many of our ancestors have died to protect a basic right like this?

1770s: Revisionists Trash the Founding Fathers

The prevalent message started with Cicero, then John Locke, who was considered to be the founding father of the principles of liberty, and later reiterated in the Cato letters. What happened? Revisionists called the *Treaties of Two Governments* a museum piece! (i.e. it's outdated!). Locke (long dead) had become a menace to the established order, and they bitterly regretted that the works of this "exploded author" had not been burned after they filled their usefulness in the 1688 "glorious revolution" in England,. Indignant "are the Closet Reveries of an author, to direct the Operations of Government, to over-rule Parliament?"[27]

---

[26]Terence P. Jeffrey, www.cnsnews.com/news/article/65600

So much for the principle of liberties they clung to in the past. When these principles conflicted with their current agenda, *one had to go.*

2010: Revisionists Trash the Founding Fathers

David Barton, the founder of Wallbuilders, has spent most of his adult life documenting our Founding Fathers and the foundational principles of this country. The web site www.wallbuilders.com has extensive information and articles regarding revisionist examples. Another good source is the book *Revisionism: How to Identify it in Your Children's Textbooks.*

"The philosophy of the school room in one generation will be the philosophy of government in the next." Abraham Lincoln

I'm sure you've heard the statement, or opinion, that the Constitution is outdated (Kind of like a ... museum piece). What interests me, is that no one says exactly *when* it was outdated. Was it last year? The 1980s? How about the 1960s? I'll bet that if you were to press someone for an answer, they would blurt out a date prior to their birth, probably even much earlier than that. Why? Because what they really mean when they say the Constitution is out of date, or that the founding principles are out of date, is that they *never* actually believed in them in the first place. Think about it—how much political traction, or just plain old *respect*, would you get if you said, "I have never believed in the Constitution or the founding principles"? Very little. You would essentially be showing your cards, hence, it is much more palatable to say, "it's outdated." After all, almost everything gets outdated, right? Records, 33s, 45s, 8 Tracks, Cassettes, and how about Beta? You see my point. When someone claims this 'out of date' theory, call them on it by finding out *when* exactly they are talking about.

---

[27] John C. Miller, *Origins of the American Revolution,* 202, St. James's Chronicle, December 12, 1774

I'm reluctant to even bring this up, because I don't want you to think I'm an Obama basher. I'll tell you right now, he is not to blame for all of our problems, not even close—our problems are decades old. I do think he represents the icing on the cake and the final straw. However, I, along with many Tea Party leaders, are actually grateful he was elected to office. Why? Because his *rapid approach* to socialism, opposed to the slow moving approach that has been in existence …, has awoken many Patriots. For that I'm thankful, even though I know it's kind of like the peeing-on-your-shoes-while-patting-your-back type of thankfulness.

When Obama said he viewed the Constitution as a document of "negative liberties" (audio tape from 2001), he was just using a confusing, conflict in terms, to trash the founding fathers and principles. It was easier to say that than to say, "I don't agree with the Constitution." He needed to keep *political traction*.

1770s: Patriots Controlled the Media

The Tories were furious—they had to stamp out this source of opposition. One Tory declared, "whether sleeping or waking, they are continually vibrating in our ears!" Since nearly all the newspapers were Whiggish, the Tories further complained that the people heard nothing but what "their ringleaders chuse they should hear."[28] The Tories (elitists) groaned that by dint of reading newspapers, even "the peasants and their housewives in every part of the land were able to dispute on politics and positively to determine upon *our* liberties."[29]

The elitist's enemy was education, they feared that an educated population, including the lowly 'peasants' and 'housewives', would ultimately determine *their* liberties.

[28] John C. Miller, *Origins of the American Revolution,* 288, *Maryland Gazette*, April 17, 1766
[29] *Ibid., Boston Evening Post*, May 22, 1769

In 1765, the Virginia Governor threatened the printer of the Virginia Gazette to keep radicalism out of his paper (so much for the 1695 law, freedom of press). The paper was shut down for four months; however, the Sons of Liberty came to the rescue by bringing a printer to Virginia to establish a Whig newspaper. After this the old Virginia Gazette threw off the shackles and became a Whig sheet as well! Now the Governor had two Whig newspapers![30]

2010: Patriots Control the Media

The media that counts, that is. TV Cable News (CNN, MSNBC CNBC, HLN and FNC), of which, the highest rated source of political news and information is Fox News, by far, often having ratings that outnumber all of the others combined! FNC, is a network clearly not afraid to report about the Patriots of today, and to expose the progressive movement's agenda. The internet, just like the colonial post, is new technology that greatly assists with today's Tea Party movement. Talk radio isn't even close! When tens of millions of Patriots tune into the marketplace of political ideologies, the clear winner is the Patriots.

What is the reaction of the 'progressives'? Do they hold dear to "our" liberties, or do these liberties just get in their way? Do they embrace the marketplace of ideas or are they afraid of open debate?

It's so easy to find out—just search the internet for "liberals attack conservative media." Here's the first one that comes up on my list.
"*NPR* and *Time Magazine* are defending and protecting their liberal reporters' public disdain and hatred for conservative journalists. NPR affiliate KCRW's Sarah Spitz and *Time's* Michael Scherer emailed their personal hostility for conservative views to their cohorts in the liberal cabal called "Journolist.""

[30] *Ibid.,* James Parker to Benjamin Franklin, May 6, 1766, Franklin MSS., American Philosophical Society, *New York Journal or General Advertiser,* November 17, 1766

FOREWORD

Scherer is the White House correspondent for *Time Magazine*. Spitz is the publicity director for public radio station KCRW and producer of radio shows "Left, Right & Center" and "Politics of Culture." Spitz openly expresses her vile dislike for conservative talk radio host Rush Limbaugh. "I never knew I had this much hate in me," she wrote in the emails obtained by The Daily Caller. "But he deserves it." Her hate language rises to the level of openly wishing for Limbaugh's death. She wrote that if Limbaugh were having a heart attack, she would "laugh loudly like a maniac and watch his eyes bug out."[31]

Hmmm ... NPR ... doesn't that stand for National Public Radio? A radio station funded and run by the Government!

You say that we could fill a book with stuff like this from both Patriots and Progressives? Ok, I understand the argument, even though I don't think you'll find as much vitriol on the Patriot side. But let's not split hairs. Why don't we look at what our government has talked about, and has actually tried, regarding passing laws that prohibit free speech! You know, 1st Amendment stuff ... assuming the Constitution is not "outdated."

For starters, look at The Disclosure Act, actually passed the U.S. House of Representatives! What's in it? Well, the law would require "special interest group officials to physically appear at the end of campaign ads they sponsor, acknowledging their campaign contributions." Remember Alexander McDougall, who anonymously printed the pamphlet in 1770? Congress must have been reading about that and thought it was too much of a hassle to squeeze the identities out of printers, TV producers, and web designers.

Does this infuriate you? It passed! In our Country! After political pressure, the Senate backed off, but *they tested the waters.*

---

[31]Quoted from an article by Emily Miller, Human Events, 7/23/2010

You might think that it's a good idea—"hey, we want to know who is behind this message." I understand and probably agree to some point. However, the rub was that it excluded certain groups that are, say, "progressive friendly." That was the unconstitutional part—some donations were allowed to be kept secret, like those given by the labor unions, while other groups were required to disclose. Darn, those pesky liberties.

The Fairness Doctrine promotes "the diversity of viewpoints expressed." It also promotes "diversity of ownership of radio stations." This long-dead bill now sits close to a defibulator called "localism." Dick Durbin (Tory, I mean D-IL.) wrote an amendment approved by the Senate that includes some guidance on how this bill could be resurrected through the concept of "localism." Wasn't it a Tory that complained the people heard nothing but what "their ringleaders chuse they should hear"?

1770s: Ridicule and Subversion of Religion

The Tories groaned that these men of God were "unceasingly sounding the Yell of Rebellion in the Ears of an ignorant & deluded people, boys who had just thrown away their satchels and who scarcely read English."[32] Just a wee bit arrogant and elitist don't you think? First, the Tories claimed that an overwhelming majority of the colonist were ignorant and deluded, since almost every colonist attended church. Additionally, the claim that these "boys" could scarcely read English is also opposite of the truth—Americans in the 1770s were the most literate and well read population on the earth: "Neither swords nor pistols, neither fleets nor armies, will be of any avail towards reducing them to obedience, if Religion shall be called in to enforce, to encourage, to sanctify opposition."[33]

---

[32] John C. Miller, *Origins of the American Revolution, 186, Massachusetts Gazette,* January 11, 1776. *Rivington's New York Gazetteer*, March 9, 1775. *Extracts of private letters from Boston*, Mr. H. to Mr. M., December 5, 1774, Hardwicke MSS. 35912, Library of Congress Transcript.
[33]

They saw preachers as threats and viewed religion in America as opposed to their imperialistic socialism. Therefore, they tried to attack it, ridicule it, then outright subdue it. Remember, these "pesky" liberties mean nothing when they stand in the way of the socialist, imperialist, or many other definitions of State authority over Natural Law.

The Presbyterian and Congregational preachers of the time told their congregations that the only form of government to which Christians could submit was a government by consent, in which the people, ceaselessly vigilant against oppression, retained the right to overthrow unjust rulers.[34] Government by consent, clearly, is one of our founding principles. Our responsibility of being "ceaselessly vigilant," though—well, we haven't done so well with that one. Another founding principle of overthrowing unjust rulers is built into our system of Government—we have the ability to throw them out with our votes, in addition to the ability to impeach elected officials and appointed Judges. The Tories were right—for them to succeed they needed to silence the American pulpits.

"Preachers were politicians and politicians preachers during the Revolutionary period."[35] To combat this, the Bishop of London urged Parliament to send a bishop over to the colonies. The government-endorsed, government-run Church of England would squelch the opposition. When word of this reached the colonies, the widespread reaction was summed up by the Reverend Jonathen Mayhew: "Let the bishops but get their foot in the stirrup, and "their beasts, the laity," may prance and flounce about to no purpose; and they will be at length be so jaded and hacked by the reverend jockeys, that they will not have even spirits enough to complain that their backs are galled."[36]

[34] John C. Miller, *Origins of the American Revolution,., 187,* John W. Thorton, *The Pulpit of the American Revolution,* Boston 1860, 16, note, 86, note, 87, 95, 98

[35] *Ibid.,* 187 [36] *Ibid.,* 188, John W. Thorton, *The Pulpit of the American Revolution,* Boston 1860, 50

The colonists knew well of religious persecution—the Protestants had been burned at the stakes in England, by a government-run, government-endorsed Church of England. That is why our founding fathers did not want our government to set up another "Church of England" type of state-run religion, although they were openly religious. The writings of our founding fathers are generously populated with very strong beliefs of the ties between morality, religion and governing. Revisionists would have to burn down the Library of Congress and sandblast nearly all federal buildings in D.C. to physically accomplish their intellectual goal—to remove all references to God from the public's eye.

2010: Ridicule and Subversion of Religion

Today, it is common knowledge that a politician who talks freely of his/her religious beliefs (especially Judeo-Christian) will be ridiculed to no end by progressives. The progressives know, just like the Tories, elitists, and socialists of the past, that their movement, their goals of a state authority over individuals, is opposite Judeo-Christian principles and Natural Law.

To subvert the freedom of religious speech today, the progressives in this country don't have a government-run church, with bishops lined up to do their bidding. Instead, they seek to subvert religious speech by stamping it out of the public's eye, starting with school textbooks.

Do you recall the recent news about the big to-do in Texas regarding the school textbook commission? There is a battle being waged between Patriots and Progressives that has been going on for decades and it is now heating up. Wallbuilders, which I mentioned earlier, provides the following example of this attempt to eradicate religion from our society.

Notice the following three examples from American history texts:

FOREWORD

We whose names are under-written [*omission*] do by these presents solemnly and mutually in the presence of God, and one of another, covenant and combine our selves together into a civil body politick. MAYFLOWER COMPACT, 1620

Is life so dear or peace so sweet as to be purchased at the price of chains and slavery? [*omission*] I know not what course others may take, but as for me, give me liberty or give me death! PATRICK HENRY, 1775

[*omission*] ART. I.—His Britannic Majesty acknowledges the said United States . . . PEACE TREATY TO END THE AMERICAN REVOLUTION, 1783

What was omitted from these important historical quotes?

We whose names are under-written *having undertaken for the glory of God, and advancement of the Christian faith and honor of our king and country, a voyage to plant the first colonie in the Northern parts of Virginia* do by these presents solemnly and mutually in the presence of God, and one of another, covenant and combine ourselves together into a civil body politick.

Is life so dear or peace so sweet as to be purchased at the price of chains and slavery? *Forbid it, Almighty God!* I know not what course others may take, but as for me, give me liberty or give me death!

In the name of the Most Holy and Undivided Trinity. It having pleased the Divine Providence to dispose the hearts ... ART. I.—His Britannic Majesty acknowledges the said United States . . . PEACE TREATY TO END THE AMERICAN REVOLUTION, 1783[37]

[37] Wallbuilders.com, *Revisionism*: *How to Identify it in Your Children's Text-book*

The first historical quote represents the intentions of the passengers on the Mayflower.

The second quote is the famous Patrick Henry 'give me liberty, or give me death'.

The third is from the Treaty of Paris, ending the Revolutionary War.

Please understand, you do not have to agree with the Christian faith. However, reading about it in historic quotes does not make belief compulsory. Remember, it is not only our history of religion that is being subverted, but also our history of the founding fathers, and principles of our liberty, *which are tied together*.

I understand if you don't have much vested in religious quotes, or care too much about the role that religion played in our history; however, when you accept or ignore subversion in one area (the religious principles our country was founded on) it makes it that much easier for the progressives to subvert what you do care for and have a vested interest in, *like your liberties!*

When I said progressives don't have a government-run church, I wasn't being completely honest with you. They do, and it's called the 501c3 *corporation*. That's right, every church in America that is a 501c3 is actually a corporation—there is no separate designation for a church. The definition of a corporation is "a legal entity created by or under the authority of the laws of a State."

Our freedom and liberties created from the Judeo-Christian faith and from Natural Law have a muzzle placed on them, via Title 26 section 501c3 of the IRS code.

Most people think that this tax-exempt designation simply prohibits churches/pastors from endorsing candidates. Not so. The reason Churches are ever so more concerned about having their tax-exempt status revoked and assets seized is because the 501c3 designation also prohibits "carrying on propaganda" or otherwise attempting to "influence legislation"!

With that definition, *anything* could be called propaganda, and could be construed as influencing legislation. Unbelievable. The following is the text from the IRS code:

(3) *Corporations*, and any community chest, fund, or foundation, organized and operated exclusively for *religious*, charitable, scientific, testing for public safety, literary, or educational purposes, or to foster national or international amateur sports competition (but only if no part of its activities involve the provision of athletic facilities or equipment), or for the prevention of cruelty to children or animals, no part of the net earnings of which inures to the benefit of any private shareholder or individual, no substantial part of the activities of which is carrying on **propaganda,** or otherwise attempting, **to influence legislation** (except as otherwise provided in subsection (h)), and which does not participate in, or intervene in (including the publishing or distributing of statements), any political campaign on behalf of (or in opposition to) any candidate for public office. [italics mine]

The IRS has been known to leave certain tax code 'dormant' for decades, and then to arbitrarily enforce it. Although the IRS has not begun to systematically enforce this gag on free speech, the gag does exist, and would punish freedom of political speech.

1770s: Borders and Foreigners Used for Political Gains

Before the Declaration of Independence was signed, one of the last Acts of Parliament was the Quebec Act. In other words, one last attempt by Parliament to subdue the "radical Tea Partiers" was to actually change the northern border! The northern border of the colonies (southern border of Quebec) was moved south to the Hudson river and extended to the Mississippi river. In doing so, Parliament claimed this was meant to serve as an effective "political check to the growing independence of our American children."[38] It was pointed out during the debate in Parliament that the Mexicans—uh, I mean, Canadians—might be used to curb "those fierce fanatic spirits in the Protestant colonies."

In 1764, the naturalization of citizenship for immigrants was used as a political ploy in Pennsylvania. The establishment in the Assembly was seeking to be a Royal Province, so to accomplish this they rounded up hundreds of German immigrants and rushed them to naturalization offices: "I have out of my own pocket spent some money for getting some people naturalized, to get some votes."[39]

2010: Borders and Foreigners

I have empathy for the illegal immigrants in this country. Most of them are escaping the harsh realities in Mexico and Central America. On a mission trip several years ago in Rojo Gomez, a village not too far from Tijuana, I noticed that townspeople could see the expanse of homes and industries of San Diego. They could see opportunity for themselves and their family, who were living in tin shacks. We have perpetuated the problem of illegal immigration because our leaders refuse to secure our southern border. Our leaders have failed to implement common sense immigration laws that allow for a realistic path for work visas and a path for citizenship.

[38] John C. Miller, *Origins of the American Revolution*, 375, *An Appeal to the Public*, London, 1774, 54. Parliamentary History, XVII, 1406
[39] John C. Miller, *Origins of the American Revolution*, 63, William Young to Thomas Penn, December 14, 1765, Historical Society of Pennsylvania, *Private Correspondence. Letters and Papers relating chiefly to the Provincial History of Pennsylvania,*

Americans will welcome immigrants that intend to integrate into our society, our culture, speak our language, and obey our laws.

The spectacle talked about today—a possible executive order from the President to grant citizenship to all illegal immigrants overnight—would be another gross abuse for political points.

I don't think most people outside of Arizona know what is going on within their border. The US Fish and Wildlife Service sent out a notice advising the public that a portion of the Buenos Aires National Wildlife refuge had been closed because it had been "adversely affected by border-related activities."

Border-related activities—what kind of "activities" do borders entertain themselves with?! Can they not simply state the truth? *This is a high traffic area for human and drug traffickers, and is a very dangerous place for el gringo.*

Apparently, the United States can't control its porous borders. That is what has happened, and is happening right now, and it's not just on the border, it's twenty and thirty miles and even deeper into Arizona.[40]

Arizona Sheriff Joe Arpaio was informed by the FBI that a Mexican drug cartel had put a $1 million bounty on his head.[41]

Rahm Emanuel, White House Chief of Staff, said, "You never want a serious crisis to go to waste. We can do things we couldn't do before." I think this also means, "you allow a crisis to build, to *become* a serious crisis, because you never know what you can accomplish that you couldn't before."

---

[40] MaryEllen Resendez, *Pinal County Sheriff: Mexican drug cartels now control parts of Arizona, www.abc15.com*

[41] Tom Blackwell, *Mexican drug cartels puts bounty out on Arizona sheriff control parts of Arizona, www.abc15.com*

I know that sounds cynical, but *come on!* What valid explanation could there possibly be for our inability to chase off these drug and human traffickers and protect our borders?

It appears to me that this crisis has been left to simmer until it boils over into a serious crisis, forcing Arizona to take action, which will then be characterized as being racist, which in turn creates victims, the victims being illegal immigrants! Of course "they" have a solution for these latest victims—Executive Order Amnesty.

What did Albrecht Ritschl say..?
A "regime change whose nature is not yet fully understood."

1770s: The Courts Used To Enforce Agenda

"The Admiralty Courts were one of the most effective and most hated instruments for enforcing the Acts of Trade."[42] The Admiralty courts removed the jealously guarded right to a trial by jury, and as such they were regarded as subversive.

There were courts throughout the colonies that upheld the Englishman's right to a jury trial; however, the Admiralty Courts did not. The Admiralty Courts were there for one reason—to uphold the Acts of Parliament. In other words, Parliament couldn't have cared less about the normal goings-on in day-to-day courts, such as who was suing who and who was getting sentenced for what crimes. However, they did care about the acts that they passed, and the "pesky" liberty of a jury by trial might get in the way.

2010: The Courts Used To Enforce Agenda

Today, without the federal courts, especially the Supreme Court, most progressive judicial fiats would simply not exist.

---

[42] John C. Miller, *Origins of the American Revolution,* 85

FOREWORD

The modern "acts" which are called programs meant to "help us" would either not exist, or would exist within the realm of whichever states wanted them (i.e. voted for them). In direct opposition of original intent, the federal judiciary in modern times has been the arbitrator of the Constitution. In fact, the federal courts have done so to such a degree that most people think that is what they are supposed to do.

The Constitution defines the role of the federal government, with the rest left up to the states. The states created the Constitution, which in turn, defined and created the federal government. In other words, the states are the parents and the federal government is the child. Does the parent tell the child what they can and can't do? Yes.

It is inconsistent with the concept of government by the people, if the federal government could simply grow in power and responsibilities *on its own*. Yet that is what has happened, via the federal judiciary.

Article V of the U.S. Constitution clearly defines the path that would allow for changes in the federal government's power and responsibilities. Please read it. Guess what—it has nothing to do with the federal judiciary. That's right, it's the *parent's* role to tell the *child* what they can and cannot do.

In case you're a little confused ... Article V stipulates that the only way the Constitution can be altered is via amendments that either Congress or the states put forward; however, regardless of who authors the amendments, the *states* are the only governing bodies that can approve constitutional changes.

That is why progressive legislation—these acts or programs that are meant to "help us," have survived, because of the federal judiciary. Not *one* progressive program has ever been introduced as an amendment to the Constitution—why? Because it wouldn't see the light of day! The states would not have approved of these massive and intrusive programs as they are defined today.

The upcoming court battle, between the federal government and the states regarding the "constitutionality" of the health care bill, is a foregone conclusion! It is a sad joke. The Supreme Court will rollover once again and side with the ever growing, progressive socialist federal government.

If the Health Care bill is such a good idea, why isn't it properly introduced as an amendment to the Constitution, clearly increasing the responsibility of the federal government? You know the answer.

Thomas Jefferson warned about this possibility in a Sept. 28, 1820, letter to William Jarvis:

> "You seem ... to consider the judges as the ultimate arbiters of all constitutional questions; a *very dangerous doctrine indeed*, and one which would place us under the despotism of an oligarchy. Our judges are as honest as other men, and not more so ... and their power [is] the more dangerous, as they are in office for life and not responsible, as the other functionaries are, to elective control. The Constitution has erected no such single tribunal, knowing that to whatever hands confided, with corruptions of time and party, its members would become despots."

Think about it, *nine justices*, acting as arbiters of the U.S. Constitution, would mean that every decision they write would change the Constitution. An oligarchy (the rule of many, by the few), is what our founding fathers did not intend. The reason Article V of the Constitution was written.

SUBVERSIVE ACTIONS: SIMILARITIES	
Tea Party of the 1770s	Tea Party of 2010
Attempt to ban political pamphlets	Attempt to ban political pamphlets
Ridicule of founding principles	Ridicule of founding principles
Patriotic Movement prevalent in the media	Patriotic Movement prevalent in the media
Ridicule and subversion of religion	Ridicule and subversion of religion
Borders and foreigners	Borders and foreigners
Courts used to enforce agenda	Courts used to enforce agenda

The political similarities and economic similarities explain why people "awoke" to what was going on, both in the 1770s and today. The similarity between subversive activities attacking grassroots movements shows the true and consistent nature of tyranny. Usually tyranny operates under whatever name causes the least suspicions—today it's called "progressive."

Something occurred to me—after reading many quotes from our founding fathers, some of which are famous, others less so, I would often think to myself, "these quotes are so amazing—they're so relevant to today!"

Now I know why! The reason they are still relevant is that they were going through many of the same things then, as we are today. Almost a full circle has happened. We are the ones and now is the time to draw that last arc of the radius. To leave the circle undone would be to deny the struggles of Patrick Henry, Sam Adams, John Hancock, George Washington and all the unknown, with their untold sacrifices and courage. I believe we are in the beginning stages of a 2nd revolution, with the stakes being just as high or higher. This revolution, thanks to the first, will be fought in the voting booths, but *fought* nonetheless.

TEA PARTY – THE AWAKENING

What is a Patriot?

That word has been used quite a bit, in this foreword, and in our culture as well. A friend of mine recently described the word as "love of country." I think love of country is a common definition, but one that falls short. Is a Patriot someone who loves oppression? Let's apply love of country to say, Russia, China, Mexico, Iran, and Iraq—all places you don't want to live! We know there are millions of these citizens who love their country even though their country and fellow countrymen have wrought misery upon each other, with genocide measured in millions. I don't think we would describe them as Patriots.

Let's get to the definition another way.

In the 1770s was everyone a Patriot? No. We all know that is true, even in my own family. My grandparents (eleven generations back), Thomas and Isabel Morehouse, arrived in Connecticut in 1630 and settled Whethersfield, then Stamford then Fairfield. An estimated 200 of their great-great-great grandchildren fought in the Revolutionary War. Men like Capt. Gershom Morehouse Jr., of Redding, CT, Capt. Solomon Morehouse of Westport, and Capt. Abijah Morehouse were *Patriots*. But then there was ... Daniel Morehouse of Fairfield, CT, James Morehouse, Theophilus Morehouse and others, who are buried in the Loyalist graveyard in New Brunswick, Canada! They were not Patriots, they were *Loyalists*.

I point this out for a number of reasons. First, the word Patriot does not exist without its *antonym*. In the 1770s its *opposite* was the Loyalist. The Revolutionary War was actually a Civil War, where Patriots fought Loyalists. The Loyalists sided with the British Redcoats, while the Patriots were later allied with the French. Battles were fought during the Revolutionary War where only Americans fought against each other, Patriots vs. Loyalists,

48

with no British or French soldiers on the field. We tend to forget that and focus instead on famous lines like "the British are coming," and the term "Redcoats."

Why did the Morehouse family fight against each other, some leaving their lands voluntarily and others exiled? Why did Patriots and Loyalists betray family, friends and neighbors? Because of the Tea Act!? The Tea Act actually cut the price of tea in half. No, not the Tea Act. We've all heard that it was because of taxation without representation, which is partially true, but that fails to explain the bigger picture.

What prompted the Tea Partiers of the 1770s is the *same thing* that has stirred up the Patriots of today.

It's All About Natural Law

This concept was first expressed by Marcus Tullius Cicero, 106 B.C. The most famous orator of Rome beautifully expressed what men already knew in their hearts, because it was imprinted upon them. Neither a Jew or Christian, born before Christ, Cicero wrote of God's natural laws, that man was born into a "state of liberty."

The concepts of Natural Law, while seemingly common sense, are very difficult to implement within a society, because they require ceaseless vigilance from their benefactors, the citizens. Vigilance against external and internal forces—the corrupting forces of power and greed.

Our founding fathers could more easily recognize tyranny and the seeds of tyranny because their world had been riddled with tyranny.

Cicero was an epic letter writer, and many of his letters survived. John Locke retransmitted Cicero's principles, combined with Judeo-Christian principles, in *Two Treaties of Government*,

1690. *Cato's Letters*, published during the 1750s and consisting of 144 essays, again carried the same message. Today, *The 5000 Year Leap* (1981), is the modern version that retransmits the powerful principles first expressed by Cicero. *The 5000 Year Leap* articulates and documents our nation's foundational principles with surprising clarity (*Please read it as soon as you can*).

Principles *expressed*, not invented, because they have been in place since man was created. The founding fathers implemented the principles of Natural Law, Anglo-Saxon People's Law and the People's Law of Ancient Israel into our founding documents, the *original* principles of our government.

Cicero concluded that once the reality of the Creator is clearly identified in the mind, the only intelligent approach to government, justice and human relations is to make laws with the existence of the Creator as the foundation.

The Creator's order of things is called Natural Law.

Cicero defines Natural Law as "true law": "True law is right reason in agreement with nature; it is of universal application, unchanging and everlasting; it summons to duty by its commands, and averts from wrongdoing by its prohibitions ... It is a sin to try to alter this law, nor is it allowable to repeal any part of it, and it is impossible to abolish entirely. We cannot be freed from its obligations by senate or people, and we need not look outside ourselves for an expounder or interpreter of it ... "[43]

How was Cicero received by the establishment of the time? He was exiled and then later murdered. *The proponents of State-given rights are not tolerant, nor are they compassionate.*

---

[43] W. Cleon Skousen, *The 5000 Year Leap*, 1981,Ebenstein, *Great Political Thinkers,* p. 133.

FOREWORD

The Principles our Nation were founded on, are extremely well articulated and referenced with sources in *The 5000 Year Leap*.

I cannot say it any better, nor is that the scope of this foreword regarding the Tea Party Movement. However, I would like to mention one principle that easily distinguishes the opposing sides of the Tea Party Movements, both in the 1770s and 2010: the principle of private property. John Adams said, "All men are born free and independent, and have certain natural, essential, and unalienable rights, among which may be reckoned the right of enjoying and defending their lives and liberties; that of acquiring, possessing, and protecting property; in fine, that of seeking and obtaining their safety and happiness."[44]

The ownership and acquiring of private property is one of our unalienable rights, and without consent, there is no power on earth that can take personal property away from an individual.

That is why our government is based on the "consent of the people." Not just a few people (an oligarchy), not every person (which would be impossible), but consent by a *majority* of the people.

Samuel Adams, considered to be the father of the revolution, minced no words when he said this of socialism and communism: "The Utopian schemes of leveling [re-distribution of the wealth and a community of goods and central ownership of the means of production and distribution], are as visionary and impractical as those which vest all property in the Crown. [These ideas] are arbitrary, despotic, and, in our government, *unconstitutional*." [italics mine]

---

[44] W. Cleon Skousen, *The 5000 Year Leap*, 1981,George A. Peek, Jr., ed., *The Political Writings of John Adams,* Liberal Arts Press, New York, 1954, p. 96.

Your Choice—Natural Law *or* Serfdom, Socialism, Communism, Marxism, Fascism and Progressivism

The Tea Partiers of the 1770s knew where the road was heading. As I stated before, they were acutely aware of the seeds of tyranny. The behavior of Parliament over decades was a slow approach to serfdom—it began its acceleration in 1763, and the tipping point was a seemingly inconsequential Act that actually reduced the price of tea.

Serfdom, Socialism, Communism, Marxism, Fascism and Progressivism are all the same to varying degrees. None of them adhere to the principles of Natural Law. Rather than unalienable rights "that no power on Earth can take away," in their minds, rights come from the government.

Specifics Please!

I couldn't agree more. We have been talking about the foundations of nations, specifically our nation. We all know that if your house has foundation problems … it's not a good thing. However, we never really see the foundation—the specifics that we look for in houses are things like style, size, quality of the craftsmanship, windows, doors and moldings.

Almost all foundation problems are discovered *after* the fact, and if you ignore these problems, you are likely to destroy your entire house. That is why it is so important to have a good foundation under your house, and to be "ceaselessly vigilant," checking for cracks and signs of erosion.

I am going to show you two examples of implementing a program like Social Security. One example is based on Natural Law, the other example is based on "socialist-progressivism." Let's see if you can tell the difference.

SCENARIO # 1

It's the 1930s in the U.S., economic turmoil and uncertainty has been the norm since Black Tuesday in October of 1929. The President, Franklin Roosevelt (FDR), has a number of ideas that he would like to implement, and these ideas are manifested in government programs designed to "help us." Among these programs are the Agriculture Adjustment Act (AAA) and the Old-Age and Survivors Insurance Trust Fund (Social Security).

President Roosevelt proceeds with getting his administration's plans/ideas drafted into legislation. Congress complies and first passes the AAA. However, in 1934, soon after it passed, a Federal Court struck it down as being unconstitutional. Two years later, in 1936, the U.S. Supreme Court upheld the lower court's decision. It looked like Social Security was headed for the same fate as the AAA, as there were three separate lawsuits pending regarding Social Security: *Helvering vs. Davis, Steward Machine Co. vs. Davis, and Carmichael vs. Southern Coal & Coke Co. and Gulf States Paper.*

President Roosevelt was enraged by the courts, both the lower Federal Court and the Supreme Court. However, what can a President do? The Constitution clearly defines separate powers between the Congressional Branch, Executive Branch and Judicial Branch. The division of power between the three branches of the federal government is and was a cornerstone of our Government. *Right?*

In 1937, less than one year later, the Supreme Court ruled in favor in *all three* cases on the same day!

What happened? Why did the Supreme Court change its mind regarding the Tenth Amendment?

Because … on February 5th, 1937, President Roosevelt sent a message to Congress requesting additional powers to appoint six more justices to the Supreme Court. He basically said that the Justices are senile, and while they are appointed for life, they refuse to retire! Also, they disagree with me!

Can you imagine today, if the President tried to push through "constitutionally questionable" legislation, only to be ruled against by the Supreme Court, and then for the President to attempt to load the Supreme Court with more justices that would be favorable to his positions!?

That's what happened, and guess what? The Supreme Court Justices *got the message!* That is when the Supreme Court stopped being the guardian of the Constitution, and started being the arbitrator—they were threatened into it.

Moving along. Social Security was sold as a retirement package, with the actual name of the Act including words like "insurance" and "trust fund." The objections to the program were two-fold: First, this program overstepped the 10th Amendment, which said the federal government was not authorized by the states to have this power of implementation that took personal property from the citizens. Second, the funds were not earmarked for a specific purpose. That's right, Congress could spend the money however they wanted! Justice Cardozo wrote the opinion from the *Helvering vs. Davis* case. This would be funny if it wasn't such a massive blunder.

Cardozo wrote, "Whether wisdom or unwisdom [stupidity] resides in the scheme of benefits set forth in Title II, it is not for us to say. The answer to such inquiries must come from Congress, not the Courts. Our concern here as often is with power, *not with wisdom*." [italics mine]

Justice Cardozo, still feeling the sting of being called a senile geezer by FDR, gave one final shot over the bow, with this scathing "ascending remark."

Not with wisdom—let's see if Cardozo was right. Since 1937

Social Security has been a tremendous revenue source for the government. It has served as a pot of riches to dole out to constituents, with an ever-increasing scope of victims—uh, I mean citizens—to serve.

Since the money was not earmarked Congress has fleeced Social Security of over *$2.5 trillion dollars* since its inception. We often hear congressmen say, "we need to save Social Security," they just don't bother to tell us that we need to save it *from them.*

I want to make sure you get this. Not only has Congress fleeced Social Security of over $2.5 trillion dollars, this money was never invested in anything to earn interest, like an insurance company or a trust fund is mandated to do! Not only are we out of $2.5 trillion, we are also out of the interest we would have earned. Today, if Social Security would simply have been managed like it was sold, it would have a positive balance of approximately *$6 trillion dollars.* In other words, even with all the money hemorrhaging out to disability, if Congress could have just been proper stewards of the fund, Social Security wouldn't be bankrupt! Unfortunately, President Roosevelt was a progressive, and like progressive politicians today, he threw in his lot with the rest of us, forced to exist on a measly serf's portion of retirement funds.

Oops, that's not right, I was dreaming. President Roosevelt was a progressive, and like progressive politicians today, who have identified themselves as a ruling class, the paltry pension checks through Social Security simply won't do!

That is why our "ruling class" of federal employees have mandatory pensions that provide benefits up to *ten times higher* than the benefits of Social Security. Thank you, your Majesties. Sincerely, Serf.

SCENARIO # 2

It's the 1930s in the U.S. and economic turmoil and uncertainty has been the norm since Black Tuesday in October of 1929. The President, Franklin Roosevelt (FDR), has a number of ideas that he would like to implement. These ideas are manifested in government programs designed to "help us." Among these programs are the Agriculture Adjustment Act (AAA), and the Old-Age and Survivors Insurance Trust Fund (Social Security).

President Roosevelt proceeds with getting his administration's plans/ideas drafted into legislation. Congress complies and creates the legislation for Social Security. Since the Constitution *doesn't* give the federal government the authority to mandate such massive program, Congress drafts their legislation as a proposed amendment to the Constitution.

The proposed amendment for Social Security is sent out to all the State Legislative Bodies for review by their House of Representatives, their Senate and each Governor's office. Also, many citizens provide oversight into the coming discussions and debates about this program.

There are citizens and State Legislators adamantly opposed. There are also ardent supporters and many in the middle. Through the debating and analyzing, a number of concerns rise to the top. The first concern is that the program is, in fact, a mandatory system, which scares many people. Other concerns are that the monies are not earmarked for their intended purpose (retirement), and that no plan exists for investing this retirement income.

After heated yet healthy debates throughout the country, in each State legislative body and many households, compromises are put forth.

Although the system will be mandatory, 80% of the contributions will remain the personal property of the contributor, including 80% of the earned interest on those contributions. That being said, there are specific investment vehicles such as stocks, bonds, real estate and commodities where the contributions will be invested.

20% of contributions, and the resulting interest from these, will reside in a collective pool to assist those whose contributions were not sufficient to sustain them or their survivors throughout retirement, and for those who have not been able to provide contributions due to health or other legitimate reasons.

All citizens, without exception, including government employees, are to be included in this mandatory program. All benefits paid out will be paid equally to each contributor/survivor based on their contributions (80% principle and interested earned), and the remaining collective pool of 20% of all contributions and interest will be paid out equally to citizens based on their retirement income level.

Since 1937, the Social Security Amendment Act to the Constitution has provided a stable retirement income source for all retired Americans. Those Americans less fortunate than their fellow citizens (although presented with the same liberties and chances of success), receive additional retirement income above their share of contributions and interest earned.

Your Choice: Natural Law or …

The argument is not about whether programs like Social Security should exist or not. The argument is that they should have followed the *Rule by Consent*, which is a principle of Natural Law and one of the founding principles of our nation.

Hopefully you can see the difference between these two scenarios. Scenario #1 is what happened—it is factual, it is history, and it was NOT based on Natural Law. Instead, it *broke* the following principles of Natural Law:

- The principle of "consent." This legislation was drafted with the full knowledge that it bypassed the consent of the people—that is why it was not drafted as a Constitutional amendment.
- The principle of "checks and balances." The Executive Branch plotted with the Legislative Branch to coerce the Judiciary Branch into compliance.
- The principle of "equal rights." By reserving posh pension plans for Congress and all other federal employees, and denying such privileges to common citizens.

These principles (and others) are all derived from Natural Law, and when Natural Law is ignored or broken, it gets ugly fast. Since Social Security was *coerced* into implementation, I think it is fair to say, that no one could have *scripted* a more irresponsible outcome of the program! Granted, Scenario #2 is theoretical; however, it is probably close to what would have happened if Natural Law would have been followed and our Constitution upheld.

It All Sounds Too Religious For Me

Does all this talk about Cicero, Natural Law, the Creator, God, and Judeo-Christian principles sound too religious for you? I acknowledge you may abhor religion. However, I'm not going to water it down for you. Natural Law does not exist without acknowledging a Creator because our rights come from the Creator. However, that doesn't mean that you *personally* have to acknowledge the existence of a Creator. Since the founding of this country, tens of millions of Americans were not compelled to believe in a Creator, yet nevertheless were the benefactors of the Creator's principles that our founding fathers used to craft this nation.

I mention this because there are many people who have been turned off to religion to such a degree that they want *nothing* to do with *anything* associated with religion. However, I briefly encourage you not to throw the baby out with the bath water. If the principles of Natural Law and of Judeo-Christian Law that were used to frame our Nation represent "the baby," the "bath water," is the sum of the botched attempts by humans to convey religious principles.

For example: the nine-month-long Salem witch trials of 1692, where thirty three people were accused of witchcraft and were killed, most by hanging, is a man-made stain on God's principles, a terrible wrongdoing by humans.

Humans, with or without Natural Law, make dreadful mistakes. However, and not to minimize any wrongdoings, you have to look at which type of government has the best track record and the worst track record: One that is founded on Natural Law, or one that is founded on State-given rights?

Let's go back 100 years, shall we?

Soviet Union: A state that would encourage progressivism, a state that does not recognize Natural Law. In 1929, they establish gun control and over the next two decades approximately 23,000,000 dissidents, unable to defend themselves, were rounded up and exterminated.

Turkey: A state that does not recognize Natural Law. In 1911, they established gun control. From 1914 to 1918, an estimated 1,500,000 Armenians, unable to defend themselves, were rounded up and exterminated, in an event known as the Armenian Genocide.

Germany: With a ruinous economy and staggering national debt, Germany, a state that does not recognize Natural Law, fell into Fascism. In 1938, they established gun control, and from 1939 to 1945, a total of 13,000,000 Jews and others, unable to defend themselves, were rounded up and exterminated. Despite the facts of the Holocaust, Iran, a state that does not recognize

Natural Law, has denied this historical truth.

China: A state that does not recognize Natural Law. In 1935, they established gun control. From 1949 to 1969, an estimated 30,000,000 political dissidents, unable to defend themselves, were rounded up and exterminated in the Chinese Cultural Revolution.

Guatemala: A state that does not recognize Natural Law. In 1964, they established gun control. From 1964 to 1981, an estimated 70,000 Mayan Indians, unable to defend themselves, were rounded up and exterminated.

Uganda: A state that does not recognize Natural Law. In 1970, they established gun control. From 1971 to 1979, an estimated 300,000 Christians, unable to defend themselves, were rounded up and exterminated.

Cambodia: A state that does not recognize Natural Law. In 1956, they established gun control. From 1975 to 1981, an estimated 1,700,000 educated people, unable to defend themselves, were rounded up and exterminated.

We could go on, because there are millions more in North Korea, Ethiopia, Biafra, Afghanistan, Rwanda, East Timor, West Papua, Iran, and on and on—*all states that do not recognize Natural Law.*

The proponents of State-given rights are not tolerant, nor are they compassionate.

These tens of millions of people were not soldiers of war—they were murdered because of their political beliefs, their level of education, and their religious beliefs. This is not ancient history; this is not a piece of medieval folklore.

It happened while the New York Yankees and other teams played in, and won the World Series, year after year.

FOREWORD

The United States, founded on a firm foundation of principles, represents the most powerful nation that ever existed. No nation has used their power for the betterment of the world like the United States. We are not perfect, but we do have sound principles that are not outdated and are worth fighting for. Not just for us, but for the rest of the world.

When the seeds of tyranny are recognized and when the foundation of a nation is showing some cracks, it is the duty of Patriots to diligently defend those sound principles.

Those Atrocities Could Never Happen Here!

Why? It's happened throughout history. In fact, there's a much higher chance that it will happen here, than it won't. You say it won't happen here because freedom and liberty are strong, but Jessica Hughes, a Tea Party leader in Texas, contradicts that. Jessica said, "We think that because we have been strong in freedom and liberty that all will be protected. However, we fail to recognize that freedom and liberty are actually very *fragile*, fragile like glass, and it is only when we choose to protect our freedoms and liberties that we benefit from their strength." *Well said, Jessica.*

"Freedom is never more than one generation away from extinction. We didn't pass it to our children in the bloodstream. It must be fought for, protected, and handed on for them to do the same, or one day we will spend our sunset years telling our children and our children's children what it was once like in the United States where men were free." *Well said, Ronald Regan*

To Summarize the Movement

The Tea Party movement of today is made up of concerned citizens. I have called them Patriots because I believe that just like the 1770s there is an antonym that exists today – it is slippery and changes names—socialist, liberal, progressive—and when there is enough light shed on it, it changes its name again.

The following is a breakdown of the phases of the movement(s), both past and present.

Phase I: A grassroots movement (people moving) coming together in public places to show their anger and frustration, just like the Sons of Liberty did in the 1770s.

Phase II: Education, as these citizens are not satisfied with simply showing their frustrations at rallies. The real story right now is that the movement is very well read and actively educating themselves and others on how to affect change—locally, statewide and nationally—just like the Sons and Daughters of Liberty did in the 1770s.

Phase III: Affect change through trial and error. Almost everyone in the Tea Party movement started out as a political novice, previously apathetic about politics. or stubbornly asleep to what was going on. As such, there will be a trial and error period. One example among many was the initial attempt to partner up with the GOP, just like the Sons of Liberty did with the established Whigs. The Tea Party movement is highly adaptable—they learn from their mistakes and move on. The movement has definitely learned that currently it's best to work within the two party system to affect change, and at the same time to be careful of the establishment's balance of power in both parties.

Phase IV: A specific unity message. The Sons of Liberty were effective in routing out the establishment in the Whigs (R).
The specific unity message of that time came together after the calling for a Continental Congress, which eventually selected five statesmen to draft the Declaration of Independence.

I believe today's Tea Party movement will get behind a specific unity message, rather than the generic mantra of "responsible government" and "limited government." Why? Because they realize that specific'laws, requiring specific votes, that implement specific actions, need to be implemented.

Electing Congressman who simply say they are for 'responsible' and 'limited' government, has not worked. Obviously, since every politician we've elected to-date has run on some platform that promises responsible actions and limited government! *Have you ever heard a politician promising irresponsibility, and unlimited government? You get my point.*

Phase V: Fight. Today's battles will be won with votes, rather than bullets, thanks to the Tea Partiers of the 1770s. In the 1770s, fighting for their specific unity message (The Declaration of Independence), they had to fight with bullets, because they didn't have *votes*. Today we do.

MORE ABOUT THIS SPECIFIC UNITY MESSAGE

Most likely, the specific unity message will be centered around State's Rights, as this is one area of Natural Law, 'rule by consent' that has been the most abused.

Brent, did you say *State's Rights?* I did, and the progressive movement is very fearful of State's Rights. You will hear them associate State's Rights with slavery! However, if you study history about the Civil War, it is evident that the Federal Government has used the slave-State's bogus claim of 'States Rights', as a basis for ignoring *real* States Rights, to further its unrestricted and unconstitutional growth.

We have to unlearn what we've been taught by the 'losing side' of the Civil War. The Civil War was not about State's Rights. It was about SLAVERY! Period.

Yes, the slave-owning States, (the losers in the war) claimed it was about State's Rights, in other words, it was politically and socially more 'plausible' to argue about State's Rights, than it was to say '**we want to continue to own other humans**'! In other words, they were 'embarrased' and 'ashamed' to argue about the real reason for the war, slavery. Instead, they devised a mask called 'State's Rights'.

In 1858, prior to the Illinois Senatorial election, Abraham Linclon delivered a famous speech that started with, "A house divided against itself cannot stand. I believe this government cannot permantly endure half slave and half free..."[45]

That speech was given two years before Lincoln even ran for President. Lincoln, sacrificed the Senate race against Douglas (Lincoln lost), because Lincoln was setting the stage for the next race (Presidential). The seven debates between Steven A. Douglas and Abraham Lincoln, for the Illinois Senate seat, were exclusively about slavery! Lincoln said to his friends "I am killing larger game. The great battle of 1860 is worth a thousand of this senatorial race."[46]

The seventh and final debate between Lincoln and Douglas, sheds tremendous light on the 'bogus' claim that has been perpetuated through even today, that the Civil War was about State's Rights.

Alton, Illinois October 15, 1858.

Lincoln "Slavery was an economic, political and moral wrong." Additionally he went on, "In the first place, I insist that our fathers did not make this nation half slave and half free... I insist that they found the institution of slavery existing here. They did not make it so, but they left it so because they knew no way to get rid of it at the time... When the fathers of the government cut off the source of slavery by the abolition of the slave trade, and adopted a system of restriticing it from the new territories where

---

[45] Charles A. Church, *History of the Republican Party in Illinois 1854-1912*: Published in 1912, page 44

[46] *Ibid.*, page 59

it had not existed, I maintain that they placed it where they understood, and all sensible men understood, it was in the course of *ultimate extinction!"[47]* ... [italics mine]

Douglas argued that it was the State's Right to regulate their own domestic affairs. Guess What? Lincoln agreed! Right then and there, when the bogus mask of State's Rights was uttered from Douglas, Lincoln didn't buy into it.

Lincoln denied that there was any parallel between the institution of slavery and other varied pursuits [rights] of the states arising from differences in soil and climate. "There had never been any trouble over the cranberry laws of Indiana, or the oyster laws of Virginia or the pine lumber laws ofMaine, or the fact that Louisiana produces sugar and Illinois flour. Slavery, on the other hand, had always been an element of discord!"[48]

In other words Lincoln said, I agree, the States retained the rights to regulate domestic affairs, but the real issue is NOT about States Rights, it is solely about Slavery!

WHY ARE WE TALKING ABOUT THE CIVIL WAR?

Granted, it would take volumes to completely go through the history of the Civil War, if even possible. However, I wanted to expose very important dialog between Lincoln and Douglas, where Lincoln completely and successfully refutes the claim (the mask) that Douglas makes about States Rights being the central issue.

I don't know if you've picked up on it yet, but you most likely will in the future, the progressive movement is all about a National Government controlling everything. State's Rights, is in the opposite corner of the ring, so-to-speak.

[47] Charles A. Church, *History of the Republican Party in Illinois 1854-1912*: Published in 1912, page 66

[48] *Ibid.,* page 68

If you recall, earlier in this book, *every* Tea Party and 9-12 group leader agreed with the following statement..., our Federal Government has grown unconstitutionally, and that is the *centerpiece* of our problems today.

Now is a good time to point out that just prior to the Civil War, the Democratic Party had long ago replaced the Tories, however, the Whig party still remained! But not for long. The Republican Party was created for *one thing*, to remove the establishment in the Whig party, who stood in the way of freedom.

Do you see? History repeats itself, therefore, we should not be surprised when our political parties do not carry the same sentiments as the people who elect them.   The establishment in the Whig party of the 1770s were obstacles, they were weeded out by the Tea Partiers of the time, and a free nation was born [but not matured], because it was the sentiment of the people.

The establishment in the Whig Party of the 1850s were obstacles to ensuring that the freedoms that were fought for in the 1770s applied to everyone. The Republican Party was created to weed out the established Whigs, they did, and freedom for the slaves was born, because it was the sentiment of the people.

In this country, neither Congress, Political Parties nor the Supreme Court can withstand the opposing sentiments of an awakened people.

To Summarize the Similarities of the 1770's and 2010

John Dickinson said this during the Constitutional Convention: "Experience [History] must be our only guide. Reason may mislead us."

I think Dickinson was trying to say that there are powerful lessons that we can learn from our past experiences and history. That if we simply rely on our ability to reason, without considering the past, it will result in the same mistakes.

When I individually analyzed the similarities between the 1770s and 2010, I was surprised, but when I considered all of them collectively, they astounded me.

I hope that you will seriously consider the significance of the similarities that exist between the 1770s and 2010. Throughout history, nations have shifted into despotism during harsh economic periods. We must rely on our experience. We know what made this country great and we know how to be the world leader in compassion, manufacturing, education, engineering, technology, services, and *fiscal responsibility*. We need to rely on our experience, our history, to return us there.

To the Tea Party Leaders

This book is *to* you and *for* you. Speaking with you and reading your stories was so much more than I first anticipated. Thank you for sharing with me, for taking up the call to defend our freedoms and liberties, for so many of you that say this is a lifetime commitment and that the Tea Party movement will not go away! Without a doubt, this has been a labor of love, love of Amercia.

I am looking forward to your feedback. After all, you've got my number, so call me anytime—*my wife is used to it now!*

In Liberty,

Brent Morehouse

I'd like to share one more thing ...

www.newpatriotpublishing.com

FOREWORD

The Lion Hunt

Do you know how lions hunt? The old lions have lost many teeth, their legs are tired and they can't run to catch their prey, so they position themselves upwind from the prey, in plain sight.

The strong, young lions are positioned downwind from the prey, staying hidden by crouching as close to the ground as they can.

With the prey in the middle, the old lions let out their fiercest roars, heard for miles. The prey hears the roars, they smell the lions from upwind, they can even see them!

How does the prey survive? If they follow instinct and run away from the sound of the roars, away from the scent of lions and away from the sight of them, they will be running right into the nest of crouching, strong, young lions.

How does the prey survive? ***They run to the roar!***

The experienced prey know that there's just a few old and tired lions upwind, and that the roars are a <u>deception.</u>

Victory for the lions happens when inexperienced prey don't recognize the deception, and they run away.[49]

The *roars* of the establishment—in both parties, in the mainstream media, in the progressive think tanks, and in the NAACP—are deceptions. They hope that the Tea Partiers will turn and run away. That is how victory happens for them.

---

[49] Article appearing in Heraldofhiscoming.com, Past Issues, August 1997

www.newpatriotpublishing.com

RUN TO THE ROAR!

Please send your feedback/comments to;
TPTA@newpatriotpublishing.com

www.newpatriotpublishing.com

TEA PARTY LEADERS

Tom Balek

I was never one to look for trouble. As a young adult I believed that most Americans were well-intentioned, wanting the best for each other and success for our nation as a whole. I was aware that there were growing political differences between citizens, but thought that the best ideas would win the day, and the United States would continue to thrive. Our nation had so much to be proud of, and had done so much good for us and for the world. What could there be to worry about?

I worked hard to be the best husband and father I could be for my young family. As I matured and aligned myself with other hard-working, conscientious friends and business associates, I began to notice more individuals whose main interest was self-interest, and whose honesty and values seemed flawed or undeveloped.

It made me question: "what am I missing?" How could the beliefs of more and more Americans be so different from mine? I've always been quite sure that the best way for all of us to succeed is the path of individual responsibility, "doing the right thing," respecting our Constitution, preserving our freedoms and being ready to fight to defend them. I studied economics and built successful businesses by making sound financial decisions, expecting the best from people, and using good common sense. But all around me, something was changing. My values and hard-won knowledge were increasingly under attack.

I watched as our political leaders began to stray from a focus on public service to one of self-promotion. It became clear that being elected was now a life goal in itself that, once won, must be preserved at all cost. Somehow, in spite of apparently meager salaries, elected officials were becoming incredibly wealthy and powerful. At some point I realized that there was so much personal profit at stake that to even qualify to run in a national election, one must sell his or her soul to one of the parties, relinquishing all independence of thought or vote. Embarrassing scandals were brushed off and excuses made for any culprit who is on "our side." Politicians pandered to shallow voters, making ridiculous promises. Half or more of our citizens were no longer ashamed to ask, "What's in it for me?"

We had become a polarized society—the "Left" versus the "Right," "redistribute the wealth" versus "individual responsibility," "apologize for being American" versus "proud of our accomplishments," "love the one you're with" versus "church on Sunday."

The media abdicated their important role in society as responsible truth-givers. Schools and universities stopped teaching honest history, economic reality, and life skills. I began to think that maybe this evolution was no accident. Our leaders started lying to us—directly and without shame or hesitation—knowing that enough of our citizens had become indoctrinated or "dumbed down" that they would not be held accountable. In fact, our national leadership had devolved to the point where they looked down at their constituents with contempt. They no longer worked for us.

I feared the November 2008 elections as they approached. For the first time, in race after race, my only choices were one candidate or another whose beliefs and values were entirely foreign to my own. The weakening of the Right had left an opening that the Left was ready to exploit. I knew that we, as a nation, were headed for big, big trouble.

It didn't take long after that steamroller election to see that the result was even worse than I feared. Our economy, our infrastructure, our security, and our future is imperiled to a greater degree every day. We shake our heads in disbelief as our principles are shredded one by one.

I can no longer waste any time trying to understand how so many people can be so dead wrong. I just know that those of us who can still think *must act now.* This is a crossroads in the history of our nation. I know that everyone thinks their time is the most important time in history. But I am convinced to the core that the intent of our leadership is to benefit a select few at irreparable cost to all others. The only means of resistance left to us is a grassroots uprising, and that is the Tea Party Movement.

In April of 2009, national news reports indicated that in some cities groups of concerned citizens planned to gather for rallies on tax day, voicing their displeasure with the radical policy changes already underway. My wife and I wondered if anybody would speak up in our small town, a place where political views are strongly held but seldom discussed, in avoidance of conflict. We made up a couple of signs and went to our local courthouse at noon. To our astonishment, about forty other citizens were there, signs in hand. It was reassuring to learn that we weren't completely alone. We held our signs high and waved to passing motorists, most of whom honked and waved back in support.

And then we, like the others, went back to work, feeling temporarily a little bit better about things.

But the onslaught of policy blunders continues, punch after bloody punch. Recession. Bailouts. Corruption. Unemployment. Nationalization of industries and the closing of local car dealerships. More bailouts. Union thugs and community organizers. Outrageous spending on unproductive government employees and programs. Removing crosses from public view. Backroom deals with lawmakers. Embarrassing gaffes in foreign affairs. Refusal to enforce our borders. Confiscation of private land. Threats to increase taxes and impose crazy environmental restrictions. Capitulation to evil rogue regimes. It seems that our leaders are intent on rewarding all bad behavior and punishing all good behavior. And every policy decision is calculated on empowering the ruling elite.

A few months ago I decided that I had to act now, as forcefully as I can. I found the local men and women who were already trying to be heard, and threw my weight in with them. I created a web site and a newsletter. We hold informational rallies explaining who we are and why we are so concerned. We offer each other encouragement and support. We are in contact with candidates in upcoming elections and sponsor candidate forums. We hold all kinds of events to educate and win over as many voters as possible to our single, focused cause: reduction in the size, reach and cost of government, and preservation of our individual freedoms. We are not racists. We are not violent. We only want the best for all Americans.

RoseAnn Salanitri

I can thank my dad for teaching me to appreciate this country and our heritage that protects freedoms and values personal liberty. I was in the eighth grade during the Cold War. At that time we all knew that communism was our enemy. However, my eighth grade teacher presented it in a way that seemed almost "Christianly." After all, helping those who are less privileged certainly is a Christian principle, and the utopian ideals of communism and Marxism actually seem to fit well into that mold. After that lesson, I went home and asked my dad what was so wrong about these two maligned ideologies. He was a true American patriot who fully understood the principles this country was founded upon, as well as understanding the pitfalls of competing ideologies. He explained the "wolf in sheep's clothing" characteristics of the "isms" and how they promise the world but deliver tyranny and oppression, as well as stifling free enterprise and killing one's work ethic. I've since come to embrace the principles he taught me even more over these last few years, and I've also come to understand what happened to others in my class and those like them who never went home and spoke to their parents about the lure of the "isms" that are now undermining our way of life. Abraham Lincoln's word seem prophetic to me when he said, "The philosophy in the classroom of one generation will be the philosophy of government in the next." We are seeing Lincoln's word play out in front of our very eyes in the philosophy of a government that was weaned by liberal college professors to be the ideologues that threaten our way of life today.

All this became a part of my inner-core beliefs—beliefs that were put on the back burner of my life as I raised my family and bought into the feminist philosophy of "You can have it all." My attempt to be superwoman and supermom kept me busy enough to stay out of the political scheme. I thought others were more capable of handling our government, and I made the mistake of trusting them to do just that. I'm now sixty years old and understand the error of my ways and the errors of others who went about life as usual and trusted others to run our government.

I didn't vote until I was forty years old—embarrassing now, but true all the same. As fate would have it, I had our second child at age thirty-seven, which meant that there were sixteen years between my daughter and my son. My daughter grew up in a school system that wasn't drastically different from the one I grew up in. However, when my son was ready to begin his school years, I was horrified by the decline in our public education. You have probably heard the story of the frog in cold water. As it goes, if you put a frog in hot water, he will immediately jump out. However, if you put a frog in cold water and heat it gradually, you will cook the frog. He'll never notice the water getting hotter and hotter gradually. I was the frog in hot water when it came to the education system my son was entering. It was a shock.

When I was in school, the level of education in our country was an untouchable number one worldwide. In the 1990s we had declined to well behind third world countries—an abysmal change.

I was there when the Department of Education was instituted and I was the mother of a young school-age boy when President Clinton tried to instill Goals 2000, which any logical person could see would result in a horrific dumbing-down of our children. Unfortunately, Goals 2000 was unstoppable, but I (along with others) did our best to defeat it. This was my entrance into political matters of sorts.

From there, I became acquainted with The New Jersey Family Policy Council, whom I've worked for on-and-off for the past ten years. My husband and I also hosted a weekly adult Bible study in our home, which was attended by a future congressman. When he ran for Congress, it was natural for me to volunteer whatever time I had available to his campaign. By this time, I was homeschooling my son and kept informed about the decline of our political system. As I taught him what we used to call civics, I was relearning it myself, and I found it both inspiring and distressing.

As the years passed, it was becoming more and more apparent that our country was in trouble, and I found myself on e-mail lists of various conservative organizations, rarely knowing how that happened. Anyway, the 2008 elections marked a watershed for many of us. Those who had been becoming active as our country declined were becoming more passionate about defending our Constitution and were very distressed about how our courts and elected officials were disregarding this document that we held in high regard. Barack Obama and his administration are the results of years of systematic political denigration and voter apathy. Those who had not been active were rudely wakened from their apathetic sleep.

It was then that one of the groups who sent me e-mails asked if I would like to organize a local Tea Party. Strange as it seems, I can't remember which group it was that first contacted me. Without blinking, I agreed. On April 15, 2009, I organized a Tea Party in our semi-rural county and was surprised by the 200 to

300 people that showed up in the middle of the week. I made a promise to those people on that day that I wasn't just going to go home and feel we did something good by gathering together and waving a few protest signs. I knew we were in trouble and that the issue of taxation was only the tip of the iceberg. As I told our group, this wasn't about being Republican or Democrat, Independent or Libertarian; this was about being American, and we had to stand together if we were going to save our country. There had to be a way to reclaim our country and I was determined to find out what that was.

I spent that summer developing our database and organizing e-mail, letter, and phone call campaigns and finally going to Washington, DC on September 12th—all to no avail. Our senator, Robert Menendez, who was often the target of our protest campaigns, paid little attention to our grievances against cap and trade and health care, not to mention illegal immigration. I also spent the summer trying to make good on my promise to find a way to reclaim our country—and I knew it had to be something that had the ability to tie the hands of the present administration. I believe I found the answer I was looking for. During the course of my research, I stumbled upon New Jersey's recall laws and found that in New Jersey you could recall a US senator. Well, to quote Chris Matthews, "A chill ran up and down my spine." I immediately realized that we had a way to keep these men and women in Congress accountable. I understood that while elections allow you to choose your representatives, recalls allow you to keep them accountable. Not only was this arrogant elitist who summarily dismissed the protests of his people accountable to us, we could actually fire him. And in the process, I knew we could shake up the rest of the elitists in DC. It seemed Abraham Lincoln was right after all—this was a nation of the people, by the people, and for the people—even in 2009!

You can check out the recall movement in NJ on our web site: recallnj.com. That's a whole other story!

Just to be clear, it will take a people who refuse to hand over the greatest country this world has ever known. You see, I found out that the only way we can lose our freedom is if we willingly relinquish it. Our founders sacrificed much so that we could be born in a country where we have the right to pursue happiness as we perceive it to be. They pledged their lives, their treasures and their sacred honor so that in the year 2010 in The United States of America, children can be born free. I say, Born Free, Die Free—nothing else is acceptable.

Fred O'Neal

I think a lot of "experts" don't have a good grasp of the motivations behind the Tea Party effort. I talked with a reporter a while ago about a survey that was commissioned to profile people sympathetic to the Tea Party movement. The survey showed they were disproportionately male and disproportionately in their 40s, 50s, and 60s (Baby Boomers). In the discussion, the reporter asked me about which one issue all self-described Tea Parties could agree on. I told him it was the size of the national debt and the immorality of one generation leaving such a debt behind for their children and grandchildren to deal with. I told him I sensed that one of the motivations behind Tea Partiers was a sense of "collective guilt" over the national debt. I told him that I, like other Baby Boomers, could almost be more accurately called a member of the "Entitlement Generation." From birth, McDonalds and Burger King told me I could have it my way or I deserved a break today. My parents, both products of the Depression and World War II (the Greatest Generation), unwittingly fed my sense of entitlement by spoiling me and seeing to it that I had all the advantages and luxuries they lacked while they were growing up. If I were the only one in my generation who was spoiled, it wouldn't have become a national problem. But, unfortunately, many other Baby Boomers were children of Depression era parents who spoiled them as well.

The end result? In almost every area of life my generation wanted what they wanted and they wanted it now. Politicians catered to our selfishness. They realized that the politician who gets elected is the one who does the best job promising the electorate they can have their cake and eat it too. Consequently, for decades Washington politicians voted in endless programs meant to please their spoiled voters, while passing the cost of those programs on to the next generation.

The net result as evidenced by the Tea Party phenomenon is that my generation, the "Entitlement Generation," has finally come to realize what our selfishness has done to our children and our grandchildren. Consequently, there's an urgency now to fix these problems before we pass on and before we pass these problems on to our kids. Hence, much of what we are doing is motivated by this sense of guilt and sense of concern for the kind of country we're leaving behind to our children.

There's no yelling at Obama and saying this mess is all his fault. This mess is *our* fault. We have to fix it. We can't trust the current breed of politicians who have been trained to give the spoiled child whatever he asks for. We need a new brand of politician who will tell the truth, the unpleasant truth, and then trust the voters to respond in terms of deciding what's best for their children.

David P. Schumacher

I have been a Republican (conservative variety) since just after Lyndon B. Johnson assumed the presidency when JFK was killed. I think I converted because of LBJ's demeanor. Can't recollect for sure. I do know, though, that Ronald Reagan was my favorite president since that time. I was disappointed with every other president as I thought they all seemed to place their policies above the good of the country. That includes both Democratic and Republican. It became a matter of voting against a candidate instead of for a candidate.

TEA PARTY – THE AWAKENING

Like most Americans, I did not learn much about the Constitution nor the Founding Fathers until my "awakening." I was, for some reason, thrilled when the Republicans took over Congress in 1994, and I expected great things. Fortunately, President Clinton moved to the middle and we put off the real nosedive to socialism for a few years. Unfortunately, many of those same Republicans we voted in in 1994 moved to the Left and became corrupted by the Washington culture. In 2007, I finally got cable television. I discovered Fox News network. I finally had a more balanced view of the nation's political news. Apparently, for many years, having only the mainstream media to watch, I didn't realize how crazy Washington had become.

Oh, the big issues I knew, but not in detail. I began to get more involved politically. But it was the Santelli rant at the Chicago Mercantile that got my mind working. Obama had been president for just over a month and had already started his push to take over businesses. I believed that Obama would take this country the wrong direction—that he would push us into a socialist society. He said it over and over, especially before and during the primaries. I was becoming fearful. Then, in early March, my daughter received an e-mail from AFA asking her if she would volunteer to help if someone would organize a Tea Party in our home town. She answered, "Yes." They sent another e-mail stating, "Great, you are the organizer!" She called me and asked if I could help her. I answered, "No!"

Two days later, I called her back and asked what she was doing with the Tea Party. She said that she had about ten or twelve folks who e-mailed her about it. She was posted on the AFA web site. So I agreed to help. We had about four weeks to put something together. We managed to recruit about four others who helped in various ways. None of us had ever tried this before, so we were flying blind. Our Tea Party was scheduled on Tax Day, April 15th, 2009. We chose the county courthouse lawn as the venue. We managed to scrape up three speakers: a city councilman, a county commissioner, and the campaign manager for our US representative. We printed and distributed fliers, sent out press releases to radio and TV. I got on a talk show with a local radio station. A sound system was loaned to us by a country band and we hoped to have 200 or so show up.

We picked 6 p.m. as a start time for the rally as most folks would be out of work by that time. We set up a registration table for folks who wanted to be kept informed about future events. At about 5:15, we were ready. Some folks had begun arriving, so we played patriotic music beginning at 5:30. Folks continued to pour in. By 6 p.m., when I started the program, there were an estimated 700 folks there! They were beginning to block the street. We never thought of closing off the street. I began the program. I was almost overwhelmed. I couldn't imagine that many conservative folks actually coming out to a protest! If I remember correctly, I started my introduction by saying something like, "My name is Dave Schumacher and I am not a politician!" I couldn't believe the response. I had to wait until it quieted down a bit to continue my intro. I then said, "I have the right to be politically incorrect tonight, and I plan to."

Our first speaker was the best. I had her back again for the second tax day Tea Party and she was the closer. By the time 7 p.m. rolled around we had over 1,200 folks at that event. Over 750 signed the registration and we were so grateful to see this movement begin to take off. Two Austin TV stations were there and several newspapers covered it. I believe there were over 800 other Tea Parties that day and I knew then that we might have a chance to take back America for "We the People." As I closed the rally at approximately 7:15, I said, essentially, that we had come out to show our disdain for our government trying to destroy our country. I told the folks to watch the news over the next few days, because they would paint us as a bunch of right wing nuts. That we were inciting folks to riot. That we were "anti-government." They would tell lies. But I say that we are patriots, trying to preserve what our divinely inspired Founding Fathers gave us.

Since that first hastily put together rally, I have been involved in putting on two more and have another one planned for July 3rd. We now have a team of folks who meet regularly to go beyond just holding rallies. We are getting involved in our government. Some have become precinct chairs, many are working with candidates, many are sending money or making calls for candidates outside of their local areas. Many of us made phone calls for Scott Brown in Massachusetts, to try to halt the health care bill as did others Tea Party and 912 groups. Even before the Tea Party planning, I got more involved. I helped a candidate for president by donating and phone banking for him. I did not want McCain nor Obama as my next president.

I think that my greatest inspiration was the 9/12 rally in DC. My son and I flew there expecting maybe 50,000 others. Were we shocked and awed by the numbers and the civility. My gosh, maybe 1,000,000 red blooded Americans traveled that weekend to ask our servants in Washington to stop the madness. We saw the response. So we march on. I want to say as I close: Thank you to all of the others in this great nation who are finally, like me, waking up. I hope it's not too late.

Paulette Michener Bockert

I was raised in a very patriotic family. My grandparents sent six boys to World War II; five came home. My brothers were both in the military. And every Memorial Day found me at special services while my friends were sleeping in or away on vacation.

I was raised to love and respect our nation's history, our country's founding, and the US Constitution. I attended Buckeye Girls' State, sponsored by the American Legion Auxiliary, and learned firsthand about the political process in our state and country.

I taught my children, at a young age, to stand at attention as the US Flag was presented—hand over heart and hats off. I instilled in them the same patriotic fervor that I carry. As a Cub Scout leader and assistant leader in Girl Scouts, I instructed young people on flag etiquette and respect. I often spoke on the subject to grade school classes.

Now my country's very foundation is being eroded and I am heartsick. When my adult children roll their eyes at me for my involvement in the constitutional, conservative movement, I tell them, "This is *my war* to fight to insure that my grandchildren enjoy life in the US as you have enjoyed it. I cannot sit idly by and allow my country to disappear. Your grandfather and his brothers and my brothers, and countless ancestors fought in wars so that you could enjoy the many freedoms that you have today. I have to try to restore it to what I have always known it to be or better. Otherwise, I cannot live with myself!"

I have a burning desire in my gut to work to restore the Constitution. I have felt helpless to return America to its founding for many years. And now others have joined me and I have a hope that is not the hope of which Obama spoke. I believe that Obama's election to president is a blessing; it is just the catalyst that some needed to get involved.

I pray that all our work is God-led and that He will allow us to prevail. God Bless us and God Bless America.

Bill Adams

My story is probably one that could be told by millions of other Americans. I am your typical American who was born in the 1950s, lived through the turmoil of the 1960s and survived the 1970s. I was raised in a white middle class family. Money for us was always an issue. My father was an accountant and never made more than $37,000 a year his whole life. Our first color television was bought the year I started college. And though money was tight in our family I always felt our life was good.

Today, I earn many times over what my father did a year, we have several cars, computers, and a nice home yet I feel a sense of foreboding for myself and my family.

I started my political life as a Democrat. My parents were Democrats. John Kennedy, Irish, Catholic you know. And I remained so until Jimmy Carter made a farce of what I thought America should be! He was the first appeaser as I look back on him! So I became a Republican. I loved what Ronald Reagan stood for—fiscal responsibility, military strength, smaller government and all was well. Then came Clinton and the Bushes.

Somewhere the Republicans lost their moral and political compass. Fiscal responsibility turned into spending sprees, government grew, and the delineation between Democrats and Republicans became blurred. The final straw for me was the stimulus package that Bush pushed through prior to the election. This proved to me that the Republicans were no different than the Democrats!

Looking ahead I decided to become involved. Prior to the Tea Party movement, I began looking at the 2008 election, and who the candidates would be. Upon researching Obama, I soon began to realize that this man was a socialist. His background was missing, and those who surrounded and mentored him all had backgrounds in communism and or socialism. I knew then that if this man got elected this country would begin the slide down the slippery slope to a liberal larger government. I had no idea despite his pre-election statement that "We will fundamentally change America" was exactly what he meant!

The record spending, increased government involvement and socialized programs signaled America was in trouble! About that time every day Americans were awakening from their sleep and realizing if they did not stand up America was doomed. The Tea Party Movement was born and that was exactly was what I was looking for! I had to do something. I had written over a thousand articles on the Yedda blog web site, but I wanted to take a more active role. I attended Tea Party rallies and spoke. Then the Tea Party Patriot Movement was born and I became an active member there also. However, due to the TPP being a 501(c), they could not endorse a candidate. This I felt was a weakness. The Tea Party Movement prides itself on that there are no individual leaders; however, I viewed that as a weakness, only for the fact that there are people who joined the Tea Party Movement looking for direction and guidance, and I felt that we were lacking in providing that. In my opinion to be a deciding voice in American politics we must vet candidates based on the Mission Statement of the Tea Party Movement, and endorse accordingly, based on the candidates stand on the issues of fiscal responsibility, free market solutions, lower taxes and less government involvement in the lives of Americans.

Not being able to do that within the Tea Party Patriots, I decided to become more actively involved with the Independent Caucus of which I was already a delegate in the State of West Virginia. As fate would have it, the State Director in West Virginia was overwhelmed with her responsibilities with the Tea Party and the Independent Caucus, and decided to allocate her resources with the Tea Party.

I offered my services to the Independent Caucus and agreed to become the State Director of the Independent Caucus in the State of West Virginia. The Caucus vets, endorses and supports candidates who support the conservative ideals of the IC, which are almost identical to those of the Tea Party Movement. I am currently in the process of organizing the state of West Virginia to play an important role in the 2010 and 2012 elections, which I feel are a "pivot point" for America!

TEA PARTY – THE AWAKENING

Patricia Crocker

I am one of nine children and was always referred to by my conservative brothers as "the bleeding-heart liberal of the family." I went to a pretty liberal college, where I met my husband, Roger, who is black (I am Caucasian). I went into the health care field as a Pediatric Occupational Therapist. I remember being excited when President Clinton was in office and Hillary Clinton was working on health care reform. I was never very politically savvy and was never much interested in our government, aside from voting in presidential elections. That all changed after 9/11. Because I work in home health, I am in my car a lot. I started to listen to talk radio after 9/11 when traveling between patient visits because I wanted to keep up with what was unfolding after the 9/11 attacks. I became acutely aware of how much news and facts I had been missing by listening to only mainstream news. I slowly became more informed on issues and politics.

After the birth of my first son, Bryant, my world was centered on him and my family. So after 9/11, I became fearful for my son, who was six years old at the time, and wondered what kind of world he would live in. Around that same time, our family also started to do foster care, and we started to care for a two-year-old child, Caleb, who we ended up adopting two years later. Through fostering other children, we have learned even more the importance of strong family values and what happens to children who do not have that kind of support system.

Fast-forward to 2008. Several things happened that transformed my life even more. The first thing was the presidential race of 2008. Even though I supported John McCain, I was at first excited about the prospect of having a black president (Barack Obama). But I was also very concerned when I started to learn about his stance on various issues. My thirteen-year-old son Bryant shares a common background with Barack Obama, being the child of a Caucasian mother and black father. What a wonderful way for him to see someone with a similar background as him make it to be president of the United States! What a potential role model he could be for my son.

One evening during the presidential campaign, my son was watching the news as I prepared dinner. There was a clip of the Reverend Wright, Barack Obama's spiritual mentor, going on one of his rants, and my son turned to me and said, "Mom would you keep going to our church if Father T ever said anything like that? How could Barack Obama go to a church like that?" It was then that I realized that this country was headed for some rough times if Barack was elected president. My fears were realized. Don't get me wrong, I celebrate the fact that a black man could be voted in as president. I celebrate the fact that Barack Obama's nine-year-old daughter does her homework at the same table that President Lincoln wrote the Emancipation Proclamation. But I am not happy that this man is our president because of his ideology and the direction he is leading this country.

The second thing that happened was the crash of the banking industry and the TARP bill that was passed by President Bush. This was quickly followed by the first bailout. When I heard the sobering statistics about how much our children and grandchildren were going to have to pay, I became a mother grizzly bear" protecting my two cubs, and knew that I had to do something other than yell at the TV set. I decided to go to the first Tea Party rally in our state capital of Montpelier, Vermont. I had never been to any kind of rally and did not know what to expect. Web sites suggested signs and the night before the rally, I struggled with what to put on my sign. I decided on, "Read My Lipstick, No New Taxes!" I took off the next day from work and nervously drove to the state capital. I had never been to the state capital before. To my surprise, there were 600 people at that rally, which is large considering that until recently there were more cows than people in Vermont. At that rally, I felt a sense of hope and exhilaration. There were actually people in the liberal state of Vermont that were upset too. I was not alone.

Following that rally, I wanted to do more. I signed up on a web site to help organize a Tea Party rally for the 4th of July. Before I knew it, I was getting phone calls and e-mails from people I did not know. To my surprise, I was listed on that web site as *the* organizer! I panicked. How was I supposed to do something like this? I had never done anything like this before. To my relief, two other women offered to be co-organizers, so the three of us set out to organize the next rally. Fortunately, after much hard work, multiple meetings, trial and error, and much sweat, the event went well. That was followed up by other events throughout the year. At one such event, I was accused by an attendee (not with the Tea Party group) *of being racist!* Pity that person when I told them that racism is when somebody suggests that my husband is a traitor to his race because he is conservative! (that did happen ... and since when should blacks not be conservative?) Recently, one of the original co-organizers of our group moved to another state. The remaining two of us continue to community organize for the Green Mountain Patriots. But we don't see ourselves as the leaders. We do help organize and facilitate, but others in our group may lead at other times, depending on the task and situation. Everyone has different and unique roles that they play. I feel honored to be with a group of people that are so highly knowledgeable, motivated, and work so hard to keep the momentum going! We will be able to take this state and country back!

Richard D. Ramsey

I got involved with the Tea Party movement because no one was doing it for me. I used to think that life kept people down and that given an opportunity most people would step up and be successful. I worked hard and as a result am in a position to help people get started and move up the ladder in nursing—I'm an RN by trade. I've heard people (some, not all) make excuses for their own shortcomings; however, through my own experience and by watching others, I feel that I am responsible for my shortcomings. Although I wanted to be a physician (I'm not) I

made excuses for not going to medical school, and when I decided to evaluate my own sense of personal responsibility, I
became a conservative.

When the Tea Party movement started in 2009, I waited for
someone to start a local chapter. No one did. I finally decided to
organize one myself. We have about twenty core members now
and we're planning more rallies in our local area. My wife is
concerned about my personal safety because of the supposed
controversial platforms of the Tea Party and local police officers
have warned me to watch what I say and do because the FBI
warns them about "hate groups" like the Tea Party.

So, why do I do this? Because no one is paying my taxes for
me; however, I'm paying for others to live on gratuitous welfare.
Because no one is protecting my home for me, but the liberal
government wants to come in and tell me how to manage my
household. Because no one went to nursing school for me, but
I'm forced regularly to go overboard with defensive medicine
until we have comprehensive tort reform. I went to college,
bought my house and I'm raising my family without help from
anyone else. I do understand charity, I've adopted a disadvan-
taged child and I give money to needy families on a regular
basis. But, what I have, I got on my own. Some people think that
government has to do things for you. I'm not one of those
people. I like the freedom to do things for myself and reap my
reward for a job well done.

Evan Queitsch

Each of us will have stories that are unique yet in many cases
you find things that tie us all together. To many of us this
movement is about leaving a better tomorrow for our kids and
grandkids and about ensuring freedom for our posterity but to all
of us this is about preserving and defending America.

TEA PARTY – THE AWAKENING

At age nineteen I enlisted in the United States Marine Corps. I arrived at Camp Lejeune, North Carolina almost a year to the day before September 11th, 2001. I was among the first volunteers from my unit to sign up to take the fight to whoever had done this to us. After all, I had family who worked in the Trade Center complex who were fortunate to be alive on September 12th and I was a US Marine and my job was to support and defend the Constitution of the United States against *all* enemies, foreign and domestic. It helped, I think, that I understood what it might mean. I'd been a student of the revolution and I knew the cost our original patriots paid for us to be free. I had also been a student of the Civil War and knew the cost that so many in our country had paid for *all* of us to be free.

Additionally, as a student of the World Wars I knew the cost that Americans had paid so that the entire world could be free. It was with the history of America and of the American military in mind that I signed up to go wherever I was needed. A year later I found out where I was going: Kuwait. I was with the advance team who arrived in Kuwait to prepare for the Iraq offensive. I drove vehicles to our forward locations and as a main battle tank repair technician I was responsible for ensuring that the gear our fighting men and women had was in the best possible shape. I also volunteered to do convoy security runs to our forward logistic support base inside the Iraqi border. I returned home after a six-month deployment just in time to celebrate my son's 1st birthday in July of 2003.

Had it not been for the birth of my son I would more than likely have reenlisted in the United States Marine Corps but after having been deployed even for so short a time as six months (I know Marines who have spent *years* away from their children), I could not bring myself to leave him for so long a time period again.

My father voted twice in his entire life and both of them were for the same man, Ronald Reagan. I found out in 2009 that this was the case, politics and voting records had never come up before.

When I asked him why he said to me, "Son, I'm not going to vote for someone I don't believe in and he is the only person I could believe in." I started listening to talk radio, researching the candidates and looking outside of Comedy Central and MTV for my news and information. I already had a background that gave me great respect for what we as a nation had come from but politically I needed to understand the entire picture and so I stepped back to see it. I knew that the Democrats were offering a transformation of America into a socialist state. Any discerning and conscious person could have seen that—the problem is that most of the voters were neither of those things and the Republican party wasn't offering much hope in the other direction. I supported Fred Thompson early on because he seemed to be one of the only candidates supporting our founding principles. Certainly John McCain wasn't doing that. When it came down to Obama vs. McCain I realized where we stood. We were in trouble as a nation but the history of the moment would triumph. I knew that Obama would win and I knew it really didn't matter except in one respect. America would finally have its answer to a question that has haunted it for decades. When will America have her first black President?

I had looked at our national situation in the months leading up to the election. I knew economically we were in trouble and that we were spread thin militarily. I knew that America had moral and spiritual questions that needed to be answered and I knew that they weren't caused by our incoming President but I knew he was going to make them worse. For the first time in my life I set foot inside my local Republican office. I wanted to help get us back to our founding. I quickly discovered that the local Republicans had no intention of doing that and it wasn't long until I would discover that the state GOP wasn't any more interested.

Then came March 13th, 2009 and Glenn Beck. I had a long commute in the mornings and would often catch the better part of Glenn's radio show. He seemed a lot like me. He'd been through tough times, dealt with it and become fairly successful.

He seemed as concerned as I was about the situation that confronted us and like me he had questions. One question I had, he had the answer to and he proved it. He set up the March 13th "We Surround Them" broadcast of his TV show and encouraged regular people to have viewing parties. I went looking for a viewing party in Delaware and I came across one being set up by a couple from nearby that I didn't know. I contacted them and I helped to organize the viewing party at their church. At first it was just a handful of us. As the numbers who were registering began to grow into the 10s and then to 50 we realized that we indeed were not alone. On Friday, March 13th we had 150 people show up and sit with us to watch. We knew that we had to do something. I had already created a web site called foundersvalues.com which was basically little more than a blog for my own thoughts. I offered to make it into something that the group could use as a web presence to attract new people. Several of us agreed to meet again and we ended up getting involved with planning the Wilmington Tea Party on April 15th. For us it was about realizing we weren't alone in our concerns and that we had valid questions. It was about taxes, spending, government takeovers and the loss of our connection to the founders. It was all of those things and we worked hard to organize the event in just a few weeks. April 15th 2009 was cold (in the 40s) and rainy in Delaware and our event was planned outdoors. Fortunately a local business owner was able to get us into an unused storefront in the location but the 1,500 people that showed up in the cold rain didn't know that.

That woke us up further and we formed officially as a 501(c)3 educational organization in June of 2009. We met with our legislators and held town halls and forums on health care reform. We also educated our group members on the Constitution, founding principles and current events. One of the most important things that we did as a group was to distribute literature. In 2009 we distributed 300+ pocket Constitutions, 100+ *The 5000 Year Leap* books, 50 *The 5000 Year Leap* CDs, 25 Glenn Beck *Common Sense* books, 20 Glenn Beck's *Arguing with Idiots* books and 20

The Real George Washington books. We have nearly matched that number already in 2010 and we have expanded our educational offerings tremendously. Also, in 2010 we launched a few new initiatives aimed at educating both adults and children on the founding of our nation. First, we hosted the first joint candidate forum in Delaware for the 2010 elections and we had candidates from every political party for the US House and US Senate attend and speak to around 100 people. Then we developed a new educational strategy and we developed a seminar packet that we call our "Innovative Founding Seminar." During the full day seminar (or split into sections across multiple days) we use the HBO miniseries "John Adams" and the History Channel DVD series "The Revolution" to tell the founding of America. We also utilize portions of the "Making of America" study guide developed by the folks at the National Center for Constitutional Studies who are also our source for the majority of our educational materials. We have also just announced an essay contest for Delaware High School Students to read the Bill of Rights and explain each of the rights that our founders expressed. The winner will have their essay read at our Constitution Day Dinner on September 17th, 2010 and will receive other prizes as well. We are also putting together a scholarship fund for students who live the founder's values every day.

We have come a long way in one year's time and we are excited about that. We also recognized that we needed to educate people on one hand and motivate/activate them on the other. So in addition to our 501(c)3 education group we created the only 501(c)4 organization in Delaware that is able to endorse and support candidates on behalf of the Tea Party in Delaware. The name of that organization is "Common Sense Communities Society" and we have endorsed candidates for county, state and national office. We're conducting polling, forming opinion papers and working hard to recruit volunteers for the candidates who represent the Tea Party message in Delaware.

TEA PARTY – THE AWAKENING

You ask what prompted me into action and the answer is simple for me: my family. I have a wife and three children with one on the way who deserve to have it better than I did. I want that for them. My knowledge of history gave me the intellectual fire-power to go out with a reference point but without my family to think about I don't believe I would have seen things so clearly. I could not let this country and the ideals that men and women fought and died for over the last 220 years fall in front of my eyes and leave that mess for my children to clean up. It simply was not an option so my only option was to fight back and to stand up for what is right. As a former Marine with a back-ground in history, there was only one choice.

In the end our country is both worth saving and able to be saved. It's up to us as Americans to make it happen and it is up to us as Tea Party leaders to lead the way. Our cause is just and our path is the way. We must push on and continue to fight. We will win.

Al Reynolds

I am a military brat and my father retired after thirty years in the US Air Force. I have lived in many states and in three foreign countries including Panama, the Isle of Trinidad and Japan, where I graduated from high school. I attended colleges in Southern California majoring in biological sciences and religion. In 1966, I enlisted in the US Navy and spent time in San Diego at the Naval Hospital as a Hospital Corpsman and transferred to Camp Pendleton with the Marine Corps. I was released from Ac-tive Duty in 1970 and returned to Los Angeles to resume college. Moved to Northern California in 1988 and worked at major high tech law firms as their MIS person for fifteen years. I retired in 2007 and moved to Illinois to be near my son and his family.

It was after moving to Illinois that I became interested in politics at local and state levels. From 2007 to the present, my real estate taxes increased each year. My property value declined during that same period and officials could not give me a sane explanation. In February I heard about the Tea Party movement in Seattle and also the event in Chicago at the commodities market also stirred my interest in getting involved in some sort of active group that opposed any more taxation. In April 2009, a group formed up in Champaign Illinois to hold a tax day rally to protest the ever increasing tax burden on the public. They held a rally in Westside Park downtown Champaign which was attended by about 400 persons including me. I had lived through the anti-war rallies of the Vietnam War era and this was nothing like the violent, radical, destructive protests that saw cars burned and stores broken into and merchandise stolen all in the name of protest. The people who attended this rally were not any particular political party members but instead were outraged property owners who had had enough taxation and were ready to voice that rage to officials in a public forum. The orderliness of the demonstration enticed me to want to be a part of it. After the rally I approached the organizer and inquired if I could join in membership to be a part of the organizing and planning of the next rally. He indicated that he would not be able to lead the next rally and asked if I would like to take over the leadership and I agreed. At this time the Tea Party movement was spreading across the US like wildfire with people of all persuasions and beliefs but one common thread linked them all: the taxation issue. A rally was planned in Washington DC in conjunction with another movement (9/12 project) started by the television commentator, Glenn Beck. A crowd estimated to be over 1 million attended and like the rally in Champaign it was peaceful and orderly—the parks and streets were left clean by the attendees. It was historic. It was symbolic of the American Spirit. It was genuine and real yet the officials denied it and called it a fraud and called the people who attended it domestic terrorists. It was this reaction of the Democratic Party, and their remarks concerning this hugely successful rally *(that voiced the opinions and concern for the welfare of the Nation)* that spurred me to seek a more viable means of change for the conservatives in my home state of Illinois.

TEA PARTY – THE AWAKENING

A million people pouring out their heartfelt concern that we were on the wrong path with socialized medicine and Cap and Trade issues and the Democratic Party would not listen and declared that they knew what was better for the people of the nation than the people did. I knew then that the only way I could make a difference was to run for office and place myself in a position where I did not have to plead with officials but could vote against those same officials on legislation that was contrary to the good and will of the people. I am currently running for State Senate, 52nd District in the state of Illinois. If elected I will give the voice back to the people in my region and they will be heard.

Amanda Norris

Until about two years ago, I didn't pay much attention to politics. I had never been terribly interested in learning more about our nation's history (every history teacher I had did a really good job of making it as boring as possible); however, I now find myself devouring books about our founders and digging for the truth behind the slanted stories that appear in our textbooks. Now, I always keep a pocket Constitution in my purse and often end up giving them away to people I speak with at the grocery store, at work and everywhere in between! A few years ago I would have probably considered someone as fascinated and passionate about our history as I am now a little "off"! I will try not to ramble ... please forgive me if I blather on too much!

My husband David and I have never spent much time watching TV ... we are always much too busy working full time, raising two pre-teens and slowly but surely remodeling every bit of our house by ourselves. We have always been very frugal and we don't buy the luxury items we want until we have saved enough to pay for them up front. It has always bothered both of us to see people living paycheck to paycheck and financing anything and everything they want.

When we would actually sit down to watch TV, we tended to gravitate toward cable news. About two years ago, we started to really pay attention to what was going on in Washington and at the state level. We were very concerned about the rate at which both the state and federal governments were growing and spending. When TARP passed through Congress, we didn't know what to think—how can they use tax money to bail out the irresponsible institutions that helped create the financial problems our nation was currently facing? Those bailouts made no sense! We try to teach our children to be responsible—and now our government is showing yet again, go ahead, make bad choices and we will bail you out! When my eleven-year-old begged for a cell phone, I told her that she would need to save up enough money to cover six months of the bill and figure out a plan to pay for it every month. On her twelfth birthday, she came to me with the money and her plan and said, "can we go get my phone now?" Every child in her class has a cell phone, but my daughter is the *only* one who pays for it herself and did not have it handed to her. We have become a society that believes in instant gratification and handouts! TARP was quickly followed by the stimulus and all of its wasteful programs and the complete takeover of our entire health care system! We can't afford to continue down this road.

The first time I watched Glenn Beck, he was talking about the Constitution. After that show, I went out and bought a book with the Declaration of Independence, Constitution, and Bill of Rights. I hadn't read (or even thought about) those documents since high school. We heard about the February 2009 Tea Parties and my husband suggested that we go to one. Our first Tea Party was on Tax Day in Davenport IA. We had no idea that there was a local group forming in Dixon IL. It was so exciting to be surrounded by such a wide array of people from all different backgrounds who all felt the way that we did! We travelled to Rockford IL for the 4th of July rally. The next day, we saw pictures of people who stood in the rain in Dixon on the 4th and I was very excited to realize that I recognized someone in that photo from my kid's school. I contacted Patty Yde and set out to attend a health care protest at Bill Foster's office in Dixon. Only three other people showed up that afternoon, but we sat and talked for hours and decided to plan a September 12th rally in Dixon. I am not a person who is comfortable speaking in front of more than one or two people, but I jumped in with both feet and spoke in front of a crowd of 300! Since then, I have been very involved in our local group. We have had a core group of about 12 people, but have since gathered an e-mail list of over 150 people (small potatoes compared to many groups, but we are very pleased to have grown to this size in this extremely liberal community). Steve Yde committed a *lot* of time in getting this group off the ground ... many of us wanted to participate, but not many are willing to jump in and take charge. We have a small, but fabulous group and have been passing the baton back and forth. I feel very blessed to know these great folks!

We have organized a few rallies, but we have decided that the best way to make a difference is to work to engage local voters in our electoral process. We organized a Voter Fair in January at our local community college before our (very early) February primary. It took just about every spare moment that a few of us had, but we managed to get twenty-seven candidates to show up and meet with local voters. We set up interviews with many of them and posted those interviews on YouTube and also created a voter guide to show voters where each candidate stood on certain issues. We knew that we would not be taken seriously by Democrat candidates as the local Tea Party, so we created a nonpartisan committee (the Sauk Valley Voter Education Committee) to sponsor the event. We wanted to keep it nonpartisan to let every side be represented and encouraged local voters to vote their values by voting for the candidate whose values most closely matched their own. Our consistent message is "forget the party" and vote for candidates of character and integrity. I am constantly amazed at the people I speak with who vote for one party or the other, but, when asked about specific issues, usually disagree with that party's stance! We are planning another voter fair for this coming September as well as a few social events, and we are looking into hosting Constitution classes and hopefully a few candidate debates.

I get so tired of people telling me that they always vote Republican or Democrat! Allegiance to one party or another is what has helped get us to where we are now! It is time for every voter to step up and fulfill their responsibility to our Republic by educating themselves about the candidates and the issues before they cast their vote! I believe it is my duty to do what I can to open the eyes of as many voters as possible and try to inspire in them a desire to learn more about our nation's history.

Unfortunately, this is going to be a long, uphill battle! It is vital that we bring back the values of personal responsibility, hard work, and a Constitutionally limited government! Our so-called representatives have been violating the Constitution for so long that they don't even bother to justify their actions anymore! We, as citizens and voters, must step up and put them back in their place and elect those who believe in and respect the Constitution. They have worked to create a dependent class and have truly waged a class war. The elites in Washington are so arrogant that they believe they know better than we do how we should live our lives. I believe that Samuel Adams was right when he said, "It does not take a majority to prevail. But rather an irate tireless minority, keen on setting brushfires of freedom in the minds of men ..." For the sake of my children and future generations, I am committed to spreading this fire in as many people as I can!

A. Elliott

I have rescued animals literally all my life ... since elementary school. That has been my lifelong passion and I have participated in some high profile nationally televised rescue and cruelty cases. Winter before last, 2009, after the '08 election, I saw the direction in which my country which headed. I learned about the

Tea Party movement that originated under President Bush ... and as I watched the Internet I saw Tea Party events popping up all over the country, I kept watching for one to be announced in Idaho Falls. My thoughts were that Idaho was so conservative that they didn't feel the need to participate. After waiting and waiting, I told my husband that I was throwing my hat into the ring and that he and I might be the only ones there ... but Idaho Falls was going to be represented by a Tea Party! It was ... we had 1,200 folks according to the police on site. It was just great to see all those people who felt helpless and simply needed someone to step forward and serve as a "nominal" head. I didn't want to be the Tea Party leader in Idaho but no one was stepping up. I now spend part of each day on the Tea Party ... with my greatest effort focusing on keeping our Tea Party folks informed. An informed electorate is a must for a free society.

What will it take to restore this country? Good and moral people—"grassroots Americans"—*must* step up and take roles in our government. Those in power *must* be held accountable *without exception.*

Andrew Ian Dodge

I got involved in the Tea Party movement by organizing the first one in Maine (April, 2009), I had noticed a map at CPAC of 2009 and Maine was the only state blank—this was late February. I certainly didn't want Maine to be the only state where a Tea Party Rally was not being held!

I continue to be involved with the Tea Party Patriots (teapartypatriots.org) as their Maine coordinator because their core values are my own. They are fiscal responsibility, limited government and free markets. I have deliberately only worked with groups that stuck to these core principles and did not muddy the water with any social issues (I am a social libertarian). I believe, as I have for most of my life, that the single biggest problem facing the US is fiscal in nature ... i.e. bloated government, high taxation and out of control spending.

The Tea Party movement is a groundswell of American people concerned with the direction in which their government is heading. After many years of merely sitting on the couch and complaining they have finally got off their derrieres and become active. It really pleases me to see fellow fiscal conservatives actively involved in their community, state and national governance. For many years those of us who did make a stand (I wrote a book called Statism Sucks! 2.0 which rails against the bloated suffocating state) felt as if it was some quixotic effort that even those who agreed with us found amusing. The Tea Party movement makes me feel proud to be American and a fiscal conservative.

To be honest, it's good to see fiscal conservatives finally out on the streets protesting. For so long, demonstrations, rallies and protests were merely the method of operation of the left. The right is finally realizing what kind of psychological effect it has to stand somewhere or address a crowd of people who believe as you do. It took them long enough but they seem to finally get it.

We have inspired the British to start their own Tea Party movement. I am advising the budding movement in the UK since I know UK politics and those involved well. I am married to an Englishwoman and have lived in the UK quite a bit of time during my life. The movement is spreading to the UK for a variety of reasons. The UK, like the US, has a large government that is slowly strangling the country's prosperity and future. It has a solid base of fiscal conservatives that feel left out of all the major parties in the country, like the US The US has adopted much of the welfare and statist ideas of the British system. Obamacare, after all, ultimately seeks to give the US its own NHS. There are clear lines of convergence between the two nations politically, philosophically and economically.

Furthermore, the idea and ideals that inspired the American Revolution and the current Tea Party movement are for the most part of British origin. Adam Smith, John Locke, Thomas Paine and, of course, the American Founding Fathers. It is not surprising that British fiscal conservatives wish to take back the ideals of the Tea Party movement and make them their own.

Andy Edmonds

I am twenty-four years old and was married on September 6th of last year. I got into politics while I was in the navy. In the military it is pretty much a given that, if you had to, you would sacrifice your life for your country. The idea made me think a little: what would I be giving my life for? So I began to do my research. I voted for President Bush both times, but found my follies in him. I started looking at our current state of the union—I saw that gas prices were climbing to almost $5.00/gallon ... I saw a war being fought, and I saw corrupt politicians making empty promises. I had to decide what I was going to do, so I started by evaluating my principles—what was I raised on, what were my beliefs. I researched on them because I wanted to be absolutely secure in my values and beliefs (not just rely on what I was brought up on). I then researched the great and not so great leaders of this nation of ours. I researched policies and laws, and even dabbled a little into the conspiracy theory world (if there weren't people who questioned everything, then a lot of truths that are now known would be lost). I read the Federalist Papers, Plato's Republic, and books about our Founding Fathers. I read quotes from the founding of this great nation and what it was meant to be and quickly realized that this country was in no way the image that the Founding Fathers envisioned for us.

So what now, I asked myself. I went to a Tea Party rally in 2009, and it inspired me! Expecting a couple hundred people in the small town of Westminster, MD, close to a thousand people showed up. Signs waved, and through the mess of our daily political lives, there were nothing but smiling faces! A few months later my fiancé and I moved into our new house ten miles north of Hanover, PA. My political education grew and my liberties continued to shrink ... tax day was coming around again. I was looking into the closest Tea Party for my wife and I to attend, when the thought came into my head, "Why not Hanover?" So it began! I expected forty or fifty people and thought it would be similar to the year before where it would be people standing on the street with picket signs ... boy was I in for a surprise. I called the local police chief and explained my idea. He told me that if I expected forty or fifty, to plan for a hundred, and suggested a park in town. The city council approved the rally and the next day it made the front page of the local paper.

After that I received e-mails, phone calls, and letters to my house ... some praising, some putting me down. I printed flyers and went around pitching the idea to local businesses, most of which supported the cause. I started a Facebook page and listed the event on every Tea Party support page on the Internet. I told friends, co-workers and family and asked them to spread the word as well. I found a place where I could rent a podium and extended an invitation for speakers at my rally. I thought having speakers would increase the credibility of the event, and sure enough, people accepted. I had state representatives, local college students, constitutional scholars, democrats, republicans, and independents. I bought a hundred pocket constitutions to hand out at the rally, thinking: "How can you defend your rights if you don't even know what they are?" I even bought a book for people to sign so I could get an accurate count of how many people were there. My wife stitched a 4' by 8' banner that said "Hanover Tea Party 2010." Both of our families pitched in to buy several cases of water and a ten-gallon tub full of ice to give out to people at the Tea Party.

The day arrived! The Tea Party was big news in our little town, and it spread quick! The rally started at 4 p.m. and people began to arrive with their signs and folding chairs at 3 p.m. while I was setting up! Roughly 400 people flooded the park! There was a group of high school kids that came on their bikes. There were people young and old, military vets, and even members of the Oath Keepers group that showed up. One of the speakers made a comment that the group of people listening thought was prejudice, and they booed him off the stage! I believe this was a good thing because it showed the Tea Party wouldn't stand for the bad stuff that the media tends to paint our movement with. We had a voter registration table, a table with a petition from a local author, and the pocket constitutions went quick. Throughout the day I enjoyed many good speakers, good handshakes and hugs, and lots of discussion on how "We the People" can take this country back.

The Tea Party was a success! People learned a few things and most of all realized that *they can* be involved in making things better. Since that rally, a number of us have created a meet-up group that we have named the Hanover Tea Party Patriots. We focus on educating the public, getting people to vote, and getting people involved. Though it was a tough and stressful experience to organize this event with only the support of my family, it was also very fun and I felt accomplished a lot. The Tea Party movement is one that is close to my heart and I honestly believe it is the only chance we have to take this country back to its roots and rebuild the faith of "We the People" in this great nation of ours!

Ann E. Lindholm—An American Soldier's Wife

My husband and I met in September of 1999 when he hired me as a personal trainer at his gym. Love at first sight. We were married in March of 2001. He not only shared vows with me but my five-year-old daughter as well, whom he adopted. A few months later some very evil perpetrators, terrorists, attacked our nation on our soil. This is a day, a week, and a year which I will never forget. Our lives were changed in ways we had not expected. Not only was our sure feelings of freedom forever depleted, but our personal lives were about to change in some very serious ways.

My husband had a very difficult time sitting and watching from the sidelines as our nation debated ways in which to defend itself. He knew without a doubt that he had to go forth and volunteer in the war against this brutal enemy. I will not lie. At first, I was not on board with my new husband going off to war. However, God is sovereign and good. He worked on me and melted my heart. I knew that this was what my husband had to do and was called to do. I began the powerful prayers of a wife and relied on God's wisdom and faithfulness to get us through the next six years at least, which I knew would end up being more. Eight years later, we are still stationed in Savannah, GA and my husband re-signed once thus far. He is a soldier in an elite unit of which I will say no more.

This is my story to tell. Here is where my part comes up. As my husband deployed on mission after mission fighting for our freedom I felt empty handed and helpless. I felt the need to do my part. As the elections drew to an end for 2008 my heart recognized the dreadful future which was about to be ours. My heart literally ached for days up to the election, during, and after of Barrack Hussein Obama. I literally felt sick to my stomach and deeply concerned for the future of America, its people, future generations, and most especially my children and my husband as he continued to fight this war. I knew things would significantly change for him as would change the dynamics of success "over there."

Nonetheless, recognizing what was about to begin taking place in our nation, my disgust and rage transformed into a call to action of my own. In watching the Fox News Channel and listening to Glenn Beck on the radio I heard there was going to be a Tea Party, or rally, in a city near me and others were taking place across America. No question in my mind arose and I knew that I would be present that tax day, babies and all. By this time, we had three more additions to our family, bringing the count to four children.

My oldest daughter remained in school, although we contemplated taking her out for this event. It wound up just being the three babies and myself. Blazing hot, stifling humidity choked the air on that historic riverfront on Rousakis Plaza in downtown Savannah, GA on April 15, 2009. Over fifteen hundred people were present. From that day on, I knew that my life had changed. The tears of American pride and goose bumps that I had as a child were back five-fold. I imagined the feelings I had were similar to that of our Founding Fathers and the wives of those who forged new frontiers for a new free country, America. I was destined to put forth all I had to fight and preserve the liberties and freedoms which we all grew up knowing. I was able to understand that the legislation being passed and the out-of-control character of the current administration was going to send those liberties and freedoms up a river. That April 15th I met the lady who put the rally together, Marolyn Overton, and we quickly became friends. To this day I am still involved with the Savannah Tea Party, handle their web site, organize rallies and fundraisers, and I became a delegate with the Independence Caucus, a partner with Chatham County Republican Party, a member of the Executive Committee as the New Media Chairperson, a Committee member on Chatham County Republican Party, assist 13th Colony Patriots with their events, am involved in the vetting process of potential candidates, an Associate Member of Veteran Defenders, a Toastmaster with Hostess City Club, and became involved with political campaigning. In addition to all of this I was already writing and blogging for my own web site. I was approached by the editor for The Cypress Times and became a featured columnist with them. I have been holding town halls/forums for the purpose of informing the community about local school board budget cuts and other policy. Through all of this activity I became very interested in our homeland security. So, I have gone back to school full-time through Central Texas College, taking my classes on-line. I am seeking an Assoc. of Applied Science in Homeland Security. I also do research and prepare research documents on such subjects as health care reform, stimulus funds, economic stimulus packages, local government activity as well as homeland security.

I have been approached and encouraged many times to run for Congress or for office in some capacity. I have politely turned all of these requests down thus far, as I am still a mom of three very young children and a teenager with a husband who is gone most of the time fighting in the war. Simply put, it is not my time. Nor do I feel called to such a position at this time. I feel much more effective in doing what I am doing. I feel as though a major field in which Americans are lacking is the field of participation and knowledge with the political process. I have been engaging with fellow Americans of the minority groups and am finding some astonishing facts. I am in the works of a very interesting project and hope to see an America which is more engaged than ever. We the People must reclaim the Republic by learning how to manage our employees, the elected officials. This I feel is more important than running for office, at this time. So for now, I stay put. I remain a freedom fighter and a thorn in the side of this socialist administration. This is my story and I'm sticking to it. I am not going away until I can no longer fight for freedom.

May God bless America and all of her people.

Jamison Faught

In April of 2009, I was 19 years old, one year out of high school. I had a younger sister (16 1/2), an older brother (24 1/2), and we all lived in a loving home with our parents. I was homeschooled my entire life, and part of our education included learning about our government (my favorite subject in school was American History). We visited Washington D.C. several times in my school years, and the vast amount of history there overwhelmed me. We tread in Washington's footsteps at Mount Vernon, saw the chamber where Daniel Webster spoke so eloquently, sat in as Senators debated legislation, visited the Smithsonians, saw the monuments, and stood inches away from the very document which gave birth to our nation - which so many great Founders actually signed. We were there in DC for George W. Bush's second inauguration in 2005 (see later on for why), and stood in the huge crowd for a special event of national importance - the swearing in of a President.

In addition to Washington, my family visited such places as Plimoth Plantation, Boston, Lexington and Concord, Philadelphia and Independence Hall, other Revolutionary War battlefields like Cowpens and Kings Mountain, Civil War sites such as Gettysburg, Antietam, Manassas, Fredericksburg, Chancellorsville, the hallowed grounds of Arlington, the Korean and Vietnam memorials... places that speak of our rich heritage as Americans, and the God-given freedoms and liberties that have been defended and bestowed upon us by preceding generations at great cost. We have also studied and seen what happens when those freedoms are ignored, or otherwise not recognized - the most poignant of which was our visit to the United States Holocaust Memorial Museum.

I have always at least enjoyed and understood the rudiments of politics. When my siblings and I were younger, we liked to play with Legos. We actually have a fully operative economy and representative government running, complete with elections, a President and cabinet, a Senate and House, bills, debates, stocks, businesses, along with the police and criminals and train wrecks and battles that accompany the All-American child's play. I remember to this day some of the more interesting political intrigue in our "Legoland" - most notably when "I" lost a race to an outlaw!

In 2004, our family doctor, Tom Coburn, decided to run for U.S. Senate in Oklahoma. My older brother became the first full-time volunteer on his campaign, and my family became heavily involved in volunteering. We stuffed envelopes like machines, made phone calls, knocked doors, waved signs, marched in parades, and celebrated victory - all as a family. Upon Coburn's election in November, my brother went on staff with him (and was in DC for a year, before coming back to work in a local Coburn office - hence why we were in DC for the '05 Bush inauguration).

In 2006, my dad (George Faught) was asked to run for State Representative. My dad is a simple, hard-working, self-employed carpet cleaner; he's not from a privileged wealthy family, he's not a lawyer, he's not college educated - his family was poor, he works with his hands (and has the scars and aches to prove it), and he's gotten his degree from Life, not some university. My dad is the epitome of the American Dream. Through a series of miraculous God-driven events, he was elected in a district that had never voted in a Republican (22% were registered Republican) in state history. Our involvement in politics exploded. You never truly know how full time public service is until one of your family members gets elected - it is a 24/7, consuming job that involves the entire family.

You also never really know how dirty politics is, and how disgusting it can be, until you see it from the inside. My family saw it from the federal level with my brother on the Senator's staff, and on the state level with my State Representative dad. You never truly realize how much good people are needed to be involved in politics until you have personally experienced politics for yourself.

The events of late 2008 and early 2009 brought the American political environment to a full rolling boil. The American people were outraged at their government picking and choosing winners, bailing out some, and taking over private businesses. They were outraged at government spending at levels so great, and so unprecedented, that the figures could scarcely be digested. They were outraged at the fact that they were being ignored by arrogant politicians who were out of touch with reality. They were outraged with Republicans, and they were outraged with Democrats.

But most of all, *they were outraged with themselves*, for letting it get to this point.

I was among those who were outraged for those reasons. I had had enough, and I wanted to do something about it. I started a political blog (www.MuskogeePolitico.com) in late July of 2008, and had been keeping up with the news. It's what bloggers do. When I first saw Rick Santelli and his now-famous "rant" on CNBC, I felt a connection with his passion and frustration. Then the first wave of Tea Parties began taking place, in February of 2009. Calls began taking place for local "Tea Parties" to go on nationwide on April 15th. I felt like I needed to do something, so I searched on the main Tea Party sites that had sprung up on the internet, to see if someone was organizing a Tea Party in Muskogee, OK, on April 15th 2009. Nobody was. That was my signal.

I jumped in, and decided to be the local organizer. I imagine that it shocked my parents, because I'm not a very outgoing person. I'm not a people person. I'm not the type to organize events like this. But this was something I had to do. I began to work on organizing the Tea Party - set up a Facebook group, made event pages on the various Tea Party websites, bought a domain and newspaper ads (all with my own money), and worked like crazy to get people there, at noon, on a work-day.

I had no idea what to expect. For all I knew, we'd have 20 people there, and the whole thing would be a tremendous flop. I showed up early to the location for our rally (a plaza downtown), in order to set everything up beforehand. A handful of folks were there to help set up, mostly people I had lined up to man sign in tables and things like that. Then they started coming. A group of veterans on motorcycles. A mom with her small children. An elderly couple. Workers from downtown. Retired po-licemen. Doctors. Construction workers. Retired senior citizens. People who had driven over 80 miles to come. They just kept pouring on in.

The parking lot next to the plaza filled up. The parking lot be-hind the Civic Center filled. The lots next to the Civic Center filled. People were coming from everywhere! I was floored - these were everyday citizens, most of whom had never been to an event that was remotely political, much less a rally or protest like this Tea Party was! They were Republicans, Democrats, Independents, and people who weren't even registered to vote.

We had 250 people from 36 communities with an 80-mile radius attend that day. Our little bullhorn didn't have the volume for folks on the outside of the crowd to hear.

Since that day, I have organized five major Tea Parties, and our group has grown and grown. Over 1,650 concerned Americans have come to our events, and we have now formed a Political Action Committee. We have made our voices heard. We will not go away, and we will not stop until we return our country back to the Constitutional principles we were founded upon.

For too long we have stood idly by while politicians were drowning future generations with insurmountable debt. For too long we have said nothing when Congress has gone on drunken spending spree after drunken spending spree. For far too long we have done nothing to stem the tide of fiscal irresponsibility in our elected officials. No longer! Now is the time that We The People must put our foot down, and shout "Enough is enough!" We will not tolerate this sort of behavior any longer!

It's exciting to see how the American people are getting engaged in the political process, and demanding accountibility from our elected officials. Citizens are realizing that they can actually make a difference in the course of our nation, and they're taking ownership once again. 'We The People' are making our voices heard... loud and clear. My wish is that my descendants will know that I did not sit idly by as my country was taken apart piece-by-piece. I want them to realize that I stood up for them. I want them to know that I did everything in my power to preserve liberty for them, and for those who follow them.

Anna Diaz

I am a third generation Mexican descendant, American. My father was born in Cotulla, Texas and was a WWII veteran who fought in the European campaign under the direction of the Rainbow Division of the army. Both my parents were born in Texas (mother born in Thrall, Texas) in the 1920s. Their parents were born here in Texas as well and their parents before them migrated to Texas from Mexico when they were accepting those applicants. What history I know of the United States I learned in elementary and junior high school. My father would always remind us that we are not Mexican Americans—we are Americans.

When I went to high school, civics was a required course. I remember studying the Declaration of Independence but very little of the Constitution. As I understand it today; it is not required. That is why our country is in this mess—the dumbing-down of our children on American History and the US Constitution.

I could see some of the things President Bush was doing in office, making more Executive decisions instead of leaning on current legislation or working on legislation to make changes. It didn't seem right to me. During the 2008 campaign, I really didn't like McCain because he is a progressive, not a true conservative, and the GOP was not selecting the true conservative candidates. Which explains the poor quality of candidates and the reason why Republicans are spending like Democrats and are not controlling the budget.

Hopefully, they've learned their lesson. I worked to defeat Obama because I could see behind the façade and had read about his history and where he came from. I kept telling everyone that he was not good for the USA. To no avail. Then Obama began to accelerate his socialist agenda and that was what urged me to do something. So I attend a protest, my very first protest—I had never done this before—but felt the urge to attend the protest on Tax Day 4/09 in San Antonio, TX.

One day I was reading the blogs I frequent and local news online, from a small paper in the rural town of Beeville, Texas. I saw an announcement that a meeting to form a Tea Party in Beeville was to take place late in August, 2009. I went to that meeting with a prayer that God would use me and that it wouldn't be a radical group but a right thinking and godly group of people with common sense and the big picture of what we have to do to get our country back to the Constitution.

Well, I went and I was elected President. I was not expecting that. In that meeting we came up with our mission statement and our goals. We emphasized educating the populace of our community. We held town hall rallies, candidate rallies, Tea Party Tax Day rallies, and invited the public. We have made new friends and contacts and have a list of 100+ members who get informative e-mails from the president and the secretary. We've gone through activist training, US Constitution training, and some of us have gotten involved within our local precincts, which is a great way to take our local government and state government back to following our state Constitution. I ran for precinct chair in my precinct and won. My next assignment is to canvass voters within my precinct, educating them as much as possible. To get our country back, we need to encourage our Tea Party members to get involved with the precinct chair activities.

"To preserve the republican form and principles of our Constitution and cleave to the salutary distribution of powers which that [the Constitution] has established ... are the two sheet anchors of

our Union. If driven from either, we shall be in danger of foundering."
– Thomas Jefferson, June 12, 1823

Anna M. Kroyman

You asked what did I see, hear or experience that motivated me to get involved? Rick Santelli!

If you watch Fox News, then you know who he is. Rick motivated a lot of people to begin paying attention that day.

I was raised in a Democrat family. I can recall the precinct captain picking up my mother and two aunts every election day to drive them to vote. He gave each of them five dollars and a brand new garbage can appeared the following Monday. That was my political experience growing up. Religion and politics were never discussed and considered taboo.

Throughout my life people talked politics at work, but I never got involved in those conversations. It was taboo. I didn't watch the news, had no knowledge of events and couldn't converse intelligently. Therefore I simply ignored them. I acted like I didn't care rather than didn't know. As long as nothing changed for me why should I bother to vote? I still had to go to work the next day, didn't I? That's the way it was for fifty years, until 1998.

I was at my boyfriend's house one evening. Jack was a solid Republican and his TV was tuned to Clinton's impeachment trial every night. Boring! I was standing in the kitchen doing dishes one night and suddenly from the front room I heard "oral sex." What? Did he change the station! What? No, he still had the trial on. So what exactly did I hear? I began to listen and Jack began to explain. I went home that night and tuned in C-SPAN. I was riveted to this lewd event going on in our White House. Two little words perked my ears up and it changed my life. I began to pay attention. Thank you Bill Clinton!

So in 2000, I voted for the *first time in my life*. The year of the "chad." Don't ever let anyone tell you that one vote won't change anything. I like to think that my one vote, plus all the "chads," made all the difference that year. First time I voted, first time anyone ever reneged on a concession. The lesser of two evils won.

I liked a lot of things George Bush was suggesting. Then 9/11 happened. Bush was a great wartime president. He protected us and encouraged us to be strong and resilient. I didn't agree with everything he presented. But all in all I believe he did the best he could with what he had to work with. Our country was at war and our economy was beginning to suffer. Republicans had control of the House and did absolutely nothing to make things better for us. Things were beginning to change and not in a good way.

Then in 2007, the Democrats took control of the House and Senate after twelve years of nearly unbroken Republican rule. The fight was on! We the people didn't seem to matter at all anymore. It was a fistfight between the parties. Nothing was accomplished. Sure, Bush handed out the first stimulus with excessive pressure from a Democratic congress. I believe he was railroaded into doing it *now*! Right now! Or the entire world would suffer the effects.

There was so much hatred for George Bush that a man, little known for anything other than "Community Organizing," came out of *nowhere* and offered "hope" and "change." The media jumped on that along with college kids looking to change the world. What they didn't ask was: *What is that change*? Hope is simply anticipation and expectation. But the most important questions weren't being asked. On November 2, 2008 Barack Obama was elected President of the United States. Many began asking, "Who is Barack Obama?" We're *still* waiting for the answer.

TEA PARTY – THE AWAKENING

In early 2009, Rick Santelli, the On Air Editor for CNBC, set out on a rant to expose the bankrupt liberal agenda of the White House Administration and Congress—specifically, the flawed "Stimulus Bill" and pork-filled budget. During Rick's rant, he called for a "Chicago Tea Party" where advocates of the free-market system could join in a protest against out-of-control government spending.

A few days later, grassroots activists and average Joe Americans began organizing what would soon become the Nationwide Chicago Tea Party effort. On February 27th, an estimated 30,000 Americans took to the street in 40+ cities across the country in the first nationwide Tea Party protest. There was little media coverage but Santelli's rant played on for months. Fabulous!

Early in 2010, people began to see radical changes in America. Suddenly we heard things like "too big to fail." The government stepped in to bailout banks and investment houses—billions and billions of our hard-earned tax dollars. People became outraged that their children and grandchildren would be slaves to the government with this type of spending. Next, the car industry—also too big to fail.

Since when has any business ever been too big to fail? If your greed takes you down that path then you deserve to fail. Our president took private industry to a level unknown to this great country. Obama fired GM's CEO! When has a president of these United States ever had that kind of power over private industry? What's coming next?

I felt this great country of ours was headed down the road to socialism. Government was taking over private industry and no one seemed to care. Government was changing our country and ignoring our Constitution. Our Founding Fathers' magnitude of wisdom saw this coming when they sat down to write. Could we ever find enough people today with this kind of wisdom to run for office? Can "We the People" do anything to stop this vast takeover?

By late summer I began to search the Internet for a local Tea Party. I found the web site TeaPartyPatriots.org, the mother of Tea Parties nationwide. They were listed by state, so I searched in Indiana and found Defenders of Liberty in Indianapolis. This was two hours away from Monticello. Same distance to Chicago. That just wouldn't do. So I waited, and waited, and waited. There were a few more Tea Party listings in Indiana but no contact information.

During all this research I discovered so many things were out of order. Things I never paid attention to before. Today it was news. I asked myself: Is Congress completely out of touch? Or have we just been oblivious all these years? As long as we have our jobs, our vacations, and accumulate our wealth. As long as we can purchase our gas, food, TVs, etc. *We've simply not paid enough attention!* This didn't happen overnight. We have no one to blame but ourselves.

In December I organized the White County Tea Party Patriots group. My very first member, Laura, was so excited and grateful to me for creating a local Tea Party. If only everyone could capture the enthusiasm of Laura we'd live in a much better place.

An old neighbor, Shannon, offered his small office for our first meeting on January 18, 2010. Sixteen people showed up. Sixteen! I still get goose bumps thinking about that day. People came from all over surrounding counties to attend our tea party.

We discussed organization and direction. We decided to offer a Constitutional Study Group within each meeting.

Our primary elections were May 4th. I decided to contact all the candidates running for our two Congressional Districts and our US Senate Seat. From March 8th until May 3rd, White County Tea Party Patriots hosted twelve candidates. We had State Senators, Congressmen, etc. I couldn't believe how encouraging they all were towards the Tea Party. We allotted an hour to the candidate to speak. Twenty minutes to tell us about themselves, twenty minutes for prepared questions and open forum for the rest of their visit. We made history in this small town of Monticello, bringing these candidates into our little back yard.

Our mission is to inform and educate people. The media and our politicians have portrayed Tea Parties as radical obstructionists, hateful and racist. *They could not be more wrong!* Let me tell you who we really are. We are salt of the Earth people from numerous Indiana Counties. We are parents, grandparents, aunts, uncles and kids. *We are you!*

We are united by shared concerns about the direction our country has taken. We believe that adherence to the US Constitution will result in a limited federal government, fiscal responsibility and free markets. We recognize the strength of grassroots organizing powered by activism and civic responsibility at the local level. Our mission is to organize like-minded individuals, educate and inform others based on our core values, to secure public policy consistent with those values, and to positively affect the outcome of elections.

Creating a local Tea Party has relieved a lot of my frustrations. I can see that many of our members who came in angry and frustrated have now found a purpose. There's a long way to go and we will do our best to uphold our Constitution.

Today our Tea Party has 120 registered members. Our local newspaper has finally acknowledged our existence after I shamed them for months. They deprived the residents of White County of a once-in-a-lifetime opportunity to meet with these candidates right here in their own little town. Shame on them! Today they cover our events.

The way I see it is this. On one end, we have: *People who don't care.* On the other end: *People who have stopped caring.*
And then we have the center: *Tea Party people.* We are the patriots that have left the couch and wish to make a difference. Wherever this great country ends up, at least *we* know *we* did everything *we* could.

I love America! I want my grandchildren to live a better life than I did. If I utter just one or two words that might perk up someone's ears to begin paying attention, then I've done my job well.

"The time is near at hand which must determine whether Americans are to be free men or slaves".– George Washington

Toni Backdahl

I am a wife, mother and grandmother. My professional background is in Operations, IT and Accounting.

Like a lot of people, I started watching things more closely after 2000. I wondered why election integrity hadn't improved with all the hype of fraud and neither had the border issue ... Then I started wondering why we paid these people to waste our money arguing, throwing each other under the bus and blocking each other's agendas ... then, I started wondering why they had an agenda that was contrary to what I was taught their agenda should really be ... then came the bid for POTUS '08 and a crash course in the history of US politics, then Obama won!

I was online and stumbled onto Top Conservatives on Twitter (Michael Patrick Leahy and Rob Gaudet, two of the original founders of this chapter in the movement). I signed up for TCOT Action Project and after Santelli's rant on CNBC we had the first conference call to coordinate a nationwide effort on 2/27/09. In March, I pulled the permit, recruited and coordinated a team of 20+ people who put on the first tax day rally in '09 where we had 7,000+ people attend. We then had rallies on 7/4 and 9/17.

We also coordinated a bus to D.C. on 9/12 at the last minute ... I coordinated the Health Care Freedom rallies in August where we had hundreds of people show up at Klobuchar, Franken, McCollum, Peterson, Paulsen, Kline, Walz and Bachmann's offices (thanks to all who showed!). The 2010 tax day rally was all grassroots and we had 3,000 ... not too shabby. Thanks to all who have sponsored and helped!

Fredrick Lindner

Robert West started the Arapahoe Tea Party and began gathering more members with hopes of finding political candidates to run for the 2010 race. My name even got tossed around; however, my wife swiftly put an end to that idea! How I got involved? I was pretty busy with work and a family at home; however, I had been increasingly worried about increased spending in early 2009. Then in the summer of 2009, the House bill of Cap and Trade was rammed through Congress in around a week's time without much debate. This was the panic switch for me. Since my educational background is in Chemical Engineering and Civil Engineering, I have been absolutely convinced that the misleading science of "global warming" will lead to economic disaster. I rapidly became active in several groups looking for a role to fill. Mr. West then moved to Texas and left me with a small group of around ten members to move forward with. We quickly came up with a short six-month game plan and focused on some events and rallies. In that time we grew membership and forwarded several candidates in forums. We then became active in our local delegate selection process and practically overwhelmed the Republican Assemblies with the largest activism based group seen in recent history. We are almost halfway to our goal of 300 members, at which time we will begin forming committees and making a solid impact in Arapahoe County and city level with help from some older activism groups.

TEA PARTY LEADERS

Arthur Bedford

I spent nearly forty years working for the USA.F., the first
twenty-eight years as an enlisted man in the communications
intelligence field, and the remainder as an Air Force civil service
intelligence specialist. I was never politically active in all those
years but considered myself a conservative. One issue, illegal
immigration, began to bother me. I could not understand why
our own federal government refused to enforce its own laws, and
worse yet, stifle the efforts of the states on the border with Mexico to assist in the enforcement. When I finally retired in 2005, I
joined the Texas Minutemen Civil Defense Corps (MCDC) and
traveled from our ranch in San Augustine, TX with a fellow
member to the border at Mission, TX for a three-day border
watch. I believed that I was helping the enforcement effort by
reporting illegal alien activity to law enforcement. That was not
the case. We were sitting on top of levees, completely in view of
everyone to see. It seemed as though we were there to be interviewed by the press rather than actually doing anything.

I left the MCDC and joined the Texas Border Volunteers, a
group that also had once been part of the Minutemen but also
had been disenchanted with the group. They conducted serious
border watches just north of the Border Patrol Checkpoint, south
of Falfurrias, TX, on US Hwy 281, seventy miles north of the
border. We performed our watches on private ranchland, employed military-type tactics, used night vision equipment and
tactical communications to report the invasion of illegals from
not just Mexico, but from seventy-five nations to date.

We spent our own money to do it. It cost us about $300 each for
a four-day watch and we conducted ten watches a year—eight 4-
day watches and two 10-day watches. I felt good that I had done
something—made an impact. The more I thought about it, however, the more I realized that we really hadn't done anything.
The federal government was returning the illegals back to where
they came from to try again, the Republican-controlled state

government talked big about making it hard for illegals to live in Texas but did absolutely nothing about it.

I started studying states like Arizona and Oklahoma that had tough anti-illegal immigration laws. It was then that I found out about initiative and referendum rights—how Arizona passed their first real piece of immigration legislation through ballot proposition by the people of Arizona, *not the legislature.* I attended a seminar hosted by an anti-illegal immigration group, Coalition for Immigration Reform (CFIR) in Austin, TX. One of the speakers at the seminar was from Oklahoma and she spoke about Oklahoma's new tough anti-illegal immigration law and how she got a state senator to sponsor it, and it passed. I asked her what she would have done if the senator had not sponsored it and she immediately said that her group would have used the initiative process. I then studied I&R and realized that this was a right Texans should have, especially when our legislators are unresponsive. I then became an I&R activist. I visited the head of Texans for Initiative & Referendum Rights in Austin and told him that I wanted to help. The leader's name is Mike Ford, and he had moved to Texas from California twenty years ago where he was active in the initiative process there. He was nearing eighty years old and the first words out of his mouth after I told him I wanted to help were, "Good, you're in charge." I am now the chairman for the group. Our web site is initiativefortexas.org.

Since most Texans have never heard of I&R, I started on a one-man educational crusade, giving presentations to any group who would listen. Glenn Beck, who I believe is the founder of the Tea Party movement in this country, was promoting citizens to start 9-12 groups at that time. I received an e-mail that a 9-12 group was forming in the nearby city of Lufkin, TX. I attended their first meeting and volunteered to give a presentation at one of their future meetings. The interest in the group grew at a rapid pace and soon the group came up with a new name "The Founders Alliance," led by a gal named Jessica Hughes. The Founders Alliance sponsored a huge tea party in the city of Nacogdoches on Tax Day, 2009. Nacogdoches is a very small city and when over 2,000 people attended, I knew the time was right for getting the people involved in obtaining I&R rights for themselves. Most were (and still are) angry that our government is not listening to the will of the people, that their representatives are not representing them, and that they feel their liberties are slowly being taken away from them. On July 4th, they had another tea party in Lufkin, TX with over 5,000 in attendance. I was able to have a booth at the event and hundreds of people signed up to support I&R rights.

Since then, I have spoken to three additional Tea Party groups in Northeast and Southeast Texas and support for I&R has grown even more. It is tremendously uplifting to see people finally getting involved in their own government, to take it back to the Constitution and to where the Founders would want it to be. As a result of the tea parties I have spoken at, three resolutions to get a pro-I&R plank on the Republican Party of Texas Platform for 2010 made it to the State Convention earlier this month. I got to testify before the Platform Committee and move for an amendment to the Platform on Convention Floor, with over 14,000 people listening. We were defeated, but I am not disheartened. They elected a new Chairman for the Republican Party of Texas who is pro-I&R, so on we go.

We are living in uncertain times and our freedom is at risk. I continue to speak at Tea Party events and now my wife and I are organizing a tri-county Tea Party this October for our rural counties of Shelby, San Augustine, and Sabine, TX. We never thought we would be doing anything like this. We are both in our 60s. I pray our youth will understand what is happening and take up the cause. It is their future that is at stake.

Margaret J Hyland

It was not long after Obama's inauguration that he reversed George W. Bush's stand on abortion. It was then that I knew I had to do something more. I couldn't stand the thought of abortion running rampant in America. More and more, there were alarming things coming out of Congress and the White House.

It began to seem like every day there was some new legislation that attacked the freedom and rights of individuals in America, and that socialism seemed inevitable. Every day, I would get more and more frightened and angry that the government was growing and the private sector was unemployed or taxed to death. I could see the growth of public unions, the cronyism in the administration, and the way the administration undermined all that was capitalism and free enterprise.

I had always been timid when it came to politics. I never liked to venture an opinion one way or another. I was afraid people would alienate me if I differed from them. I was busy also, raising my two daughters by myself, and had little time to watch the news, read newspapers, or go online to get more informed. However, I, and many others probably, felt that the country would pretty much take care of itself, as the government in general had the welfare of the nation at heart. We had the luxury, or so we thought, that it would continue that way.

Then I met my husband and all that changed. I no longer was alone, no longer had to work full time, and my daughters were grown. In addition, he was almost an expert on politics, having followed it for nearly forty years. When he asked me if I was conservative or liberal, I honestly did not know the difference. He then asked me how I felt about a few topics, and my answers clearly revealed that my beliefs were conservative. I began exploring the Internet and learning about the ins and outs of politics in the US, and the world in general. We began following the candidacy of Barack Obama vs. John McCain, and I knew this was a very momentous election. I instinctively had misgivings about Obama and couldn't trust him. I chose to vote for McCain because I believed he was the lesser of two evils, and that my vote did indeed count.

Needless to say, I was disappointed when Obama won the election. This was honestly the first time in my whole life where I felt fear and a sense of doom for our country. The Internet was a strong source of information and a powerful medium to find less biased news and articles that didn't appear in the main news agencies. It became evident that the truth was out there, and most people were not aware of it. It became important to me to try to awaken as many people as I could. I learned many were liberal and so set in their blind devotion to Obama that they couldn't or wouldn't open their minds to alternate information, or even a different perspective ... including my brothers and sisters. It was like talking to a blank wall. If I approached them about taxation and how it was destroying our middle class and our economy, they would say things like, "I like government and taxes. We need more. The government will take care of us. We need to save the planet." Appealing to logic was useless. The number of people on unemployment and unemployment extensions is unbelievable! The administration was turning previous workers into lazy wards of the state.

One day, when totally frustrated and angry about the direction our country was headed, I emphatically told my husband we needed to "do something." He said, "OK, what?" I said we needed to start a Tea Party. He agreed, although neither of us knew what we were in for. At that time, there was only a murmur across the Internet about Tea Party Protesters, and we set about to try to create one in Astoria.

My biggest problem was that I was new to Astoria, and hardly knew anyone. I had met a long-time member of the North Coast Republican Women, who was open to sharing her contacts with me to get the word out. So we set out to hold a Tea Party on April 15th, national Tax Day. We sent out e-mails, made phone calls, put up flyers and tried to get the word out. I had never done anything like this before. We had no idea if this would be successful, or even how to measure success. Our theme was taxes and excessive government spending. We felt pride in joining many others across the nation. We had thought that in this small, mostly liberal community, we would be lucky to have fifty people show up. We were amazed and heartened that 300+ came to our rally on the Post Office grounds. We overflowed into the street and caught the attention of a team of reporters from our local (liberal) newspaper. They interviewed many people, video-taped part of the rally, and actually did a good job on reporting it on the front page of the paper the next day. We found out these reporters knew nothing about the rally and just happened by that evening. Our impromptu speakers addressed the crowd from the back of a pickup truck. Taxation made the crowd roar with applause because of recent tax increases nationally, as well as locally. There were people of all political persuasions in the crowd. The signs people carried were wild and creative and illustrated the frustration and confusion of the conservatives toward the government. It was clear to us this was going to only be the beginning. The rally was respectful, well mannered, and patriotic, with red, white, and blue everywhere.

We were relieved and pleased to know there were so many conservative people in our community! Who would have known?

Since then, our database has grown astonishingly and we have held numerous smaller rallies and other events as well. I began sending out e-mails to those interested in balanced national news, keeping them abreast of the relevant Internet articles and videos, which evolved into a twice-a-month e-newsletter. I hosted a professional seminar on the Constitution and a large number of people attended and requested we do it again, so we are in the process of organizing one for September. My husband and I are now members of several coalitions in Oregon, such as Oregon Tea Party, and when possible, we attend conferences, seminars, and other rallies to keep informed of the national Tea Party movement.

Our 2nd annual Tax Day Tea Party was successful, as well, and instead of lack of interest, people were even more energized and angry about the government and its policies. The success of the

Tea Party rallies and communication made us a center of political attention ... and we have spoken on radio, and are now experimenting with a weekly podcast. A large number of Americans fall into the same category I used to be in—apathetic, or just uninvolved—for one reason or another. It is alarming to me that what used to be good, moral, and correct is now labeled politically incorrect, and now in the name of tolerance, "anything goes." I believe our president is a Muslim: he has shamed our military and our flag; he has apologized to other nations for his idea of our faults instead of proudly leading our nation; he has sided with communist nations; he has ignored our national boundaries and federal laws; and he has demonstrated disdain for the American people. Our schools are indoctrinating our students into socialism and rewriting history; our churches are slowly being phased out or infiltrated with liberal ideology; society is being misled and taken over by special interest groups such as environmentalists, gay marriage activists, pro-choice activists, and radical Islamists; our energy resources and economy are being destroyed systematically; and instead of the truth, our airwaves and newspapers are brimming with propaganda and outright lies. The government has taken over the education system, the health care system, the banking industry, the automobile industry, and will soon try to take over the air we breathe and exhale through Cap and Trade legislation, which has been proven by thousands of scientists to be based on the *hoax of global warming!* Corruption is wild in our current administration; taxes are sky high; babies are being aborted (murdered) at an alarming rate; morals are being discarded; our borders are no longer secure—terrorists cross them daily; Islamification is threatening to turn our nation away from the Founding Father's godly principals and into a Muslim nation; our Constitution and Bill of Rights are being destroyed, and I could go on and on.

I feel, at once, honored and burdened to carry this movement. As you can see, I've become aware of the issues that have been building for many years, and are amplified now with this Congress and administration. *I cannot and will not go back to being unaware!* Our future is too important! Every day, the administration attacks from a different direction, and yet the mainstream media presents it all as if nothing is wrong and the liberals just lie about it. I will continue to do my small part to spread the truth and attempt to arouse people to see what America was meant to be, how it was founded on godly principles, and how it is being stolen from us. My fight is for my country of which I am very proud, and in honor of our military past and present, our children, and our future generations; and I am committed as ever, but now I am more focused and prepared to debate and demand politicians return this nation back to its constitutional heritage. I would like to think we will continue to live a life of freedom. I hope it is not too late!

Barbara Gonzalez

I will start this story by saying that I was never very politically savvy. I voted when I reached my 30s, but didn't pay as much attention as I should have. Along comes Barack Obama and now I am interested! I was interested because he was young and inexperienced, and yet, I could see that something was happening. People were being captured by his youth, promises of hope and change, and his way of delivering a speech (on teleprompter, of course), and people were just being mesmerized. I didn't think this was going to be a good thing. I started to follow everything I could during the campaign. As many have, I learned many things about Barack Obama that were screaming "this man should not be the leader of the free world!"

One day, I was watching the news and Rick Santelli was on "ranting" about the bailouts and how people should have tea parties. Something clicked. I asked a couple of friends to help me organize a tea party and we decided on July 4th. We found a great location and went ahead and promoted it.

It was a beautiful day and I was quite happy to see over 250 people show up. We had a sign-in sheet and collected about 250 e-mail addresses. Towards the end of the rally, I noticed people heading towards the highway with their flags and signs and heard horns honking like crazy. More people stopped to see what was going on. We did this on the road for a couple of hours after the tea party.

When I went home that evening, I looked at the list of e-mail addresses and thought "now what?" I keyed them all in and sent everyone an e-mail saying, "We are the Bayshore Tea Party group." I asked them if they wanted to do that "roadside rally" once a month, and someone replied, "how about once a week?" Since that day, we have been doing our "roadside rallies" every Sunday for a couple of hours each time.

A year has gone by and at this point, people honk as we are arriving and still parking our cars! Our group has grown since then to more than double. We now have an informal leadership, as we want to stay as grassroots as possible. During the primary Congressional campaigns, we were approached by several candidates asking for our support. We decided to have the candidates come and talk and take questions over three sessions. We then had an online ballot and voted for the candidate that we thought best represented us. We knew that in order to have a chance of winning off the county line, there would have to be something to differentiate our candidate from the GOP-supported candidate. We decided on putting "Tea Party Approved Republican" on the ballot. Anna Little from district six and Dave Corsi from district twelve agreed to do this. For the first time in history in NJ, a candidate won off the county line. Anna Little won as the Tea-Party-approved Republican. Dave Corsi lost by less than 1,000 votes. Our candidates spent under $20,000 compared to half a million by the GOP candidate. The people saw us on the road week after week and knew what we represented. During the last few weeks of the campaign, we did our roadside rally with only the signs of our candidates. People noticed. They related to us. Now, with this victory, we must work even harder. We must help Anna Little defeat a very liberal incumbent. I think we can do this ... I really do. Hopefully, I can finish this story after November by saying we had another victory! For now, I will close in saying God Bless this awesome, beautiful country and God help us defeat the progressive movement that means to take our freedoms away. FREEDOM!

Barry Willoughby

I remember the very first Naples Tea Party on April 15, 2009 like it happened yesterday. There were 3,000 American patriots in attendance and exactly one year later, on April 15, 2010 we had another rally. This time we drew between 7,000 and 8,000 people. It was an affirmation that the Tea Party movement is truly grassroots and will not fade away anytime soon, in spite of what the Senator from South Carolina said recently. Shame on you, Lindsey Graham. Do any of you political elitists have any idea what the Tea Party is really all about, how it was conceived, how it spread like a wildfire and how it became the most influential political force in such a short time in our nation's history? Let me help explain it to you.

The following story is not just about me. It represents the voices of millions of Americans who have the same concerns for our country and have worked just as hard to restore and help preserve the values and principles that made America exceptional. To all of you I have met over the past two years (there are too many to list), toiled with, laughed and cried with..........what an adventure. You became part of my immediate family and no words can express my love for you. It remains to be seen if we will change the course of America, but our times together have changed me forever. From the bottom of my heart, thank you for being a part of my life.

My name is Barry Willoughby and I am sixty-seven years old. I have been married to the same woman (Jackie) for almost forty years, helped raise four children and have nine grandchildren.

I attended college and enlisted in the United States Army Reserves, receiving an honorable discharge after serving six years. I have been retired for the last few years, after starting and operating a small business both in Oregon and Wisconsin.

I was never active in politics, other than voting in every election and making an occasional campaign contribution. My late father was a conservative, so I tended to lean that way early in my adult working life. Although, I did vote for Democrats on occasion, including Jimmy Carter. I happen to like his "peanut farmer" story and like many Americans, fell out of favor with Richard Nixon. I also voted for Ross Perot, thereby helping to assure victory for Bill Clinton. That was the last time I voted for someone other than a Republican, although it was the lesser of two evils on many occasions.

Ronald Reagan awakened my political senses. For the first time, I became aware of what it meant to be a conservative. I became a staunch supporter of less government and fiscal responsibility. I had to balance the budget in my own business and household ... why couldn't the government be held to the same standards?

The Reagan years were great for me and my business. I didn't need to dwell on government control of my life. Things like Social Security, Medicare and other government entitlements seemed vague and distant. Not once in my entire life have I had to go to a government agency for assistance. In fact, it has never even occurred for me to do so. My view is that charity comes from the individual heart ... and the government has no business in the charity department.

The first time I became aware of the brutal power of government was when the county I lived in forced an employment tax on my business in order to pay for a mass transit system. Not one employee would be able to use the system and not one customer would use it to patronize my business. And yet, it was the collective will of a few in power that forced me into something that had absolutely no benefit to me, my family, or customers. Welcome to the world of collectivism and the power of government.

After Reagan, things started going downhill for America in a hurry. The secret meetings to create a national HillaryCare health care plan, the shenanigans of Bill Clinton, the further decline of our moral compass and the start of a complete lack of accountability from elected officials confirmed my belief that government was not the solution … it was the problem. For the first time in my life politically, I cheered when the Republicans took over control of Congress under Clinton, thereby neutralizing the progressive agenda for the time being.

George W. Bush, of course, was a mixed bag. For the life of me, I don't know how he got elected. Having moved to Naples, Florida upon retirement, I was able to follow the "hanging chad" fiasco first hand. What a revolting display of politics running amok. It was at this time I lost all respect for the Democrat party and realized the means to an end can include lying, cheating, and any other dishonest tactic to gain a political advantage.

The Bush years were filled with divisiveness the likes I had never known. Even the Vietnam War era seemed pale in comparison. I spent a great deal of time trying to defend Bush, but also spent much time criticizing him. The argument coming from the Left that Bush could do no wrong in the eyes of conservatives is a total fabrication. I mean … good grief! Bush was in charge of the executive branch, the Republicans controlled Congress and Supreme Court appointments would assure at least some neutrality. Why was Bush so inept at getting some major things accomplished? Things like Social Security reform, securing our borders, enforcing the rule of law and stopping the massive growth of government spending?

These are issues that have always bugged me about Republicans. They finally get control and they blow it. The perfect storm that was brewing for Democrats weighed heavily on my mind throughout 2008. I became disgusted and angry at the same time. The thought of Hillary Clinton becoming our next president was almost too much for me to comprehend. Never in my wildest imagination did I even consider the possibility that a Marxist like Obama would have a chance. In fact, I was silently hoping he could overtake Hillary.

When the impossible happened, I started to realize the implications if Obama were to actually win the election. The nomination of McCain, someone I've always considered a "good ol' boy," further dampened my spirit. Only the Sarah Palin pick got me energized and I decided I had to do something to vent my frustrations. During the summer of 2008, I made a couple of signs at the urging of my son David and his two friends, and we started standing on busy street corners warning the passersby what a mistake it would be for America to elect a radical Marxist for president. David is a former United States Marine and is now a firefighter along with his two friends.

I still remember my first sign. It said, "Wealth Can't Be Multiplied By Dividing It." It was the first time in my life that I took to the streets to express my political feelings. Horns would honk as cars drove by, giving all of us a sense of accomplishment. Others would give us the middle finger salute and yell obscenities at us as they passed by. As far as I know, we were the only ones in the Fort Myers/Naples area standing on the street with political signs advocating less government, less spending, stop the bailouts, and please America wake up … don't elect a collectivist. This lasted up to the election.

After the election, there was a feeling of disbelief. Could America really be discarding the values and principles that had made our country the envy of the world? Could we really be abandoning the Constitution and rule of law in favor of a majority mob rule democracy? My feelings of angst, along with that of my friends, made me anxious to say the least. Obama was moving like a speeding bullet trying to force his agenda upon us. If we thought Bush was a spending machine, we had not seen anything yet. The stimulus plans, private company takeovers, talk of cap and trade were unprecedented in such a short time. I began to feel like I was all alone in my thinking, even though my friends shared the same beliefs regarding Obama.

Then, one day in February, 2009, I happened to tune in to CNBC to see how the stock market was doing. I was fortunate enough to hear live the famous Rick Santelli rant, as it has become known. It was an amazing display of emotion, honesty and warnings. When Santelli threw out his famous line about it's time for Americans to wake up and have another tea party, it hit me like a lightning bolt. My mind began racing and I knew instinctively I had to become engaged and organize a tea party … whatever that was!

During the next few days, I got together with four other people, including my son. We were sitting together at a large table in a restaurant planning to organize and hold a tea party. We had absolutely no idea how to organize a Tea Party, but knew that it involved an open display of protest against our government. There were no web-sites on how to hold a Tea Party, but we knew we had to attract like-minded people who shared the same concerns and disgust that we did.

A few weeks later, the Tea Party concept began to take shape. People were talking about it on talk radio and cable news. My group decided to hold the first Naples Tea Party on April 15, 2009. I remember my son saying we had better attract more than ten people to join us, otherwise he was going to give up on the idea. We all agreed with him. We decided to hold our Tea Party at a very busy intersection in Naples. There was a large public grass strip that separated a service road from the main drag that runs through Naples. Parking was adequate and there was plenty of room to stretch out.

TEA PARTY LEADERS

We did not know that three other groups in the Naples/Fort Myers area had formed and were planning to do exactly what we were doing. But, once we started to promote our April 15th Tea Party, we learned through the grapevine about the other groups. One group was holding their rally a week earlier at a public park in Naples. Two others picked April 15th. It was decided that our starting time of 12:00 p.m. to 2:00 p.m. would remain in place. Another group would hold theirs at 3:00 and run till 5:00. Finally, the last Tea Party of the day would be that evening in Fort Myers, which is thirty miles north of Naples.

We had no organizational chart, no bank account, and yet we set out promoting the first Naples Tea Party. One person concentrated on utilizing the Internet and started building an e-mail address book. I stood on busy street corners with my son, along with another recruit, and passed out flyers describing the Tea Party. We would work during the peak rush hour traffic for three and four hours at a time. In order to draw attention, we had some colorful signs in the ground that said...

DISGUSTED?
JOIN THE
NAPLES TEA PARTY
ON APRIL 15th

At first, it was very slow going. We were lucky to pass out two or three flyers an hour. People had no idea what we were talking about. "What's a Tea Party," they would say. It was actually pretty comical trying to explain it to some people. As the days passed, things started to pick up. We were able to recruit more people into the group and it became a word-of-mouth campaign. Someone would tell their friend, they would tell their friend ... and so on. Our e-mail address book continued to grow daily. Talk shows were really talking about the new phenomena known as the "Tea Party Movement."

TEA PARTY – THE AWAKENING

One could almost feel the excitement in the air as April 15th approached. We had learned that hundreds of other Tea Parties would be held all across America. A few were held before April 15th and that only bolstered every other Tea Party group. The pundits were desperately trying to define this movement in terms of a bunch of angry Republicans getting together to stop progress.

On the eve of April 15, 2009, I called everyone and said, "well, we've given it our best shot. What will be will be." We had no idea how many people would show up. The first Tea Party in Naples held the week before drew around 500 people. The organizers seemed very pleased with the turnout and we were hoping to at least match that. Needless to say, I had great difficulty falling to sleep that night.

My wife and I tossed and turned all night. We finally got up, relieved that the weather was going to accommodate our first Tea Party. A severe Florida thunderstorm was the one thing I worried about more than anything else. We arrived at 9:00 a.m. at the Tea Party site and started setting up. We put up a canopy and a couple of tables to display some flyers.

Our other volunteers started arriving shortly thereafter. We had people that would circulate and gather names to add to our e-mail list. We also set up a sound system with speakers, from which we would play the national anthem and patriotic music throughout the event. We placed small American flags into the ground and hung a brand new "Naples Tea Party" banner for all to see.

We also set up an area for people to throw tea bags into a container and sign a petition that we intended to send to Washington. Our simple petition was a one-page document with a picture of Uncle Sam pointing his finger. It read: "The call to action has been answered. On April 15, 2009, at the Naples, Florida Tea Party, patriotic Americans acted to make their voices heard. We the people … do hereby sign this petition opposing far-Left and socialist elements that compromise the centerpiece of the federal government's current agenda, including massive government spending and taxation, limitations on religious freedoms, wealth redistribution, amnesty for millions of illegal immigrants, government run health care, free speech restrictions, weakening the Second Amendment and environmental extremism that undermines faith, family and individual liberties while expanding government control over us."

It was now 10:30 a.m. at the intersection of Pine Ridge Road and US 41 in Naples Florida. The sky was clear, the patriotic music was at full volume. Would anyone show up? People in cars drove by with quizzical looks on their faces. "What the heck was going on?" their expression said. Some cars honked as they drove by, as if to say, "I'm with you Naples Tea Party." Our contingent of organizers and volunteers took our Tea Party signs and stood on the street waving to passersby.

At 11:00 a.m., three television stations showed up with satellite equipment and reporters. The Collier County Sheriff's Department also arrived with about fifteen law enforcement officers and spread out. Nothing like this had ever happened in Naples before, so no one was going to take a chance on missing out on the action. Newspaper reporters began to interview people as the crowd started streaming in from all directions around 11:15 a.m. By 11:30 a.m., we knew that the first Naples Tea Party would be a resounding success. At 12:00 p.m., the official starting time, there were over 3,000 people lined up along the street with their signs and banners.

The playing of the national anthem at noon was one of the proudest moments of my life. Tears welled in both eyes. Words cannot describe the emotions of being surrounded by thousands of like-minded patriots with one thing on their mind … take back our country. Traffic was backed up for miles. As people drove by in their cars, they gave a thumbs up and honked their horns continually until they passed the last Tea Party patriot.

The atmosphere was unlike anything I had ever experienced. Everyone I talked to felt the same way. They were all saying that if was so nice that there were others who felt the same way they did. They were not alone. The makeup of the Tea Party was truly grassroots. Even though the event was on a weekday, there were several families in attendance along with working men and women who took a long lunch hour. There was no visible anger, no obscene or inappropriate Tea Party signs and no altercations of any kind.

People were lined up to sign our petition by the hundreds. We ran out of flyers and the container holding all the tea bags was overflowing. People were courteous and respectful of those around them. They laughed, cried and whooped it up. I will remember it always. And then, at 2:00 p.m., the place started to empty. No one needed to be told to police the grounds. The site of the Tea Party was left cleaner than the way we found it, unlike Washington DC after the inauguration of Obama. By 2:30 p.m., everyone was gone and my wife and I drove home completely drained physically and emotionally. "Now what?" we asked ourselves.

We learned that there were several hundred Tea Parties on April 15th. You wouldn't know it by the press. Our event was well covered, but crowd estimates were grossly underestimated. Only Fox News had adequate coverage of this historical event. The Left yawned and Obama completely ignored the whole thing. The looming question was indeed, "What do we do now?" We had a list of names to decipher in order to add to our e-mail list that would take some time, but some things needed immediate attention.

Independent groups were forming and were represented at the Naples Tea Party. These groups included the 9-12 Project, One

TEA PARTY LEADERS

Nation Under God, World Changers, The FairTax Group and others. I started getting a lot of calls and e-mails saying that we needed one voice speaking for the Tea Party movement and all the groups should merge into one unified voice. It was decided to hold a "council" of group leaders in order to explore the idea.

There were twenty people at the "council." Within ten minutes, it became apparent that Tea Party people are very independent and don't like to be told what to do. The discussion disintegrated into twenty different ways to do things. The original quest to merge into one group with one voice would not work. Each group had their own mission statement and political agenda. Speaking as an organizer of the largest Tea Party in the area, I suggested to keep the Tea Party separate from all the different groups. Let the groups support one area Tea Party and participate at Tea Party functions. The Naples Tea Party could then direct people to groups that best filled their needs. That is exactly what we did and it has worked out very well for over a year.

Many groups that support the Naples Tea Party have their own web sites. We are not so fortunate. We started out with no organizational chart and no bank account ... we remain that way today. Things like Facebook, Twitter and all the other social networking devices are things I deliberately avoided. I have enough problems managing the e-mail account, let alone answering to some goofball on Facebook. There are Naples Tea Party members that have dabbled in it and I do not discourage it. If they wish to increase their list of contacts and provide the information, that's fine with me.

I have registered with the major national Tea Parties. We list our events and contact information. We have recruited new members using this method. However, we never intended to join hands with a national Tea Party. We don't like the idea of a centrally organized Tea Party with a few people elevated to positions of leadership and power. The local Tea Party groups all across the

141

country are still the heart and soul of the grassroots Tea Party movement.

Along the same line, we have never advocated a third party. Many of us remember when Ross Perot help defeat George Bush senior. My feeling is we have enough problems with the two main political parties ... why do we need another one to muddle things up? I take the position of the founders when they warned against letting political parties lead the political process of our Republic.

During the summer of 2009, the Naples Tea Party was very active. Working with all the groups, we were able to attend town hall meetings that made the national news. Who can forget some of the town hall meetings that summer? We confronted groups like MoveOn, ACORN and OFA. When we got wind of one of their rallies, we were there with our people. On July 4th, we participated in the parade in downtown Naples. We provided a float that depicted Washington crossing the Delaware, had a colonial color guard, played patriotic music and had over 500 marchers walking with their Tea Party signs. It was quite impressive.

On September 12th, many of us went to Washington DC to join over one million people at the national Tea Party. You can view my entry which describes the experience of a lifetime. We also organized a Naples Tea Party on the same date and drew our largest crowd to date. Over 5,000 patriots braved the inclement weather and showed up that Saturday morning.

The fall elections were not only thrilling, they were inspirational. It was finally apparent that the grassroots Tea Party movement was a force to be reckoned with. The Scott Brown victory in Massachusetts was a Tea Party victory. This was exactly the shot in the arm that we needed that fall. Every other election went our way except the congressional race in New York. I honestly believe the Republican Party blew that one and had they endorsed Doug Hoffman, New York's 23rd District would be held by a Republican. The governor's races all across the country were Tea Party victories.

In early December, 2009, I started the Naples Tea Party Blog, in partnership with our local newspaper, the Naples Daily News. We decided it could be a good vehicle to reach more people and allow Tea Partiers to express their opinions. One problem that would soon come to the surface was the ability of our opposition to also make comments. The savagery from the Left soon became apparent with their hate-filled comments. But, if anything, it energized the Tea Party members because they could see firsthand how demented and out of touch with reality the progressives were.

Early 2010 saw ObamaCare rammed down our throats. The "nuclear option," was used by the Democrats for the first time in history to pass a piece of legislation of this magnitude. The Tea Party movement was able to postpone it for over a year, but in the end, progressive thuggery won out. It was a huge disappointment for the Tea Party movement. Socialized medicine had been the number one issue for such a long time and many hearts sank the night of the vote. I quickly pointed out to our people that we may have lost this battle, but we have not lost the war. We had to keep engaged and press on.

When Arizona passed their immigration law, the Naples Tea Party decided to hold a rally on June 5th. We met on the steps of the Collier County Court House and had some Tea Party supporters give some speeches instead of standing on a street and wave signs. Again, see the Naples Tea Party Blog for a full description of this event. All of the speeches were magnificent and some are included in the blog entries.

A few weeks later, we again participated in the Naples July 4th Parade. We built another float and had over 500 marchers with signs wave to the crowd along the parade route. We passed out copies of the U.S. Constitution, provided patriotic music from live singers who performed on our float and generally had a wonderful time. Those who were physically unable to march with us lined the street with their Tea Party signs and cheered us on as we passed them by. For the second year in a row, we were the hit of the parade with our display of patriotism and love for America.

Throughout the remainder of 2010, our emphasis will be a continuation to find and promote the right candidates for this year's midterm elections in November. In the State of Florida, we have made a huge difference for several candidates, including Marco Rubio and Colonel Allen West. Rubio was 40 points behind Charlie Crist when he talked to the Naples Tea Party group last year. He surged into a huge lead and forced Crist to switch political affiliations. We always knew Charlie Crist was a RINO and now we know he will do anything to get elected. We are hoping for a Rubio victory in November.

It is now late August and we are preparing for our last 2010 Tea Party of the year to be held on October 2, 2010. Our goal is to have over 10,000 people join us, making it the largest Tea Party yet in our area. The event is exactly one month before the general election in November and we'll soon see if the Tea Party movement can change the power structure in congress. We are passing out flyers to promote the event that say............"What has happened to America? We no longer assume that our children will have it better than we did. Career political leaders have no sense of what the people are feeling deep down, so let's show them in October and REMEMBER IN NOVEMBER. Freedom is not free. Spread the word with friends and family if you value saving America. Bring your Tea Party signs, flags and banners to preserve our individual freedoms that come with personal responsibility. GET ENGAGED!"

In conclusion, let me end with the very first Naples Tea Party Blog entry. I titled it "The Spirit Of 1776 Is Alive Today."

"The grassroots Tea Party movement started from one small spark that ignited events unprecedented in American history. What caused such a rapid grassfire of public outcry has not been fully explained, especially by a liberal biased media intent on using crass characterizations depicting those who participate in the Tea Party movement.

We've heard it all. Tea Parties are an "angry mob" made up of right-wing extremists trying to block "progress" initiated from a populist president. And so, it follows that anyone who participates in a Tea Party is a "racist," because if you don't like the great things President Obama is doing, you have to be a racist. Then came the sexual slurs that liberals take so much delight in throwing around. Yes, we've heard it all.

Nevertheless, our nation has been captivated by a united band of millions of disgusted citizens who recognize that the leaders of our country have gone astray. They have abandoned the principles and values that are the cornerstone of what makes America great. They are shredding the US Constitution with the expansion of government to the point it will soon control every aspect of our lives if we the people let it go unchecked.

To that end, we the people have come together and formed the Tea Party movement. We are going to take back America, and in particular Washington. We are going to hold those in Washington accountable and make it clear they work for we the people. If you are disgusted with the direction our government is headed, it's time to do something about it. Join with millions of other patriotic Americans and get involved in the Tea Party movement.

There are many opportunities in the Tea Party movement besides standing on a street corner holding a sign. We attend town hall meetings, political special interest rallies, attend meetings from a variety of conservative groups where we educate ourselves with information relative to the crisis we are facing.

Remember, the spirit of 1776 is alive today. The Tea Party movement *is* that spirit."

Emily Barsch

I'm not sure where to begin, but I have always heard that we are products of our environment. I was raised in a conservative Christian home and can remember, as a child, hearing my parents occasionally speak about different Republican candidates and President Eisenhower. My father was a Lieutenant in the Navy in WWII and actually saved a fleet of ships in the Battle of Leyte Gulf. Unfortunately, he passed away when I was 8, so I remember very little about his politics.

My mother was from a very small town in central Kentucky about two and a half miles from Lincoln's birthplace. I spent my summers up there and we visited the "Lincoln Farm" frequently. My grandfather was especially proud that his grandmother was present when Lincoln was born and helped pick his name "Abraham" from the Bible. Obviously, Honest Abe is my favorite president.

My mother was remarried to a man who served in WWI and was very patriotic. He would get choked up just listening to Souza's marches. My stepfather was an American history buff and an avid reader. His bedtime reading choice was "The Story of Civilization" by Will and Ariel Durant. I can remember my parents talking about Kennedy and their dislike of him. During the Kennedy and Johnson years, my aunt touted the fact that we were distant cousins of LBJ. I was already beginning, at that time, to develop my political preferences and I didn't want the LBJ connection to be disclosed to anyone.

As a teenager in the 1960s, my stepfather often told me that our country would destroy itself from within, as the Roman Empire did. As a conservative, I was sure he was right, but as a teenager, I didn't think much about his warning. I didn't agree with the protests in the 1960s, because I supported the war in Vietnam. I thought it was our duty to save them from communism. I became disillusioned with the war when I realized that we weren't "in it to win it." I was disgusted with the fact that it had become a war of political correctness run by the politicians and not by the soldiers.

I married at a young age and, like many of us, life and family became my focus. I voted for Nixon in my first presidential election. To this day, I don't think he would have had to resign if he hadn't lied about his involvement in the Watergate scandal. I respect him for having the grace to resign, unlike others (Clinton) who got away with lying to the American people. I continued to vote, conservatively, but never really paid any attention to what Congress, the presidents, or the Supreme Court were doing to our Constitution.

The Clinton/Lewinsky scandal woke me up for a few months, but it was 9/11 that was my first real wake-up call. I began listening to conservative talk radio. Glenn Beck had an afternoon show, originating in our area on WFLA, and I became an avid listener. Unfortunately, he left several months after 9/11 to move on to bigger and better things but I still only listen to talk radio.

My second wake-up call came with the financial meltdown. I had supported George Bush and the Iraq war, but did not realize just how easily he had been swayed by the Democrats and progressives in Congress with regard to immigration, entitlements and pork barrel spending. The more I listened to talk radio, Glenn Beck on CNN and Fox News, the more I began to realize that we, the people, needed to stand up and take this country back from the politicians that were only focused on their own power and greed.
I was appalled by Obama's radical ties and became extremely worried about the outcome of the election. McCain wasn't too much better, due to his "progressive" ideologies, but Sarah was a refreshing change. After Obama's election, it became more and

more apparent that the people would have to emulate the forefathers to put the government back in our hands.

I'm not sure how, but I heard about a Tea Party rally in the park in downtown San Antonio, Florida. My husband and I decided to go, so we gathered up the flag and went to check it out. There were about 100 people there. The microphone was opened up and I wound up speaking for a few minutes on excessive government spending. As we had provided our contact information, we received an e-mail asking us to participate in a new Tea Party group. There were no options: in order to help save the country, we had to participate.

The East Pasco Tea Party Patriots were formed, and started with about six to ten of us meeting once a month. On July 4th last year we held a rally in downtown Dade City, Florida, with music, political speeches and ACORN. That's right, ACORN showed up trying to get petitions signed. Needless to say, they didn't stay around too long. There were approximately 450 people in attendance. Just prior to July 4th, I wrote a poem "The Rise and Fall of the Constitution." I read my poem during the program. Also, my daughter (twelve years old at that time) spoke about the TARP and the stimulus plans and how the incurred debt would affect her future.

Several of our members had the privilege of attending the 9/12 march on Washington, last year. My husband and I had never had the opportunity to visit DC and it was awe inspiring. However, the participation of over 1 ½ million conservative, grassroots patriots was the most amazing thing I have ever seen. We were so proud to be included in that event. Coincidentally, during the preparation for the trip, we discovered that we had known the Florida Coordinator of FreedomWorks for many years, not realizing his involvement with that organization. Upon our return, I wrote another poem about the experience.

Our group has now grown to over 250 on our mailing list, with at least 100 members attending each meeting. We have had to change meeting locations twice to accommodate the growth. We have been blessed to have wonderful, educational speakers address our group, including a retired Michigan Supreme Court judge, a terrorism consultant to WestPoint, local political office-holders, and local politically active attorneys and physicians. This year, the East Pasco Tea Party Patriots will be donating pocket Constitutions to all of the 7th graders in our county, who are mandated to take a new Civics Course in middle school.

Recently, I was honored to be invited to a round table discussion with Newt Gingrich. There were approximately twenty-four Tea Party and 9/12 leaders invited to discuss their stories. It was an interesting and informative meeting. I am happy to report that I was impressed with the fact that Speaker Gingrich spoke only briefly, but listened intently to our discourse. During my story, I expressed that I had not protested in *the* 1960s but, since I turned 60 last year, I am now protesting in *my* 60s.

It is my desire to make a difference, regardless of how small, in preserving and maintaining our freedom, as outlined by the Founding Fathers, and our God-given unalienable rights. I have considered running for office, but I am not sure if family commitments may inhibit that process. Until that time, I will continue to encourage and grow our grassroots campaign through the East Pasco Tea Party Patriots. I will also actively support candidates whose platforms support the US Constitution and all of the privileges and rights contained therein.

Becky Gerritson

My husband, Eric, and I are the founders of the Wetumpka Tea Party (WTP), just outside Montgomery, AL. I was raised in Colorado. My life is dedicated to being a wife and homeschool mom. Eric was born and raised in California. He served in the United States Air Force for twenty years. It was the Air Force that brought us to Gunter AFB in Montgomery, AL. Eric retired in January 2005 and currently works as a civilian contractor for the Alabama Army National Guard. We now consider Wetumpka, Alabama our home.

Our daughter is fourteen and has become quite politically active over the past fifteen months (not all by choice). She can talk politics with any adult and even hold her own with Glenn Beck or Keith Oberman (although I don't think Keith is an adult nor knows much about politics). She is a beautiful godly young women and we are very proud of who she is. She has been a great help to us in the WTP. She hands out fliers, works registration tables, helps us set up for meetings, and even sings the National Anthem. She often acts as our domestic engineer too as she cooks and cleans for our family since often times we are too busy with Tea Party business to do it ourselves.

I was never involved in politics until the last year of the Bush Administration, although I have always been very patriotic and pro-American, and I always vote in the general elections. During the months leading up to the 2008 election I started doing research on the candidates and became very concerned about Obama as I learned more about him and his far left leanings. I was also very bothered about the bailouts in September 2008 and the direction our country was turning. All of this led to the "awaking" of my activism.

Our intrinsic motivation comes from our Christian faith and the belief that the Lord has put us in the position so we can be a light to others. We believe with all of our hearts the Lord wants His people to stand up against tyranny and stand up for His morality and His principals. Some Tea Parties focus only on fiscal issues, however, the WTP does not shy away from social/religious issues, and our members embrace the passion too.

After the massive spending during the eight years of the Bush Administration, the bailouts of the banking industry and then the

$1.8 trillion dollar stimulus package in February 2009, the American people had had enough!! On February 20th we watched Rick Santelli of CNBC, on the floor of the Chicago Board of Trade go into a spontaneous rant against the out-of-control spending in Washington. We, along with other citizens around the nation, were motivated by his words and decided to hold Tea Parties of our own.

In March 2009, we had heard about the plans for a Tea Party in Montgomery. Eric suggested we hold a Tea party for the residents in Wetumpka, so they would not have to travel to Montgomery. As we got ready for our April 15th rally, we frequently called the local talk radio station in attempt to get the word out and "rally the troops" in our area. My daughter and I distributed fliers to homes and businesses around town. I wrote with shoe polish on my car the date and time of the event. On a gorgeous April 15th at noon, we held our Tax Day Tea Party at Gold Star Park located next to the peaceful Coosa River. We told ourselves we would be satisfied if 50 people came, but to our astonishment we had 420 peaceful, friendly, law abiding citizens show up with signs and flags. We opened in prayer, sung the National Anthem, and played the Tea Party Anthem by Lloyd Marcus. We had invited two local homeschooled young men, Preston Kennedy and Dave McCrosky, to speak about liberty and our out-of-control tax system. They were amazing and the folks absolutely loved them. The youthful enthusiasm and amazing grasp of history and economics wowed everyone in attendance. Eric and I both gave speeches about current legislation that was slated to strip away more and more of our God given and Constitutionally mandated freedoms.

Attendees signed three Gadsden "Don't Tread On Me" flags; one for 2nd Congressional District Congressman Bobby Bright and one each for Senators Jeff Sessions and Richard Shelby. The flag we signed for Senator Jeff Sessions now hangs respectfully in a black-rimmed frame in his Senate office in Washington DC. Our event concluded with all 420 able-bodied attendees walking down to the river and throwing in handfuls of tea, symbolizing the Boston Tea Party in 1773. Since that April day fifteen months ago, our lives have never been the same.

The Wetumpka Tea Party held numerous events throughout 2009, ranging from a "Patriots in the Park" event where citizens came to the park on a summer evening and listened to southern music and speeches on the health care and the cap and trade bills, to some health care forums, a citizen protest at the ABC affiliate in Montgomery for bias reporting, and a "Grannies and Grandpas against Health Care" rally outside Congressman Bobby Bright's office.

On September 6th of last year we held an evangelistic in nature "Reclaim Rally." The event's focus was on Reclaiming America's Christian heritage. Our nation's history proves we were built on Christian principles and it is imperative that we return to those same principles if our country is to ever going to turn around. Charisa Hagel, a homeschooled fifteen-year-old young woman, gave an inspiring speech and Judge Roy Moore gave the keynote address.

Our favorite event was when we chartered three buses carrying 150 people to the 9/12 March on DC in September 2009. That was the most amazing event any of us had ever participated in. There were almost 2 million Americans from all 50 states protesting the out-of-control spending in Washington. Participants were young, old, all races, creeds, economic backgrounds. Our buses arrived in Chrystal City just outside of Washington DC early Saturday morning. From there we walked to the nearest Metro Station where we joined thousands of others who immediately overwhelmed the subway system. When we descended underground into the Metro system we were not prepared for what we saw. It was jammed full of people trying to buy tickets to the Freedom Plaza where the march was to start. Because of that, it took forever to get our tickets. After getting our tickets we proceeded to the platform and were again amazed when we watched a train pull up to the platform and it was so full of people wearing patriotic T-shirts and holding T.E.A. Party signs and flags that they couldn't open the door to let anyone else on.

It got even better as *three more* subway trains just like the first one came by before one finally had some room for a few people to get on. We would cheer and wave at each other through the windows as the trains pulled up. People on the tightly packed platforms and over full trains grinned ear to ear as they watched their fellow American brothers and sisters unite on this unforgettable day. There was an excitement among us that I can't describe. I get goose bumps even now as I write this. The march was to begin at noon at Freedom Plaza but the DC police made us start two hours early because there were so many people crammed into that area. As we walked towards the Capitol building, we were at times literally so tightly packed that we were shoulder to shoulder with each other, and believe it or not I never felt safer. These were the friendliest people I have ever seen.

Everyone was awestruck at the amount of people. It was so exhilarating finding out what state people had traveled from. We made friends with people all over the nation that day. Some I e-mail on a regular basis now. Some people from our Tea Party group even ran into Eric's cousin and family from San Diego California! His cousin recognized the "Don't Tread On Me" Wetumpka Tea Party shirts and asked if they knew Eric and me. Our friends relayed the message to us once we were back on the bus later that night heading home.

The most amazing part to me was when we sang God Bless America. Two million people with one voice standing in reverence and singing as it echoed off the Capitol building down through the Washington Mall in waves of unmistakable pride. It was incredible! A Washington DC Park Patrol worker told a group of people from our Tea party that he had *never* seen so many people on the Capitol grounds before. It was amusing to watch the police—they appeared to be having a great time observing us and speaking to us and not having to worry about arresting any rabble-rousers. I think they were dumbfounded that we could be so friendly since the mainstream media had made us out to be crazy radicals.

We're just regular folks who obey the laws, work hard at our jobs and at raising our family. We just want to restore the core values that this country was founded on: limited government, hard work, personal responsibility, free market-capitalism, ingenuity, etc.

Something else that shows how classy and respectful Tea Party people are is that after the rally they left the grounds in pristine condition. There were pictures taken of the grounds after the rally and set alongside pictures of the grounds after the President Obama's inauguration. After the inauguration there were piles of trash everywhere and apparently the city spent millions of dollars and many days cleaning up the mess. The pictures of the grounds after the 9/12 event looked just like they did hours before the event. Everyone picked up their trash and belongings and had total respect for the Capitol grounds and what they represent.

The Wetumpka Tea Party will be chartering buses again in August 2010, for the Restoring Honor Rally hosted by Glenn Beck and also for the March on DC events on September 9/12, 2010 hosted by Unit in Action and FreedomWorks.

In January we invited Keith Carl Smith, *The Conservative Messenger*, of Trussville, AL, to give a presentation on being a "Frederick Douglas Republican." He is an African American who demonstrates how the federal government is the modern day slaveholder and "We the People" are its slaves. He goes back to life of Frederick Douglass and explains what the Republican party used to stand for and how Frederick Douglas was actually the father of the Republican party before Abraham Lincoln. Keith explained Douglass's four life-empowering values:
1. Respect for life

2. Respect for the US Constitution
3. Limited Government
4. Personal Responsibility
I highly recommend watching this presentation on the Wetump-ka Tea Party web site: WetumpkaTeaParty.com. It's a powerful history lesson that every American should watch.

We held our second Tax Day Tea Party on April 15, 2010. This time we 760 people! We have held numerous other events not mentioned since our first Tax Day Tea Party in 2009, to educate our friends and neighbors about our history and about current legislation that is being pushed and passed that is stealing our freedoms. We have been so encouraged to get to know the members of the WTP. They are dedicated, passionate people from Wetumpka, Montgomery, Prattville, Tallassee, Millbrook, Titus and other outlying towns. We have made so many new friends and have been truly honored to stand side by side with them over the past fifteen months.

A New Chapter for the Gerritsons

As active Tea Party organizers during 2009, we became increa-singly aware that the truth of who Tea Party people are and the values that unite them is not being portrayed accurately by the mainstream media. So in April Eric and I stepped down from Leadership within the WTP and started a state-of-the-art satellite webcasting company called MyeDecision (MyeDecision.com). Our goal in forming this business is to bypass the mainstream media and take the message of limited government, fiscal and personal responsibility, accurate American history and Biblical truth to all Americans and people all over the world. We also hope to use this technology to help get conservative leaders elected, by webcasting debates, campaign dinners, fundraisers, etc. We will broadcast Tea Parties, activist trainings, town halls, etc. MyeDecision allows viewers to make educated decisions about the issues and candidates without the mainstream spin.

In closing, if you were to ask me would I have ever thought I would be where I am today, doing what I do? I would have to unequivocally state "No!" Again, if asked, "Do I regret the sacrifices our family has made?" I would again reply "No!" This has been the hardest and most stressful fifteen months of our lives but I believe that we, along with all of the patriotic members of the Wetumpka Tea Party, are making a difference. We are so proud to be part of this historical citizen movement and look forward to it getting bigger and bigger so we can restore of founding principles and get back to responsible governing run "by the people, for the people."

Please check out the Wetumpka Tea Party which is now organized by Loretta Wakefield at WetumkpaTeaParty.com. Visit our web site, MyeDecision to see how we can help you broadcast your event or message.

Ben Rice

I am from Chambersburg, Pennsylvania. I am married and have three kids who range in ages from five to ten. I work for Franklin County within the 911 center and have done that for ten years. I love serving the citizens of the community that I live in.

I have been active in Republican politics since I was fifteen, volunteering in local campaigns. It has been a hobby of mine for a long time.
My political beliefs have always been to put your ideals before party. In addition, the Republican party should be the conservative party, which as a whole still holds conservative values within its platform. The problem has become that Republicans have ignored this platform and have become more Democrat-lite than opposite of the Democrat.

Locally, I am part of a group of staunch Constitution-loving Republicans that have worked to reform our party from the inside. In doing so, we have held three local Tea Parties that have given our citizens a voice to stand up to the power grab that has existed within our government at all levels. Although these events were organized by the party, we did not hold back on Republican officials that supported increased spending, bailouts and economic stimuli that burdened my childrens' and grandchildrens' economic future.

Currently, I am working with the patriots that came out to our Tea Parties to organize into a nonpartisan group. We are in a "make or break" time in history. If we allow the statists to take our country we will lose everything that the Founding Fathers wanted for this great nation.

I feel the Tea Party movement should be a movement of the grassroots that reforms the political process. It will be more successful than forming its own party. By getting involved in the local committees the Tea Party will move mountains. This is a revolution that the establishment fears more than anything in history.

Beth Mizell

To think back at "what got me started" was startling to me, since I'd never really thought about it.

I live in a rural, mostly low-income parish in south Louisiana. We'd moved to a farm in this area about twelve years ago after living in a more affluent parish nearby for twenty years. Upon moving here (we'd grown up in a nearby town in this parish) we learned that no one really knew about the funding for roads or schools or community services in general. The general feeling was that the citizens really could have no effect in how things were being done or the direction the parish was going. I decided to attend a Parish Council meeting (that's our governing body) mostly out of curiosity. At that meeting, our parish president at the time (Toye Taylor) was suggesting that the parish have an Economic Dev Commission appointed. I knew we already had an Economic Dev group and thought why would we need another? When the motion was made and the ordinance brought to the public's viewing there was one line at the bottom that stated this commission would have the right to take private property for "economic development purposes" as deemed by this commission. Well, that became a real issue after it was made known to most citizens, the majority of whom never read an ordinance or attended a public meeting. The next meeting for the vote on this ordinance was with a packed, standing-room-only crowd in attendance. At that meeting (which was on YouTube for a long time and may still be there) several members of the public let their feelings be known on that part of the document. At one point when asked where the commission's right to take property for economic development came from, our parish president replied, (as he pulled a booklet from his shirt pocket) "This right here is my right—the constitution gives me that right." He was asked to read that line—which we knew didn't exist as he was applying it—and he refused. Anyway, this is where my interest and passion started.

From there, we had a little incident called Katrina that affected our area. After that, the public's eyes were opened to the need of oversight of public officials. In my small community I worked on an incorporation proposal to have our area made into its own municipality. My involvement with most issues is to educate the public and try to arouse interest in issues they have no knowledge about, but would be appalled if they knew what their elected officials are doing.

I am a Republican, and the current president of our local Republican Women's group, but have a lot of interest in the Tea Party because of the energy the group has in getting things done. That's how my interests progressed into Tea Party involvement.

Betty Blanco

"Something is wrong in America—terribly, horribly wrong. I can feel it. When I lay down at night, I get a real sick feeling inside. When I examine this feeling, it's like bells going off whenever I think on finances of our government.

Now I feel a rumbling beneath me. It feels like an earthquake.

It is the American people waking up from their slumber.

Wake up, Wake up. The enemy is coming. Rise up, America; let your voices be heard. We will not go silently into the night. We will not sit down and shut up. We are the silent majority no more and with the help of God, we will turn this country back to its foundations."
– Betty Blanco, April 15, 2010

These are the opening words that I said at our Tea Party in La Junta, Colorado on April 15, 2010. These words are burned into my heart. From these words come my passion. They were given to me in the wee hours of the morning and I believe them to be God inspired. I never dreamed that the Tea Party would ever be something I would do—never— but what do you do when you are called to do this? (Excuse me while I choke up.) This calling, to the Tea Party, is very humbling to me just to say the least.

People kept saying to me, "Something has to be done (about this out of control spending government)." Even my pastors were saying this. When I prayed about it, I felt a prodding to do a Tea Party. "Why not you?" I heard. I argued. "I can't do that. I could never get up in front of all those people and do that and besides that, I wouldn't know what to say." Then I heard, "How do you know that I didn't put you here on earth for such a time as this?"

Since then, I have been determined in my heart to do the very best job possible to promote the local Tea Party for God and to be of altruistic service to the local people and to have their voices heard.

TEA PARTY – THE AWAKENING

Bill Dietz

This is not my story only, but the story of a great many hard working, taxpaying American citizens. I am sixty-two years old. Growing up we had six boys and six girls, and Mom and Dad. Fourteen of us sitting around the table at mealtimes. We were farmers, went to church every Sunday, said our prayers before every meal and at bedtime. We grew up in a time when if you worked hard, didn't lie, cheat, or steal, you would get ahead to live the great American dream no matter what your occupation was. Taxes were low in most areas. Very few fees, license, and permits. It was a Free America.

I should write a book and call it, "While we were working or Sleeping"—bad things were taking place behind the scenes. Our public servants were becoming tyrants, giving themselves large pay raises, lavishes retirement pensions, huge expense accounts, besides all the perks they could swindle out of any lobbyist that came along. Government unions were moving into the Police force, Fire Department, and Educational system and others. We kept working and sleeping, getting up every day to go to work, paying our mortgage, paying for our kids education, and pay our taxes, fees, and permits for everything under the sun. It became very discouraging to keep up the grind: cut here and cut there, work longer hours, clip out coupons.

One day I heard Rush Limbaugh saying the things I had been saying for several years—finally a voice in the media that spoke up for the common man. Next thing Fox News came on the scene with fair and balanced news. Then I went to a Rockford IL Tea Party organized by David Hale and listened to many patriots speak and realized I was not alone. I could not help myself. I got in line and said my few words of concern about the socialistic direction our country was going. People say, "Someone ought to do something." I thought to myself—why not me? I have an old school I converted into apartments with a meeting room. I talked to a few conservative friends of mine and also a friend who admitted he is a tax and spend liberal, yet he is sick of the way the country is going! We had our first meeting February of 2010 with thirty people showing up. We had up to seventy show up from five different counties. We are expecting more numbers in July. Now two more Tea Parties just started up within twenty miles of ours in Lena IL. People are worried that the Free America we grew up in is quickly vanishing, and we are afraid that our kids and grandkids will not enjoy the opportunities and freedoms that we had. This may be the first generation that will be worse off than the generation before. All you have to do is look at the National Debt Clock and see the $13+ trillion debt, which translates to over $42,000 per citizen or $119,000 per taxpayer. When you figure in the unfunded liabilities, it is over $109 trillion or $353,000 per citizen, or as near as I can figure $1 million per taxpayer! Now if that is not enough to make you want to vote the tax and spenders out, then you are part of the problem and not the solution.

Bill Maryberry

Late on a warm afternoon, Richard and I were out on his back porch sipping on cold iced tea after moving some furniture around for his wife. It was April Fools' Day of 2009, of course. The conversation quickly turned to politics and the inevitable "This country is in serious trouble" repartee. It did not take long to get to the usual frustration of We Little People had little hope of changing things. Then it started: Maybe, just maybe, we could call attention to the issue. You know, stir up some trouble.

We became more exited, and in twenty minutes we had a plan. Richard would get busy calling the folks needed to get a site, permits, security, and permissions. He is active in Veterans' Affairs and called his buddies in DAV, VFW, and local veterans' groups. I did the media and public notifications. I also thought the local GOP would of course be glad to help. I was wrong.

Within a few days, Richard had permission to use our local

Veterans' Park, had called a friend with a flatbed trailer, and rented a PA system. I had letters out to the two local weeklies and the local bigger town's daily, wrangled a radio interview, and called the Republican Party honcho. They paid for one advertisement, which appeared in the paper completely changed from submitted.

Our first effort was a great success considering it was put together in fifteen days. State patrol had blue lights; motorcyclists with ponytails brought American flags; pictures were made which showed up in newspapers. We had an aquarium for donations and over four hundred dollars showed up.

The GOP secretary/treasurer wanted the money "to help finance conservatism" and send some people (county Republicans: basically her) to Washington for the 9/12 rally. She got her feelings hurt when she didn't take "Uh, no, dear" for an answer. "Hell, no" finally worked, marking the end to the relationship between Tax Protest and the county GOP.

We began planning The Second Annual Tax Protest six months in advance. I signed up with several *bona fide* Tea Party organizations, carefully recognizing the differences between the Tea Party (political organization) vs. TEA (Taxed Enough Already) parties, which are events. The Republican Party steadfastly refused to participate. Since I am also a noisy member of that august group, they suffered my appearances at their meetings to hand out fliers, daring them to rule me out of order.

Along came some other return-to-conservatism groups: GOOOH, Project 9/12, Constitution Party, Freedom Project, Neal Boortz's marching minions, etc. We made the clear decision for this Tax Protest event to remain dedicated to the single issue of onerous taxation, coming down squarely on one side of the tax and spend equation. We stayed committed to keeping attention on economic good sense, veering away from splintering ideologies. We did not want to join any other campaign for whatever else; we are a protest event, not an organization for any other political, social or financial issue.

The contributions from 2009 paid for a few advertisements for 2010 in local papers and online. Facebook was helpful, and full-color fliers were distributed. The phone rang and e-mails were exchanged.

Our three best speakers then hinted they might back out: "Too many Republicans." After making it clear they were free to bash the GOP, they enthusiastically brought more people and made very good speeches.

The event of April 15, 2010 went very well. The speeches were on topic and nonpartisan, the fire was poked up, the crowd was responsive. State congressman showed up and national candidates sent surrogates. Not a single local politician came.

There were a few flies in the ointment: the reporter from the neighboring college town was friendly then burned me in print; our invitation to the open microphone got out of hand; the local Democrats tried to sabotage us with counter-publicity; the local Republican leadership made not the slightest attempt to show up for the issue; and contributions were scanty. Our polling shows the contributing dollar is being splintered.

We have already begun preparations for The Third Annual Tax Protest, anticipating that taxation will be even worse by April 15, 2011. I've continued to make a pest of myself at the county Republican Party meetings and events, already handing out fliers. Our Facebook page gets a few new members every few days.

My friend Richard is active in alternative conservative groups, having given up on Republicans. We agree completely on conservatism while disagreeing entirely on how to revitalize it. My decision has been to remain a Republican squeaky wheel, working to return this old, entrenched organization already in place to conservative principles. Richard has simply chosen a different tack and works from a different angle. As long as taxes are reduced and spending is viewed as having to be limited to what is available, how we get there matters little. The worst scenario will be if outrageous spending continues, followed by hocus-pocus dreamed up to pay for it.

Limited taxes make for limitless growth; revenues follow. We cannot spend out of debt, multiply wealth by dividing it, or give to someone without first taking from another.

Dee Saddler

I refer to myself as "the reluctant volunteer" because I have not been involved in politics for years. Yes, I did my patriotic duty and always voted (hopefully for the best candidate), but that was the extent of my involvement. Like many Americans I was naïve in thinking those elected would protect our voice in Washington.

My feelings about the 2008 elections were mixed. Neither party seemed to offer the solutions I thought the country needed and when Mr. Obama won, I cried. I cried because my intuition told me his color did not matter, his faith did not matter, but I would literally get sick every time he appeared on the news. He was not the man to bring about the true "change" we needed.

Shortly after the elections I received an e-mail about the story of Kitty Werthmann and the struggles she witnessed in 1938 Austria. That e-mail left a lasting impression on me and I started watching Fox News and inhaling any book that might give me a clue as to how I could make a difference. Ironically, one of the books I was reading at the time spoke about the *10 Measures of the Communist Manifesto* and the list only confirmed the pattern

Kitty described as Hitler took over Austria. By this time our new administration was using some of the same tactics.

I believe it was Glenn Beck who mentioned the "cycle of government." The cycle starts with *liberty,* moves to *complacency,* then *dependence,* then *tyranny* and finally *revolution.* It wasn't hard to see where America was in the scheme of things. By now I had made the decision that the Tea Party Patriots was the group for me. I firmly aligned with their mission statement of "fiscal responsibility, limited government and free markets." My father served in the Navy in WWII and had instilled these beliefs in us at a very young age. Now I just had to figure out how to help. I traveled seventy-five miles on April 15, 2010 to see what one of their tax rallies looked like and came home with the idea that I just needed to start a local group. The best way to learn is to teach or organize and so I did. Our first meeting in May produced six loyal patriots. I was pleased to have that many attend since our entire county is only 5,000 strong and the nearest town has less than 200 people. Our June meeting made my spirit soar with twenty-two potential patriots arriving. It's not the numbers that impress me, but the enthusiasm these people have for "taking back America." The most common remark I hear is, "It is so good to know I am not the only one that feels this way."

In conclusion, the journey has been short in terms of time, but I have come full circle now. Plan A was to create a local group, help them find the right candidates and keep them posted on the issues at hand. Plan B was to fill my larder, buy ammo, clean my guns and find a bunker (go to the mattresses in *Godfather* terms. But then I found Plan C which is the best one of all—The Holy Bible. My Bible study group just finished reading the Book of Daniel and we're now getting ready to study Revelations. This step puts it all in perspective for me and gives me the peace I was looking for when I started this journey. I can't wait to see what the next chapter will bring.

TEA PARTY – THE AWAKENING

Tom Tillison

I can still recall the depression that slowly swept over me on the evening of November 4, 2008, as the election results were beginning to prove that America was indeed buying into the *hope and change* of Barack Obama. You see, I was one of the few that had actually done my homework prior to the election and knew exactly what Obama represented, who his mentors were and what his views of America were.

I went to bed early, not being able to bear the results any longer and woke up early the next morning with a sinking feeling in my heart. I was having trouble coming to grips with reality. I couldn't believe that the American people had just elected a man that saw our country as fundamentally flawed and in need of such radical transformation.

I asked myself, "Did I do everything I could to affect the outcome?" I had spent the time to educate myself—I even donated to the GOP in support of their candidate. Yet, I knew I could have done more, and I made a commitment to myself at that very moment that I may wake up four years from this day with the same sinking feeling in my heart; however, I will be able to look at myself in the mirror and say, "I did everything within my power to bring about a different result!"

Why all the drama over a presidential election? Because I knew that America was in trouble. I knew that we were at a pivotal point as a country, and that the principles upon which this nation was founded were on the brink of extinction. And, upon that moment, I embarked on a new direction. For far too long, I stood on the sideline. I ignored my civic responsibility ... like so many others, I worked hard, took care of my family, and spent my leisure time enjoying the fruits of my labor. I left "politics" to others, but no more!

I had no idea where to start, but start I did ... and now I find my-self doing things I never would have imagined just a little over a year ago. I've sat down with House Minority Leader John Boehner, NRCC Chairman Pete Sessions and every local candidate running for office knows who I am. I co-host a weekend radio show called Tea Party Patriots LIVE, and I'm the editor-in-chief of an online conservative news site orlandopolitical-press.com. I organize tea parties, protests, rallies, and events designed to educate and motivate my fellow citizens. I am a grassroots activist, a community organizer, an antagonist, if you will! Hell, I even learned what a "hob-nob" is!

In fact, I have gotten so involved it's become a full time job. The time constraints have gotten so demanding that I even went part-time at my job, taking a significant financial hit. I make this choice because I believe we are at such a critical time in our na-tion's history and because of another awakening I had. My mother passed away this past December, and, as I sat there in the church staring at her as she lay in the casket, it occurred to me that when the day comes that I am lying there, it will not matter at that moment how much money I have in the bank. What will be far more important is the impact I had on the world around me.

Additionally, I was blessed with my first grandchild this year, and I want her to know the same America that I knew, to have the same opportunities. I do not want her to look back at this pe-riod thirty years from now and ask, "Why didn't my grandfather do something about what was happening back then?"

So, do something I am! And, I am just getting started, as my goals are long term in nature: to educate the public on the issues of the day, to help motivate them to get involved and to work together to hold our elected officials accountable. I do not be-lieve that our politicians are to blame for where we are as a nation, instead, we the people are responsible. When you allow the fox to guard the henhouse, the outcome is predicable, therefore, how can you fault the fox for doing what comes natural?

We are Americans, though, and I believe in my heart that we will rise to the occasion. Having come to learn so much about our Founding Fathers, I will leave you with a quote I came across a while back that has become my motto:

"All tyranny needs to gain a foothold is for people of good conscience to remain silent."
– Thomas Jefferson

Brandon Benson

The first step of getting involved was deciding which Tea Party organization to really be a part of. Nebraska already had several 9-12 Project groups, and I'm a member of those. I wasn't necessarily looking to start a new group, rather to put my education and experience in new media to work for one of the national Tea Party groups. I noticed that the state did not have a listed coordinator for Tea Party Patriots. I volunteered for the position and have been the coordinator since mid May. Since there hasn't been a state leader for the TPP in Nebraska, I have found mixed reaction. Most seem really content with their local, small groups. I think that's great, but at some point there needs to be interaction and planning among these groups—not to cannibalize each other, but rather to be on message and be efficient in spreading the message. I have plenty of work to do in this facet of the cause.

While I support and respect the tenets of the 9-12 Project and have participated in the Tea Party Express stops, I found myself more aligned with TPP. I feel that Tea Party Patriots has a better mass appeal and concentrates more on the issues of fiscal responsibility and promoting smaller government. The social issues are important but I think our crisis right now is in the areas of size of government and fiscal issues. We need to correct those issues first, then move on to such things as immigration. I think education is an important secondary step too, especially when it comes to American history. In that regard the 9-12 Project groups are doing an excellent job, especially from what I observe here locally and statewide.

As far as the Tea Party movement, specifically with Tea Party Patriots, I think the loose organization helps and also hurts. And perhaps that's universal across the movement. If there's one thing I could change it would be that—better organization from the top. While the current setup provides for excellent solutions and development of the cause from the bottom, that is, the individuals in their communities, it also can be somewhat inefficient and make the movement appear too vague. However, I am confident that the current setup will work and we'll see leaders rise through the ranks all across the Tea Party movement and pave the way for a restored Constitutional government in the United States.

What I've been doing is acting as a liaison from the national leaders with TPP and state groups and organizations. I also try to keep people updated via Twitter and Facebook of events and information. I have also started my own Internet radio program on BlogTalkRadio.com to supplement my web site. We have in the works a state organization called CCON (Conservative Coalition Of Nebraska) to help link all the groups and be a central location for news and information. I'm also working to put my video production skills to use by taping the local and state events and posting them online for the public to view. One of the things we need to do is bypass the mainstream media and show Americans who we truly are. We are not racists, we are not uneducated backwoods rednecks. What we are is a true cross section of America coming together to protect everything that makes America and Americans great.

One of the amazing actions specific to Nebraska has been that the 9-12 and Tea Party groups have been meeting weekly at

Senator Ben Nelson's office to protest. This has been going on every week—rain, snow, or shine. I'd like for everyone outside of Nebraska to know that most of us here are fed up with stuff like the Cornhusker Kickback. Maybe it would have helped Nebraskans ... but at a cost to others. And that type of government is not acceptable, and we won't stand for it. We will stand on principle.

I think the Tea Party movement is about principle over politics. It's about individuals stepping up, putting aside that fear of being vocal, and defending our American founding and our way of life from outside and inside forces. One of the features on my web site I have started is called "AmeriCANS vs. AmeriCANTS." I think that's the best way to sum up the Tea Party movement. We are AmeriCANS. We are the ones who say we CAN get it done! We're not victims and we refuse to have our traditions and history revised and transformed into something that is un-American. I think we've lost much of that rugged individualism. In order to fix that it's going to take brave individuals at the local levels to correct each bit piece by piece.

Tracy Wilson

I am very happy to tell you how I became involved in the Tea Party movement. I am a thirty-eight-year-old mother of five. I recently went back to teaching at the elementary school level. I have been interested in politics from the day I was old enough to vote, and even before. I have always been conservative, and the election of Barak Obama along with a Democrat majority really disturbed me. I love black folks, so it was certainly never a race issue for me. I did not believe that Obama was qualified to be president, and I stood absolutely opposed to many of his policy plans.

I do receive e-mail from Christian organizations such as the American Family Association. In the spring of 2009, they (along with a number of other groups) sent many e-mails supporting the

Tea Party movement. Finally I decided to see what was going on in our little community. I obviously did not carefully read what I was filling out the on-line form to do, because when I thought I was requesting further information, I was actually signing up to be a coordinator.

I totally believe that God is involved in our lives, and He was that morning. Not long after I did this, I got a call from a power-house senior citizen in my county named Betty Downey. Betty informed me that she found me listed as the Currituck County Tea Party Coordinator, much to my surprise! This dear lady had not had any real political involvement, other than voting, and at age seventy-eight, she was on fire! That morning, two unlikely candidates became the start of the Currituck Tea Party move-ment. Betty and I share a commitment to the Lord and a common love of country. We found a great group of patriotic Americans who joined us for our Tax Day Tea Party in April of 2009. We also had a Patriot Liberty Day Party on the 4th of July last year. Many individuals spoke on chosen Founding Fathers and how we have strayed from their plans for our nation.

Since last summer, Betty had a near death experience with her heart, and I went back to teaching. We were thrilled to connect with a couple of new key players this year who had more time, energy and focus than we did to plan the event. I was able to speak again at the Tax Day event this year, which was a great thrill for me. That's it in a nutshell!

Brian Aeschliman

I am not actually sure where I developed such a love for my country beyond the fact that it is the greatest nation that has ever been. Its conception and birth alone is an amazing story and when you take time to truly learn about our history it becomes nearly impossible to deny the possibility of Divine intervention. I am someone who believes in the existence of God Almighty and the role He has played in making the United States the nation that it is. I also believe that we have succeeded so well for so long by being a nation founded on many of the pillars of Christianity and by recognizing that we do owe much if not all that we have to the God who has seen us through so much adversity and blesses us even today when we have become so undeserving.

As long as I can remember the sight of the American flag and the playing of the National Anthem gave me goose bumps. Often times I have trouble singing the entire song out loud because it becomes so emotional for me and as I have more opportunities to travel to other countries I become even more grateful for where I live. As I have gotten older and become more aware of politics and how it has affected changes in our country, there have been many times that I have been disappointed in some of the decisions that have come out of Washington, but never too overly concerned about any of the changes taking our country in a totally different direction. I guess I, like so many others, have sat by and let "the little things" go on unchallenged even if I felt it was wrong. As a result I feel that I am also to blame for allowing my country to have taken the turn that it has but not anymore.

For me, becoming involved in the Tea Party is a way for me to express that not only do I feel that the government has lost touch with the people it was put in place to serve, but that time has not changed the fact that the framework that was originally put in place that made us a great nation is still the framework we should be building upon to return us to the nation we once were. Less government, free markets, and fiscal responsibility: how can any of those things be seen as a bad thing? Furthermore, in the Tea Party group I have organized, we realize that unalienable rights begin with life and that to allow the termination of a guiltless and innocent life violates the most sacred of them all. We also feel that to remain one nation under God and to continue to prosper as we have, our nation must still include God.

Never before have I been more sickened by what is coming out of Washington. To me it is a disgrace that our government resides in a place named after our first president who was a truly selfless man who knew the role that God played not only in his personal life but in the creation and protection of our nation. Most of the career politicians of today do not seem that they would have been worthy of even caring for George Washington's horse. As for those that say that the Constitution and the Bill of Rights is outdated and no longer applies I would say that I disagree and it appears that more and more people everyday come out that disagree as well. I am not asking for anything new, I am demanding that the people of the United States have returned to them what the government has taken away bit by bit for so long now.

I am taking my message to the streets, literally. If you happen to find yourself passing through Topeka, Kansas and see someone dressed in a colonial outfit holding Tea Party signs, that would be me doing yet another thing I feel I have to do. If it something to help the cause of returning the power of the people back to the people I am willing to do whatever it takes. Too many people have given their lives for much too long for me to just sit back and watch as our country is run down by a select group that has forgotten that it is "we the people" that they serve and that I will continue to fight under a Constitution of a country that I love so very much. Why am I in the Tea Party? Because there is no other choice for me. In the Declaration on Independence it says:

> We hold these truths to be self-evident, that all men are created equal, that they are endowed by their Creator with certain unalienable rights, that among these are life, liberty and the pursuit of happiness. *That to secure these rights, governments are instituted among men, deriving their just powers from the consent of the governed.* That whenever any form of government becomes destructive to these ends, it is the right of the people to alter or to abolish it, and to institute new government, laying its

foundation on such principles and organizing its powers in such form, as to them shall seem most likely to affect their safety and happiness. [italics mine]

Most sadly, I feel that the current government has become destructive to these ends. Now I can only pray that the silent majority will unite under a common voice and a common action and begin to right the wrongs and return us to kind of nation that God intended for us to be.

Brian Bertha

My story is pretty straightforward. I spent most of my working life working sixty-hour weeks and not paying much attention to politics. I am a registered Republican and have been since Barry Goldwater. My favorite president was Ronald Reagan. I am a Vet and after Jimmy Carter, was very happy to have someone in the White House that made me proud to be an American. I still didn't get involved other than voting in the general election.

I retired in 2005, did some work on the side for a couple of years and tried to spend time with my children and grandchildren—something I didn't do much of during my working years (much to my regret). I didn't pay much attention until Bush Junior's second term. Some of the things he did concerned me—the Patriot Act, for instance. I did not like the fact that it did not state it was intended for foreign nationals. I started to distrust our leadership at that point.

Enter Barack Obama. I naturally looked at him very hard during his campaign. I was not happy with John McCain because of some of his positions and his "friendliness" with Ted Kennedy and company. The only reason I voted for him was Sarah Palin, who at the time seemed a breath of fresh air.

I attended a couple of the early Tea Parties (local) and decided it was time to get involved. Not so much for myself but for my kids and grandchildren. Initially I was concerned mainly with the debt but thanks to Obama that quickly expanded to Health Care and cap and trade. I actually read HR 3200 and was appalled at what I found there.

After years of yelling at the TV I finally got off the couch. I was still in limbo as I thought I was pretty much alone in my concern. Then came 9/12/2009. I went to DC and was totally amazed. I've been in large crowds before—Yankee Stadium during the pennant race and Giant Stadium many times. The crowd was an order of magnitude larger. Upon hearing the MSM suggest the crowd was around 70,000, I was flabbergasted. I looked at videos and just calculating the areas covered with a conservative density I came up with over 600,000—and that was just early in the day (people were still coming when I left). End result, I was totally energized! Everyone was pleasant, polite and pretty much of one mind from all over the country. Some had traveled 2,500 miles. Mine was only a seven-hour drive.

At some point during this I started watching Beck. I had been watching O'Reilly who I still watch occasionally but Beck got me doing my own research. I had always been interested in history but now I read with intent. *The 5000 Year Leap*, books on the founders, The Federalist papers, anything by Sowell and William Williams etc., and of course, the Constitution many times over. I took a class by Bednarik, read his book *Good to be King* and an activist was born.

I said I read HR 3200 also the cap and "rape" bill. Looking back over time, I was amazed at how far we had come from the founders. The focus on case law and activist judges vs. common law which has stood the test of time for centuries. Regulation, restrictions, special interests strangling freedom and liberty. As a veteran I said to myself—I cannot let this stand. I owe it to those who came before me and gave all to secure my freedoms. How can I do any less for those who will follow me?

I could quote many of our founders but will leave that to others. I will simply say I will do everything in my power to turn this Marxist tide and ensure that we are on the path back to the Republic our founders envisioned. I am a firm supporter of the Constitution and our Republic, and will defend it with all that's in me. I swore an oath when I went into the military. I meant it then as I do now.

When I go to Tea Parties I don't fly the Gadsden flag, I fly the Culpepper flag. It too says "Don't Tread On Me," but it also says, "Give me Liberty or give me Death" This was attributed initially to Patrick Henry but millions of Americans still believe in it. I hope we turn things around in November for all our sakes. *Silent no more—Wake up America*! Now is the time to stand up and be counted once more.

Bryan Luster

I got into the Tea Party movement in February of this year. I have never been very politically active other than voting, but was tired of screaming at the TV and felt I needed to get involved in some way. I began searching the Internet for a local Tea Party group. I knew there was a rally in 2009 so I figured there was a local group. However, I was unable to find one locally, so I teamed up with an Occupational Therapist and decided to informally create one on the electronic media applications like Tea Party Patriots, Facebook, etc., and see what kind of response we received. It has been pretty tremendous and we had a Tax Day Tea Party Rally April 15th, 2010 at the Craighead County Courthouse in Jonesboro, AR with approximately 500 attendees. We currently have another event planned for July 14th with Dick Morris in conjunction with Americans For Prosperity Arkansas and Answer To Us radio. We currently have 307 members on our Facebook group page.

TEA PARTY LEADERS

Carl Edwards

I have been acutely interested in the political world since the 1960 election. I was thirteen, and I was devastated when Nixon lost. Read into that what you may, but I've been hooked ever since. If there's such a thing as a natural-born conservative, it would be me. That doesn't mean that I'm a hard-nosed, uncaring guy, but I'm convinced that the conservative mindset is far more in sync with reality, particularly when it comes to fiscal matters. Social matters are important too, but the debt and the deficit are the biggies. All else will become moot questions if our economy is in tatters.

I've always kept myself current with national and international events, but I've never been an active participant in the political process with the exception of voting. I've always voted even in the primaries, and I have usually cast informed votes. I never became more active because I was always busy with working and taking care of my family. There were any number of very legitimate reasons for not being more involved. But even though my conscience is clear, I know deep inside that this mess is our fault. It's our fault, because while we were slugging our way through life, we failed to keep our government in check. Remember reality? Well, reality dictates.

Our government had been slowly creeping out of control, but the November election in 2008 was a bucket of cold water in the face. We were completely unprepared for Mr. Obama's hell-bent march toward socialism. The press, with only a few exceptions, had failed to vet him. First, his stimulus packages, followed by his nationalization of large corporations. Then there were the energy and health care monsters bearing down on us. They gave us the feel of an enemy army's relentless onslaught. Then something wonderful happened! 9/12 happened! More than 1 ½ million protesters on the steps of the Capitol happened! These were all like-minded patriotic Americans, and suddenly we didn't feel so alone. Finally, there seemed to be a ray of hope. Maybe we could defeat the beast after all, because we had the strength of our numbers.

Nothing has been the same since. I got involved in a Tea Party in Bradford, Pennsylvania, which was where I worked. That group has done well and continues to increase its strength. The only problem was that my wife and I resided across the border in New York State. We searched high and low for a Tea Party closer to home. We couldn't find one, so we and four other very capable people started one. We've now been in existence now for three months. I must say that this last three months has been one of the most challenging periods of my life. But it's been challenging in a good way. I'm using certain old skills to the utmost, and I've been required to develop some new ones. As for old skills, I'm mostly referring to my preparation for and experience as an army officer. That was a grand time in my life, but it was *so* long ago. The leadership skills are still there, but they're a little rusty. Then there's this computer thing. Going into this I was completely computer illiterate. I had some idea of how they could augment an endeavor like this, but I didn't even know how to turn it on. I didn't know how to access e-mails, and I certainly didn't know how to send them. It's only by the grace of my wife's incredible patience that I have achieved any semblance of competence. I still have to call her at work a couple of times a day with elementary questions, but that happens less and less.

We in our core group are still in the midst of building this organization. I'm not even sure if we're out of the woods yet. Sometimes, things seem so iffy. But I'm guardedly optimistic. In the meantime, we blindly forge ahead, trying to tackle one situation after another. All this while we're trying to figure out what works for Tea Party building. We're in uncharted territory. There are no books. We can't turn to those above us for guidance, because there's none above us. That's because this movement consists of thousands of small, autonomous groups all around the country. But a number of things unite us both within the group and between the groups. First and foremost is love of country. This is one of several absolute universals. I'm not saying we have a monopoly on patriotism, but we are all, to a person, intensely patriotic. Then there's our embrace of the US Constitution. It's the greatest political document ever written, and we're doing all in our power to remind the country of that. As we study it we see the beauty of its symmetry. We recognize that without it our nation may have never achieved its greatness. It's not the sole reason for our greatness, but it's a big one. We also see that so many of our problems could have been averted had we not deviated from the course so wisely laid down by the Founding Fathers. The blueprint for this course was our Constitution.

At the top of our agenda is: smaller government, energy independence (not to be confused with cap and trade), term limits, a balanced budget and a strong national defense. The two items that cause us the most concern, though, are the march toward socialism, which infuriates us, and our incredibly huge debt, which scares us to our very core. We seem to be rallying around these two above all others. I don't think it's coincidence that these two issues most threaten our way of life.

Carla Bonney

How did I become a Tea Party organizer? I have been asked this question multiple times, and though each of our responses will vary slightly, I think there is going to be a common thread ... sheer panic.

The very first activities I did as a Tea Party individual was before the movement started. When the primaries gave us John McCain and Barack Obama, I started paying attention. I looked at some of the radical ideas that Barack Obama had embraced. His church affiliation was obviously full of half-truths. His background was sketchy and his experience was minimal. When I looked at some of his writings, I had concern. But I know I am preaching to the choir.

The very first thing I did was respond to an e-mail I received from the Republican Party to make phone calls to swing states. I started calling every afternoon at about 3 p.m. So, I found myself calling North Carolina, Wisconsin, Pennsylvania, Nevada and maybe one other swing state that I don't remember. I did this every day. The Republican group supplied the phone numbers, and I ended up with making approximately 760 phone calls. I could tell that the tone of the country was, "I have always voted Republican, but we need change."

I then went on a bus trip to Henderson, Nevada to walk districts. It was obvious that Obama was going to win.

After Obama was inaugurated, he began acting as if he was going to be a "moderate." People were relieved. However, within a very short time, he began his course. It has continued strongly ever since.

Rick Santelli had a rant in February, I believe. He addressed the president. It cost him. But he also got very popular. He said to the president, "Mr. President, are you listening?" We don't want to pay for our neighbor's house. And the rest is history when he said, "We are going to have a Tea Party in July, and you can join us."

When I got a Tea Party invite via e-mail, I signed up for every city in Ventura County. The first Tea Party in Ventura County was April 15, 2009.

We have hosted five major rallies, and many smaller ones. We have attended political town halls, we have counter-protested. We have started web sites, and we now have three Tea Party groups in Ventura County that all feed into the larger group. We have had TV coverage and multiple newspaper articles. We have a really great group. Everyone is an integral part of the group, and they help with time and money. Everyone is into education, and informing others with breaking information.

We work with other Tea Party groups in California. Our web site is venturactyngttia.ning.com. We're mad and *not going to take it anymore!*

Carmen Fructuoso-Canter

I organized the Chino Tea Party out of frustration that no one had taken the task. Truth be told, I am one of those individuals who have so much on her plate and so little time. It was a struggle. I was apprehensive, a little anxious, and a little intimidated. I hardly ever took on a leading role on anything except caring for my parents and being a cheerleader in high school! Oh, and I also had a mild case of stage fright when I was asked to sing in one of our town fairs—I got up behind the curtain and started shaking. I thought to myself, "Where did that come from?" I don't know. So, you see, I took on this task because I felt compelled to find representation for myself—even if it had to be from doing the organizing myself. I decided to join with Chino Hills Tea Party to get more visibility and to split whatever cost it would take to print flyers, post ads and announcements, and get the group motivated.

The Chino Tea Party started off with an announcement in the local newspapers for meetings and events. Our first meeting was at my home in Chino. I invited a couple of co-workers and their spouses. After just several calls, my home was full! Amy La-Bruyere of AnyStreet.org was there to assist me, and Laura Boatright of TeaPartyIE.com was there to be the guest speaker, she provided everyone with a booklet of the Constitution. Since then, we have had meetings every month until we joined forces with Chino Hills Tea Party to hold events and meetings together. Every time I post a public announcement in the local newspapers, I get more calls. Although I get a few callers here and there, the current membership invite friends and families to attend our meetings. Getting the word out is a task, but we will be growing for as long as our politicians fail to understand what this country is all about, and that what they are doing, is destroying this great country.

I have friends and relatives that are very liberal. I cannot understand the logic. Hearing them complain about the state of the country, they sound conservative ... but when you start talking about "party talking points" they parrot what you hear the Democrats say. It is very frustrating. I totally believe that they do not even know they sound conservative when they complain about taxes, government and the economy.

My personal story: I was born and raised in the Philippines. My grandfather worked for the US Navy in Subic Bay for several years as an engineer. He told his children stories about America, talked highly about Americans, and taught my father the true meaning of democracy. My father imparted this knowledge on us. My father owned a small business and understood what the government can do to make it succeed or make it fail, and his goal was for this business to be there for his children. When Marcos imposed martial law in the Philippines, my father was scared for us twelve children. He did all he could to save up money, and had to hide his wealth from the politicians in the Philippines. He found ways to send his money to America. The fear he had of Marcos taking away his wealth, his business, and the corruption that was the norm in Philippine politics drove him nuts. The "People Power" rebellion that took Marcos out of power motivated him to get us children to America. Sounds familiar? It took twenty years for the people to finally revolt? If it worked in the Philippines, I truly believe it could work here. The difference is that the people in the Philippines had nothing to lose. And the soldiers were God-fearing people. Even after being ordered to attack the protesters, the soldiers would not. In fact, they bailed and left their tanks and their posts. Here in America, the media is in bed with the politicians. The politicians here pander to special interest groups, and for me, that is corruption. I never knew it could happen in America. What happened the past few years? Has America really been asleep? Or was it tolerable the past several years until now?

You have to understand ...I hated History in school, and I was a single mom raising three children. I learned politics through my ex-boss' father. Staff would have lunch together in the shop and he would always educate me about America. Such a smart man. His name is Robert Austin. He also lives in Chino. He explained to me why my taxes were going up. He explained to me about liberalism vs. conservatism. Then came Clinton. I always believed that our politicians were not corrupt here in America, not like the politicians in the Philippines anyway. But Clinton ... that's when I was faced with the realization that our politicians here *are* corrupt. How could the Democrats rally around a president who clearly lied under oath, abused his power by having sex in the White House, and revealed highly confidential information during his trysts with Monica Lewinsky? How could they stand for someone who has demoralized the status of the American president? It was shameful. It was appalling. It was to me a major disappointment. And for him to be allowed to run a second term? Preposterous. Clinton was the reason I started following politics, watching the news, and listening to Rush Limbaugh in the morning whenever I was in the car driving anywhere.

I realized how ugly politics can be. I realized that politics is as intoxicating for the Democrats as drugs are to normal people. The Democrats fight for this power to push through with their radical agenda. I can't believe how far they would go—legalizing late term abortion really hurts me. As a mother of three children, I cannot get myself to look at killing fetuses as a "woman's right." For Democrats to carry a slogan of "the people's party?" OMG! Are the innocent babies not part of "the people?" Am I, as a registered Republican, not one of "their people?" If they are "for the people" as my daughter-in-law says they are, why do I not feel like they are representing *all* people? I don't get it.

So, my motivation to do what I am doing is a long story. It didn't happen overnight. It is not for fame or recognition. It is not because I wanted to run for office like some people ask me. I would be more than happy attending someone else's meeting or someone calling for a rally and I show up. All these years of frustration. I attended last year's April 15th rally in front of Chino City Hall. This year, I wanted to do the same. I knew that there was going to be a rally in Chino Hills ... but that is where I work, and I did not want to rally in the City—I just felt that it would be disloyal and a betrayal to those I work for (Call me crazy.). So, I assumed there would be one again in Chino, and I invited some friends and my husband to rally there again. We showed up and drove around and no one was there. I could not take the frustration anymore. So I pledged to my friends and my husband that I have had enough. I would do whatever it took to organize.

A few weeks before I organized the Chino Tea Party, my friend Jim Milliman passed away. He, too, was a teacher to me. We met during the George W. Bush elections. He was blogging and I started blogging as well. I read more and more of his comments and they were truly insightful for me. He had such wisdom, and I was very impressed by him. We started exchanging e-mails. He taught me a lot through blogging and e-mails. After about two years, I scheduled a trip to San Diego and decided to pay him and his wife a visit. We remained good friends all these years.

My husband, too, is a conservative teacher from Ohio. I don't think I would have dated him if he was a Democrat. I just didn't feel up to arguing about politics in a marriage. He is an English teacher and he minored in History. So, I guess, I had three teachers who taught me what is right and wrong in this country as far as politics and how the country is headed for disaster. This is *not* what was in my grandfather's dream. This is *not* what was in my father's dream. This is no longer what I know of America. We have come a long way from the America of Bob Hope.

I flew out to Washington DC by myself to attend the 9-12 Rally. It was the most exhilarating experience in my life! I felt I was doing my part in joining "The People's Power—American style." It didn't seem like there was *that* many people there until I saw the video on TV. I got a call from my husband and friends while I was listening to the speakers in front of Congressional House. I met so many folks and listened to their stories. So many different stories, but they all boiled down to finally saying "enough." People have had it! They have had enough of the inequities and the injustice. The Tea Party is here and it won't go away. The Tea Party is telling the politicians that we will *not* be the silent majority anymore. *That* is what I am saying. *That* is why I am doing this. Whatever Obama is, whatever his citizenship is, whatever his agenda is ... all I know is: this country had better find a way to impeach this man and get him out of office. I can see the Philippine government in the way he wants to run this country. It is *not* the kind of country you want to live in.

Carmen Kulp

I became involved with the Tea Party movement because of the dedication I saw in Margaret Hyland, a true Tea Party Patriot. She runs the Astoria Tea Party and does a great job of keeping that party alive.

I researched the AFP and Tea Party web sites and signed up for Margaret's Astoria e-mails. After looking over the AFP and listening to them at a few other meetings, I decided they were more Republican-party focused than I liked. I am a registered Independent and firmly believe the two party system is a large part of our country's problem.

Margaret is a Republican, a Christian, however; she looks at the whole and makes a clear and logical assessment. Her drive is not to elect all Republicans or dismiss everything the current Congress and administration is doing—just most of it! Her drive is to educate people in Clatsop County and get them to pay attention to what is going on in local, state and federal government, to voice their opinion, to speak up. She is not looking for them to agree 100% with her, just to know what is happening, act when needed and vote with common sense.

Her commitment led me to look into the Tea Party movement web site. What I like about the movement is that like Margaret, no one is trying to force any political agenda. All they are doing is getting more Americans aware of what our responsibility is within our government system, aware of our rights, our Constitution and what is happening to our country because we have not been involved.

So my friend Terry got us linked to the Tea Party Patriots web site, started a newsletter and I set up the e-mail account. We got together with a few people, did the tax day rally in Scappoose. Now we need to get focused on the November election. There is a small group of Columbia County people, mostly Republicans, who are Tea Party and AFP members. A challenge is to get these loyal party members to see that both parties are part of the problem, and to stay focused on the primary issues, that we really need to oust all of them out—every single Congressman/woman needs to be defeated. Clean the House and Senate and start fresh. They have a tendency to get on their 'God-kick' as I call it, up in arms over postage stamps, coins, Pledge of Allegiance, most of which is not a real issue, in my opinion.

Most important from my view is—Americans have lost the true purpose of America, of capitalism, of freedom. When did capitalism and profit become evil and socialism good? When will we learn our nationality is *American*? We will learn it when we stop listening to the politicians, the special interest groups and the media (liberal and conservative), when we start to use common sense and realize all people are created equal and that equality is not measured in material wealth but in human wealth.

Christian Hidalgo

I joined a small group of local residents to organize our Rutherford County Tea Party in February of 2009. We were motivated by stories of other Tea Party events around the country and believed it was time to speak up. We planned our event for April 15, 2009 on the historic county courthouse. We expected a few hundred but got 3,000+. An impromptu protest took place after our event just a couple of blocks away at Bart Gordon's office. Hundreds attending our event marched to his office and protested for over an hour. Our representative, Bart Gordon, had been in office for 25+ years and his voting record had become more and more liberal over the years. Many remembered him as a conservative Democrat but had become disillusioned with him. Our April 15, 2009 Tea Party was an open mic event with patriotic music and lots of angry voters. The success of this Tea Party led to our second Tea Party on July 10, 2009. We developed a theme and web site for our second Tea Party, which was, "DumpBartGordon.com." We decided not have our event on the 4th as so many others did because we didn't want to cause attendance conflicts for those wanting to attend our event. The July 10th event was a success as well as over 1,500 showed up, just as angry and outspoken as before. Shortly after the July 10th event I got personally attacked by the local Rutherford County Democratic Party on their web site as well as through various blogs, etc. Because I was the front man at both events they did research on me and discovered I was in an installment agreement with the IRS for unpaid taxes. I've never defaulted or been bankrupt and when my tax issue was raised I immediately began paying the IRS back. Their supporters even developed a web site called DumpNavigationAdvertising.com in order to destroy my livelihood. They began an e-mail campaign to my clients telling them they would boycott their business because they did business with me. They issued a media alert or press release that made it all the way to Keith Olberman's MSNBC show where I was named one of his "Worst Persons of the World"—*a true badge of honor!* They attempted to silence me by smearing me. It didn't work and shortly after their attempts Bart Gordon announced his retirement which almost ensures we will have a conservative representative for the 6th District. I attended other local Tea Parties and even attended the September 12, 2009 Tea Party in DC, where I saw the greatest mass of humanity I've ever seen peacefully protest out-of-control government. For several months after 9/12 I went dormant due to exhaustion but in the spring of 2010 I joined several other Tea Party activists who had not been part of our original Tea Party group in organizing a April 16th Tea Party here in Murfreesboro. That event was much different than our previous tea parties because we emphasized political and social education and activism. We invited patriotic activist groups to display for free as well as local candidates. We had 1,000 show up and believe we accomplished our primary goal of taking all of the Tea Party passion and turning it into activism.

I'm married and have a seventeen-month-old son. I was born in the south and raised in Middle Tennessee. I went to art school as well as received undergrad at UT Chattanooga. I'm an amateur documentary filmmaker and been fortunate enough to film projects in England, Israel, Liberia, China, Mexico, and throughout the US.

Christi Carden

I had been paying close attention to the 2008 presidential campaigns and election. I was upset by Bush's financial bailout in late 2008, very upset with Obama's stimulus bill, and was worried about where the majority party was going to try to take our country. In February 2009, I read on Michelle Malkin's web site that a nationwide Tea Party was being planned. I went to the web sites people were using to sign up to try to find one in Huntsville, and contacted someone who gave me a number to the conference call the organizers were using. I was on the conference calls leading up to the Nationwide Chicago Tea Party on February 27, and ended up going to Nashville for that Tea Party because no one had scheduled to hold one in my city. On the calls after that, Tea Party plans for the second nationwide Tea Party, on April 15, 2009, were formed. When I saw, once again, that no one was scheduled to organize one in Huntsville I stepped up to do it.

It was organized simply through myself acquiring a permit and through citizens who contacted me to help. My contact info was put up on taxdayteaparty.com and because of this hundreds of people contacted me for information, and to help and be involved. Through those contacts, I secured a stage, sound system, American flag, speakers, a minister who led an opening prayer, and a group willing to sing the national anthem. It was amazing to see everyone work together so quickly to make this happen. Approximately 3,000 people attended the Huntsville Tax Day Tea Party in 2009.

After this, I founded a nonprofit organization, The Huntsville Tea Party Movement, Inc., in order to take donations for future Tea Parties and other events and endeavors. Over the past year the group acquired approximately 2,000 e-mail contacts, and has used donations to hold other Tea Parties and Constitution Seminars, and to distribute pocket Constitutions and informational flyers. We went to August Town Halls and local physicians organized a local doctors' rally, to participate in the Nationwide Doctors' Rally against government-run health care last November. We sponsored the local doctors' rally and provided the stage and sound system. We are set up as a 527 organization, so our organization is able to endorse candidates. I personally endorsed (not the organization) Mo Brooks for US Congress in District Five in the recent primaries, and so did Chad Capps (the man who I asked to run the organization when I stepped down) and Deborah King (founder of the nearby Athens Tea Party.) Mo Brooks beat the incumbent Congressman, Parker Griffith (who had switched from the Democratic Party to the

Republican Party in December of 2009), without a runoff on June 1st. We are now busy preparing for a special election in July and the general election in November.

After the 2009 Tax Day Tea Party I also became a State Coordinator with Tea Party Patriots, teapartypatriots.org, and a member of the National Leadership Team of the Nationwide Tea Party Coalition, nationwideteapartycoalition.com.

I stepped down from my leadership roles in all three organizations in mid-March, but am still involved. Chad Capps is now the president of the Huntsville Tea Party Movement, and he and the leadership team are doing a fantastic job.

Chrissy Prazeres

I was one of those Americans that was "asleep" on the morning of 9/11/01. I had been busy with my own little world of raising my children, going to work, and making plans for the weekend. When I watched those towers come down it horrified me. I was glued to my TV set for days, then weeks, then months. I began to hear about the "left" and the "right" in our country and what their vision of America was. I became furious when I heard Americans saying that it was our fault and that we were to blame for the attack. I never knew that these people existed in our country. I was shocked! It was then that I woke up.

I continued to watch the news on a daily basis and listened to conservative talk radio every day on my way to and from work. What an education I received! I realized that a lot of what was wrong with our country was being perpetrated by a small, liberal minority. I supported George Bush in the next Presidential election and supported him throughout most of his presidency. Yes, I admit it—I drank some of the "conservative Kool-Aid." It wasn't until I began to watch Glenn Beck that I realized we had progressives on the left ... and the right.

I supported John McCain during the 2008 elections only because the alternative was unacceptable. The thought of having Obama as president scared me. I listened to his campaign speeches; I saw who he had around him and who his "friends" were. I knew what he would do to our country. I barely slept during the campaign season and cried the night he was elected.

I joined an online organization and got involved right away. Why? My children. The thought of my children losing their freedoms and living in the country that the "far-Left" had envisioned for them was more than I could bear. I would walk through fire for my children and I know that if we do not win this war on our freedoms ... that I just might. I believe that God had a hand in the creation of the United States of America and that we are blessed. Anyone who is against what America, our Founding Fathers, and our founding documents stand for must be evil. They must not win. Our country must be saved. Losing is not an option.

I love my country and, in my opinion, there is no one like the American people. We are, in general, good, decent people who want to live in peace. We are the most generous people in the world with each other and with others around the world. Not only do we send our money overseas, but our soldiers have spilled their blood on foreign soil fighting for freedom around the world. We must all stand up for ourselves, each other, and our country!

Cindy Lucas

My story goes back to the Reagan years. I've always had a conservative viewpoint when it comes to government. I was reading conservative authors and listening to conservative talk radio. After moving to Florida in the mid '90s, I became an activist. My first experience was when Bill Clinton came to our town for a fundraiser. I contacted Free Republic and the Florida "Freepers" contacted me and we planned a protest. Over 300 people showed up and media did a poor job on the attendance numbers and failed to report the real story. In 2000 when George W was elected I felt hopeful. However, when W shook Ted Kennedy's hand and joined him in passing No Child Left Behind and the Prescription Drug Program, I became leery of W's position. After 9/11, I felt compelled to support our country, especially our troops, and give the administration another chance to prove themselves. However, there were red flags at every turn, so I started reading some of the writings of the conservatives like Tom Deweese, Henry Lamb, Phyllis Schafly and Barry Goldwater. A friend of mine, Jim Stack, was the person that introduced me to some of the books that I read. It became evident to me that we were on a course toward global governance.

During 2004 – 2005, I started watching Glenn Beck. I had felt a change in our basic country coming for several years. Small towns and family were no longer important. History, as I was taught when I was younger, was no longer taught in the schools. My father was a history buff and I was raised in Monmouth County, New Jersey where the revolution still lived for those who wanted to visit the sites. Glen was talking about the same thing that I was feeling. When he asked everyone to read Skousen's *The 5000 Year Leap,* who had also written *The Naked Capitalist,* I realized that Glen knew what I knew about the movement to one world order and global governance.

When he called for us to get together to watch his show in March 2009, I contacted about a dozen or so people ten days before the date. I had a local restaurant set aside a small back room that sat approximately twenty people. That afternoon, I got to the restaurant around 4:30 p.m. The crowd was starting to show up. The 20 I expected turned into 150 people who all shared the same feeling. When Glen said that he'd be back to us by September 12, the 9/12 group was born. I didn't run any ads for this get-together to watch the show. It was all done by word of mouth. Today we have several thousand people that we communicate with as well as other groups.

We question candidates about their position on global governance and one world order. Anyone who believes that this is an alternative for our constitutional Republic can't be supported by our people. Our common belief is that our forefathers created this Republic and our Constitution to live on forever.

As a side story, just this week, the small community in which we live (pop. 4,300) had two proposals for sustainable development and sustainable transportation. Both those proposals were tabled until the commission had a chance to read the U.N.'s Agenda 21!

Allie

I started it out of sheer frustration. I was listening to the news one morning and just couldn't take one more word! I got up and went online looking for a group in my area and couldn't find anything, so I started one on my own. This was on February 28, 2009, and by September 2009 I filled two charter buses for the rally in DC!
I'm tired of our non-representing representatives walking all over our Constitution. I'm tired of being told to sit down and shut up. I'm tired of my tax dollars going to stupid things like a study on homosexual behavior in bars in South America or studies on a salt marsh mouse. I'm tired of paying for other peoples bad behavior (bailouts, abortions, etc.). I'm tired of paying and paying and paying taxes. I have been *Taxed Enough Already*!

I believe that for every Tea Party Patriot, there are ten people who share the same values. I have people come to me all the time and say things like, "I agree with everything you've said, but what can we do?" I tell them to start with joining the "team," but they don't/won't, for whatever foolish reason they can come up with. They are afraid ... of what I don't know. I'm afraid too. I'm afraid there won't *be* an America for my grandson to grow up in.

We are a 912 group, although we wholeheartedly support the Tea Party in their efforts. A 912er has 9 principles and 12 values we live by. If you can agree with 7 of the 9 principles, you are a 912er.

Principals :
1. America is good.
2. I believe in God and He is the Center of my Life.
3. I must always try to be a more honest person than I was yesterday.
4. The family is sacred. My spouse and I are the ultimate authority, not the government.
5. If you break the law you pay the penalty. Justice is blind and no one is above it.
6. I have a right to life, liberty and pursuit of happiness, but there is no guarantee of equal results.
7. I work hard for what I have and I will share it with who I want to. Government cannot force me to be charitable.
8. It is not "un"-American for me to disagree with authority or to share my personal opinion.
9. The government works for me. I do not answer to them, they answer to me.

Values: honesty, reverence, hope, thrift, humility, charity, sincerity, moderation, hard work, courage, personal, responsibility, and gratitude.

Clifford Atkin

I became involved in January 2008 by focusing on several inequities that were affecting the taxpayers. We had no voice; this was the reason for the original Boston Tea Party. I felt our country was heading for a disaster. The Tea Party Movement was not on the horizon then, but there were signs of some simmering among "We The People." I spoke to many citizens and they were distraught, angry and felt their voices were not being heard.

It did not matter to them who was in office. They felt helpless. The movement started to ferment and really began to acquire critical mass in February 2009. Many attribute it to Rick Santelli who ranted that we needed another Tea Party.

However, there was an underlying unease in the populace and there were beginnings of some Tea Party activity. I began to realize the growing concern of those who pay the bills. Many people I spoke with were very adamant at the course of government. A great majority of those who came to Tea Parties were middle-aged, old-aged and some were Democrats who voted Democrat their whole life. This was not an Obama thing, this was a socialist thing. These people realized the socialist agenda of Obama and company and all of those who came before. This was the exact opposite of what the country needed.

The big Tax Day Tea Party, April 15, 2009 was an eye opener for me. In Hartford, CT close to 5,000 patriots showed up. We had many speakers; I didn't realize how grassroots this was. The event organizers were ahead of the curve. There was an open mike session and they allowed me to speak. And I did, only for one minute. I quoted Barry Goldwater: "Extremism in the defense of liberty is no vice and moderation in the pursuit of justice is no virtue." This excited the crowd.

A friend of mine—honestly, I don't know how we met, but it was a few months before—asked if I would help organize a Tea Party here in Woodbury, CT, which of course I said I would. It was a success. I spoke for about five minutes. This excited me; my speech castigated big government and defined the scope of what big government has done to our rights. Since then, I have spoken at approximately ten to twelve Tea Parties, including two this past weekend (July 4). I am well received and have asked to speak because of the content of my speeches. I was one of the main speakers at the Tea Party held in Boston on July 4, 2009 at Christopher Columbus Park. Again, I do not take credit for organizing any of the major Tea Party events. However, I was a participant in the "Dump Dodd" movement here in Connecticut.

For months I among others protested with signs, flags and the like. We met Dodd at every corner, every venue. Dodd finally called it quits!

We have made a difference so far and will continue to do so. Our movement is not a tempest in a teapot. It has legs and will continue to move in the right direction. We are now vetting candidates before we support them. In November our alliance will be at voting venues. We will be manning phone banks and passing out flyers.

The movement is heading into November, but our major force will be in November 2012. That is the big enchilada. It is our hope and prayer that someone with the ability to lead this country in the right direction comes forward. We are patiently waiting. Time is running short. A true American patriot, such as George Washington, need make an appearance soon. Because if our country does not change in the next six years, all hope will be lost. The future generations will wonder what happened to the United States of America.

Clint Sanderson

I am a seventy-two-year-old American that loves his country. I have been a Tea Partier since 1955 when I joined the US Navy—I raised my hand and swore to uphold and protect The Constitution of the United States of America, the very core of what has made America the greatest nation on earth. I am appalled when so many of today's so-called leaders swear to defend the Constitution, then without a second thought, trash it and attempt to destroy it. At age seventeen when I made that commitment, I meant that vow, and to this day, I remember the moment. I believe today's heroes are the young men and women who serve in our military are still the best defenders of our heritage.

When today's Tea Parties began to emerge, I applauded and joined. I want to see the efforts grow. I believe in the basics— less spending, much smaller government. I hope and pray that "Tea Party Leaders" don't overreach and shoot themselves in the foot.

As to the question about what it will take to restore our country—it's going to take a strong, smart, tough-love president (not the one we've got), and political leaders all over the country with those same attributes to convince Americans to sacrifice in order save the nation for future generations. The real battle comes in fighting corrupt labor unions that have no concern for the policies that bankrupt our country, *and corrupt politicians that have no concern for the policies that bankrupt our country!* Labor union members are not the problem, they have been led to this point and they must be convinced that some parity with other workers is necessary. Tough job ahead.

Morality or "Gods Law": Our country has lost so much, the list is long. The most obvious to me is abortion. Like labor union members who are brainwashed to believe America can sustain entitlements, women who have abortions are not murders, they have been brainwashed to be OK with abortion. It's simple: when you take the life of a human being, it is called murder. When you take the life of a yet-to-be-born human being, our laws call it a "choice." Amazing!

Seth Cocquit

I organized a Tea Party at my now alma mater Monmouth College in Monmouth, Illinois on April 15th, 2010. Monmouth College is a small liberal arts college of about 1,400 students. I would have to say most are liberal minded. I didn't mind holding the event on campus. One good thing about my college is that it encourages to look at all sides of an issue and to respect other views. I was a senior at the time when I organized the event.

I was laughed at, I was scoffed at, and I even received hate mail for doing what I did, although the hate mail didn't come from any student at the college. I don't regret any of it. The event I organized had a turnout of about 200 people. Most of the people were probably thirty-five years old or older.

However, there were many college students that did attend; some out of interest in what we were doing, some out of getting extra credit for going to the event and writing a one-page summary about it!

We only had one hiccup in our event when a man wearing a white T-shirt with slander written all over it showed up and started arguing with the elderly people that were sitting in their lawn chairs about Fox News or something.

The elderly people started to sing "America the Beautiful" while he kept yelling and swearing at everyone. Being the organizer of the event, I tried to calm him down and tried shaking his hand. I showed the man some respect and asked him to do the same to the other folks at the event but he wouldn't have it. He kept yelling, "Why should I show you any respect for what you're doing?!" I kept asking him, "what are we doing?" He wouldn't answer. He was just trying to stir up trouble. He failed to do so. The only trouble anybody was causing was his. Nobody took any force in making him leave. I believe he finally got the point after he realized he wasn't affecting anybody and gave up.

Other than that we got right on with the event. We had a Republican candidate for Congress, Bobby Schilling, an economics professor, a couple students, a judge, and many local people get up and say what needed to be said. All of them were sincere in what they had to say.

What motivated me to do something like this?

Well, honestly, what prompted me to action is my belief in a government that should have limited powers, promotes economic and civil liberties, and doesn't spend its country into oblivion. Essentially, I had come to a point where I said, I am young, I am able, and if I want to change the direction of my country then I'm going to have to do something about it. That's when my seed was planted, and just like a seed grows, so does my involvement in this movement. I wake up every day knowing there is something big going on in this country. Some days I'm anxious and other days I'm eager. However, every day I am optimistic that there are men and women out there ready to change the direction of this country. This country was founded on very simple but very powerful principles that we have drifted away from significantly, and that is also what keeps me motivated. Liberty is a strong rock to stand on. Liberty is popular. Liberty is powerful and allows a man to make his own destiny. The more government grows, the less power and freedom that man has to follow his own dream. I will say that it does take courage to speak your mind, especially as a young conservative but if you can change somebody's mind, it is worth it to talk, it is worth it to lead by example and it will be so worth it if we get our government under control and taxing and spending responsibly.

Colleen Owens

I'm a stay-at-home mom and had always thought I was a person that kept up with the news and always voted. Now I know that I was really oblivious to what was actually happening right under my nose.

My feeling of unease probably began when we were purchasing a house in 2005 and the mortgage company asked if I wanted a conventional loan or an interest only. I thought they were joking—how could interest only loans exist? Then I saw in the news that 60% of the mortgages were interest only. I remember talking to my husband about how insane that was, and that a lot of people would probably lose their house when they had to start paying the principle. But I did nothing else at the time.

Probably the next thing that caught my attention was during the primaries for the 2008 presidential election. When it was just Clinton and Obama remaining, the television became the Barack Obama show 24/7. The cable news covered his speeches in their entirety. Shows like Entertainment Tonight would do gushing stories about Obama and his family night after night. Network news covered him like swooning teenagers. Any coverage of Hillary was never in the same glowing, hero-worshipping terms as her opponent. This made me start looking into his background, because it was so obvious that the media was so in the tank for him. I've never seen anything like it in my life. This was the beginning of my eyes finally being open to what was happening to our country.

The financial collapse in the fall of 2008 was followed by TARP, government takeover of the car companies, then the stimulus. The deficit was ballooning and our president was saying the government was our savior (he being the Messiah). The shift from billion dollar deficits to *trillion* dollars was trivialized as no big deal.

I attended my first Tea Party in Richmond on April 15th 2009. I continued following the news in depth and my frustration and anxiety continued to increase. The Richmond Tea Party had a potluck in November 2009 and I started going to meetings. I became the chairperson for the Tax Day Rally committee for 2010 and also became a member of the RTP leadership team. We are in the process of planning a Virginia state convention along with other Tea Parties across the state.

I don't know if the Tea Party movement is too late to turn this country around, but I do believe we are this country's only hope of stopping the progressives from bankrupting this country and turning us into socialist serfs of the state.

Conni Robinett

I think my story is similar to many that I have been hearing this past year or so. I never was very politically active. I only started listening to talk radio when George W. Bush was elected to his second term. Because of the Florida recount fiasco I tuned into talk radio to keep up with what all was going on in that situation ... then I was hooked. I enjoyed listening to Rush Limbaugh and Sean Hannity to stay informed, but still wasn't someone who called my congressman to voice my opinion. That all changed when Barack Obama was elected. Of course I was nervous about how he would do as president because of things he was saying, and hearing about the people that helped shaped his thinking and worldview. But I didn't fully understand how radical he was until I began seeing what he was doing to my America.

One day while listening to talk radio I heard the clip of Rick Santelli shouting ... saying things about how awful these bailouts were ... how you in essence you were paying for your neighbor's house that they couldn't afford in the first place. He went on to say something about how the American people should have another Tea Party and let Congress know that this was unacceptable. As the days went by and I kept hearing that clip play, and hearing that some cities were organizing Tea Parties ... I knew I had to get involved and be a part. I wasn't hearing of any Tea Parties in my city of Abilene, TX, so I checked with a friend of mine who is connected with the Republican party here in Abilene. He gave me the name of someone to call. I made that call and got the name of two ladies that were in the beginning stages of planning a rally here in town. So, of course I called those ladies and got involved with the planning of our Tea Party here in Abilene. Word was spreading and I began getting e-mails and phone calls from strangers, wanting to know more information and wanting to be involved. The rally was a huge success.

Then I began to hear talk of a march that would be held in Washington DC that following September. It wasn't in my budget to go to DC, but I just felt this need to be a part of this historical time and felt the urgency to let my voice be heard in Washington. So with my husband's blessing, Heather (one of main organizers for our Abilene rally) and I made plans to travel to DC. We weren't traveling on the same day so we made plans to meet up in DC (along with a friend of hers named Ilene).

I had never traveled on an airplane this distance by myself. My flight was to land at Dulles airport. So, I had to find transportation from the airport to downtown DC, which was around twenty-five miles or so (the easiest solution of getting a taxi was not in the budget at all).

To those that are regular travelers this doesn't seem like a big deal, but I was definitely stepping out of my comfort zone by doing this. When I got to our hotel I quickly checked in and dropped off my bags. Heather and Ilene were out in the city visiting congressmen's offices. I couldn't sit still waiting for them to get back. Again, stepping out of my comfort zone I asked the concierge for a map of the city and located where my congressman's office was.

I took off out the door and into the city by myself ... on a mission to let my voice be heard by as many senators and representatives as I could see before the offices closed for the day. On the way to the first one I met up with Heather and Ilene and we headed off together. We visited the offices of Reid, Boxer, Pelosi and our own Texas senator John Cornyn.

The following morning was the day of the march. As we walked to the beginning place, we began seeing hundreds, thousands of people ... already marching towards the capital grounds. Word trickled through the crowd that the march had to begin earlier than expected, because of the mass amounts of people that continued to show up. The police told the organizers that they must begin walking, because otherwise traffic was being blocked. It was surreal to be marching down towards the capital building, surrounded by thousands of people. It was kind of funny too because as conservatives we're used to following the rules, and not making fusses. Most of us had never participated in anything like this before and didn't know exactly what to do. Are we supposed to shout out, sing, wave our signs and flags ... or what exactly? Every now and again someone would start a chant and the rest of us would join in ... still unclear about how to do this whole "civil unrest thing." Ha! We finally made it to the end place and listened for hours to different speakers. Heather and I were near the front and I would look behind and all around me and saw seas and seas of people. Again, it was a surreal experience. I texted my brother Dale during the rally and told him that they were estimating about 1 million people here, and how incredible it was. He texted back that there was nothing on the news about it. Of course that was disappointing to hear ... but not surprising.

Back in Abilene I was now calling senators (not just my own) on an almost daily basis, letting them know where the American people stood. Also, mass e-mailing the list we had acquired from putting the local rally together, and making sure others knew what issues were being voted on currently and who to call in the Senate etc ... we were making sure to let Congress members know that the Tea Party movement is here now and we the people plan to take our country back from the politicians.

As we neared the next April, the health care debate was heated again and I felt the pull to have a rally again on tax day. Heather and I started organizing again ... a little bit more experienced now with one rally already under our belt. I even volunteered to speak at the rally. That is a huge deal for me, because public speaking terrifies me. But, again I felt the need to step out of my comfort zone. This rally went well too even though it rained on us. To see close to 1,000 people standing out in the rain listening to speakers and singing "God Bless America" was inspiring. It makes me have hope for our country's future.

The Obama administration is doing all they can to "fundamentally transform America" (As Obama himself said he wanted to do about five days before the election.).

We the people know that America is the greatest country on earth and plan to reclaim it in the November elections. Never again will we "fall asleep" and let our elected officials have the run of the place. We are awake now and are on guard, protecting our freedoms and the Constitution of America.

Connie Sherwood

My husband and I have been involved in politics from our living room couch ... for thirty years! Yes, we always followed what was going on through news programs and talk radio. So nothing was so shocking when Obama won the election ... we expected it.

What was shocking is the grandstanding and the total ignoring of his past record—mostly about his stance on abortion and the push for partial-birth abortion when he was a senator. The lack of investigation into his background, the lack of political experience and the favoritism that was displayed was what totally caught our attention throughout the campaign season. We both known we were in for so great changes if he won the election ... and lo and behold ... he won!

The immediate spending frenzy set us on a whole new path ... and we knew it was going to be a rough term with Obama and his cronies. The frustration of the outrageous spending lead us to the first Tea Party Protest in Belmar, NJ on April 15th, 2009. The weather was cold, wet, raw icy rain ... and 1,500 people showed up. We were shocked and knew for sure the country was on an upswing towards sanity in government, controlled spending and getting our voices heard. Part of the group broke off into Jersey Shore Tea Party and we began our local group in Toms River this past January called "Ocean County Citizens for Freedom" because we wanted to have a greater influence on our district's congressional race. Unfortunately "our" guy didn't take the primary ... but we have learned a lot and we are a lot wiser now than when we began. We have well over 250 members and we are expanding all the time.

The founders of our group are Clark and Connie J. Sherwood of Bayville, NJ, and Nancy and Ted Peterson of Toms River, NJ.

Craig Kline

My wife and I have not always been conservatives. We both graduated from one of the public indoctrination centers called a public school. We also came out of broken family childhoods of blue-collar generational working Hoosiers and my grandfather was very active in the Democrat party as a real conservative Democrat. Well those days are over and that party has been totally hijacked by radicals. It was underway while he was alive but there were several like him that kept the party from freefalling toward communist-type leadership. Papaw voted for Reagan.

I, though, was young and did not care a whit about politics until after about ten years of marriage when I became a Christian. Yes, I am one of those "born again believers," a washed in the blood of the lamb follower of Christ who believes the Bible. God then not only changed my alcohol, tobacco using and doping activities, He changed my entire worldview. This was and is the best and greatest event in my life.

Bush was a relief to me after enduring the immorality and corruption of the Clinton administration, but even GW disappointed me with the term "compassionate conservatism," as I discovered that meant big government moderate Republicans in support of a welfare state. I did and still know he was right on our military response to 9/11 and continued defense of the US from Islamic terror and he was not afraid to name it so. But I disagree that Islam is fundamentally a peaceful religion, as a literal reading of the Koran will attest.

Bush's office was dignified and honorable and I feel he left it that way. My family's activity in the Tea Party began when the televised rant of the Chicago exchange was watched on You-Tube after the TARP and other bailouts began. This was actually before Obama took office.

Yes, I say family because all five of our homeschooled children are as much a part of the movement as my wife and myself. I am now close to fifty but the kids are the ones that are going to suffer most from all this irresponsible and reckless spending, crippling regulations and future taxation.

We began to watch Glenn Beck and now are praying Sean Hannity will give up his talk radio and TV career to take on a higher calling, the US presidency for 2012.
Do I think he can win? You bet he can and he has been personally challenged by this sitting occupier of the White House. He is the best communicator since Reagan and there is no one that reflects those conservative ideas better than Sean. The Tea Party should plead with him to run and propel this guy all the way!

Darla and I have been active since almost the birth of the Indianapolis Tea Party and it is two hours north of us. We attended the 2009 and the 2010 April 15th Tax Day Tea Party at our state Capitol building. We have been to many other rallies including the 9-12 march on Washington, which was probably the best and greatest encouragement we have received. Hey, we are not alone! The more names they call us, the more determined and energized we get.

Tired of the propaganda from the media and government, we are now networking and building a huge underground structure of multiple groups loosely connected but powerful and with a common cause: "take our country back." This I know is going on everywhere.

We intend to return the nation as close to the founders' intent as possible. And they left us maps of how to do it. First we have the Constitution that so many are sworn to uphold but treat it as toilet paper, then we have all the historical documents such as the Mayflower Compact, the Declaration of Independence, the Federalist Papers and the personal writings of the founders, plus much is carved in stone in the monuments in our capital.

The progressive socialists have made a grave error—they are counting on the ignorance of the American people to allow them to turn us into serfs, but they should have destroyed our history first because the truth can easily be learned and difficult to erase from the minds of a free people.

We have since started a group in our local community and are networking with surrounding groups to have an effect on the November election at all levels—local, state and national.

If you come to my city of 6,000, my house for now is the only one flying a Gadsden flag beside the stars and stripes.

And the text says what we mean as free men and women: "Don't Tread On Me."

David Leopard: My Tea Party Story

In February of '09 after watching TV re: TARP funds, the stimulus bill, and losing 36% of my retirement, I was getting upset and did not know what to do. I ended up acting out my frustrations by writing an editorial to the Dallas Morning News and it is quoted as follows:

> **"I'm Tired of Being Silent"**
>
> I am not one who would normally write an editorial but I am now because I am not at all happy with what has taken place in our country re: loss of financial savings to my family, my friends and obviously to millions of other Americans. Why are we not up in arms about this? I am a member of the "Silent Majority" age wise and I am tired of being silent while business executives and legislators, (who were to provide oversight on all of this financial/mortgage business), did nothing at our expense. I am sick and tired of hearing about what is going to be done to straighten this out. Stimulus package? Stimulate who? It is not going to stimulate my retirement. I am going to be nonpartisan when I say—why are the American people (rich people, poor people, middle-class people) not screaming and hollering about what has happened (particularly those who have lost their jobs by no fault of their own).We are all suffering as a result of this. I guess we have no mechanism to turn to so that our voices can be heard. Or, maybe nobody is upset with what has taken place as I am. I don't want my tax dollars to be spent this way, but it does not do any good for me to holler at my US senators and congressman since they voted against this stimulus plan. Now what? I am so frustrated that it is gotten to this point—we need to stand up and be counted. How do we do that? Or is it so late that we will just have to grin and bear it? Sorry. I can't do that anymore.

This editorial actually got published and I contacted my friends about it.

Within weeks my wife told me she had heard on the radio that a group of people were going to get together at the Knights of Columbus in East Dallas to talk about starting a Tea Party regarding their frustration with what was going on. I decided to go to find out who these people were and if they were some right-wing kooks or just ordinary Americans. To my surprise, about 300 people showed up and a couple of guys along with a local radio announcer and columnist talked to us about getting involved and doing something about what is going on. It turned out the people who showed up were ordinary Americans, young and old. There was some discussion and then we broke out into different groups re: our expertise, interest, etc. (public relations, signage, security, entertainers).

Because of my security background (former Corporate Security Executive) I signed up to be involved in security. As a result of this and other meetings, we got about 10,000 people to show up at Dallas City Hall on April 15, 2009. I was one of the security people managing the crowd. We had speakers, music, etc.

After that event there was some discussion about planning an event on July 4. About ten of us formed committees and met at different restaurants to plan it. We had no money, no staff and so started from scratch to get volunteers and to solicit donations from individuals. As a result, on the 4th of July, 37,000 people showed up at Southfork Ranch north of Dallas! I was in charge of security and had 120 volunteers working for me during this afternoon and evening event. Michelle Maulkin was our keynote speaker.

Bob Keller

I have been aware of the slow shift toward progressive ideas for a while. Like everyone though, it wasn't too alarming. Gradual changes don't often prompt too much response. Besides, we are still living a good life in the USA for the most part.

TEA PARTY – THE AWAKENING

When I was in the US Navy boot camp in 1977, we learned about the oath that we swore to defend the Constitution of the United States. We learned of the consequences of dereliction of duty, espionage, sabotage, treason, and sedition. These crimes were serious and had ultimate consequences. It was no small thing that we were swearing an allegiance and making a promise to defend this document with our lives. This impacted me and I would talk about this with other boots. Would you die for the Constitution? For our country? For the flag? I got mixed responses that would really puzzle me. It stuck with me for years.

Fortunately I never had to see my real response to these challenges. Through the years, I've heard much of the Progressive's stealth agenda's and how liberals and conservatives have yielded to more and more of the demands to change our country and Constitution to become global and less sovereign as a nation. As talk of the new world order and so many conspiracy theories have clouded the glorious landscape of the great USA, it was too great an order to handle.

Again, gradual changes have kept most of us at a less than alarmed state of disbelief. When the buildup to the 2008 Presidential election began, there were the usual critiques and rants. Along came the most unknown person charging into this arena that America has ever witnessed. I had long listened to Glenn Beck and a little Rush Limbaugh. Sean Hannity, Laura Ingraham and Ann Coulter were all reporting on BHO from the beginning. Fox News and other conservative talk show and news personalities were augmenting the coverage. Knowledge of BHO ramped up to expertise levels overnight. The problem was that the mainstream media was not covering in the usual fashion. In elections past, all the stops were out for all media entities covering every little blemish and scar on every candidate. This time, it was a hush. It was a murmur. It was quiet and deadly silent. What was going on? A great deal of apologies and attacks on the conservative news sources but nothing aggressive on Obama.

We all watched as the lamestream media were systematically giving Barrack Obama a bye on this run for office. It was incredibly depressing to see the entire media (that used to pride itself on being the fourth branch of the government with its checks and balances to the actual three branches) gag on the directives of the powers that have gripped Washington. In late February 2008, I was watching The Glenn Beck Show on Fox. He told us to go to MeetUp.com and start a local group of people like ourselves and others to join these groups and get together across America on March 13th to watch his show. He would reveal a special project that they were beginning. It was called the 912 Project and it was going to be big. So, I signed up on March 9th with the Akron Ohio group that was begun by Amy Schwan. I also joined the group in Lake Mary Florida where I would be on March 13th visiting my sister and would attend there. The information shared that night on the 13th was profound.

After returning to Ohio, I began attending the Akron meetings. We began committees and I became the Communications Chairman. We had much activity throughout the summer of 2008 locally protesting and writing letters to editors, Congress and holding local educational meetings the entire year. Many of our members attended Tea Parties and many other types of rallies and meetings throughout Ohio and especially North East Ohio. The web site Summit912.org was created for blogs and articles by members. We also began planning to attend DC on September 12th as well as planning our own Akron Tea Party for August 19th in Cuyahoga Falls Ohio, where we drew an estimated 7,000 attendees and broadcast live on WHLO with their talk show voice Matt Patrick who served as our MC.

On June 24, 2009, at 10 p.m., ABC aired an exclusive from the White House covering the Health Care Bill that was being worked through Congress. We protested this outside the Cleveland affiliate WEWS 5.

TEA PARTY – THE AWAKENING

My sign read:

American
Broadcasting
Censorship
… the opposite side read:
June 24, 2009
The Day Open Debate
Died In America

In October, I began holding meetings for the express purpose to educate and inform about the Second Amendment. We chose a name of Ohio Second Amendment Group and began holding bimonthly meetings and soon started planning for an event with Sheriff Richard Mack that was held on March 13th, 2010 at Green High School just south of Akron. We had a crowd of approximately 500 that was the final stop of a tour that we had set up with four other 912 groups around Ohio. Creating the Sheriff Mack Tour of Ohio, these groups shuttled him around the state in a weeklong whirlwind tour speaking to five crowds in five regions. We are planning two more educational events in Akron.

There is a ten-year-old girl, a five-year-old boy and a two-year-old boy that I call grandchildren. It deeply saddens me to see the way this great nation is going. Many levels of leadership throughout our country have been infiltrated by progressive/ Marxist believers. The agenda is aggressive and relentless to take control of this country's institutions and resources and turn this once glorious body of freedom and liberty into a typical run-of-the-mill communist state. I have dedicated the remainder of my life to working for these kids' future freedom and liberty. God help us if it's too late. Though it may be too late, I will always work for truth and liberty.

212

TEA PARTY LEADERS

David DeGerolamo

Like the majority of older Americans, I was raised to believe in the American dream. You went to school for a good education, worked hard to raise a family and saved for a future retirement. The problem with this life is that I abrogated my responsibilities for public virtue to political parties who had lost track of the founding principles of our great nation. The result of our inaction has resulted in career politicians who have sold our country's future.

The reason I now have to literally fight for our nation is simple: our children deserve a better future than the one that they are going to inherit. The media have labeled this fight as "The Tea Party." I like to think of myself as a Patriot trying to restore our Constitution. Most of the people who are involved in Tea Party groups, 912 groups and other assorted patriotic groups have one common bond: They believe in the United States and want to secure its future.

How can we effectively restore our country? Most people look to Washington, DC as the solution to our problems. These people are using elections as an excuse instead of a solution. A national debt of over 130 trillion dollars will not be overcome by any election. Our problems are the result of corrupt government, an educational system whose purpose is to indoctrinate instead of educate, and churches who are more concerned with a tax exempt status than instilling morality and virtue into our society.

Our Founding Fathers understood the role of religion. We have elected poor politicians with few morals and are now reaping the consequences. However, we also have allowed our schools to become propaganda centers and our churches to become havens for social justice. Imagine what would happen if even 10% of our clergy actually assumed their responsibility to God and the congregations. Most of us do not even realize that the Revolutionary War was called the Presbyterian War in England.

Once we understand the root causes of our country's descent, we can then take the necessary (and required) courses of action. I had to read *The 5000 Year Leap* to understand the founding principles upon which our country and Constitution were based. After reading this book, I took a look in the mirror and realized that my inaction was destroying our country. I could no longer blame politicians as most of the country is still doing. I then came to the very hard realization that the solutions to our problems are not going to be easy or quick. In fact, we know what needs to be done and most of the country is not willing to accept the hard facts. Part of this is due to the successful infiltration of our schools over the past fifty years by what many now call a "progressive" agenda. The label does not matter: our young adults are ready and eager to sacrifice their freedom for an ideal that does not exist. We can wrap socialism up into a nice package but the final price to pay is tyranny and slavery.

How can we succeed? Everyone must understand that freedom is not a commodity that can be compromised. Any loss of freedom is unacceptable and must be considered slavery. The educational system in our country has successfully removed our founding principles from its curriculum in order to produce a new generation of socialists who "feel" instead of "think." Is the concept of freedom so elusive that we now have to bargain for our future?

Why do I fight for my country? Because "Our lives, our fortunes and our sacred honor" must be more than words if we are to save our children from the chains of slavery.

David Doll

I am a sixty-five-year-old engineer working as a consultant in the field of commercial aviation maintenance. My grandson is currently serving in Afghanistan.

I have been interested in political philosophy and its relationship to morality since reading Ayn Rand's *Atlas Shrugged* at the age of fifteen. While I have always been interested, I have never been involved. My concern over the gradual slide of this nation into socialism turned to alarm after the Obama elections. At my age I am facing increased taxation, decreased energy supplies, increased intrusion into the way I live my personal life, erosion of my income and savings by inflation, and the loss of availability of medical care.

Like you, I attended a local Tea Party rally. At this rally they called for volunteers, and I decided to exchange sleepless nights for action. I became a member of the Teller Tea Party central committee. We organized several very successful rallies. I built a web site and started programs such as "The AARP Business Reply Brick" which found constructive use for all the junk mail our seniors received from AARP. However, I found that this was not enough. I reasoned that if we were to change our government, we must change the people in government. Therefore, I organized a committee of volunteers to review and rate all of the candidates running for office. We researched the offices, designed question sets and called in all of the candidates from county clerk and recorder to governor.

At this point I ran into conflict with our central committee. They wanted to "stay pure" and avoid politics. I saw this as impotent noisemaking. I broke with the Teller Tea Party and formed the Teller County Tea Party. They could continue with the popular rallies. I would join the fight to get principled, competent, conservative candidates elected, and I would do this by using the machinery of the Republican party. We kept our Tea Party small, and developed a new web site candidatereports.com to present candidate information and our endorsements. We campaigned for caucus positions and representation on the leadership council of the county Republican party. We were successful.

TEA PARTY – THE AWAKENING

We are currently deeply involved in the race for sheriff in our county because we believe that we have to earn the right to clean up the state house and Washington by cleaning up our own backyard. We also continue to work for our whole slate of candidates. Our success at the state Republican assembly has demonstrated the power of our approach. The purpose of the expensive ads purchased by special interests to sell candidates like soap powder is to dispense information. We can do that more cheaply and effectively on a person-to-person basis than a blizzard of annoying ads. When we demonstrate this at the next general election, we shall have made a strong first step toward displacing these special interests. If we follow up by firing politicians who lied to us, we shall make a strong second step.

David Kellett

I got angry at my government when our representative from the State of Wyoming, Barbara Cubin, who was retiring, decided to accept whatever she was offered by the Bush Administration and voted against the wishes of the State of Wyoming. By that I mean she voted to pass the first stimulus package. This infuriated me. I was looking for something to do and a way to get involved and couldn't find the right method until the Tea Parties began.
I researched the Tea Parties online and found that my State didn't have one in my town of Powell, WY. I decided to get involved and get one going. My wife and I began hanging up posters around town and got a call from our local newspaper. Through them we announced a planning meeting in which eight couples showed up and we planned out our event. In less than two weeks we got over 200 people to show up for our event.

After the first event I realized that we needed to start communicating with other groups around the state and we began making contact with them. We organized a meeting and we've kept up with the events going on around the State ever since. We share knowledge and information with wonderful groups like the

Wyoming Patriot Alliance, Cody Tea Party, Sons of Liberty, Goshen County 9/12, Wyoming Liberty Group, and others.

Because of the work that has been done, many people who are truly educated on the founders' original intent are now running for offices across the state and our goal is to make sure we have an educated and involved electorate from now on.

Deborah Hughes

To be awakened and shocked by the direction our country was going was so upsetting to me that becoming a Patriot was my only option to help save the future for my children and our nation. Being shy, timid, and a stay-at-home mother was all I had known for quite awhile. To step out of my comfort zone was very hard, and I had no idea the passion that lay inside of me. It was as if God was sending me a sign—it's time to wake up and see the truth. Take a stand and do my part for God and country.

I knew that things were bad and asked myself, how could I do anything to help? I started telling family and friends how bad things were and that they should wake up and prepare, as things would get much worse. I also started to send e-mails and make phone calls to politicians to try to get them to hear my concerns. I knew I had to do things differently when I realized that no one was listening to me, that they really didn't care how I felt, that it's all about what they think is better for me, and that I don't know any better. Now there was a very angry mom, and God knows you don't anger moms!

I asked myself: "Where are all the people? Don't they see what's happening?" I started watching the news and tried to find other news sources by searching the Internet. I started looking for opinions and articles outside of the United States to get a feel for the way people in other countries saw things. During this time I saw a man named Glenn Beck on CNN. He was talking *to* me, not *at* me! I felt compelled to keep watching and listening to his message: "Constitution, say what you mean and mean what you say, do your own research, learn history, both parties are at fault, and common sense." That is what I found to make more sense than anything else.

Then 912 was introduced in March 2009 when Glenn Beck moved to Fox News. I searched for a 912 event and ended up at a church in Newark, Delaware to attend the first meeting for 912. My father came from Ephrata, PA to attend with me. It was a great wake up call. Everyone brought food to share and we had a nice meal and like minds came together.

I decided to keep trying to find a group closer to Delaware County, PA and ended up at a few more start-up groups until I finally found a man who had started a 912 group in our area. He came once, and then never came back, and the group of five was falling apart. I recruited a few people who lived in our county from the other groups I had attended, and a few more people came on board. We named our group the Delaware County Patriots. Our first meeting was in August of 2009. Since then we have grown to about 700 members as of 7/1/10 and still have many people to wake up. We are learning and working very hard to get people involved in the process so "We the People" have the power, and use it to stop the takeover of the progressive politicians wanting a big government to take away our rights.

The most important point is that we instill in our children the need to be diligent in protecting their freedoms. We are teaching them with God's love to know and appreciate freedom. God bless America and our troops.

I am a fifty-year-old computer geek and I work a full-time job and volunteer almost thirty hours per week on behalf of the Tea Party movement.

TEA PARTY LEADERS

Debbie Dooley

I became involved with FreedomWorks in 10/08 because I strongly opposed the TARP and they were one of the only groups that opposed it. I felt like I was without a political party. The Democrats were too liberal and the GOP had strayed from the Reagan conservative principles. I was very angry about some of President Bush's fiscal policies. I was really upset in January and February 2009 when bailouts after bailouts were passed. It seemed never ending that our country was now rewarding irresponsibility of companies and persons and the taxpayer was footing the bill. I became a grandmother in December 2008 and was increasingly concerned about my grandson's future. I felt if the country continued on its course, he would have less freedom and less choices when he was an adult.

I felt hopeless that I did not know what to do to change the course. I then heard Santelli's rant and I knew what I had to do. I called the FreedomWorks DC office and told them I wanted to organize a Tea Party in Georgia. They gave me information about a call that was to be held that night to discuss organizing Tea Parties. This was organized by groups and activists all over the country. I was one of twenty-two people on the first call to organize the first round of Tea Parties on 2/27/2009 and I have been active ever since. We never dreamed the Tea Party would create such an impact!

Millions of conservatives nationwide suddenly were awakened and active. Senior citizens were attending their first protests. We had 300 at our first Atlanta Tea Party that was held in the drenching rain on 2/27/2009. It was raining so hard while I was speaking that my speech seemed to melt in front of me.

At our next Tea Party, held on April 15, 2009, we had over 20,000 in attendance and Sean Hannity broadcast his show live!

I spoke at the 9-12 March on DC both at Freedom Plaza and at the Capitol. That was an incredible experience. When my plane arrived at the airport on 9-11, there were Tea Party activists at the airport arriving from locations all over the US including Hawaii. I remember thinking that we may just reach our goal of 50,000 in attendance.

We held a rally at Freedom Plaza beginning at 9 a.m. on 9-12 and we would then march to the Capitol beginning at 11:00 a.m. I arrived at Freedom Plaza at 8:30 a.m. and just halted in my tracks at the crowd that had gathered. I realized at that time that the crowd was much larger than we ever imagined or planned for. The park police told us at 9:45 a.m. that we had reached "critical mass" at Freedom Plaza and we would have to begin our march to the Capitol much sooner than planned. We began to march at 10 a.m. People from all walks of life, ages and racial background were there. We were all Americans that wanted to return the government back to the people. We had over one million that attended the 9-12 March on DC. That is an experience that will be with me as long as I live.

In closing, I will quote Thomas Jefferson: "When people fear their government, there is tyranny. When government fears their people, there is liberty." The Tea Party movement will bring back liberty to our great nation.

Dee Park

Here's the story of how it happened for me. Who am I and what would lead me to get involved in the fight of my life. The roots began, perhaps, back in 1951–1952 when I worked on Eisenhower's bandwagon. He was running for President, and I was thirteen going on fourteen years old. I did not do much, but I remember stuffing envelopes and being convinced 'Ike' would be right for our country. Time passed and I kept up with some of what was happening politically in America. I read articles and books about heroes of the United States in history and economics and government.

And then came the 2008 campaign for President. Obama? Who? What? McCain. Hero. We learned a bit more and then lots more about both of those ultimately successful candidates who would face off for the presidency. Neither was perfect, but as I read about, watched, absorbed the views of those two, I became convinced that Barack Hussein Obama was a wolf in sheep's clothing, a charlatan, a fake, and someone who might well bring down America.

Some of us became alarmed and talked with others. We read more books, listened to television—I discovered Fox News and marveled that some in the media, perhaps most, were unwilling, unable to see the obvious direction we would be led in if Obama and his crew were elected.

No sooner had the election ended and the swearing in been completed than Obama's congressional followers began their Health Care overreach beyond compare in modern times. We three women—really more than three, but fewer than ten—met, talked, planned and organized our first in-public rally, for Southern Pines, in North Carolina, on April 15, 2009. The Pilot sent a reporter and photographer to cover our planned event, the front page story attracted much attention, and on April 15th there were 1,000 folks there at the Post Office, rallying and carrying hastily made signs proclaiming "Taxed Enough Already" and "Honk If You've Had Enough."

Getting our name, Moore TEA Citizens, building a blog, getting leadership roles assigned and accepted, and determining next steps came later. We met in a still-small group of fewer than fifteen, and rallies were planned. We were given time on WEEB, a local talk radio station, for four times daily commentaries, five days a week. An hour a week on the air, venting. Super. We called those talks "WEEBies." Now we have bylaws and

501(c)4 status. We're more formal, but still just as passionate about the issues we resonate to. Health Care. Cap and Trade. Financial Reform. Czars. Presidential Edicts. Congressional Entitlements. Congressional hutzpah. Presidential assumption of kingly rights and privileges. *How dare they.*

September 12, 2009: I was there. One of over a million people gathering from all corners of America and beyond to rally, wear our hearts on our sleeves, and get strength from one another for the fight that still is developing. We've been back to Washington five times over this past year, and to Raleigh and other rallying places to protest at congressional offices, on state office lawns and to march, march march. We have stood outside of NC legislators' offices rallying.

In less than a year we gave away the first three thousand copies of the Constitution in parades, in offices of lawmakers, and to friends and family members.

We have organizational trappings—brochures, flyers, membership cards, and position papers. We have collected countless petition signatures on a wide range of legislative issues.

We've taken bus trips to Washington and back, occasionally up and back on the same day. We are Moore TEA Citizens. My own identity has merged with that of this wonderful organization. We're all in this together. It's a struggle I'm committed to seeing through to the end—hopefully, prayerfully, a peaceful end of return of American freedoms. We must prevail. Sometimes I get the question, "How long will you continue with this project? *As long as it takes to reclaim America.*

As we said at that first rally, I am "mad as hell, and not going to take it any more." It's a time of great peril for this country and its people. I am not the same happy housewife I was in the past—most of my reading is about dangers America faces and heroes of the past. An alarming number of the 168 hours in each week is spent working on Moore TEA business. Planning for the next caravan, the next newsletter or alert to go on the web site and in e-mail form to our members.

Diana Benjamin

I've been involved with the Tea Party since March 2009—by accident. After the February Tea Parties I found a web site and signed in thinking it was for information. Within fifteen minutes I got a call from a lady excited that I was "going to have a Tea Party." Speechless, at first I said no, but it only took five minutes to change my mind. If not me, who? I called her back and started planning for 4/15/09.

I've followed politics and news for many years, but I was the kind who thought politicians were idiots and threw things at the TV. I really had no idea what I was doing, but honestly God put the whole thing together for me. Not knowing if anybody would show up was scary, but from the e-mails I was receiving I figured at least 100 people would be there. 500 showed up. I was the only speaker, concentrating on three topics:
1) Read the Constitution
2) Stop spending money now
3) Quit redistributing wealth.
The crowd went nuts! We called the White House and left a message—In unison we yelled, *Stop spending money now!*"

Then the hard part—God was telling me to say, "Come back to me" and "Pray For the Country." I'm speaking to 500 relative strangers and God wants me to preach! Again the crowd went nuts. These were Christians that knew as I did that this is God's country and He is the answer.

That day I got lots of e-mail addresses, media attention and the attention of the GOP who tried to co-opt the movement (unsuccessfully!). It's been a wild ride ever since and shows no sign of letting up. It's cost me a lot because I've neglected my business, but saving the country is more important than money.

Diane

I'm another one of "those people" who was never politically active, or even aware, until recently. There are many thousands of us out here, and thousands more than that still hungry for information and education on how to get us out of this mess.

Raised in a Democrat household, I really wasn't awake and aware of how the machine really works. I can recall hearing the grown-ups talk of how this or that legislation was affecting our lives at home. My Dad cussed Ronald Reagan for being a "Union buster." My first vote for president went to Jimmy Carter!

My "awakening" began when I got a job (with the federal government, no less), and began commuting an hour each way to my duty station. I tuned in to talk radio on my drive, and a love-hate relationship with Neal Boortz began. I first thought he was some sort of loon—a Limbaugh Lite (I still can't stomach Rush). Neal's humor pulled me in, then he started talking about the FairTax. Whoa! What's this?! This thing make *sense*! I began reading up on it, bought the book when it came out, and have been a volunteer for them ever since.

I listened to co-workers talk at work, many of them conservative, and while some of their talk started making sense to me, my liberal side was stubbornly hanging on to the emotional side of the political world. I still wanted to save the whales, feed the hungry, house the homeless ...

Then one day, Neal was talking about a book that turned him around. *Atlas Shrugged* by Ayn Rand. I like to read and thought I'd give it a go, so I ordered a used copy off Amazon.

Wow!

Suddenly, it all made sense to me! We *can* feed the hungry and house the homeless *without* government interference! These "problems" are supposed to be taken care of on a *local* level, and still with no government involvement! Americans are the most charitable people on the planet, and *we can do this*, if government would only get out of our way.

Recalling my Dad's "dislike" of Reagan, I could now see both sides of the coin. In a job I had before this government gig, I was a dues-paying union member. Being outspoken, I was invited to attend the negotiations between the union and "the company." Boy, was that an eye-opener. Here were these union men, supposedly looking out for "their workers," and on the last day of our week-long negotiations, we were told to *stay out in the hallway* while they went in for final negotiations! *Huh*?! They came out with a contract in which they'd conceded on some points that we'd felt very strongly against. All that week, we'd been taken out for dinner, "wined and dined," and were evidently supposed to feel privileged that we were spending workers union dues on lavish meals. When many of us had a problem at work on which we thought the union should be jumping to our defense, we'd usually be met with a lukewarm response and half-hearted attempts to "help." I realized most all their fervent "support the union—we're for you" spiel was pertaining to us paying our union dues. Well, as Neal says, "Horse Squeeze!"

I am now *pro*-Constitution, *pro*-smaller government, *pro*-fiscal responsibility and accountability.

I am also still a union member, though I haven't paid dues for almost ten years. Go figure—with the federal government, you're a member whether you pay dues or not, and I opted to no longer finance their meals and business trips.

I am currently organizing our second annual rally at our state capitol. We had eight days to plan the first one as we took the reins over from someone advocating the disruption of a union parade on the same date, prior to the rally. I told them if they had a problem with the union to protest at the union's HQ, *not* at an annual parade which held legal permits and at which children would attend.

As a result, we didn't have time or funds to arrange for many speakers at our first rally, so we turned it into an "open mic" event for the attendees. Wow! That will now be a tradition of our rallies—that was a most empowering experience! Most all of the people that came up to the mic that day had *never* spoken in front of a dozen people, much less the 300+ we had in attendance that day. This gave them the courage to go out and speak up about their views in day-to-day life, and it was wonderful!

I fight for the FairTax, for state sovereignty, for all our rights as secured in the most brilliant document ever put to paper—our US Constitution. I am working to get statesmen elected to office, not more politicians.

Dodie Preston

Having retired after forty years as a registered nurse and a health care administrator, I turned to what had been my goal for several years. I gave up pantyhose and makeup and became Betty Crocker. I sewed, quilted, cooked and gardened. And, I turned on C-SPAN. Whew, I honestly could not believe that those people on the House floor and Senate floor were acting to represent me.

My husband, also retired, and I began venting our frustration at what was happening in our country and evidently we had an impact. A stranger showed up at our door saying that he was venting his frustration to someone who told him ... you need to go talk to the Prestons! Living in a rural Indiana county (total county population of about 25,000) and Lynn, a community of 1,100, we are geographically and population-wise in what they call "fly-over country." We are not exactly a politically focused area. After he left, Ron and I decided to get some friends together, just to discuss issues. This was at the same time Glenn Beck was starting his 912 Project and encouraging people to get involved. We labeled our meeting a "liberty meeting."

We had our first meeting April 1st of 2009. Two weeks later we attended a Tax Day Tea Party Rally in Indianapolis. What an experience. To stand with thousands of others and say the Pledge of Allegiance! To be among kindred spirits who felt as we did! We did not see one hateful poster, we did not hear one foul word and we did not see as much as a cigarette butt on the statehouse lawn as we left. We were impressed and we decided that as citizens we had a responsibility to become involved.

Although our group is fiercely independent, we did join the Indiana Tea Party group and adopted their mission. We had speakers from the Freedom Maker Coalition, liked their philosophy and became a part of that group. Our group has been meeting for over a year now. We meet twice a month and have about 140 people on our e-mail rolls. We average thirty in attendance at our meetings. The group has:

- Sent pink slips to our members of Congress and to Barney Frank, Nancy Pelosi, and Harry Reid.
- Provided free copies of the US Constitution to high school government students and have handed these out free at fairs, community activities and to community groups.
- We have had local and other elected officials attend our meetings to discuss their responsibilities and our expectations.
- We developed vetting questions for candidates for local office in our spring primaries and had fourteen candidates complete our questionnaires.
- We have had floats in parades, written letters to the editor, provided local news coverage of our activities, and provided speakers for community groups.

- We have attended rallies and seminars to learn from others like ourselves.

How has all this impacted me? I am doing some things for the first time in my life: writing letters to the editor, speaking to groups, researching and organizing to make sure we provide factual, accurate information, calling and writing to congressmen, arranging for speakers, posting notices of meetings on all available bulletin boards, taking an American flag to new business owners, contacting candidates for office to share the expectations of the Tea Party. Perhaps I am trying to redeem myself for all those years I simply was not paying attention. My grandchildren cannot visit without receiving a civics lesion.

As the most important election of our time draws near, we are developing work groups for door-to-door canvassing on the issues. Our group continues to grow, slowly but steadily. We focus on the need to inform people of what must change.

Herman Cain said it recently:
- We must *stay connected*—they are trying to separate and divide us and they will continue to do so
- We must *stay informed*—don't let them tell us after the fact
- We must *stay inspired*—we must believe we can take back Congress and our country. They will continue to try to tell us we cannot do this. We Can!

Don Forward

Don't know where to begin because I am just a retired construction worker that has worked all over the USA, Russia, Saudi Arabia, Indonesia, Nigeria, Venezuela and Ecuador. During all this time I followed Titusville and Florida politics, voting absentee when I had to vote. But I never got really upset until 2008 when we lost Congress—well, not too much, but I really started to notice the change.

G.W. Bush started sliding under the train and the last straw was TARP. I got so mad at the Republican party that I tore up the card and joined GOOOH. I got started in the Tea Party by listening to Beck and then checking the web and found Brevard Tea Party. I printed a BTP logo, put it on my car and went to stand on the corner to protest, to do *something*! That is when I met Connie Smith. She gave me a sign to hold: "Say NO to Socialism." I carried that sign to all the street rallies for a year until finally a lady in Port Orange asked me if she could have it.

I joined Space Coast Patriots in Merritt Island, Florida as there was nothing around Titusville. I would travel sixty miles away just to go to a Tea Party meeting. My wife was getting a little tired of me being off so much so I started "Titusville Patriots" out of three people that had had a Tea Party April 15th rally.

Many people know us as protestors, but we are not protestors, we are informers. Stop and think of it, signs are informative, make people think, and hopefully charge them up. The best thing we have done to date is we all got together and put up a billboard. A group of us came up with $6,070 to put it up for six months on a busy highway. There were many donations of $20 to make the amount. We had a great time meeting under the billboard for the photo. It is a bonding picture for us—we are proud of our accomplishment.

Forming a group on a shoestring is rough, especially in finding a place to meet. Mostly we meet in restaurants and there have been some flops and some good times. Last weekend was our best event yet. With two weeks planning we put together a "Florida Stands With Arizona" BBQ picnic. All the speakers had to stay on the theme of "immigration." One after another they told their stories, which were great. Some made us laugh, some brought tears. Small events like this is what makes it all worthwhile. Now at the end of almost every meeting I feel that way. I just don't worry about the numbers anymore. So, for a retired construction worker turned informer, I strive every day to learn to become a better informed voter and pass on what I learn to anyone that will listen or read. It's the least I can do for this great country. Our forefathers spilled too much blood for us for us not to try and keep our country free.

Donald Jakel

I began looking for a Tea Party rally in Michigan soon after seeing Rick Santelli's rant live on CNBC in February of 2009. That rant was the birth of the modern Tea Party movement. I found a rally on April 15, 2009 in Grand Rapids and attended with 2,000 other outraged patriots who believed that the explosion of government spending, bailouts and control over our lives needed to be reversed. I asked to attend a steering committee meeting after that rally and was invited. I did not want to spend my time on just protests and rallies. I asked them if they were ready to take tangible action to fire incumbents and find and elect fiscally responsible replacements. They said yes, then asked me to be their treasurer. We have grown from four founders to 1,800 members and continue to grow steadily. We are organized as a non-candidate section 527 group for primarily educational purposes. We do not endorse candidates. I found Independence Caucus and was hooked after viewing their videos at icaucus.org describing the corruption in both political parties and the solutions using constitutional principles.

We have grown to over 12,000 volunteer members nationwide and over 650 in Michigan. We have invited over 100 Michigan candidates to enter our comprehensive candidate endorsement process. The process includes eighty questions about the Constitution, character, and legislative process. If they qualify, they are interviewed by four or five members for 1½ to 2 hours on the record. If there are two or more qualified candidates running for an office, we have an online member conference and a vote among all our Michigan members to decide who is the best to endorse.

We are quite certain that every endorsed candidate will represent our principles and they will work for we the people rather than big money special interests. Thus far, we have endorsed twenty-three constitutional conservatives in Michigan and will vote on another ten races very soon. Our primary is August 3rd and we are now in campaign mode to get our candidates elected. We won't win every race, but everyone we do win will lead us back to our founding principles of a constitutionally limited govern-ment and help restore free markets and the opportunity to achieve the American Dream without the fruits of our labor without being confiscated through high taxes.

We are passionate and committed to continue to improve and grow both organizations and I, for one, plan to be an activist as long as I live. We will also become watchdogs to hold our elected officials accountable. If they managed to lie to us or get sucked into the corruption, we will work twice as hard to get them out of office as we did to elect them.

The beauty of the Tea Party is that we are locally autonomous and not tied to any of the national organizations that are vying for control of the movement. We are all volunteers and we will not be controlled. Our group is a member of the Michigan Tea Party Alliance which is about thirty Tea Party or 912 project groups which communicate and coordinate with each other to learn best practices and to sponsor statewide events.

Donna Shaver

I'm a Ron Paul Republican. I was a registered Democrat who paid no attention to politics and wasn't interested. My new (at the time) boyfriend Dennis told me about Dr. Ron Paul ... that was May 2007. We joined a local meet up group (meetup.com) for Ron Paul supporters and did sign waves and made signs, etc. We also went to SC and saw him speak. We became great friends with the supporters here. We're still all friends today and members of Dr Paul's *Campaign for Liberty* group. We're all very active locally now.

The very first modern Tea Parties (after the original one in Dec 16 1773 of course) were during Ron Paul's campaign! Be *sure* to cover that! Dennis and I participated remotely by making donations to his campaign. He raised over $6 million in one day!

I helped throw a huge Tea Party in Union County NC last year on 9/12/09. Some 450 people attended. The speakers were excellent! Dr. B.J. Lawson ... Dr. Mike Munger ... and six others!

Doreen Finkle

What initially prompted me to wake up to this calling was the fact that last year our government passed the stimulus bill(of which I am still angry about). Prior to that, I was also annoyed at our government, media, and education but have never acted. I was just a stay-at-home mom with a teaching degree in elementary and special education raising two young children. I thought that if I minded my business and just went to vote that things would change. Being my level of education and all of the years I went to school and places I've traveled and lived, I do know something—and something that went completely wrong.
I went to our local 2009 Tax Day Tea Party and put my name on their e-mail list. I went to their meetings, found out there were others like me and noticed that there was no youth! This was contentiously brought up at every meeting and I suddenly realized that some of the elderly did not know how to connect with the youth. So I went to work. I knew that colleges would not openly accept a movement like this so I went backdoor and found some holes and found some very serious frightening problems on our campuses.

On November of last year we had our first Tea Party at Rutgers University, the State University of NJ. Great idea that was, yes! Was there something missing—you bet ya! This university has

25,000 students. We had only about 50 show up. So I asked, "Where are all the college conservative students?" I went to work again and found out that close to 37% of NJ colleges are missing representation on campus. Meaning there are no college Republicans or like group such as Libertarians. There are around 100 colleges here. So I asked why. I contacted Dave Horowics' office. They claimed that the movement has to come from within the college itself. Furthermore, it is harder for the conservative movement to maintain any kind of conservative group because these groups require an advisor who is willing to take the group. The advisor must be a professor or administrator. Horowics has said that the ratio of liberal professors to conservative is about 7 –1. In some cases about 30–1. And so the students get discouraged.

So what we plan to do is to grow laterally outside the college and inside. We plan to put boots on the ground around the state and will cut in and recruit students. By law now, if the student is interested, the colleges are "obliged" to do their part for the student and provide that advisor.

Wherever that is not the case, now, we will "sue" at taxpayer expense. During the five months of operations, we have come across several serious "egregious behaviors" existing on our campuses that have been reported.

Also, during the course of the five months in operation, we have held campus rallies at Rutgers and traveled to other college campuses throughout the state. We are activists! We will not allow our youth to continue to be brainwashed in this manner.

This operation, while only five months old, is now forever!

Robert Rowland

What does it take to stir Americans to give up their daily routines, take time from their families, friends and jobs and realize that the way of life we take for granted may be precariously close to being taken away from us? What does it take before we realize that we must find a way to preserve our nation, for ourselves, our children and our grandchildren? When is it that average Americans, who have no previous political influence and no notoriety, decide to rise up in the tradition of our forefathers from over 200 years ago, and start to form liberty groups to oppose their own government?

Throughout our history events have happened where the threat has been so imminent and so clear that Americans knew it was an immediate call to action. Pearl Harbor is an example often used to highlight a direct and real threat to our nation, but when did the threat of losing our liberties, losing our founding documents and constitutional protections, and being overrun by our own government become evident to us? When did we realize the unthinkable—that we have a government no longer Of the people, By the people and For the people, and that we have a president who does not believe in the America we have taken for granted for so long? When did the constitutional separation-of-powers government, the safeguard we assumed would protect us forever, evolve into one overpowering, liberty-threatening bureaucratic mass, and why didn't we notice?
It didn't happen suddenly. We've all been too busy to notice that our liberties and our nation was changing, moving away from all the things we always believed would be there forever. It's hard to say exactly what got our attention. It started slowly, with little periodic changes under several administrations, but culminating with the swearing in of Barack Obama, who at first had many believing and others hoping that he had been honest in his campaign rhetoric about only wanting the best for America. In many ways his blatant turnaround from those campaign promises has been the cold water in our face that was needed to see through the subtle march our government was on to socialism and making our Constitution totally irreverent. Perhaps if President Obama and the current Congress hadn't forced national health care on us, or he not been so obvious in his appointments of

czars with pasts that most Americans know are not in line with our values, or if he had not begun to toss aside alliances with allies and friends like Israel that most Americans know are critical to our nation's safety. If he hadn't openly used terms like "redistribution of wealth" or spent more taxpayer money than any president in history, then maybe we would still be asleep. So in a sense, Barack Obama may be the spark that re-lit the flame of liberty in our hearts and minds.

I was one of those asleep in my comfortable world of middle-class America. At fifty-seven years old, I had been blessed with all the gifts a free and prosperous America offered. With two grown sons, two grandchildren, and a wife of thirty-seven years, a nice home in a rural area of Colorado, five acres, a good paying job of twenty-eight years, three cars, a tractor and two horses, life was good. I always voted when the weather was good, I sat around the TV watching Fox News and had plenty of commentary for my family and friends and happily assumed no matter what they did in Washington it wouldn't really affect me in my comfortable little rural nest. I was wrong. First I started to hear our new president say things that caught my attention. I started to pay attention to the Reverend Wright saga and thought, "Well they voted this guy in, that's what *they* (us) get." Then he picked up the pace, and then health care, surely he couldn't get that through. Now he's messing with my doctor and I'm fifty-seven years old, this is personal.

One day shortly after they used a loophole in a congressional procedure and surprised us all by passing this monstrosity, I got mad. And as I was standing at the meat counter at the local market in our rural town talking to some neighbors and waiting for pauses between all of our ranting and raving to say my piece, it hit me: "It's time to do something, this is serious, this guy is not who he says he is, and though I haven't read the Constitution since junior high school, this sounds like a violation of it." I drove home thinking, "I've been complaining about this government for months, but it's doing no good, it's time to find a way to get involved." It was a Friday evening when I talked to my thirty-five year old son in the living room. I said to him, "We have to do something, we need to get involved." Since I'd heard about this Tea Party movement, and knew a little history including something about throwing tea in the harbor some time back, I said, "I'm going to join the Elbert County Tea Party." So I proceeded to my computer to Google it and sign up.

I found our county didn't have one, so I started to look at other Tea Party web sites in the area and started to realize they were grassroots groups being started and organized by regular folks like me. I called to my son to come into the office and said, "There isn't a Tea Party in our county, what would it take to build a web site and start one?" I had no idea what organizing a Tea Party meant, but it seemed like a good idea and it was serving to release some of that frustration and nagging fear I was having about how serious a threat this government was quickly becoming. With my son at the keyboard, I pulled up a chair and by Sunday morning we had build our web site from a free template we found online. We set up an e-mail address and for $12 secured the name and address with Go Daddy. Another $60 hosted our web page with one of the online hosting services. I called my friend from the market encounter and said, "You and I are the founding members of the Elbert County Tea Party. Tell your friends."

I then took the liberty of sending an invitation to all of my friends and neighbors in the county and asked them to spread the word. The responses came quickly: "Sure, add me to the list, we've got to do something" (though none of us knew exactly what that was). I made up some flyers and hung them around town. By the next week we decided to have a meeting, picked a date, stopped by the old school in town and got their permission to use the gym on a Saturday morning in April. We went to work, meeting with folks I didn't previously know who were now e-mailing and offering assistance. We started to talk about structure, what our goals were, and one evening I sat down and put together our mission statement. Now we had purpose. It was starting to make sense and something inside us was stirring as people started to realize we had a responsibility to respond to what we believed was a government against the people, against us, a government with leaders who no longer listened or cared about what we thought or believed in.

About seventy-five folks showed up at the first meeting where we gave speeches and asked each and every person in the bleachers what they thought and what they expected of a Tea Party. The response was terrific and our patriotic spirit had been re-ignited. We set a date and promised another meeting the following month. I started to call and e-mail our politicians, not actually thinking they would return the call or e-mail, let alone thinking that they would come to a meeting out in the boondocks. They responded quickly and agreed to come to our meeting in May. Our congressman in Washington, Mike Coffman, was our first speaker. Greg Brophy, our senator in Colorado, along with our representative in the Colorado House, Cindy Acree, and candidate for governor Scott McInnis all showed up, spoke and took questions from our group, now over 250 strong. Attending at their own request, the candidate for US Senate and former Lt. Governor Jane Norton appeared on stage, spoke and answered questions from the crowd, many now wearing apparel with our Tea Party logo.

As the momentum kept building, I was flooded with e-mails and requests to be added to the e-mail list. We were getting calls from media and the candidate's campaign staff members asking to speak at our next meeting and asking for endorsements. This Tea Party thing had suddenly come to everyone's attention. Our 3rd meeting saw Tom Tancredo, former Colorado Congressman and Presidential Candidate, along with Scott King, Congressman from Iowa, and the other leading candidate for Colorado Governor Dan Maes. Many of the local elected officials, commissioners, county clerk, treasurer, assessor, sheriff and candidates for office could be seen in the crowd of over 350.

TEA PARTY – THE AWAKENING

We've now scheduled our 4th meeting in July, the last one to be held before the primary elections in Colorado on August 10, 2010. I am now attending leadership council meetings with about thirty other liberty group leaders in Colorado as we plan strategies about how to grow the movement statewide. Our Tea Party has launched a program called "adopt a candidate." We are supporting three candidates for the Colorado House who are out of the district but have a good chance at recapturing seats currently held by liberal Democrats. We're offering classes to members (now estimated at close to 400) called "Restoring Moral Government," including lessons in American history and civics, along with some simple economics as to why our country and our dollar is in deep trouble, all with an overlaying theme of our nation's religious roots. We've all reacquainted ourselves with the US Constitution and we're distributing copies of these founding documents and asking folks to read them.

We had ignored our country and our nation's safety for too long. We honestly believe that we can and will take our nation back from those who would transform us into yet another socialist, liberty-denying nation. We aren't naive, we know those forces are strong and we know nothing is assured, but America is awake again. Whatever our differences are as a people, we once again are coming together with a common national purpose. There are deep political divisions, wider and more strongly entrenched than perhaps any other time in our history. We know we must prevail, we must be able to tell our children that they too will live in a free America. We will tell them what we did today, why we had to do it, and that it will be up to them to not let it happen again. They must know they cannot forget this time and that they cannot fall asleep.

Elizabeth Sotallaro

"How did you get involved with the Tea Party?" is both easy and difficult to answer. Easy because it seems so natural, right, and

God-driven that I'm compelled to do what I do ... and difficult to put into words that completely explain it.

I was rocked to my core on 9/11 when Islamist terrorists killed so many of our citizens on our own shores. It woke me up. Something very basic had changed. The US was complacent and we were paying the price. I've loved my country with all my heart all my life, and described myself as a patriot for over twenty years. I've been lucky enough to travel outside the US, and have seen firsthand what countries without freedoms like ours are like. I don't want that for the United States.

I read about our true history, about *all* American patriots, black and white. I learned how the Progressives have lied for generations about our Founding Fathers and the very details of our wonderful history. How horrible that they pervert our great American Dream by lying about or omitting altogether so many great American patriots and their heroic deeds!

I got involved with the Tea Party movement because I believe We the People will bring America back to her roots and cause her to be strong again. Our Founding Fathers, in their brilliance, always knew we would need to fight to keep our freedoms, but I had to learn it firsthand. God's hand has blessed us and we must carry that blessing into action. If I love America, I must do everything within my power as a free citizen to protect her and save our freedoms. I will not stand down. This is difficult—difficult to accept, and then to take action—I never thought I'd be "that person" ... but it's easy, because it *is* the only thing to do. I love God, my country, our freedoms. I will not stand down.

Pam

I have been a right-leaning person all my life, but not very active other than voting in all elections. About ten years ago I was recruited by the local Republicans to join their committee in my small town of about 5,500 ... they were having trouble finding warm bodies to do committee work. So, I did my duty: sold tickets for the chicken dinners, helped local people get elected, etc. Then I decided to run for a town supervisor seat against the incumbent Democrat, without much chance of success, but I couldn't stand to see him run unopposed. I lost, but in the process created a simple web site and the name "Gardiners Right," and started collecting e-mail supporters. Mostly Republicans, but not all.

Meantime, the local Republicans and I started to be like chalk and cheese. I wanted to send strong letters to the editor of local newspapers to criticize the local town board members ... but the Republicans never wanted to "rock the boat." If they didn't have candidates for office locally, they were willing to back Dems instead of going out to find good candidates. When we lost a local election even with three good candidates for town offices, I contacted some people from the neighboring Republican committee to find out their secret for having gotten their candidates successfully elected. I was blasted by Gardiner Republicans for "airing our committee's dirty laundry," and accusing them of being lazy in the election. The committee sent me a letter asking me to resign ... which I would not do, to their consternation. I wanted to work to get candidates elected and was willing to fight for it. They were not, and wanted to just "get along," as they felt compromise with the Left was the way to not alienate the populace.

Meantime, I'd been steadily getting more upset with the national Republicans, and Bush, for the TARP and other bailouts. Then Obama got elected, and I cried. In the early months after the election, the bailouts, the turn to socialism, and the takeover of private companies was appalling. I found myself watching Fox News every night and yelling at the TV in frustration about what was happening to our country and I wanted to *do* something.

I heard somewhere about the Tea Parties that were being held first in Chicago, then elsewhere, and I found the Tea Party Patriots web site. They offered a way for local Tea Party organizers to post and promote a Tea Party in their locality. I saw a few other Tea Parties being organized in New York. There were no requirements or rules ... just do what you wanted, post it, and become an instant community organizer. I decided to organize a Gardiner Tea Party for April 15.

That was March. I immediately quit the Gardiner Republican Committee—on my own terms. If they wouldn't organize the Right politically, I would. I had about 250 names in my e-mail list, which were local/regional Republicans for the most part, but also non-enrolled Independents and Democrats (the old-time lunch pail Dems) who were just as scared as me about the direction our country was going in. I picked a location for the Tea Party ... on the Rail Trail which intersects the main state road (Main Street) that runs through Gardiner in the hamlet. Technically, it was a public park, and it had political history as well, since the town paid a land trust $70,000 to purchase the old rail bed/trail, and it was considered a political boondoggle. So the site was politically significant as well as being accessible, free and smack dab in the middle of the hamlet.

I posted the Tea Party on the national Tea Party sites I could find. I put a press release out to all the local newspapers. I put up flyers in all of the local stores gas stations, markets, that would let me. People nationally were using the national Tea Party sites to locate Tea Parties near them for April 15. I started getting calls right away—from as far away as Brooklyn, Westchester, Sullivan, and other counties throughout New York State. The New York Post contacted me and did a story about the Tea Party.

So, with April 15 looming, I was nervous ... about what to do, what to say, and if anyone would show up! I had visions of being on the site in Gardiner all alone, with my sign that said "Founders Rule!" I decided to keep the agenda simple. I created a "We The People" petition, with a list of about ten issues that we had with the government—bailouts, TARP, takeover of private industry, Congress not reading bills before signing, etc." We would salute the flag, say the pledge, honor the military, and I would talk about the items in the petition and how Obama and Congress was stripping our Constitution and transforming our country into something we didn't recognize. Then we would symbolically shred some tea bags, of which the ends would be collected to send to our senators, congressman and Obama.

The day came, and my friend and husband helped me set up the table with the petitions and get the flags in place at the Rail Trail. I was realistically thinking that 50 people might show up, and in my heart I was hoping to have maybe 100. Then they started coming. I started the Tea Party on time, and they kept coming. It was hard to estimate the crowd ... but before it was over, several people told me they did head counts of about 350 people, and the signatures on the petition confirmed that!

We had people with handmade signs, and a full color guard from a local chapter of Gathering of Eagles came to join us. People were angry, but mostly frustrated. I kept hearing that they wanted to do something, but didn't know what, and that the Tea Party gave them a way to express that. Mostly, people wanted to feel that they are *not alone* ... and they wanted to be heard by someone ... anyone ... in the government. I think the best moment at that first Tea Party was when our Town Supervisor (Democrat) drove by the crowds of Tea Partiers lining the main street in his pickup ... and you could see his jaw drop to his knees at the size and intensity of the crowd.

I added a lot of names to the Gardiners Right list and am now regularly speaking to a group of 500+ people with all the same fears, concerns and thinking. I go to town board meetings and report on what is happening locally and regionally, promote other rallies as well as my own for Gardiners Right gatherings, and generally keep a line of communication open for the "right" thinking people. Also, I let them know that we are working to reverse the damage that Obama and company have done. I've had Tea Party gatherings on July 4, September 12, (2009), April 15, 2010 and upcoming on July 4. I will keep taking it to the street as I tell people what are doing is really just using our First Amendment rights to speak freely, assemble peaceably, and petition the government with our grievances.

Since then, I'm reading and studying what I can about the Constitution, and hopefully becoming and helping others to become better Americans. I have confidence that the US, the greatest country in the world, will survive the Obama's damage. I give him credit for one thing only—waking up the sleeping giant which is the American people to not become complacent over the liberty we enjoy and are in fear of losing.

PS: I always chuckle when I hear the Left accuse the Tea Party movement of being secretly a prop for and being funded by the Republican Party ... which could not be further from the truth. There is nothing behind the movement other than thousands of individual organizers, like me, all doing their own thing, but with one goal in mind ... to take back our country.

Gene Miller

Last week, in Troy, MO we had our first ever Tea Party rally and we've been tying up some loose ends since then and trying to get organized for the local 4th of July parade as well.

Let me start by saying my wife and I have been married for twenty-four years and in the fall of '09 I thought it was all coming to an end mainly because I was an OTR truck driver—but that was only part of it.

In January '09 I started to hear the murmurs of Tea Party rallies. With a lot of time on my hands driving, I was hearing the likes of Limbaugh, Beck, Hannity, Ingraham on the radio and was finally coming out of the left-wing media-biased funk.

Needless to say, when I would get home and unload all my "new knowledge" on my wife, that after several months of hearing me rant, it became very apparent that we were going in different directions.

Well, as luck (I call it that now!) would have it, I had an injury to my neck and have not driven on the road in a semi since early November '09. *Hang with me there is a point here!*

With me sitting at home healing and listening to Fox News, my wife has now seen the light!

Long story short, this is a small version of what is happening all across our great nation. *People are waking up!* This is not a Republican vs. Democrat thing, it is about holding our elected officials accountable to the *Constitution* of the *United States of America* and the religious beliefs it was based on at that time! Our country could function so easily if the government would let it! *God bless and save our country!*

Spencer Leiter

I have been aggravated with government spending and growth for decades. While studying for my MBA at Purdue University in 1989, I was privileged to take an economics class taught by Dr. Horowitz. If you could say that there was a theme to his class, it was that government spending, especially for social programs, doesn't help the intended group of individuals, and brings down the standard of living for the entire population. Dr. Horowitz's used material from various sources to reinforce his points. He introduced us to the writing of Milton Friedman, Thomas Sowell, Walter Williams and many other economic experts. I have been reading and studying these peoples' writings ever since.

During that same period of time I took a finance class. One of our assignments was to project the cash flow for Social Security and Medicare. It became very apparent, even back then, that neither of these systems could continue to exist without some major changes. The numbers indicated that eventually they would collapse. Yet, no one in Washington will even talk about it.

During George Bush's term, my frustration increased tremendously. I was boiling mad. We had elected a Republican House, Senate, and president. This president had promised reform of the Social Security system, the education system, and fiscal responsibility. None of those things happened. Midway through his second term, during a speech club event (Toastmasters International), I gave a speech expressing my confusion over why the liberals didn't love Bush. He had increased spending for the department of education, implemented a prescription drug program, and increased spending for many other social programs. I pointed out that he had done more to implement the liberal agenda than any president since LBJ. I am still mystified as to why they hated him so much.

Then came the collapse of the economy. It was obvious to me that the whole problem was caused by government programs. The source of the housing bubble, and thus the predictable bubble burst, was caused by Freddie and Fannie. The auto industry was also having problems. Part of it was their own doing when they gave their workers benefits that they couldn't afford. However, the government also played a role. Bush implemented a tariff on steel. Thus American car companies paid more for steel than their international competitors. The high price of gas was also hurting the auto industry. Gas prices are dictated by supply and demand. Government had limited supply by restricting drilling. Thus even though auto industry's wound was self-inflicted, the government inflamed the wound so it couldn't heal.

Then came the government bailouts, the stimulus package, the wasting of money, and the accelerated increase in the debt.

When I had thought it was as bad as it could get, it had suddenly gotten a lot worse. I became, and still am, scared for the future of our country.

In February of 2009, I was on a pig hunt with a friend. While driving home, I asked him if he would be interested in having a Tea Party in Bloomington. The question was really spontaneous. I hadn't really thought about it before. I just thought it would be fun. He was enthusiastic about the idea. Right there in the truck we picked April 15th because it was tax day. We didn't know that that would become a day for Tea Party rallies all over the country.

Bloomington is a very liberal college town (Indiana University). It is often referred to as the Berkley of the Midwest. I optimistically hoped we would get 100 people to show up. My family predicted at most 20 people. We didn't do much advertising. We created a Facebook event, set up an e-mail account, and created a web page. We also made an announcement through the letter-to-the-editor section of the local paper.

About a week before the event, it became apparent that something was happening. We started getting a lot of hits to the web site, and a lot of e-mails. You could tell this thing had energy. Normally when you do something like this, you have to search for people to attend. In this case it was the other way around. They were looking for us. When they found us, they told their friends. It grew like a fire in the wind.

When the event finally happened, we had over 1,000 people show up (We documented over 750 in one picture before the event even started. The local paper said we had about 200). We hadn't planned any speakers or any activities. Someone in the crowd yelled that we should march through town. So we did. We had a string of protestors six or seven blocks long zigzagging through the downtown area. Nearly all of them were carrying protest signs or flags. It was fantastic!

During the event, I was asked repeatedly, "What's next?" We hadn't planned a "next." We were just a couple of pig hunters who thought it would be fun to organize a Tea Party. We didn't plan or want to be leaders of a movement. But George Washington didn't want to be commander of the army in the revolution or to be president. When the people asked for him to do it, he did. The same with me. Hundreds of people asked me to keep it going. So, I did. That is how I became a leader of the Bloomington Tea Party Movement.

Jim Billman

Here is my story. I was employed by a large drug company (Schering Plough), which later sold to Merck. During the past ten years I was the facilities manager for the Allentown, PA facility, making a good living and great benefits, working hard to support my family. My last day was March 31st, 2010. The facility was closed and 10,000 people in our facilities all across the country lost their jobs when Merck bought out Schering Plough. *Many of these jobs went overseas.*

I really started to consider what would be there for the youth. I looked at my children and grandchildren and wondered: if we keep going on down this path of socialism what will be there for them?

I have a beautiful wife and five children as well as three grandchildren. We were blessed and we had an opportunity to start our own real estate business back in 2002 and have done fairly well so far considering the state of the economy.

But I look and wonder where are the younger people going to go to get good jobs that will carry them and their families through the years? Not everyone will have the same opportunity we have had. All of the good manufacturing jobs in this state are pretty much gone! All of the steel industry in PA—tens of thousands of jobs have gone overseas.

There are not more than two factories left in Reading, PA that employ more than 1,000 people. We used to have Dana Corporation—about 5,500 people. There was the Glidden paints manufacturing facility—3,500 people and Lucent Technologies—6,000 people. We were one of the biggest textile centers on the east coast—thousands more jobs all gone overseas!

There is hardly anywhere in this country where a young worker starting out in the workforce can get a good lifelong job with good benefits to carry them and their family into retirement! I saw the writing on the wall a long time ago and became interested in politics back in the Clinton years but there were not too many willing to listen back then—everyone thought things were just great and kept their eyes closed! During the Bush years a few cried foul at the Patriot Act, his bailouts, etc., but not much else. Once Obama was elected people finally started waking up and seeing that he was leading us into a path of utter destruction: appointing his czars, bailing out the banking industry, taking over two of the auto industry giants, his stimulus, etc., etc. I started to get involved in the Tea Party movement back around April 15th, 2009, when I was invited to a tax day protest at the Gus Yatron postal facility in Reading, PA. After that I was asked to captain a bus to Washington DC for the 9/12 rally. A few of us saw a great need in the Berks County area for a Tea Party movement that was about more than just rallies and protests.

In October 2009 we formed the Berks County Patriots and invited everyone we could to the Riveredge Hotel for our first meeting. There were about twenty or twenty-five people at that first meeting. So we held a meeting each month for a few months and at each meeting the people from the previous meeting would invite others and our numbers grew quickly.

We were busy reviewing legislation, etc., and really letting the people know what was happening, not just protesting the issues. Then in early January 2010 we decided to run an ad in the local papers for a meeting at the Leesport Farmers market in Leesport,

PA. The ad said anyone Republican, Democrat or Independent who is fed up with government is welcome to attend. To our surprise we had so many show up to that January meeting that we had to turn people away—the hall only holds 1,200!

Right then and there we knew we had something and we struck a common cord with the people. We started having monthly meetings on the third Thursday of the month at the Leesport Market and had many guest speakers. Since that first meeting we have grown our numbers to about 2,000 members and have hosted a candidate forum with one Governor candidate, 5 Lieutenant Governor candidates, one Senate candidate and numerous local office candidates.

We had a "Meet the Sheriff Night" so our patriot members could meet the sheriff and understand the gravity of the housing foreclosure problem in our county (35% increase from this time last year) as well as various other county issues. We have confronted or exposed several local and state candidates as well as some holding office concerning misuse of public funds, inappropriate actions, etc. We currently have an active education committee teaching the federal and state Constitution in home study groups all across the county. On July 22nd, we are holding a family preparedness expo at the Leesport Farmers Market to educate and inform our patriot members about what you will need and what to do in the event of a natural disaster or other regional/national emergency. We are sponsoring another bus trip to Washington DC on August 28th for the Glenn Beck rally for the troops (four buses full so far). We have an active legislation committee who has reviewed current legislation pending in the state and either got behind the sponsors in support of it or confronted them publicly demanding answers about it. We have even written a resolution and had it carried to Harrisburg to be reviewed by a couple of state house members concerning the taxpayer-funded pension issue (one has agreed to carry it to the floor for us!).

TEA PARTY – THE AWAKENING

We are not about party politics, we are about honesty and integrity in our public officials. We do not want machine politics on either side of the aisle anymore! We want/demand that those in public office uphold the Constitution and look out for their constituents, and not get fat off the land and line their own pockets, so to speak. We are not going away; we will continue to grow our numbers and work to effect change in our sphere of influence.

Mark Leyva

Early 2009 the conservative e-mails were talking about a Tea Party coming to our areas in April 2009. After weeks of going to the Tea Party Day web site to watch for a rally in my area, it never came. So I decided to hold a Tea Party in Lake County, IN. I was reluctant at first, because I have been a candidate for US Congress in Indiana's first congressional district. However, I decided to hold a Tea Party tax rally at our local county courthouse. I didn't know what to expect but I made buttons and had T.E.A. signs made. We had about one hundred and fifty individuals attend. I took names and e-mails that day and told everyone that we would have a web site up as soon as possible.

Later that day, April 15, 2009, I went to Valparaiso, IN where there was a much bigger Tea Party rally to support the movement. It was great—they had speakers and microphones to have individuals speak. I took advantage of an opportunity to speak; it was an electrifying feeling. I started working on a web site and a place to have meetings for the Tea Party. Later that July 4th we had our second Tea Party at Wicker Park, one of the local parks in Highland, IN. It turned out pretty good for a rainy day—we had about eighty patriots. The best story of that day: I was not sure what I was going to say at that Tea Party. That morning, while I was on the treadmill working out and watching TV, I started to pay attention to a show about the Founding Fathers, how twenty-six of the fifty-four signers went to seminary school. For years, Congress spent one to three hours a day reading the

Bible! Also, the first public Bibles were printed by our government printing office, and that schools made Bible study a mandatory class. This was my inspiration to talk about at the Tea Party.

In the process of growing, I started communicating with other Tea Party leaders and later we joined together to put a ten-group Tea Party rally together in Warsaw, IN. It was a success. We decided to put a coalition together called the Indiana Patriots Coalition. In January of 2010 I worked with three other Tea Party leaders and put on a Reclaiming America Tea Party rally. It too was a very successful event.

We are networking and growing as time goes on. I have juggled many hats as I ran in an eight-man race for Indiana's first congressional district and was the winner and am now working to defeat a twenty-six-year liberal entrenched congressman that we need to defeat in November!

Michelle Fowler

Our group, the West Texas Patriots, was started about eight weeks ago. Our focus is on community involvement. At the time that we started this group, I was on the board of the Odessa Tea Party.

We volunteer with H.O.T. (Honor Our Troops), Patriot Guard and the Welcome Home Committee in support of our troops. We also regularly contact our representatives about local, state and federal issues. We have a web site that is very new, and we use the web site to inform the community about what is going on and focus on important historical facts. This week we are spotlighting black Founding Fathers and the emancipation in celebration of Juneteenth.

We consider ourselves the local watchdog group also. This May, we came across an article in the local paper about a new charter school opening up for this next school year. It turns out that this school has ties with a radical Islamic imam. In researching, we have found schools all over the United States that have been started by followers of this imam that connect. We have found that these organizations are involved in money laundering through various Turkish organizations that are mainly store-fronts. We are in contact with people all over the world that have been researching the connection between these schools and this imam.

We are attempting to network with other groups to really make a difference. Especially here in Texas, we feel that we (Tea Party/9-12 groups) should have had more of an impact on our primary elections. I guess you could say that was the turning point for us. We were tired of the rallies and the regular meet-ings with the same people, it was too much like preaching to the choir. Like our motto says, we want to "Inform, Encourage and Empower" our communities. So instead of them coming to us, we are looking for ways to reach out to them.

James Mason

It actually started when I was listening to the radio back in May of '89. There was this talk radio host who was pointing out warnings and facts about liberalism and how they were taking over the Democratic party. He didn't have a gripe about Demo-crats so much as he did with liberals and their agenda. I was a Democrat at the time and soon changed parties after realizing what he warned about all came true. It was Rush Limbaugh.

After the 2008 election, it was apparent the Obama was not going to be subtle about making policy changes, and that he would not honor his campaign promises and that he intended to do whatever he wanted—no matter what the majority of the na-tion wanted. His speeches to the AMA were followed by notices from the White House to the AP saying that any statements made by the President were not to be taken literally. To me this was unheard of, after his promises to have transparency in his policy making. He even made sure that the American flag was to be removed during some appearances, along with any religious artifacts that were around. It was almost like he was unafraid to reveal to the world that he hated our flag, our Constitution and our nation. He was even alienating our allies and befriending our enemies. Something was terribly wrong with this administration.

In mid-January it was apparent that the Ted Kennedy's Senate seat was really in danger of being won by Scott Brown instead of the heavily supported campaign of Cowley, and I then decided that the Tea Party was more than a flash in the pan. They were for real and the will of a huge chunk of the nation was supporting their agenda. So as southeast Nebraska did not have any representation, I started the Tea Party of Nemaha County.

Jane Kenny

I am seventy-one years old and I am a Tea Party organizer in Bluffton, SC. Do you know why so many Tea Party patriots are older Americans? It is because we're the only ones who remember a time when our nation was truly free … we remember a time when the government structure was closer to the model outlined in the US Constitution. Older Americans can remember getting a paycheck that had us taking home most of the money we earned. We remember when there were no sales taxes and no government-imposed hidden taxes and fees on everything from wills and estates to fishing licenses.

Our younger years were a time when the free enterprise system was indeed free, not restrained by heavy-handed government regulation and taxes or obstructed by government-created monopolies and even outright government ownership of private enterprise under the guise of public-private partnership. We remember when we didn't have a burdensome national debt, when

we had the largest and most productive middle class in the world, and we lived happily within our means. To proud and self-reliant Americans, government handouts were anathema.
We studied civics from elementary school on up; we know our Constitution and Declaration of Independence. We even memorized the most important sections. We understand our responsibility as American citizens. We the People are the government! Older Americans remember fathers, grandfathers, uncles and brothers who went to war to defend the freedoms guaranteed by the Constitution. Our generation knows that to preserve the Republic—we must limit government intrusion on our liberties lest we morph into tyranny. We learned about civic responsibility by example at home and in school.

When Barack Obama came to power, it didn't take American citizens long to rally in an historic way. Millions gathered together spontaneously in Tea Party groups all over the nation. It was a unique phenomenon … clearly a protest from citizens who do not want their country converted to Marxism. It's that simple.

Prior to the election of 2008, it did not take much independent research to learn that Mr. Obama is a lifelong avowed Marxist, despite what the political spin was saying on radio and TV. Now, after just eighteen months under President Obama's leadership, we are well on the way to a transformation to Marxist political, economic and social policies.

Will the Tea Party movement be able to gain enough momentum to take back the Congress this year and reclaim the administration in two years? Are there enough American heroes to step up and pledge their lives, their fortunes and their sacred honor in order to protect and defend the Constitution from all enemies foreign and domestic? That's what it will take. I'm a realist, not a conspiracy theorist. I ask myself how we came so far, so fast—from American patriots like Eisenhower and Kennedy in the White House to the Marxist who now resides there and insists he will fundamentally transform the Republic? The answer can only come from our children and grandchildren who know so little about civic responsibility.

In 2008, our children voted for a political American-Idol-style rock star who, devoid of substance, was created by a dazzling advertising and promotional campaign. At the same time our grandchildren were being taught to sing songs idolizing Obama as the beloved leader. Reflecting upon how two entire generations of Americans are allowing themselves to be deceived, the phrase, " ... forgive them for they know not what they do," comes to mind. Our system of self-governance could very well die off with my generation.

I am convinced that the Tea Party movement is the only force that can save the Republic from the fundamental transformation to Marxism that is already underway. If enough American patriots courageously rise to the challenge, have enough bravery to identify the domestic enemy and pledge their commitment to stay with the struggle to fully restore the constitutional Republic, it will be America's finest hour!

Janet Smith

I attended my first Tea Party rally in Tampa, FL to express my displeasure with the way the government was taxing us and spreading the wealth to those who are not willing to work. I have since attended a rally in Indianapolis, Indiana as we split our time between FL and IN since being retired. I am very upset with the progressive agenda and Obama's far left agenda taking our country down the path to socialism. I think we are in deep trouble with all of the government spending and raising of taxes all around us. I sometimes felt alone in my convictions but with the Tea Party I found others who were also concerned and wanted to do something to make a change.

I want to see this country taken back by the people and the government alerted to the fact that the senators and representatives work for us and not the other way around. I think it is important that we elect true conservatives who respect the Constitution and actually follow it instead of making up the rules as they go along. We need less government and not more. When I attended the National Tea Party convention in Nashville, TN in January 2010, I was energized by the enthusiasm of the people there who were very concerned about the direction this country is headed. Sarah Palin delivered an inspiring speech to the group, and I met the chairman of the Indiana State Tea Party and his wife. With their assistance we have started a Tea Party group in this area called the Greenfield Area Tea Party and we hope to make a difference locally as well as nationally.

Jannie Hornby

My husband and I had been reading the news (he's a news junkie) and watching the tube and talking to our friends and complaining all the time for years, and I mean before the big "O" got in office. So I told him enough was enough, either we actually *do* something or quit complaining! That very week there was a meeting of our local "Americans for Prosperity" and we went. We all talked about our feelings about what was going on with our country and it came out that most of us were independents or at least not supporting either party. We decided that we wanted to have a local Tea Party the week before Tax Day to advertise the Tea Party at the Oregon State capital on April 15th. No one wanted to organize the rally so I volunteered. Keep in mind this was our first meeting and I didn't know a soul at this meeting. My husband raised his eyebrows but didn't say anything. I spent the next three weeks contacting all the local radio stations with calls and e-mail. I managed to get four appointments to talk on three stations. I also got info in the local newspapers and on all the Oregon Tea Party web sites. The week before the Tea Party we got together at a beautiful farm and in one of the shops built 20+ Tea Party signs. The day of the Tea Party we had around 150 people, which is a lot for this area! We had a pickup truck for the speakers and a sound system that the speakers used to rally the troops. We even had a ten-year-old boy speak about the pink slips he was handing out to give our government officials for not representing the people. We had so many wonderful signs and gave a prize to the sign that was voted the best one. After the speakers we walked the streets with our signs and got lots of great response from the public.

Jason Adams

I am twenty-four years old, from the Seattle area (Stanwood, WA). I have been very politically active since I was seventeen. Now I am an active member of the Mount Vernon Tea Party, Camano Island 9-12 group, and I am the founder and coordinator of Liberty Forever. Although I have been very active in helping candidates that share my values get elected, what got me involved with Tea Party groups is the lack of fiscal responsibility in our government. I do not believe that Obama is responsible for the whole mess but he is sure making things worse. The US has been electing irresponsible candidates for decades. The Tea Party Movement is just a group of regular people that make up a mix of Democrats, Republicans, Independents and Libertarians that want to change the course that our once great nation is heading towards. My group's sole purpose is to help and improve communication between other Constitution-based groups (An area that the Tea Partiers have been very weak in). What I believe the focus of the Tea Party groups should be is protecting freedom, liberty, and supporting responsible candidates and lower taxes. The constitution should be applied to all laws immediately and all that fail to pass what our great Constitution stands for should be repealed. A great man once said:

> The liberties of our country, the freedoms of our civil Constitution are worth defending at all hazards; it is our duty to defend them against all attacks. We have received them as a fair inheritance from our worthy ancestors. They purchased them for us with toil and danger and expense of treasure and blood. It will bring a mark of

everlasting infamy on the present generation - enlightened as it is - if we should suffer them to be wrested from us by violence without a struggle, or to be cheated out of them by the artifices of designing men.
– Samuel Adams

Jeff McKeown

First of all, I believe I was spurred on by the acronym itself, Taxed Enough Already. I feel that we have come to a point in this great country of ours, which I honestly do believe is the greatest country in the modern world, where it will quickly go away in our lifetime if we don't step up to the plate and say enough is enough, or to steal the phase from the movie *Network* from 1976, "I'm as mad as hell, and I'm not going to take this anymore." Or, we will sit idly by and continue to see our freedoms taken one by one in the name of peace, protection and equality.

I believe that we now have a government that has used situations of the past nine years to further the cause of government control and socialization. I do not believe that our Founding Fathers ever desired our country to come to this but I also believe that they understood that it would if we the people did not maintain control of our government. I do not believe that our government should be allowed to mandate health control against the wishes of the majority of its citizens. I am against some of the measures that they continue to institute in the name of prosperity and a better place to live. The current oil spill situation in the gulf is an example of the government using situations to mandate their agenda, like a six-month moratorium on drilling and the opportunity to destroy any idea of drilling in Alaska.

I do understand the ramifications of the current spill but I also realize that according to the numbers they have been giving us concerning the amount that is leaking out that we should not be dependent on foreign oil and the only way we can be independent is to discover safer methods to extract it. They continually want to set in place restrictions that have forced manufacturing out of this country and into others that do not have all of the regulations that cost businesses so much. We are also at the point that they are pretty much encouraging people not to work but to just allow the government to provide for their needs such as housing, food and medical.

I am tired of sitting back and allowing these things to keep happening at a cost to all of us who are legal working citizens.

Our government cannot continue to create new taxes that allow them to take more of our money so that they can distribute the wealth to those that choose to not do anything, and they cannot continue spending money that we do not have.

I am also an advocate for our Second Amendment right to bear arms, but as we have seen over this past year, our government will try to limit our ability to have ammunition. I do know because I have seen it myself that there is already a signed treaty that gives a date by which firearms in the United States will be eliminated. I do not plan to stand by and watch this happen, but our government knows that if the people have no way to defend themselves then they can control the people. Call me crazy, but I honestly believe that there are things in the works to bring about so-called financial crises that will cause individuals to consider giving up their firearms in order to feed and house their families.

These are some of the reasons that I choose to be involved.

Jen Ezzell

Getting involved in the Tea Party movement was not something I contemplated ... it was something that just happened. The Stimulus Bill of 2009 was the final straw. Over the years I have not been politically active, like most of the people involved in this grassroots movement. But from time to time I was "irked" by things that were happening to our country, by our government.

There was a book *The Buying Of America* that went into how corporations were buying influence with our elected officials. That book infuriated me so much that I couldn't finish it, yet it made a lasting impression on me. How lobbyists (many of them former congressmen, staffers, and/or family members—working for corporations, bankers, and special interest groups) were undermining America as a whole. Large farm businesses were getting regulations in place that actually favored them over the small family farmer, for one example.

Every time Congress would impose regulations for the "good" of the country, it would make me wonder who was getting paid off. Never really found that answer, but one thing was for sure ... it was going to cost us more in increased prices for goods, services, utilities, etc.

In 2007, Congress tried to get their "comprehensive" immigration reform bill passed. It would be the first time I became active in speaking out against what the government was trying to do. It was the first piece of legislation that I would actually completely read, but not the last. It was a real eye opener into why there have been claims that some of the laws Congress writes are unenforceable. In one section they stated they would deport the criminals (illegals who were gang members) ... okay ... I could live with that ... then a hundred or so pages later the bill stated that all gang members had to do was produce a note saying they would not be involved in gang activity. If they did that, they could stay here. Unbelievable!

In 2007, Congress also passed the Farm Bill. The amount of pork that was put into this bill was unbelievable. Nancy Pelosi made sure that everyone had a piece of the pie to ensure a veto override, as President Bush had stated he would veto it. In this Farm Bill was the increase for corn-based ethanol, a product we are forced to use. Ethanol (just like a filler) added gasoline is not economical for use ... not only does it add to the price of gasoline, but we get less gas mileage per gallon ... hence we get hit with a double cost for our fuel usage and no benefit. All compliments of our government meddling.

In 2008, gas prices were skyrocketing while Congress sat and twiddled their thumbs. The average American was hurting. For some, they were losing some of their freedom of movement. For many they were losing their precious, hard-earned dollars to rising energy costs and higher food costs. As their disposable income started to disappear, fears of losing their homes started to increase.

Global warming was the rage and very few seemed to want to speak out against it. Those who did were excoriated and ridiculed. Many members of Congress either supported the GW talking points or shied away from saying anything due to the fear of being ridiculed. *Where were our leaders?*

In the summer of 2008, Congress passed an "emergency" war-spending bill that included a whole new education program for veterans and also an extended unemployment compensation package. The education program was not an emergency war-spending item—it should have been included in the Defense budget. The unemployment compensation package also was not an emergency war-spending item—it should have been passed on its own. But neither was done correctly, because then Congress would have to either raise revenues (taxes) or cut spending to pay for it, as Nancy Pelosi had promised that they would follow their "Pay Go" policy. The stuffing of emergency spending and other sleight-of-hand tactics is something that only Congress can get away with, all the while blaming the president for the fiscal mess. Congress writes the rules, makes up the spending packages, and can override a president, if they have the votes. They are not blameless in the mess we have on our hands.

In the Fall of 2008, we had a new term in our vocabulary: "TARP." The majority of America was against it, but Congress passed it. This was the second time I became involved, making phone calls, sending e-mails, and calling into radio shows with my concerns.

From there the pace picked up. Bailout became the new watchword. After the swearing in of President Obama, there were executive orders being signed, the Stimulus Bill started picking up steam ... all the while Americans were saying ... no ... stop it ... slow down. The Democrat congressional representatives turned deaf, blind and dumb to the people they represented. They followed their party line, special interest groups (think Unions) and donors.

The Stimulus Bill represents the biggest wasteful spending bill this country has seen, as it was not for the improvement of our country but for the betterment of special interest groups and a slush fund for Democrats. The whole way it was being promoted: shovel-ready jobs, the timed release of the money (instead of an immediate infusion of dollars, it is spread out over years), and many of those receiving the money (colleges with hundreds of millions to billions of dollars in endowments, receiving millions for research) just doesn't pass the smell test. It stunk then and it is still stinking today, with none of the promises of stopping unemployment or creating jobs.

In February 2009, Rick Santelli made his now famous rant. A couple of weeks later there were Tea Party rallies in forty cities across the country. I decided then and there that I had to do something. I heard that there were plans for another rally on April 15th. I was fortunate to connect with some people (I did not know any of them) in CT who were also working to have a rally in Hartford. From there I met Rich and Lou and we went on to plan a Tax Day Tea Party in Norwich for April 15th, 2009.

For all intents and purposes, in my mind, this was just going to be a one-time event. A time to let others, who felt like we did, get up and exercise their First Amendment right. I am not sure why or when we decided to collect names of those attending, but we did. Our list grew from our 3 names to over 400 on April 15th, 2009, to now over 1,400 people in Eastern CT.

Then came the cap and trade bill, followed closely by the Health Care Bill. What was becoming quite obvious was that our elected officials were not going to listen to us; instead they were going to follow Obama, Pelosi, Reid and the progressive liberal agenda. An agenda that is anti-American, goes against our Founding Fathers' vision and goes against the Constitution.

Our goal, as Tea Party patriots, has been education ... whether it is a bill coming up, incumbent voting records, candidates running for office, or even about the Constitution. We try to keep our list members informed with the actual bills, reports from various think tanks, government reports, etc. The best weapon we have is our knowledge and using that knowledge to share with others. We all are responsible for overseeing our government and we need to take on that responsibility now.

We are seeing our country fundamentally change—our children and grandchildren will not have the freedoms or lifestyles that we had. They will have to pay, not only with their hard earned dollars, but now, it seems, with their health care.

I could not just sit by and let things happen. If we succeed in changing back some of the erroneous bills that have been passed ... and not just from the last year and a half ... our children and grandchildren will have a chance to succeed. If not, I hope that we inspire them to pick up the battle where we left off, to continue the fight to return our country back to the promise our Founding Fathers gave us. At the very least they know that I and many others in America tried to stop the onslaught against our liberties.

TEA PARTY – THE AWAKENING

James E. Page

I suppose like most people my age, I have not been overly concerned with politics nor spent too much time with the direction of the country, other than to occasionally make it a topic of water cooler discussion. I have been aware over the last forty years or so the creeping intrusion of an ever-expanding federal bureaucracy. It seems almost immune to what political party is in control. As it grows, it feeds on more regulations, fees, permits and taxes by many other names. Also, the rise of "political correctness" and the push for self-esteem, so we can all feel good about mediocre and mundane accomplishments.

Again, like many people my age, after a few months of the Obama administration, did I ever get a wake-up call! I did not support or vote for Mr. Obama, in fact I wrote a letter or two to the opinion page of our local paper pointing out some of the problems I could foresee. It soon became apparent my apprehensions would pale to reality. Men of extraordinary intellect and vision gave their talent and in many cases their lives to birth this great nation. We have withstood civil war and struggles that have led to world wars, and now it seems we are under attack from a few politicians that intend to change the very foundations that have served us so well. Capitalism is under attack! It seems our great statesmen have been replaced by very shallow politicians who put their selfish ambitions or misguided philosophies ahead of service to the country.

I felt I had to do something, to take some action beyond worry or talk. A Google search turned up two or three people in my area also interested in becoming a part of the Tea Party movement. After an exchange of e-mail and phone conversation, five of us met and formed our group (the Terre Haute Tea Party). Our next meeting a couple of weeks later saw an increase to around twenty in number. We took this core group and organized our first rally on April 15, 2009. We got out information using flyers with all the appropriate information plus a Gmail account, word of mouth, and a letter to the editor that I wrote. We had a sign-making meeting a couple of days before our event, for those that did not bring their own. I painted a large Tea Party sign to identify us.

The rally was to start at noon that day. I must admit being nervous about showing up. This is something I really never dreamed I would do. My name was out there for all to see in my letter to the editor. Was this thing going to flop? Would there just be a small number of participants? Would we be outnumbered by Obama supporters? To my pleasant surprise our numbers were well over 200 enthusiastic Tea Partiers.

We have had two more rallies since and our number have continued to grow. Personally, I have called the White House several times, and I have sent many e-mails and faxes to representatives and senators expressing my serious concerns about the plight in which we find ourselves. There have been more letters to the editor, and I have sharpened my skills of persuasion with facts I glean to persuade those I come into contact with. I try to be pleasant and brief—I realize "we" have not all "seen the light" yet. I am probably more alarmed by the national media and their bias and dishonest reporting. If they would do their job, I might be able to get back to my water cooler conversations.

Zan Green

Where to start? Why? I had to, just knew something had to happen, status quo wasn't working. Similar to why we march on Washington in September. No one (in DC) was listening to us from the local level. Then they didn't listen at their front door—Obama even left town. So we continue to fight. Yes, fight—this is a battle for our very way of American constitutional life. Just this week a publishing company was found posting a disclaimer to the US Constitution—http://bit.ly/9H94nQ. If they can erase who we are and where we came from, they can declare who we are and who we are to become.

The Left (socialist, communist, Marxist Left) have been organized, dedicated and relentless for the past sixty years and they saw a large opening and tried to push the whole agenda through at one fell swoop. We the people noticed, finally. I happened to remember one very distinct lesson from history class in the fifth grade (back when teachers were also patriots) and that was that if America fell, it would be from the inside. I knew then—not on my watch. I am a housewife and mom with no formal education, no career, just a red, white and blue American gal from the heartland that knows she is in the right, and that we, America, are in the right. We are the last best hope for all that want to be free. Life, liberty and the pursuit of happiness.

I have watched my husband for the past twenty-eight years work his way to the top of his profession. He started life in a wood frame house his father built with his own hands. He was raised in rural Mississippi, educated there, joined the Marine Corp and put himself through school. Now he is what the Left calls "rich" and they want his life's work fettered out to someone that had the same opportunity and did nothing to improve their lot in life. Wrong, wrong, wrong.

Tired? Yes, but I will never, never, never give up. I hope I have the courage and the talents to keep my group motivated, active and focused enough to make a difference. But let me make one huge point—I may have put the ball on the field, but the team moved it forward. We the Rainy Day Patriots have a very talented pool of volunteers, and they also are very dedicated and driven. To them I owe much.

How we got started. On Twitter in late 2008 to early 2009 a gang on #tcot (Top Conservatives On Twitter, tcotreport.com) started talking about having a Tea Party. Ideas ranged from mailing in tea bags to DC to sending in voided checks with the department amount written in as payment on them. We were mad and venting until Rick Santelli's rant and the movement to have a physical Tea Party started. I opened a one-page web site linked to #tcot, posted it on Twitter and had about five people get in touch with me. I called the local talk radio shows and announced where to come and what to bring (a sign). About twenty folks I never met before showed up. It was a cold, stormy day, February 28th, 2009. It rained and blew and a tornado struck about a mile south of us. We jokingly called ourselves a bunch of rainy day patriots, and the name stuck.

Everyone wanted to meet again and the Tax Day Tea Party of '09 was being talked about—we had over 10,000 show up! Since then we have had four major Tea Parties, several Instant Tea Parties, gone to DC several times, held candidate forums and become a force in the local political scene. We have a very active web site, rainydaypatriots.org, six delegations in other counties and a membership of 12,000 plus. We grow every day.

We get frustrated, wonder if we are making a difference, and rethink our agenda from time to time, but we never discuss giving in or giving up.

Ray Jones

I was a "War Baby," a Baby Boomer. I was born in Arkansas, just after World War II. My father served in the Army Air Corps. Thus I lived and grew up in a time of patriotic fervor in this country. We never failed to say the Pledge of Allegiance and hear a prayer in school. And we sung patriotic songs in school. I am a Tea Party patriot. I love the Constitution and the United States. And I love the Republic it once was and can and should be again. Correction: it *must be again*!

I attended the September 12, 2009 Tea Party March on Washington DC, along with 1.7 million other common decent patriots who also love America and her Constitution, and are shocked and appalled at the current state of our nation, and especially of our government. A government that is supposed to be "Of the People ... For the People ... By the People!"

I learned a lot from my stepfather, also a WWII veteran. I learned about honesty, integrity, a good work ethic, hard work, honest pay, and the value of a good education. He was a wise old man. We called him Poppa Kirk. He believed in buying American-made products. He was a machinist at a roofing mill, the salt of the earth, a lunch-box working man, and made a living for his family.

I am a Chemical Engineer. And I work in the field of "Alternative Fuels," the so-called green fuels that hopefully will help America survive and remain free and prosperous even as oil someday begins to become more scarce. However, people should know. We are a long, long, long way from replacing oil as our energy source! Liberal progressive pipe dreams of "Clean Energy" are still merely dreams and their common lies are means to gain control of the energy sector of our economy. We *must not* ever let them do this!

How did I get involved with the Tea Party movement? For years I watched sadly as the liberal socialists took over the important sections of our nation, as our school systems became mostly liberal bastions of propaganda and socialist indoctrination centers. It wasn't quite as bad when my daughters were growing up and in public school down south in Arkansas. But it had already begun. Now as my grandchildren are in school and most of them in high school, it is very bad. They are confronted daily by liberal nonsense and political correctness. It is quite sickening.

I began to understand that Obama was not correctly vetted by the DNC as a candidate for president under the qualifications of the Constitution, it literally made me ill. Those who understand the true realities of the term "natural born citizen" know that you must not only be born in the USA, but *both* your parents must also be citizens. So we have a usurper in the White House.
And when I heard about the organizing of Tea Party events all across America, I planned to attend the local event, and I pre-

pared signs to take with me. I attended the local Tea Party events, and I also attended the September 12, 2009 march on Washington DC along with 1.7 million others from all across America. This was one of the most thrilling events of my life, next to marriage and the births of my children and grandchildren. And I plan to attend the event this year. I wanted to attend the first Tea Party convention but work related events prevented that.

I have organized web pages on Tea Party Nation, and on God and Country USA. I also regularly visit several other Patriotic Conservative web sites to keep up with what is going on. The web groups I organized and moderate are called "Minutemen of 2010." This is a group for members to keep updated on polls and news related to the critical elections of 2010 (and maybe beyond). The Minutemen of 2010 seeks to interject their own funds as collective volleys of dollars via individual contributions to conservative candidates for critical elections at critical times. The members send their own contributions in concert with the group to be a more effective impact for a particular candidate.

I advised FreedomWorks and Tea Party Patriots to arrange to broadcast the speakers at the 2010 September 12th march on Washington, and to advertise this to attendees so that all people in the huge crowd could hear the speakers. That was a minor problem at the 2009 march. So many people showed up that they could not get close enough to hear the speakers. FreedomWorks prepared for a crowd of 50,000 and 1.7 million showed up! My hope is that this year … 5 million plus will show up for the rally.

That's my story. I plan to remain active. I get the Whistleblower magazine. I watch Glenn Beck, Hannity, O'Reilly and Stossel on Fox News. I watch PJTV also. I plan to actively work for the flipping of Congress from liberal socialist to true conservative … to restore our nation to its representative Republic form of government, and to restore the government to limited government operating under the restrictions of the Constitution. God Bless America and Don't Tread On Me!

Vicki Towles

During the late spring of 2007 as the primaries were ramping up, I began paying attention to the Democrats as I felt certain Hillary Clinton was destined to become the first female president. I'd heard of Barack Obama, but hadn't researched or followed him despite his sudden burst onto the scene. The first time I saw him debate, I was shocked that anyone could consider him presidential material due to both his inexperience and his responses to the questions posed by the moderator, Charlie Gibson. I was immediately drawn to his body language and incessant back and forth head movement as he delivered his responses. I'm no Hillary Clinton fan, but her performance was head and shoulders more presidential than Mr. Obama's, so I blew it off thinking he had no chance of winning the primary.

Then came Iowa. The Clinton's were suddenly on their heels and in a defensive mode. I found it entertaining, as I realized that as a young Democrat of the '80s and early '90s, that the Democratic party was not the "party of the people" as they claimed, but instead was the party of "we know better than you how you should live and we'll do anything to have the power to run your life." Long story short, that is when I started researching and following Mr. Barack Obama.

My research left me very, very concerned about his agenda for our country. So I knew the day had arrived for me to do more than I'd ever done politically. John McCain was leaving a trail of ashes on the primary trail and I knew that even though I didn't prefer him among the Republicans, I'd have to support him against Obama.

Obama and McCain won. I was very disappointed and dispirited. How could so many Democrats elect a man with so little experience, whose history is somewhat a mystery because he suddenly just "appeared?" And how in the world did John McCain, the epitome of "stale, GOP establishment" slide to victory?

Ugh. I just dreaded campaigning for McCain and there were even days I told myself I wouldn't. But on a cold Friday morning, my spirits were catapulted by the announcement of Sarah Palin as his running mate. I signed up at the Shelby County Republican HQ the next week and began campaigning. Florida was a swing state so I signed up to volunteer in Miami and took a week of vacation from work to do my part down there. Two friends and I flew down from Memphis and were truly amazed at the hospitality and kindness we received from the volunteers in Miami. This GOP field office was mostly comprised of Cubans who had personal stories from dictator Castro's (lower case intentional) revolution. The passion and fear in their stories validated my feelings about the threat posed to liberty and individual rights by Obama. One couple, Marta and Orlandos, invited us to their home for dinner where we were treated like family. She was a former Democrat who heard all this "Hope and Change" rhetoric before, but this time recognized it was a dangerous slogan that could lead to an erosion of individual freedom. We were strangers, but we were family because we were there together to fight for freedom.

Election night was a bummer and I jumped off the merry-go-round of politics for a few months. When Rick Santelli's rant went viral, I came alive. Finally, someone from the mainstream media bravely spoke up and verbalized what so many Americans were screaming at their televisions. I went online to get information to host a Tea Party in Memphis and found that someone had already secured it. In early March 2009, a group of strangers met at a Perkins restaurant and began organizing a Tea Party rally for April 15.

The energy and camaraderie was unbelievable. For a group of folks who'd never seen each other, much less known one another, to come together and successfully coordinate a Tea Party rally was nothing less than amazing.

We knew this event was for something bigger than ourselves and we gave it our all, unselfishly. Why was this successful and why did I get involved? Because there were no "by-laws, memberships, fees, committees" and there was only one requirement: protecting individual liberty. Anyone, no matter his or her religion, color, gender, or orientation was welcomed to participate as an *American*. All the issues that we Americans bicker over are secondary because at the end of the day, the common thread we share is *the power and freedom of the individual*. We have been called horrible names and accused of ugly actions, but none are true. All the video footage produces no evidence of these false accusations. The people in the Tea Party movement welcome *all* like-minded Americans, regardless of race, gender, religion, orientation, etc., who believe in this special land we call the United States of America.

A lot has happened since our first Tea Party. We've got several Tea Party groups in the Memphis and Mid-South who remain active in educating and empowering individuals.

site.thepatriottrust.us
midsouthteaparty.org
thememphisteaparty.com
tiptoncountytnteaparty.com
fayetteteaparty.com
wethepeoplewesttn.com

I've been to Washington, DC six times since last September to protest the out-of-control government assault on the individual. I've met some amazing people at these rallies who came from all corners of the country. Many who fled oppression and immigrated to come here. They were so kind to share their stories so that Americans might wake up to what is happening.

Several of us in the Memphis area are running for office in the upcoming election. We are not politicians but we are moved to get more involved. I'm certain this is happening all across America. People are stepping up to the plate, risking ridicule and personal attacks, to get into formal positions of power so they can lead according to the principles in our Bill of Rights and the US Constitution. We are not perfect, nor are we polished, but we have heart, courage and love of country that will lead us to victory. This Tea Party movement is not about anyone's personal political gain, but instead is about protecting the rights of the individual. "The price of greatness is responsibility." The people in the Tea Party movement understand this.

Vernon Brossart

Right after the election 2008, I bought Mr. Obama's two books and *The Obama Nation* and read them. I also read his comments on the campaign trail with Joe the Plumber—we could build coal plants but be taxed out of business. North Dakota depends on coal for its energy. That would kill us. I became very concerned. I had been hearing about Tea Parties and I attended two rallies, July 2nd and 4th, in Montana.

After returning home, I wondered why no one in Williston was talking about them. So I called the organizers of the rallies I just attended and asked them what to do. They said, start one yourself! I got a place to meet, picked a date, July 18th at 7 p.m., made up fliers and put them out all over the city. Meeting night came. I was told that if I got six to ten people I should be happy, but forty concerned citizens showed up. By the way, they were all leaders, not followers, so we decided to have a 9-12 rally at Harmon Park, then formed committees: budget and finance committee, food committee, guest speaker committee, committee for advertising, committee for honor guard, committee to take care of children so their parents could be involved in the rally, etc. We ended up with seven speakers and covered many topics such as global warming, cap and trade, abortion, religion in schools, health care, our forefathers, the progressive movement, and more. We also came up with nine of what we called the Tea Party Williston's concerns. Also attending were the three Democrat/Progressives, congressmen from North Dakota. Total attendance was approximately 1,018 (Williston is a town of about 13,000). After the rally, we formed watchdog committees to monitor city and state legislatures, the park board, city commission, county commission, etc. We believe that it was because of us that Senator Dorgan decided to retire!

We also vetted a good man to run against Earl Pomroy. He should beat him handily. We have also started the recall of Kent Conrad. They say we can't do it but we will see. Conrad has voted for every bill that Pelosi, Reed and Obama have come up with, which 70% of North Dakotans don't want!

Paula Slow

I was born and raised in the Midwest, specifically Minnesota. I came from a typical middle-class family. My father was a politician but an honest one. He truly represented the people of this Republic. He served as mayor of two different cities, state senator, county commissioner and many more positions. His example is what I follow.

The people in government today, do not understand the value of integrity and working for the people. It has become a place for lawyers and self-seeking individuals to push the people down so *we* can work for *them*. That way, they can stay in power and rule us even longer. That is why I am involved in the Tea Party movement, here in Williston. This is a group of everyday people who have integrity and understand that our country was based on us being the ones in power, and not these power-hungry corrupt individuals. Alas, we have let them take over. Some of us have decided that we are not too busy to take our country back to its roots. Where we are free men and women, able by God's gift to make our own decisions.

I so enjoy spending time with these good, hardworking people involved in our local Tea Party. They live the values this country was founded on every day. Values like helping your neighbor, working hard, sharing your wisdom and your material goods with less fortunate people, and caring about what goes on in your town. Not seeking to gain personal profit from "helping" others.

We get things accomplished in our Tea Party that amaze the other people involved in the movement. This is due to the leadership we have in Vernon Brossart and the people who are just willing to seize an idea and go with it, fighting with their whole hearts to preserve the true freedom we are daily losing. We are in a battle for our very way of life and we take that seriously. Our privilege is that we have been able to live and grow up in this country as free men and women and enjoy life and prosperity.

So in closing, please know that we are just like other people across the country, people who appreciate what we have had and want to preserve it for future generations. When I see this freedom of life being taken away, I do have moments when I cry and truly grieve for what is being lost.

Tony Raymond

I am a thirty-eight-year-old husband and father, who up until September of 2009, was not very active in politics. One Sunday morning at church, a good friend of mine, Janelle Nagy, had just returned from a 9/12 rally in DC and was fired up. She asked me if I would help organize and plan some local events and I decided that it was a good way for me to become politically involved. I have always voted Republican, but have been deeply disappointed in the progressive trends in the party. Over the past nine months, the Northern Illinois Patriots (NIP) have grown from 3 to 225 members, had over thirty-five events, and been featured in several national papers. I believe that this is just the beginning. Our leadership team (yes, we are not shy about being leaders) is working on a patriot's voter guide to help citizens in November mid-term elections and I am working on building a coalition among leaders of conservative groups. I am blessed to have so many committed patriots around me who love our country and believe that we must be aware, get involved and make a difference. God bless America!

Fredrick Main

I am a seventy-nine-year-old veteran of the Korean War era and a retiree from the aerospace industry. Back in April 2010, I attended a formative meeting of a group wishing to form a Tea Party organization in the Milledgeville, Georgia area. The people at that meeting were strong in their opinion that the country was moving in the wrong direction and I agreed with them. They were, however, without an experienced leader and, in a moment of weakness, I offered my services. It has been a wonderful experience. We have doubled attendance at our monthly meetings over the past three months and we have had congressional and state candidates come to our meeting to speak to us. Not too bad after only five months. We will continue to grow to be a positive force for rational spending policies, constitutionally limited government and personal and economic freedom for our citizens.

Thomas Beach

Thanks for contacting me. I would be glad to share with you my experiences and Tea Parties. My personal story is probably a shade different from other Tea Party leaders and organizers. I started an organization called Concerned Citizens of Lawrence County. Lawrence County is located about forty-five minutes west of Huntsville, Alabama. Even though this organization is very much a Tea Party organization, it wasn't intended that way. Actually, Tea Parties didn't exist at the time. Ironically, it wasn't Obama or his ilk that helped catapult the creation of this organization, it was created because of the failures of the local Republican party. Also, the pillars of this organization might be similar to those of today's Tea Parties, but the foundation is clearly different. I'll explain, but I need to start at the beginning.

I live in a county that has never seen a Republican win a single office in any city, community or municipality. This county was created in 1818. We have a obscene unemployment rate, high school graduates with 8th grade reading levels, a population rate in the single digits with a four-year degree or higher, and no industry has came to this county in the last fifty years. I could go on. I wanted to use the dire situation here as a platform for the local Republican Party. After the 2008 loss, I attended the next meeting with the local GOP members, which were only a handful of people. Then I came up with ideas of how we can increase the standard of living here, but each and every single idea was decided against. Each and every single idea was based off conservatism. Actually, the exact words given to me were that if I wanted to raise the standard of living in Lawrence County, I needed to buy the local high school counselor lunch and ask them to do a better job. This was their only idea. This was their answer to making things better. I was disgusted and left.

That meeting took place on a Thursday. For the next few days I talked with friends and people that I knew and by the following Sunday I had 200 members in my organization. It was strange to go talk to a public servant by myself about an issue and get ignored, then turn around and come back with 200 people in a small community. They tend to act like they were always for your idea and your best friend.

I believe the key to get a couple hundred people together was defining conservatism. I knew things nationally were getting worse, but what was really bad was that I saw society pushing

God away. Since I didn't have Obama's ear or a national audience, I had to concern myself with preparing for tough times here locally. I know that if you push God's hand away, His blessings go away too. We as a nation are asking for a world of hurt and it's going to get worse. This is important because I came to the realization that our natural rights come from God. If God has no place or simply doesn't exist, then the issuer of our rights becomes government. This is what makes America so exceptional. The Constitution reflects this philosophy because it inherently limits government and protects our God-given rights. I know we are in trouble as a society and nation, so I did what I could and started this organization to prepare Lawrence County, Alabama for tough times. You prepare by raising the standard of living based on conservative solutions. I believe you cannot have prosperity without conservatism. What we need to do is simple: 2 Chronicles 7:14. It's really that simple.

Thelma M. Homer

I am seventy-seven years of age, and have lived most of my life right here in Elko, Nevada, now a town of about 40,000 but when growing up, much smaller. I never engaged an interest in politics until 2005 – 2006, when amnesty for illegals was proposed, and I began searching my computer for pertinent information. It was the pictures, the sheer numbers, that alarmed me. They had actually come out of the shadows making demands on our country. I joined numbersusa.com and fairus.org. The statistics were overwhelming. I began studying the laws and the lawmakers. Then came the Tea Party movement. I signed on to their web sites, as I did to congress.org in order to e-mail my congressional representatives about current events and laws. I finally began to know what I didn't know.

Prior to the last election, all presidential candidates came to speak in Elko and I went to hear them all—McCain, Hillary Clinton, Ron Paul and a very impressive Sarah Palin, with the exception of Obama. I began to write a letter to the editor of the local paper: holding to their requirement of one a month, no more than 350 words. During the Obama Care protest the Tea Party bus tour came through, and at that event I set up a table handing out my essays and letters to the editor, toll-free numbers for Congress and important web sites. Many came by and chatted. I mentioned to a few of them that we should get together and discuss political issues and especially to learn about local and state candidates, as I was beginning to be more informed about federal policies than those closer to home. I needed more input. I realized that force is in the numbers and we could accomplish more than I could alone. In February of this year, four of us finally met and decided that we should do something for the April 15th tax protest. In March we decided to start the Tea Party of Elko, and now we have grown to approximately thirty members, but it is only June. It was our desire to further the common good and the general welfare of the people, and to talk, inform, and take action on the issues and topics relevant to the Tea Party movement. We are a new group, learning as we go. We meet the first Wednesday of every month at 10 a.m., but we are acquiring new members regularly as they learn about us, so we may have to go to an evening meeting to accommodate those who work. We must grow the membership as we need volunteers who will work actively, leaders who will energetically organize the teams of volunteers to achieve our goals, and even observers—those who actively follow what we are doing and share our views and just spread the word. We need to become more visible and we need to become *the* channel that voters respect. I hope we can educate by having a class here on the Constitution, by having speakers, by marching in parades and tax-day protests and freedom rallies.

We are all agreed that this administration's agenda is detrimental to the pursuit of happiness by the American people, that it is leading us down a road to socialism or worse, and it is undermining the fiscal future of our children and grandchildren. We have to stop the spending. We must have state's rights and individual freedom to choose. We have to do something about the

47% of the American people who pay no income tax. We should abolish the income tax and adopt the Fair Tax. We need to abolish the fraud in Congress, do away with the pork, banish lobbyists forever, eliminate illegal immigration and put a moratorium on legal immigration until our country gets back onto firm fiscal ground. We need to send Congress a message, strong and clear by this November. Vote all incumbents out!

I retired after thirty years as a real estate broker, and have since written four books of poetry, all of which have been handbound, limited issues, self-published. The first one was later nationally published by Whispering Pine Press. So I have kept busy. Maybe that is what keeps me young.

Mary Bengtson

The Highlands Tea Party was born at an American Party of Florida meeting in March 2009. It was announced on Barry Foster's local talk radio show that at their next meeting they would be forming a Tea Party and it was open to the public. Although there was not a big turnout, after their old business they asked for people willing to volunteer to chair the Tea Party. There were four of us who raised our hands: myself, Lester Lob, Dick Fankhauser and Jim Skaggs. But there were others who were there and they came to Tea Party meetings from the beginning: Mike Barry, Barry Foster, Bill Youngman, Don Elwell and David and Candy Foxworth, who were willing to help and do whatever it took to get this movement going. With demanding schedules, Jim Skaggs and Dick Fankhauser could not make it to every meeting, and Les and I, with a desire to grow this movement as fast as we could, worked together and had meetings at Beef O'Brady's every Monday night. Les chaired the meetings, and with my background as an old school paralegal, I knew shorthand, so we agreed that I would be the unofficial and unelected secretary. We all had our jobs. Dick was the T-shirt, smock and 50/50 guy and still is today. Les became the information guy and still is today. I became the networking person, and obtained the Tea Party e-mail address and the web site which was maintained by Barry Foster until Verwayne Greenhoe took it over a few months ago. I generated the agendas, took and transcribed the minutes, and disbursed them to all the e-mail addresses we had gathered as more and more people started show up at our meetings. As a group we planned and coordinated events, and I drafted and disbursed flyers by e-mail and by hand, among a myriad of other things. We all helped each other—whenever we ran into problems or issues we did not know how to handle, there was always someone to step up to the plate and help. Whenever we needed entertainment and couldn't find enough, there was Barry Foster. And when a speaker had to cancel the morning of an event, there would always be a patriot to step up, such as Bill Landes. As I said, I was the networking person, but little did I know how beneficial my networking would be. We actually had people from The Tea Party Express at our event on the circle in November 2009 because of one of my contacts, William Gheen of ALIPAC in North Carolina (Americans for Legal Immigration PAC). William knew a few of the people touring with The Tea Party Express, knew they were ending their tour in Orlando at the time of our event in November, and contacted them. We had the Rivoli Revue and author Bill Owens at our rally, free of charge. Our keynote speaker that day was Robin Stublen, the Tea Party coordinator for Punta Gorda, Florida. I'll never forget him asking me, "Mary, how did you get them here?" and I told him the story. Our roots have always been grassroots. We discussed it immediately and decided we wanted to remain grassroots. With that decision came the discussion of incorporating. There are pros and cons to incorporating and after weighing them all we decided to remain grassroots. However, this particular Tea Party movement has been blessed. We have our own stage thanks to the carpentry skills of John Larsen, we have a sound system available to us whenever we need it through David Foxworth, and we have several microphone systems for our meetings paid for by donations. We have grown from a group of 9 or 10 to a group of about 450, with an average of 100 showing up at meetings, and between 200 and 300 showing up at events. That's huge for just a year and a few months in a small community. We have migrated from one meeting place to another to accommodate the growth. I hope it keeps growing. I personally do not believe that our movement's job will be done even if we get a majority of conservatives in Congress in 2010. We still have a lot of damage to undo, and I suppose it will be a process that I will not see to its fruition during my lifetime— that's how much damage has been done and how far we have strayed from the country our Founding Fathers intended for this great nation.

Ted Pearson

My introduction to the Tea Party has been fairly recent. I had become interested in the issue of global warming a couple years back and investigating the facts and reports from both sides of the debate landed me firmly into the "Deniers" camp. The ensuing scandals, exaggerations and continued black-box calculations from the IPCC, Al Gore and IPCC scientists made the case remarkably clear that there is a profitable scam behind the carbon offset community. When the US government ignored and excluded debate of the issue, I became more focused on the administration under Obama and found the Democratic Party to be almost completely involved in this charade. As I had been fighting against gun-control legislation at the state and federal levels for some time, it became apparent that the same deaf ear from the Democratic Caucus on this issue was also defying public opinion on man-made global warming.

When the debacle of Health Care came onto the scene, I became aware of the Tea Party. Working through this system of like-minded individuals has given me a sounding board to discuss issues outside of the contemptuous name-calling and race-baiting that I encountered on so many of the major media news pages. The contemplative debates I have found on conservative web sites have focused my research and understanding of both sides of the ideology, and as I learn more, I try to pass this information to others, receptive or not.

This is where I am today. I have a small group of patriots who I keep in contact with in a group called ArkLaMiss Tea Party—we are having our next event on July 3rd in Louisiana. We will be "Getting Out the Vote," handing out information packets provided by a foremost global warming fact publisher, serving refreshments/snacks and publicizing our Tea Party web page. I have great expectations for the Tea Party movement and the eventual removal of the progressive powers that currently have our country by the neck. We will bring this country back to the constitutional Republic it once was for the sake of our children so they can carry the torch forward.

Sylvia Curry

I am a proud patriot protestor (fifty-two years old). I attended my first ever protest at the local White Hall Arkansas Tea Party on April 15th with my 6 yr old granddaughter (I have the local newspaper article that quoted my granddaughters' sign and picture) I also attended the Tea Party bus tour stop at the capitol in little rock on Sept 4th where over 1000 people gathered to share information, pledge allegiance to the flag and sang America the Beautiful and God Bless America (there was little news coverage). Griff with Fox News skipped our Tea Party. After speaking to other "patriots" at the little rock rally and listening to the Tea Party speakers I decided to go to the 912 DC march. My family was very concerned about me attending a "political protest" (we don't do that in our family). I invited my prim and proper sister to go the 912 DC march; she agreed to accompany me so she could "keep me from getting into trouble." My fifty-three-year-old sister who lives in Louisiana was amazed at the amount of patriots, the range of age of the patriots and most of all surprised by the peaceful atmosphere. After the rally we went to dinner; two hours later I had the taxi drive by the capitol grounds so I could proudly show my sister how clean the streets and capitol grounds were left by the patriots. I explained to her we all bring garbage bags and cleanup the areas after a rally: "We don't need the government to clean up after us." You didn't see those pictures or that story covered by any media. I can proudly say my sister has proclaimed herself a "patriot" in the mission of reclaiming our "out-of-control government." The 912 DC march has been misrepresented by the mainstream media and the clueless politicians." The Fox News ad was correct making the statement that the "mainstream media" did not cover the story; they showed pictures which represented the 1% minority of kooky radicals but they did not spend enough time going into the crowd of the hundreds of thousands of patriot protesters to find out the real motivation of the patriots. They don't even know we refer to ourselves as patriots. Since we don't have a "leader" to speak for us, let me explain the "patriots" principles and beliefs, and what I understand as our mission. Go to the912project.com for the details of the 9 principles and 12 values "we patriots" hold true and the 5 pledges for Congress. Nancy Pelosi, Harry Reid and the offensive name-calling members of Congress should be afraid of the 912 patriots. Our mission is coded as "2010-2012-2014"; we patriots plan to vote all corrupt members of Congress out of office regardless of their political party. That will send the message "we the people" have "awakened" and are reclaiming our country." The corruption that has been going on in the Congress for the past fifteen years is unacceptable and we patriots are going to return our country to the principles the founders clearly stated in the four page Constitution. That's why we marched to the capitol and not to the White House. Now the intellectually superior commentators want to call us "racist"— here's a fact for the Ivy League educated out of touch talking heads—Congress consists of 86% whites and 8% blacks, according to the web site congress.org. We patriots follow the examples of Gandi and Martin Luther King in our journey of "peaceful protest." No one has mentioned the fact that there were zero arrests made on Saturday 9/12/09; maybe the reporters could find some of the police, firefighters, and paramedics on duty that day and ask their observations of the patriots' overall behavior.

I'm a proud army veteran—mother of two, grandmother of 3—hard working small business owner (twenty years), and taxpaying American patriot. My involvement in the 912 patriot movement is steadfast and ongoing. I pass out literature and information to anyone who asks and since I wear patriot shirts and pins every day I am asked daily what the Tea Party movement means. We patriots are truly a grassroots movement and our roots come from the wise founders of this great nation. Bill O'Reilly, Glenn Beck, Sean Hannity, Mark Levin, and other media outlets (conservative blogs and political web sites) have helped gather the information that has awakened American patriots. The other media has ignored the truth and we believe the mainstream media has turned a blind eye, which we believe makes them irrelevant and part of the problem going forward. Government corruption is part of everyday business in our nation's capitol and we patriots are on a mission to "take back our country." Glenn Beck, Sean Hannity, Mark Levin, Michelle Malkin, Sarah Palin, Mike Huckabee, and the other famous patriots who have helped give us the information about the corruption did not participate in the 912 DC march because "we the people" do not need to be led by anyone.

Glenn Beck is the author of The 912 Project—he reflected and identified the feelings of American patriotism on 9/12/01 which we patriots identify with today. All we patriots needed was a wakeup call—thank you Glenn Beck (FYI—I started watching Glenn on CNN) and God Bless America.

The 912 DC march was the beginning of the second American revolution.

TEA PARTY – THE AWAKENING

Sharon Calvert

Below is a little bit about my story and how the Tampa Tea Party group was started. I have been a member and now also an organizer of a Tampa Town hall political discussion group since Jan. 2004. We meet once a month for lively discussion and debate on politics and hot topics of the day. We also had an e-mail distribution list where we could send out and make comments on articles of interest outside the lamestream media. I've always been interested in politics. I have an older brother who has a Ph.D. in Political Science who is in academia, and is on the other side of the political spectrum than myself. Some of the folks in the town hall group were already part of activist organizations such as Fair Tax, Minutemen, and FreedomWorks. That started my involvement to take a more active role in political issues and campaigns.

I did not like all the spending President Bush did and in 2008 was *appalled* at TARP. TARP, I believe, started the undercurrent for what eventually became the Tea Party movement. The pork-laden trillion dollar stimulus package, written by the radical left Apollo Alliance, was the springboard for everyday citizens to stand up and oppose Obama's agenda. At that time, the Republican Party would not stand up to Obama/Pelosi/Reid and when we heard Santelli's rant it sparked an instantaneous combustion that We the People can and will *oppose* the insane spending and moral hazards that Obama/Pelosi/Reid were ramming through, even while a majority of Americans *opposed* the stimulus bill. I was petrified at what this spending would do to the livelihood of my children's future and I was bound and determined to fight for their future and the future of this great country. Santelli's rant lit the fire for a few of us to plan Tampa's first Tea Party on February 27, 2009 in front of Senator Nelson's office in downtown Tampa. We had no web site, we only had our own personal distribution lists and that of the town hall group and we had all of three days to make it happen. We contacted those we could and ended up with close to a hundred people who came and some who just spontaneously joined us. We gathered as many e-mail addresses as we could at that event and the next day we started the Tampa Tea Party group and began planning our next big rally of 2009, Tax Day Tea Party. We actually held two rallies that day in a downtown park and with no advertising but word of mouth, e-mails and distributing some flyers. We had 2,000+ people attend. We saw crap and tax pass the House and knew health care was going to be a center stage of the Obama agenda. We formed a coalition of grassroots organizations in Florida and began fighting Obamacare last summer. That coalition continues today and continues to grow as more and more groups are formed and leaders participate in our twice-a-week calls. Attending the 9/12 Taxpayer March on DC was one of the most inspiring events I have ever attended. Together with the Tampa 912 Project, we took about 200 people to DC from the Tampa Bay area. However, we were virtually ignored by the media *until* Scott Brown won in Massachusetts. We do get some media attention now. A 60 Minutes producer interviewed John and myself and we actually had their film crew on a bus we chartered down to Fort Myers for a Marco Rubio event. Unfortunately, the Tea Party segment on 60 Minutes never aired because we were such ordinary Americans getting involved in the political process. It has been so exciting and refreshing to see so many people of all ages who are for the first time becoming involved in politics, and who are truly concerned and frightened of the direction this Congress and administration is taking our country. We are now turning to GOTV for 2010. We realize that we must *change* who is representing us at all levels of government. We have also begun focusing on more local and state issues and races to gain successes as we move forward to change who represents us in Washington. As stated above, we are specifically taking on a one cent sales tax referendum that will be on the ballot in Hillsborough County to fund Light Rail and ensuring the public is informed about each candidate's position on this issue. This is a direct pocketbook issue and another reason and motivator to get folks to the polls. Members of our group have joined the local Republican Executive Committees as we intend to reform the party from within as we are not supportive now of a third party. I have a full time job and most of my spare time is spent organizing, coordinating and communicating Tampa Tea Party activities and information. I wake up each day knowing that it is one day closer to Election Day 2012 when Obama will be voted out of office. That and the future of my children help me stay focused at a time in our history I never thought I'd see.

Chris Lewis

I took a roundabout way back to the Tea Party. I ran for county council in 1998 after graduating college. I became the first person in Wicomico County Council history to get enough signatures to run on the ballot as unaffiliated. I learned a lot— enough to despise politics!

Fast forward to 2009. I now have two small businesses and four children, and about to write a check to the government for more money than I am able to keep for my family. Frustration does not go far enough. I have followed politics but stayed away because of what I learned when I ran for local office—the corruption, lies and power-hungry people involved. However, at this time, I could not stay out. I put the word out and people came and helped out and we had over 700 people show up in the pouring rain in our small town.

I thought the Tea Party would be a great way to get the voice out for regular people who were fed up of what was going on. And it did. There are a lot of people upset about the way things are going in this country, most of these people work for a living, and supply the government with the money it needs to grow.

I believe the Tea Party is just a step. The next step is for regular Americans to run for office and try to take us back to when government represented the people and knew the *people* were the lifeblood of this country, not the government. That is why I am throwing my hat in the ring once again for county council, even though I still despise how politics works. It is time for a change, and the people who attended the Tea Party all over the country, will help bring that change about, at the expense of career politicians!

David Hale

I couldn't believe what I had gotten myself into the morning of what I thought would be our one and only Tea Party. I was actually protesting something for the first time in my life and to boot I was leading the protest. For me, getting in front of a crowd wasn't the problem, it was the fear that was strangling me over how the government was going to react locally to us daring to speak out and defy them. We had started our Tea Party the year before with a Facebook page, a MySpace page and an e-mail address after a few pitchers of beer and hot wings, sick of George Bush and his government and the government in general with their high tax-and-spend policies. Our plan was to march down State Street over the State Street Bridge right in front of the register Star newspaper offices and throw tea into the river even if only the four of us showed up. Well, it fizzled out. None of us followed through. At least not until a year later when Rick Santelli called the nation to protest using the Tea Party metaphor which stopped being a metaphor when we had another meeting over beers and wings and decided to actually do it.

I sat there at the protest site of the coming Tea Party literally strangled by fear. Fear that the police would show up and break it up or worse yet that there would be violence. I had spoken with the Police Chief and made him aware. We had no permit and had no plans to get one. Would they throw me in jail? Who knew what could happen from there. It was raw fear as I sat there in my car two hours before our event in the drizzly 45 degree April weather. Then, one of my cofounders showed up.

There was something about that moment when I wasn't alone anymore, despite all the meetings we had conducted prior and all the press and e-mails and phone calls, there was something about the moment at that site that melted every fear and I knew that the reason why we had organized a Tea Party were legitimate and real and honorable and worthy.

We were not starting an upheaval. None of us knew exactly what to expect in that first protest where about 300 people showed up. Police were everywhere and they were actually supportive. It was unbelievable. It was a display of the strength of our institutions that they could be challenged even in such a small way and yet respond with such restraint. Many of us thought that first protest would be filled with baton-wielding police and tear gas, but they were not. They were filled with laughter and peaceful anger. People were shaking hands and trading e-mails and sharing notes. Every one of them picked up their tea—their litter and their hearts were left where they stood. We were protesting, participating in this event no matter what in order to make a statement. We were participating in the life of our nation with any statement, even if only silent in the rain and cold. Rest assured this was a grassroots movement and the media did something so extraordinarily different. They told the story. We all had expected the media to do what it could to keep it quiet despite the terrible frustration with this government, and I think it has been that way for quite some time before Obama with Obama magnifying it by a thousand in these past months he has been in office. The tone in America was vastly different than the frustration with the Clinton administration's shenanigans. We all wanted to make an impact this time around, immediate and large, and make it all better, and make all the "bad things" that were happening, like the trillion dollar bailout, go away.

We would not do that even with 15,000 Tea Parties in one day. We hope we will do that with diligence. We will do that if we remain vigilant until 2010 when we can make a difference at the polls. That is what we were all saying from the beginning. We all agreed that it would be a steady, consistent and constant effort unlike any we have ever undertaken and it will not be for those who quit running the race. One day was not going to change history this time. In 1773 it did. But one day and the next day and the next will in continuing to make that difference everyday to bring real change—the kind that brings us home to the Constitution.

Robert Maynard

I am a native Vermonter and have been involved in the pro-liberty movement for quite a while. My background is in engineering, but my hobby is the rise and fall of civilizations. I have noticed that when individual liberty gives way to an expansive role for government, civilizations tend to decline. An expansive role for government not only threatens individual liberty, but also crowds out the voluntary institutions of civil society. The concern that the US is following along the same path to decline has lead me to get involved in numerous groups over the past twenty to thirty years aimed at reigning in government to its constitutionally mandated role. It seemed that we were not getting very far and usually had the same crowd at our events. There was a concern about attracting new faces, but that concern rarely translated into success.

This was changed with the rise of the Tea Party movement. Suddenly there were people active who had not been politically active before. Many were concerned because they had young children and they feared for their children's future. These people came from all walks of life and most had full time jobs and children to take care of, but they found the time to become active and take a stand for liberty. The coordinator of our local Green Mountain Patriots is a working mom whose husband works as well. When she is not working or taking care of her children, she is organizing events to promote the cause of liberty. We are not incorporated, but our meetings and events attract members from a cross section of pro-liberty groups. When something needs to be done, a team of volunteers form to take the project on. A large section of the group actively participates in such activities.

Although we do have coordinators, the decision-making process is one of consent on the part of the group as a whole. Our group strongly buys into the notion of a "leaderless movement." I get the impression from talking with Tea Party activists from around the country that this is a notion which most are in favor of. The other point that we try to stress is that we are not simply reacting to policy which we disagree with, but actively promoting the principles of ordered liberty that made our country so free and prosperous. We believe that these are timeless principles which are relevant to the problems we face today.

Robert Cavanaugh

The Tea Party movement caught my interest on July 4, 2009, when I attended a local rally. I am a lifelong conservative and always voted Republican, but felt disenfranchised by the Republican Party after the years of reckless spending and growth of government during the G.W. Bush years. I was also shocked by the President Obama agenda which only offered promise of even greater spending and government growth. I wanted to get involved in any effort to turn the nation around and head it back to fiscal sanity and constitutional law. During the July 4th rally, I found that most attendees felt the same as I did. In August 2009, I became chairman of the local group which boasted 800+ members and I began plans to organize buses from eastern NC to attend the 912 March on Washington. We eventually sent five busloads to DC and our membership has since expanded to nearly 1,500 patriots. The 912 March on Washington was spectacular and all I had hoped it would be. As leader of our local group, I felt it important to set the example since we were encouraging people to run for public office. I entered my name in the Republican Primary for the US House of Representatives and campaigned against an eight-term congressman. With a very limited budget and no name recognition, I garnered 15% of the vote. I felt it very important to not use or abuse the Tea Party as a stepping-stone during the campaign. If I won, I wanted to win on my own merits as a candidate, not as a Tea Party leader/personality. I do plan to run again in 2012.

With the primary elections over with, our group decided to endorse and support the winners of the Republican primary elections. Our goal is to take back the federal legislature from the Democrats in order to halt their agenda and also to win the statehouse after 112 years of Democrat control. I have been working with the local Republican leadership to synchronize our efforts into one "machine."

Our April 15, 2010 local Tax Day rally drew a crowd of over 2,000 and we are currently planning an Independence Day Rally for July 3rd where we will also kick off the next campaign to enlist bus riders to the next 912 March on Washington.

I believe the Tea Party movement is having a huge impact on American politics and that its influence will continue to grow. I see my task as helping to keep the movement grow and maintaining the enthusiasm and commitment of current members. 2012 will be a pivotal year in American politics and the future of our country. We must succeed in moving the government to the right of center and begin restoration of constitutional law and rehabilitation of the nation's financial well being. Then begins the long arduous task of unwinding government dependence and restoring the principle of self-reliance among our people.

Randy Dye

Where do I start? My first involvement with any conservative movement started two years ago when I was sitting at home reading the local newspaper here in Chatham County, NC. I noticed an article that our county commissioners passed an I.C.E. Resolution that prevented any county agencies from contracting with I.C.E. law enforcement, thus declaring our county a safe haven for illegal immigration. Then, I was walking downtown Siler City (yes, the same one The Andy Griffith Show always talked about) and saw my Sheriff's photo on a Que Pasa News-paper on the front page about Chatham County being a safe haven!

After checking into the resolution, no public input was involved in this resolution! I obtained a copy of the BoC minutes and found the only input was from the ACLU, La Raza Council, El Pueblo group and a few county HR folks, which led to this news clip wral.com/news/local/politics/video/4625851/

That was my first encounter of a Tea Party movement activity as I researched on how I was no longer being represented by my elected politicians. The rest is history and yes I've spoken at many Tea Party protests since then. Check out our web site at ncfreedom.us.

Leon Howard

I am like most of the "silent majority" in that I sat on my butt and yelled at the TV because of the stupidity I would see being voted out by Congress but rarely even wrote a letter to my repre-sentative or senators. Apathy? I think that is probably what it was with most Americans. The summer of 2008, we had Barack Obama and John McCain running as the presidential candidates for the two majority parties; I, like many Americans, studied the candidates as best as I could by searching for information online but it was very difficult to get excited about either man—you had progressive and progressive-lite running and, according to your political leaning, you were going to be voting for the lesser of two evils! About standard since Ronald Reagan: The Dems have been taken over by the progressives and the GOP tries to act like conservative 'progressives' (an oxymoron if I have ever heard one). After looking at Obama's voting record in Illinois and the US Senate, the church he went to, and listened to several of his speeches, I concluded and told my friends that I "would hold my nose and vote for McCain because Obama scares the hell outta me!"

Then McCain picked Sarah Palin for VP! I had told my wife the night before he made the announcement that she would be the best pick he could make but I didn't think he'd have the guts to do it! Now, I felt I could vote for McCain without holding my nose! Then came TARP! I screamed at the TV: "*No! Let them fail! That is how the free market works!*" The Republicans in the House were not letting it pass; the Senate was balking at passage; McCain suspended his campaign to go to Washington "to save the day!" we thought. He reverted to his RINO ways and brokered a "deal" to pass it! Had he stood with the fiscal conservatives, we probably wouldn't have ever had this secular socialist in the White House and we wouldn't be in the financial mess we're in now and the Tea Party movement would have never got off the ground!

But I'm still home, frustrated, angry at D.C. (the "District of Criminals!") and hoping McCain/Palin will win but with McCain's capitulation on TARP, the media's hatred of Sarah Palin, and their obvious bias for Obama, the American people were saddled with one-party rule! In one way I was proud the nation had elected a black president but truly worried that the man was at best a socialist, at worst, a Marxist! He is sworn in, January 20th, 2009, and the first thing he wants is a "stimulus bill" to stimulate the economy! I am a student of history and I knew, as many Americans knew, that would lengthen the recession, not shorten it, so I began writing my representatives to tell them, "No! Leave it alone and it will correct itself in a few months!" They passed it anyway and immediately start talking about passing national health care legislation! I knew then that my worst fears about Obama were true! Michelle Malkin called for demonstrations in Arizona when Obama was there, calling them "Porkulus Parties"—I thought the signs were great but that wasn't something I could get my teeth into. It took Rick Santelli of CNBC to call for a Tea Party after hearing that Obama wanted to use some of the stimulus money to pay for people's mortgages to excite me to something I could see would be a national cry! It was a success in Chicago and I could feel the excitement through the TV—this was something to get off the couch for!

The following week, I started doing Google searches for "Tea Party" and had hundreds of hits but most were about the original Boston Tea Party; I did another search for Washington state Tea Party and found several hits. I went to each web site (there were three) and registered as the coordinator for the tri-cities, Southeastern Washington, looking for more like-minded Patriots and ideas on how to start our Tea Party. After I registered at the 3rd site, I received a confirmation e-mail from them saying Ross Burton had registered at the same time on their web site but they supplied us each with the others contact info so we could coordinate our efforts. Ross told me he registered as coordinator because like me, he was looking for others. However, because he worked full time, he would rather I be coordinator (I am a retired Nuclear Security Officer).

While he and I were still trying to figure out what to do next, I was notified by e-mail from the Washington Tea Party web site that Jerry Martin was looking for somebody to work with on the movement. I called for the three of us to meet and start our plans for a demonstration on April 15th, 2009; this was March 3rd, 2009, at the time of the meeting in Denny's in Richland. That first meeting was the blind leading the blind, trying to come up with plans that would attract others. We planned a follow-up meeting for a week later, again at Denny's and there were eight new folks that contacted us through the Washington Tea Party web site! I had advertising experience from twenty-eight years before this, so I volunteered to get the PSA advertising out there. We didn't have any money but knew we didn't need any money for a demonstration in a city park. Our problem would be attracting enough folks to make us newsworthy!

I sent out e-mails to all my friends telling them what we were doing. Ross and Jerry, plus the other eight, did the same thing and names started pouring in. By that Friday, we had compiled a list of 100! We thought we had died and gone to heaven. 100 of our friends were going to join us! The local 912 Project leader contacted me and wanted to know if his group could join us for the demonstration. I was ecstatic—that was 100 more! Now we were up to 200 in three weeks. I sent a fax out to every TV, radio, and newspaper in the area (there is only one newspaper!) announcing our upcoming Tax Day Tea Party and we called ourselves the Tri-Cities Tea Party. As the coordinator, I was interviewed by one of our news radio stations and the newspaper; Jerry Martin was interviewed by our other news radio station about what we were doing and why. We still hadn't figured out exactly what we were except that we were nonpartisan because both parties were to blame for where we were at. We the people were at fault for returning the same slugs back to Congress! We knew we had allowed the government to stop following the Constitution and knew, instinctively, that was a major part of our overall problem. We also knew that the federal government was spending too much and the debt they were accumulating was unsustainable. Knowing that, we somehow got through the interviews with good comments from friends who listened.

On April 14th, I showed up at the park where the demonstration was held the next day, just checking out where we would have the podium and mic set up and the newspaper caught me there. I asked if he was there checking out the park before the event and he told me he was there taking pictures for another story but he wanted to take a couple of pictures of me for the reporter who would be covering the story the next day. He asked about how many folks we were expecting and I told him I expected almost 500! I fudged the number somewhat but I did feel that would be close because others usually show for things like this that you don't know about. April 15th: The event was scheduled for 3 p.m. to 6 p.m. and we agreed to meet at the park by 2 p.m. to set things up. By 2:30 p.m., we had over 500 in the park; by the time the event started, we had over 1,200 in the park! We were floored!

I felt we actually had a chance to change the direction of the nation! The handmade signs hit all of the points I saw as the road to tyranny. We were not alone! Glenn Beck said that and I wanted to believe it but until I saw those faces and those signs, I had my doubts. Six of us had decided to give a ten minute speech on what we saw wrong with the direction the Congress and administration was taking us in and in-between speeches we decided to have open mic for protesters to vent their anger. We figured we would have to give our speech twice over the three hour period. Our last speaker didn't even give his speech! The open mic was absolutely eye-opening!

We had an open mic speaker from Canada, a naturalized American, warn us of the woes of socialized medicine; another from Great Britain with more horror stories of socialized medicine! Next we had a businessman from Romania; he had looked out his hotel window because of all the horn honking and he said he realized what this was from some news reports and decided to come rally with us. Again, this was an American *by choice*; he immigrated legally, took the required tests and naturalized. His message was an inspiration to me:

> Do you know why I am an American? It wasn't to make a lot of money; I could have gone to many other countries to make money; the richest man in the world is from Brazil! So no, it wasn't riches I was after! I became an American because I wanted *freedom*! We are the freest nation in the world and I can see us losing it day by day with this socialist in the White House!

We had other speakers on every subject you can think of that this Congress was trying to rush through and shove down our throats but the American from Romania was my favorite! Except my daughter-in-law—that's when I truly saw the light!

My son Rad and his wife, Sasha, were late in arriving; they got there about halfway through and Sasha had that deer in the headlight look about her—she was frightened! To understand that, you need to know that Sasha is from Uzbekistan; Russia conquered Uzbekistan in 1860! My son was explaining to her that here in America, we have the God-given right to protest our government's actions against us but it is not a concept she could grasp immediately. I, like most Americans, never gave it a thought but my son understood her fear because he went to Uzbekistan and saw the government corruption firsthand, so he consoled her. I was busy with other activities and left them for about thirty minutes; when I got back to where they were, Sasha was sitting at one of the tables we had set up in the park, *smiling.* She was holding a *"Taxed Enough Already"* sign and had two other signs propped up in front of the table and she said, "Dad, would you take my picture?" I said, "Sure, but why?" She said, "I want to send a picture home to my family because if I did this at home, I would be gone the next day and you would never know where!" I wept.

I realized *then* that there was more at stake than Obamacare, cap and trade, Wall Street bailouts, car company bailouts, and all the other financial disasters this administration and Congress had set as their goals; we were on the road to slavery and/or gulag-style indoctrination! My commitment level went up several notches at that point to find the new Congress and to flush the 535 already in Congress and start with true statesmen, citizen legislators as our Founding Fathers had envisioned! That has become the driving force to the Tea Parties: *Change the face of Congress in 2010!*

This is a fight for survival as a sovereign nation, the freest nation on earth, and to retain our *individual* God-given rights! Our individual God-given rights is why we are the freest nation ever; our founding fathers were free-thinking philosophers and applied individual rights where every other country spoke of collective rights! When we speak as a collective, we have just put the government above the people! And that is what this administration and Congress are attempting to do. "Party" is not the answer because the progressives have infested both parties; "progressives" is the new name for Marxism, socialism and communism! As Clint Didier, the man I hope will replace Patty Murray in the Senate this year said, "Both parties have been taking us down this road together; the only question, right now, is do we want to go over the cliff at 85 miles per hour or 45 miles per hour?" Obviously, he's not the party favorite—he's running as a Republican but he takes his marching orders from the people; the party doesn't like that, so they're running a RINO against him in the primary election in August! Hopefully, the people will prevail but this one race isn't the litmus test for freedom because Washington state has been in the progressives' hands for a long time. It has taken the progressives over 100 years to get us to this point so 2010 is only the first step back from the brink.

I am almost sixty-eight years old; the majority of the Tea Party members are retirees, or soon to be retirees. Herein lies our biggest challenge: Attracting young people to the cause of freedom! It is my generation's fault that young people don't know what our Founding Fathers had in mind for the nation; we just *assumed* they knew about the history of our founding documents. The "progressives"—I hate that term! There is nothing "progressive" about these Marxists! Everything they want to do to us has been done countless times in countless nations and failed every time! But they refuse to accept countless failures as failure! "Progressive?" No! "Regressive" fits them much better! The Regressives slowly took over our education system and have altered and erased the history books to reflect their philosophy and we allowed them to do it. Scrubbed clean is the brutality of Stalin and Mao! Communist philosophy is all sunshine and roses—capitalism is hallmarked by greed and is bad. The Declaration of Independence isn't included as a founding document and the Constitution is referred to as "out of date," "dated," or "almost irrelevant" to modern times!

Herein lies our path back to freedom and individual rights: *Education!* We are sponsoring classes on our founding documents. Sound boring? It would be if history was made boring but with the right instructor(s), the history of our founding documents stirs the rebel in all of us; the same is true of our young people. We tricked our seventeen-year-old granddaughter into attending an NCCS Constitutional Seminar. The instructor? Earl Taylor, trained by W. Cleon Skousen, author of *The 5000 Year Leap*! After an eight hour seminar with a short break for lunch, My granddaughter remarked: "Wow! I wish he was one of my teachers!" She's not a constitutionalist yet but she wants to know more.

Our Tea Party group is very active to elect a new Congress: We have held one Senatorial Forum for the six Republicans who were running in March (It was said to be the best forum they had appeared in because of the Town Hall format); we are vetting candidates who want the Tea Party stamp of approval (We cannot endorse but we can put results of vetting on our web site and can show that Candidate X refused to be vetted); we have held over ten "Meet and Greets" for candidates for county, state and federal offices up for election. We are now arranging another Senatorial Forum for the three remaining candidates wanting to run against Patty Murray, to be held prior to the August primary. Most of our group is helping candidates by door-belling, putting up yard signs, and donating money towards their campaign.

I have taken on the issue of incumbency in our county. Getting the incumbent out of office is a task by itself: The incumbent has name recognition and a track record. It can be a formidable task, so our challenge is to try to level the playing field. The Benton County Auditor's up for reelection and I am stirring the pot over the envelopes and postage being used to get the ballots to the voters. Uh, what? The auditor's name is on the ballot envelopes; the envelope sent that has the ballot in it and the return envelope to send it back to the auditor's office, *plus* the postage to send the ballots out—over $13,000.00! Could be considered a nice Taxpayer Funded "donation" for the auditor's reelection! We'll have to wait and see how this one plays out. But that is another area the Tea Party needs to get involved in fighting—corruption! I won't be the belle of the ball over this one because the incumbent is a Republican and I was a delegate to the Republican State Convention. Oh, well!

I am in very good health and if that continues, I will stay deeply involved in the Tea Party movement until after the 2012 elections, but then I promised my wife of forty-seven years I would step back and let somebody else continue to take our country back. We have to remain committed and retake a little at a time, retaining what we take until we have our "camel back in the tent!" We have to remain as tenacious as the regressives have been for 100 years! They're getting tired and frustrated; they're sooooo close to attaining their goal of enslavement to the one-world government and they seem to be on hold! They have no idea who they are dealing with!

Our Founding Fathers gave us individual liberties and the responsibilities that go with those liberties! It is up to us to use those boxes they enshrined for us: the soap box, the ballot box and the ammo box! We've been using our soap box effectively and we are about to use our ballot box to start retaking America, which means there will be no need for the "box of last resort," the ammo box! But, if violence comes, it will come from the frustration of the Left—it will come from the regressives! For that, always "Keep Your Powder Dry!"

Patrick Simon

Back during '08 I was completely dedicated to getting Obama in office. He had me in a trance of what I thought was a great future for America. But as he took office I started to see how much he didn't care, how much he was destroying the American ideals that generations have fought and died for. I always enjoyed the idea that there was no other country like America, in the fact that we have a government that doesn't interfere with the everyday lives of the people. People are the foundation of America—we control what goes on, we tell Washington what to do, but it seems like Washington doesn't get it. I joined the Tea Party because I wanted a voice, I felt that the government "didn't get it." They didn't understand if we don't want government-controlled health care then don't force it on us!

Pat Berg

I've organized a few Tea Party rallies here, but there is no organized Tea Party. I only became politically active when Obama got elected. I realized early on that he was a danger to our country. I knew that I could not sit by and just complain about it. I had to take some action. I organized a small group of conservative women and we decided to become activists. We do all we can to support conservative candidates and causes. Hence, the Tea Party rallies. We get more and more people every time—last time over 100. That's a major accomplishment on a small island of 60,000 dominated by liberals at all levels of government.

Pam Burkardt

I got involved because no one else in our town was doing anything but complaining. We are in a pretty unique geographic location: Montgomery, Prattville (where I live) and Wetumpka are shaped like a Mickey Mouse head. Montgomery had a fantastic April 15 Tea Party last year and Wetumpka was gearing up to do a lot of fantastic things (which they have done, by the way) and we did nothing. I decided if no one else was going to do it, I would step forward and see what kind of trouble I could get into. Turns out I could make a lot of trouble!

We have the distinct honor of living in the 4th most corrupt state in the union. This is a concept I have difficulties with, being raised in North Dakota and marrying into the military. I know there are crooks in ND, and I know there is a lot of corruption in the AF, but I was sheltered from most of it. Here in Alabama, we have voter fraud, graft, bribery—you name it, we have it at least once. Through our patriot group, we were able to help root out some of the stuff in our county. The Tea Parties across the state were also able to work in conjunction with each other during the thankfully short legislative session, with some surprising results. The biggest coup we had was to push through what was considered a dead bill on opting out of Obamacare—the unconstitutional health care bill. Three of us sat in the gallery of the Senate and reported daily by e-mail and in real time via Twitter on what was happening at that time. One of the Tea Party groups held a Tea Party during the "debate" on the bill, and scared the bejeebers out of the left-leaning Republicans and all the white Democrats in the Senate. When the vote came down, the only people who voted against the opt-out bill were the eight members of the black caucus. We have found out since then that the people we scared the most at the state House were not Democrats, but Republicans. Go figure. If only we could do that to the RNC!

I feel I have failed my three daughters in this one area. I have taught them to be unfailingly polite, and to shut their mouths if they don't agree. Part of it is my upbringing (Emily Post and Scandinavian heritage), and part of it is military. I hope that they are learning by my actions that you can still be polite in a challenge, and also how to fight for their state, their country, and their lives. Their dad fought for them for twenty-eight years. Now it's their turn to pick up the standard and go forward.

Our plans in the near future involve examining the actions of the local and state elected officials and exposing wrong actions where we find them. We will be joining another group close to us (Birmingham) since they are already incorporated and have a web site. In the forteen months I've been working in our group, we have had a pretty dismal turnout. I now have a person involved who is determined on growing the group large enough for jobs to be delegated, which will be nice, but I plan on keeping my original patriot group separate from the new one. We will be the ninja/guerilla wing.

TEA PARTY LEADERS

Gregg Nicholl

In the fall of 2008 I was in my third semester at Cincinnati Bible Seminary located in Cincinnati, Ohio. The economy in this area was in an accelerated spiral and it was becoming increasingly difficult to balance work and school as I was having to work very erratic hours in order to achieve a whole week's standard wages. I had a sense that something was very wrong, not only with the economy but with our nation as a whole. TARP and the bailout of selected industries seemed to go against the grain of common sense and the American Way.

I completed that last semester in February. About this time, President Obama was beginning to push for more. I became even more deeply concerned for the future of this nation and my children. There was a sense that the black clouds of America's demise were gathering on the horizon, looming ever larger. Then I saw an announcement for a Cincinnati Tea Party to be held on Fountain Square in downtown Cincinnati, March 15th. I knew I had to be there. I crafted some signs for my twelve-year-old son and myself and headed down. It was amazing. Just regular folks, friendly folks, all there sharing the same concern. There were families, retirees, college students, black, white, Hispanic and Asian people. One of the people who spoke was Harald Zieger who had escaped from East Germany during the height of the Cold War. His speech was especially stirring as he had lived under tyranny and now he saw it creeping at America's doorstep. His appreciation for freedom was refreshing and an indictment to the rest of us Americans who had for far too long taken our liberty for granted.

Afterwards, I was infuriated by local news agencies that stated that they did not cover the event because they feared for their reporter's safety! This was so far from the truth. I wrote the station manger of a local media outlet and stated sarcastically, "Yes, your reporters had a good reason to fear—there were little old ladies, families with children being pulled in little red wagons, clean-cut college students, and just average folks that could very well be your neighbors." To my surprise, I received an obscenity-laced letter from the station manager basically stating that I had no idea what I was talking about and that my knowledge of the profession was sorely lacking. I knew right then we had a bigger problem than I could have ever imagined in America.

Attendance at many events and protests followed—Bob Basso at New Richmond, protest of Obamacare outside of Channel 9 in Cincinnati, the Dayton Tea Party. Soon, I heard that local groups were forming and I desperately sought to join a local group, but could not find one. Then, I attended the July 4th rally sponsored by the Dayton Tea Party and someone handed me a pamphlet advertising leadership training for local groups. I resolved to go.

The leaders training seminar was like being among friends even though you'd never met these folks before. The training covered a broad spectrum of issues from starting a group, what precisely your group should do, and things to avoid. On July 29th, 2009, I reserved a room at the local library and held the first meeting. I had received some referrals from both the Dayton and Cincinnati Tea Parties and worked the phones the week prior to the meeting inviting people to attend the initial meeting of the Middletown Tea Party. I was way out of my comfort zone, but a sense of urgency drove me through the plastic barrier of my fear. Fifteen people showed up for that first meeting.

The challenges have been exceedingly difficult here in Middletown. We are not welcome. This is a strong union town (i.e. pro-Obama); the sole major industry is AK Steel, a huge steel mill. At local events we have been harassed, told to leave by police who stated that event organizers "Do not want you here," and have had bureaucratic roadblocks thrown in the path of every advance. But still we have persisted.

Most troubling to me has been the reaction of people who I thought were my friends from church. I lost many due to my involvement with the Tea Party movement. Their thinking was that I needed to be dedicating my life solely to the cause of Christ; that basically, I needed to be behind the closed doors of the local sanctuary praying for Jesus' swift return. I reminded them that Jesus stated that we need to be in the world but not of the world. But this raised only consternation on their part. I was reminded of Dietrich Bonhoeffer's indictment of the German church during the 1930s. They took a similar tact, expecting that the government would leave them alone as long as they turned a blind eye and a deaf ear to the rise of despotism and turned their heads as their friends and neighbors were carted off. What kind of morality is based on self-focus and preservation at the cost of freedom and liberty for all human beings? (I'm reminded of the NRA's recent exemption as part of the Disclose Act—history repeats itself and in the end the NRA will suffer at the hand of an ever-encroaching, ever-expanding government). Nonetheless, people who I thought were my friends and co-workers shunned me.

Nancy Davis

It isn't about the party or the politics; It is about the *principle* of the thing! When I was growing up my father was very verbal about the local "good ole boys" and the politicians in general. Crooks and cheats! You don't get into politics unless you are filthy rich or want to be filthy rich. Little did I realize then that without knowing the history of something and educating yourself about events it's impossible to know what is going on.

At eighteen, I registered to vote. Nobody had to ask me if I wanted to register, made it easy by including it in driver's license renewals or even strived to convince me that my vote might make the difference in an election.

It was my right as given in the Constitution and at that age, it was a part of becoming a responsible adult. After all, the history courses taught in school covered "unalienable rights" and what that really means. We had assemblies every morning with the Pledge of Allegiance and a prayer to God. We had clubs in school that stressed family values, right and wrong, the importance of caring about yourself and your ability to make of yourself whatever you wanted, no matter what your circumstances. The government was the last place you expected to get help. Welfare and "social justice" were not acceptable. The Constitution ruled and children were taught what freedom meant.

Back then, neighbors cared, churches taught, schools educated and parents molded their children! What happened? What happened is I realized that America is still basically the same; we have simply been bought by the charisma and hype of politics. The news used to report facts without prejudice or politics. Now they present a media circus to divert your attention away from the direction politicians are taking America.

And this is the realization that hit me and made me determined to do something to attract our youth and make the age old principles of my childhood become the new facts of life for today's youth. It isn't about the politics, *it is about the principles!* The fear of the progressive movement is that without that "media circus," American's will remember the good old days, their parents, their teachers, the joy of really winning, and the Sunday's spent in church. So the mission is to destroy and reshape the American dream—but the *change* is empty!

So, I became a Tea Bagger and proudly wear the title of conservative. I will do my part to restore America, without apology.

Molly Sechrest

In a thumbnail sketch, I started out my adulthood as a left-wing hippie due to various circumstances of my childhood and the coinciding of my coming of age with the decided lurch of our country to the Left. While living as a college dropout in Haight-Ashbury in the late 1960s and early 1970s, I became more and more disenchanted with my life and lifestyle, though I hadn't a clue as to what to do about it. I appealed to a friend who gave me Ayn Rand's *Atlas Shrugged*. I was very impressed with the ideas in it and over the course of several years, I made an about-face. I learned that precisely the thing I had been taught to hate—American capitalism—was in fact the most moral and benevolent system ever developed.

Skipping ahead several decades, I retired early from a career developing software mainly for the New York Stock Exchange but also for other Wall Street firms. I married a maverick, libertarian college professor in West Texas and moved to Alpine, TX.

The first time I heard about the Tea Party movement was soon after Rick Santelli's historic outburst on the floor of the Chicago Mercantile Exchange (Wikipedia tells me this was February 19, 2009). I was watching CNBC that morning and was overjoyed to see a TV personality such as Santelli protest loudly against the overreach of the government. I soon heard that people were indeed doing what he recommended—staging Tea Parties. For several years, I had been engaged in teaching myself American History. I read biographies of many of the Founding Fathers, studied the intellectual history of pre-Revolutionary America, the foundations of the Constitution, and so forth. Consequently, of course, the notion of linking a modern protest to the protests of our nation's founders was (and is) particularly exciting and meaningful.

Mike Armstrong

Prior to beginning my college education, my understanding of politics in America went little beyond mainstream media sound bites and partisan attacks. My experiences as a student at Clarion University, however, reshaped my philosophy of government and encouraged me to become an active participant in our movement.

For as long as I can remember, I had always considered myself a Republican. I grew up in a heavily Republican area in western Pennsylvania and my grandparents were even local GOP committee members. When I left for school, it only seemed natural that I join the College Republicans. My mastery of public policy was limited and my values were inconsistent. Nevertheless, my fervor for campaign work allowed me to gain favor within the group and I was elected president in my sophomore year. I became more and more involved, eventually climbing the ladder of leadership in our county GOP to the position of Vice Chairman. I realized then that I had caught the political bug and loved my new role on campus as "Mr. Republican." I had finally found my niche. In 2008, I took on a new role that would challenge my values and political philosophy. My pastor, Rev. Keith Richardson, made the decision to run for Congress and I signed on immediately as his campaign manager. As I got to know him, I began to understand the logic behind his political convictions. For the first time in my life, politics wasn't about winning elections and attacking opponents. It was about values. My eyes were opened to a government that over-taxed, over-spent, and over-regulated its people and their businesses. I saw how our civil liberties had simply eroded before our eyes and yet Americans were doing nothing. I became critical of Republicans as well as Democrats who had led our country down its path of unsustainability.

Following the election, I returned to my place in the Republican Party only to find myself now out of place. Discontent with Senator Arlen Specter (then a Republican) and other differences with the GOP led our College Republicans to change their name to the College Conservatives. I too left the GOP and became chairman of the new student organization. The successes of the group were remarkable, from hosting a health care Town Hall with our congressman to beginning the school's first conservative newsletter. In April 2010, we organized the county's first Tea Party rally with the help of a number of local patriots. Although we originally anticipated a small event, more than 300 concerned citizens showed up to voice their concern for our country and the direction of our government. Seeing so many willing to come out and show their support was such an encouragement for me. From the success of the rally, we built an organization for local Tea Party activists and continue to plan events and initiatives to educate others and return our government to its limited scope, fiscal responsibility, and Constitutional roots. The future of our group and our movement has never looked brighter.

Mike Sabot

Little background: up until two years ago, I've been an Independent all my life, never publicly supported a candidate, never donated a penny to any political party or candidate. Most of my involvement was in the late '60s while in HS, attending a couple of protests against the Vietnam War but then joining the Army in 1970 for the educational benefits. I served seven years and was qualified as a Vietnamese and Spanish interpreter. I worked for the Army Security Agency, Engineers, MI and Signal Corp. Married twice—first time to a lady from Mexico for eight years, went though the immigration process, took two years to get the green card. Two stepdaughters and one son from that union. That son, currently serving in the Army, has been to Iraq twice with a 3rd tour scheduled later this year. Married the second time around and I've been married to her for thirty years this August.

My wife was the one who woke me up to what was happening, starting with TARP. We got upset with the bailout and got more upset with the stimulus, knowing it would not do what they said it would. Our congressman would not listen. We could not afford it. I heard about the first Tea Party, and my wife and I organized a Tax Day Tea Party in Leesburg, GA, population 2,600. I paid for it out-of-pocket—cost us about $700. The local newspaper Lee County Ledger supported us. The editor later told me that he expected five people to show up—fifty would have been a big crowd. We held it on the County Court House Steps. We had over 500 come out that day! Coverage by local TV stations. I joined the Tea Party Patriots and the Georgia Tea Party Patriots when they formed. We collected over 4,000 tea tags. Hand delivered to GA Senator Isakson at the 2nd Congressional Dinner at the 2nd Congressional Convention.

With the view that the GOP had lost its way, we joined to work to bring it back to its roots from the ground on up. I became a precinct chair at the April county convention; my wife and I were delegates at the district and state conventions. I was elected to the state committee. My wife is currently serving as the precinct chair and I as the county vice-chair. Our county GOP is now a very pro-Tea Party organization. We are currently working to do the same at the district level, by reactivating counties with pro-Tea Party groups ruining the county GOP.

We then worked with like-minded people from two neighboring counties to hold a 4th of July Tea Party in Plains GA. With the national coverage on Tea Party groups so poor and disdain from our Democratic congressman I was getting frustrated and wanted to do more. Our congressman has been in office for eighteen years and I noticed that he only got good press from the TV and newspapers. I made a vow to change that and see him voted out this year. I organized protests in front of his main district office, and anywhere he showed in the district we were there. Protests spread to the other two district offices organized by other local Tea Party groups. At his local fundraisers we showed—at some we were only a handful of people, at others we had 200 or more. At the state chamber of commerce meeting he was a speaker, and we had more than 100 protesters show up. Most of the Republican elected officials present and the Republican candidates running for office came out to speak with us. At each protest we held, the newspapers and TV crews came out. The coverage by them got more and more savable as time went on.

As the health care debate went on, we held our own town hall. Our congressman sent a representative, but none of the people there supported it. We were promised a reply to the newspapers that never came. He held his own town hall meetings, and in each one the majority were against the health care legislation. *He still voted for it.* He returned to the district for a victory celebration at each district office. When we found out about it after the first one, we had protesters at the second and he canceled the third.

We did the same with cap and trade—we overloaded his DC office with calls. A staffer told me that the calls were a 100 to 1 against, but *he voted for it.* His last newsletter to the district now says his vote was a mistake and he would never vote for the same bill again.

We don't believe him. The protests have stopped and we are now focused on working with the candidates against him, all the various groups. I write weekly letters to the editor and have them published in various newspapers. My wife and I have for the first time given money to a local candidate. We have a candidate that for the first time has been able to raise money against our congressman. He has been able to raise over $250,000 all from local individuals while our Congressman has pulled in $400,000 mostly from PAC and out-of-district people. We feel this is our only chance to defeat a man who over the last two years went from a moderate Democrat to a far-left liberal supporter of Nancy Pelosi almost 100% of the time in votes. Because of the demographics of the district makeup, this will be our only chance or he'll be in office until he retires. He still doesn't listen and when he replies to our faxes, our e-mails, and our letters, it's just his form letter reply. If he doesn't have a stock reply then there is none.

TEA PARTY – THE AWAKENING

Joan Sterling

A year ago or so I got hooked watching Fox News. To be honest, I didn't understand most of what they were saying mainly due to ignoring what was going on in government. I did like all the people who were on the cable network—Bill O'Reilly, Glenn Beck and Sean Hannity were my favorites. I started listening to Glenn everyday and I felt that I was getting an hour of a history class. I learned more from him about our history and government than I did when I was in school. The things I was learning were becoming very real and very scary to me. So, I went looking for a group that I wanted to join and I couldn't find one that I thought fit me. The ones that did, didn't seem to be doing anything. So I thought about my children and my grandchildren and I wanted them to know that I was part of making a difference for them to live a better life, and for all people to have a better life, so I started the South King County Tea Party. We're a hardworking group who continues to watch our politicians in office, because we want our country back!!

John McKenna

My story is very simple. I love America.

Joni Schmidt

With horror and a sinking feeling in the pit of my stomach, I awoke on November 5, 2008, to the news that Barack Obama had won the presidency of our beloved country. There were so many questions about his life that yet needed to be answered, but no one in a position of authority was interested in pursuing them. TARP had already piqued my interest in putting our elected officials on notice, and now all the bailouts, stimulus packages, etc. sent me over the edge! I have children and grandchildren! I want them to have the same opportunities to succeed in this nation of freedom as I had, if not more. OK Joni, I thought, it's time to finally get out there and make your voice heard—really heard.

Calling your representative obviously doesn't work, so we need to start mobilizing and taking to the streets with our message of fiscal conservatism and constitutional government. It's "We the People," after all. Will they listen if millions of us speak up at once?

I heard Rick Santelli's rant about hosting a Chicago Tea Party, and shortly after that, my brother heard about a group who was organizing Tea Parties all over the country on February 27, 2009. That was my chance. I had never done anything like this before, so I needed a support group—and some ideas! After daily organizing calls, I reserved Alamo Plaza and sent invitations to my distribution list with instructions to pass on to their lists. I packed my tea bags, the "Big Black Hole" (a tub in which to toss the tea bags), my portable CD player, Patriotic CD, and signs, and joined with about thirty other Texans to show my displeasure at the blatant dismantling of our Constitution by the leftists.

We had so much fun, we wondered why we hadn't done that before! Why did we just rely on phone calls and e-mails, instead of showing our congressman what we wanted? After the February 27th Tea Party, I turned the San Antonio Tea Party organization over to Robin Juhl to run, and I began an organization closer to home: The Boerne Tea Party Patriots. Will we make a difference? Only time will tell … *November's coming*, after all!

Kathy Abram

The reason I started the Lebanon 912 Project was not because we had a black man as president, despite what my critics say. I had slowly become more politically aware over the past decade and saw actions being taken by our government that did not feel right to me. During those years I couldn't tell you why precisely certain bills that were passed through were wrong, but I knew in my gut that the United States was headed in the wrong direction.

It began with President George W. Bush and Medicare Part D. I found it preposterous that a self-described "compassionate conservative" would allow an even larger entitlement to a broken system. It was against logic and common sense. Yet what could I do to stop it? Nothing. Next we saw TARP coming down the line. Yet again, what was going on? These programs were against the GOP's platform.

The 2008 election year was upon us soon enough. I realized that the Republican Party was no longer the party I believed in as John McCain was chosen as our nominee for president. Conservatives were faced with a "lesser of two evils" voting year for president. I decided to vote for Sarah Palin instead of the old guy in hopes that one day she would be president. But on election day we were faced with a new progressive president. I could have cared less about the color of his skin. It was the content of his character and his twenty-year affiliation with Reverend Jeremiah Wright's church. President Obama's friends were not of the same cloth that I knew. These were radicals and progressives of the highest degree. They were not Democrats. I knew in my gut that the Democrat party had been taken over, just as the Republican Party had been moderated by the likes of Senator Arlen Specter and his ilk.

I had been a fan of Rush Limbaugh, Glenn Beck, and Sean Hannity over the past few years. I didn't agree with everything they said, but I have always believed that if I agree with someone over 50% of the time then I am in good company. I did my own research when time allowed and the topic deemed it necessary. Glenn Beck had been the one I listened to most often in the morning. His entertaining style with moral fibers was enlightening to me. He didn't care what people thought. Glenn spoke of what he believed in no matter what the reaction was.

One day, Glenn had a caller on his radio show who felt like turning off the TV and radio. This man couldn't take it anymore. He felt alone as a conservative. This call was pivotal to this nation in my mind. Glenn told the caller that he would prove to him that he was not alone. "There are more of us than there are of them," Glenn implored. He soon showed us he was right—there was no reason for us to hide in the shadows anymore.

Soon Glenn announced a TV special he was going to air on Fox News Channel. It was called "We Surround Them." Fans were asked to gather their friends and families to watch this special. I took this to heart. I went online to see if anyone was holding a viewing party in my county. No one had set up anything. I kept checking for a few days ... still nothing. I couldn't handle it anymore and decided to have a viewing party at my home. I invited our friends and asked them to spread the word. Before I knew it there were too many people to accommodate in my home. The next step was to find a bigger venue. I stopped by a local pub and reserved a room with two large flat screen TVs. Soon I posted it online so others could join us.

The night of the show, I was a bundle of nerves. I wasn't sure if anyone would come. But soon my fears were allayed. By the time the show began we had forty-five conservative friends and strangers joining together to watch the program. As the show drew to a close I wasn't sure what we were to do next. He gave us no direction. I was no leader, but I knew something had to be done. I collected names, phone numbers and e-mail addresses just in case.

Glenn soon answered the call and developed the 912 Project platform. He would not be its leader but merely wanted to provide a list of values and principles that could easily guide us on how to proceed. I found that these values and principles resonated with me. They made sense and they gave power to the individual, not the government. This is what we needed. With this, the Lebanon 912 Project was born.

We now have over 300 members in our town. Our first major action was to have reformers run for the Republican committee.

I was so proud to see us nearly take over half of the committee. The GOP needs to return to its principles as well. We cannot make change happen as armchair activists, we need to get our hands dirty. We have only just begun, but I am proud to be a part of this movement.

Mary Anne Cole

In March of 2009 I saw several instances of Tea Parties and decided that I would plan one for Dekalb County. I called and asked for the courthouse steps. Friends joined and we took care of the sound, paper, speakers and singers. Some friends refused and acted as if I were crazy. I kept trying and a lady called and said that she would do flyers and distribute them just when I wanted to give up. After only a few weeks of planning we assembled with around 200 in front of the Dekalb County courthouse. I was the most surprised person there. I asked for different cities in the area and was surprised to know those representing them and many in NE Alabama. It was the first rally in NE Alabama, I learned at a later time. The Police Chief was there and came over to me during the first speaker and said he was calling in patrol cars to clear the way for us to march to Dye Creek and throw the tea in. I was amazed as they closed the main street and all the cars had to wait as we marched with the flag in the front. Two papers covered the event.

For our second rally, on May 1st, I invited all the candidates running in the June 1st primary. It was a hassle! First they could come and then they couldn't. At the event I had ten running for office, both Democrat and Republican. I was able to get a local quartet which is quite good to give their time plus the National Anthem again sung by the twelve year old. The Pledge by the Vietnam Vet and prayer by a local pastor. No coverage by one paper but good coverage in the other. I actually wrote the article and the best line was this: "This is for Disillusioned Democrats, Irate Independents and Rapacious Republicans: a Tea Party for All!"

Some Republicans refused to come because I invited the Democrats, but how better to decide how to vote than to see them side by side?

Lisa Douglas

I, like many among us today, were quite busy with my own life. I was/am raising a family of five children, going to college to receive a BA in Psychology, tending to the home, meals, laundry, husband and children. I was always active within the local school district. I was the PTO President for three years and served as a trustee on the Board of Education. Life was good, I was happy. I took a college class on American History. I absolutely loved it. In turn, I switched majors to American History and have enjoyed the last two years learning more than I thought possible about America, about our Founders, and about the trials, tribulations and sacrifices that so many before us endured to ensure future citizens a great country. Regular people doing great and heroic things—it was truly inspiring and gave me a sense of what the words "proud to be an American" really meant. At the same time I took a class entitled Media Bias. Honestly, I rarely read a paper or watched the news. I didn't have time and more to the point I didn't have an interest. I always voted, but my vote was based upon an uneducated opinion, my own. For the class I had to read numerous newspapers from across the globe to discover how the same story was skewed to their reader base. Needless to say, it was an eye opener. I'm embarrassed to say this but for the first time in my life I began to pay attention to politics, and I served in the USN! Ridiculous, I know, but it's the truth. The more I read, the more I delved into news stories, the more I didn't like what I was beginning to see.

Early in October, I had had enough and felt as if I was going to explode so I started a blog for women. Originally the name of it was Hudson Valley Patriot Moms. About two weeks into blogging I had more men than women joining my blog group so the name was changed to Hudson Valley Patriots. I start the blog to get the truth out that mainstream media was ignoring or at best failing to report accurately. I read everything, I watched everything, and I saw the major problems on both sides of the fence. It's not a Republican/Democrat issue, it's a nonpartisan issue and both sides have dirty hands. I felt compelled to shed light on that main point; I needed to make people aware of what was at stake; I worked to get factual information into my reader's hands. Since October, not only has my group grown but my blog turned into a morning newsletter filled with need-to-know information that is e-mailed to 1,027 (to date) voters six days a week.

I believe in fiscal responsibility, free markets and above all, a constitutionally limited government. My group's core values are derived from the Declaration of Independence, the Constitution of the United States of America and the Bill of Rights, as explained in the Federalist Papers. I believe it is my duty to stand with the founders and that is what keeps me inspired to get up at 5 a.m. each day to read everything I can and get pertinent information into my reader's hands. The truth shall set us free and that line is what motivated me from the get-go and continues to provide the necessary motivation to keep going, keep educating the sleepers among us, as I can relate to their bliss in knowing of nothing that will one day affect them in more ways than I can count. While I long for those "ignorance is bliss" days, I can never go back—my country and my children's future means too much to me.

Maureen Sims

My interest in politics began as a youngster, as my father was very enthused about being an American citizen. He was born in Ireland, went to China as a missionary, and met my mother. She was a missionary kid from England. The Japanese bombings forced them to leave in 1940, and my mother's entire family was placed in concentration camps in China. Fortunately, my parent's ship took them to California! In our family, tears were shed when we saw "Old Glory," and my father constantly spoke of our liberties and appreciation for the Judeo-Christian values on which our country was founded. It all came together for me when my husband served in Vietnam. It was then that I realized, not everyone had the same convictions about fighting for our country and sacrificing our lives for the liberty of others. Since then, we have raised four sons, one served in the US Navy, another is a firefighter. About twenty years ago, I heard Rush Limbaugh on the radio and found someone else was actually expressing the very thoughts that I had (ditto).

No one else was talking about it. We were all busy, raising our families, working and going to church. Upon approaching Tax Day, 2009, I was frustrated because there was no rally near our town where a Tea Party gathering was happening. I could not take the day to drive to our state capitol, Olympia, WA. My ninety-two-year-old mother lives with us and needs a care-giver close at hand. I decided that Renton City Hall would be a good place to gather and called a local radio station, KVI 570. The then talk show host, Kirby Wilbur, announced the Renton location. We had 150 people show up!

In 2010, I decided to post a rally at Renton, for 11 a.m. and 5 p.m., two more in Kent, and two more in Covington ... six in all! Each group attracted wonderful people, with positive signs and flags of all sizes! We even had a candidate come to shake hands! One group called the afternoon talk radio show and they greeted the whole Northwest! I was able to get to four of the six rallies. A wonderful person in Kent thought to gather e-mail addresses, so we are growing that list. The Internet is the main way to communicate. When Tea Party Patriots came out with their statement that they were not a third party, and wanted to work with the Republican Party, I decided to sign up with them. We need to elect conservative candidates, willing to cut Government spending and let us keep more of our hard-earned money. To be accountable to "We the People!"

TEA PARTY – THE AWAKENING

Matt Winey

I am an American citizen who has been awakened from my slumber in the last few years. I have voted Republican for many years as they have for the most part had a conservative stand. Around January of 2009 I became more and more leery of our national government as I started keeping track of what was happening in our political arena. It was shortly after that, that I first heard of anything like the modern Tea Party movement. I really didn't decide to get involved until around January of 2010 as I saw what the Obama administration was doing to our freedoms as Americans. It was then that I started studying the politics of our nation in a diligent manner. As I studied I realized that the Republican Party had become somewhat of a problem to our freedoms also. They seemed to be getting the same disease that the Democrats had, which was not really caring what "We the People" thought was right. Around February of 2010 I started looking for a local Tea Party group. But to no avail. There had actually been one going the year before, but they had somewhat fallen apart. I finally got word of one fella in my home city who had belonged to the Tea Party a year ago. He told me that it seemed that most all those who were involved got busy and had kind of dropped the Tea Party movement in Craig Colorado. We decided to try again.

I had made some flyers that we were starting a Tea Party in our area called the Bears Ears Patriots. I developed a web page in hopes some would see it and become interested. It seemed to be futile until one day, as I was at an appointment with my dentist, the dental hygienist told me her parents and a few others were still trying to make things work as the local Tea Party and were probably going to try and have some meetings soon.

About this same time a lady who was involved with conservative candidates, and had been a part of the first Tea Party, saw a flier that I had left posted at a local restaurant and contacted me. As I talked to those who my dental hygienist had told me about and the lady who had called me, we had a short meeting. From there it just seemed to take off.

We started having monthly meetings, and as we handed out fliers and had radio and paper announcements about our meetings, the Bears Ears Patriots just seemed to take off.

We are a group without a so-called president or any kind of board, but just like the National Tea Party group we are making a big difference in our area. Hopefully that difference continues until we can win our nation back.

Ken Urbanski

As for me, I am just an ordinary guy in my mid-fifties who never imagined that this is what I would be doing at this or any other point in my life. Like many Americans, I am ashamed and embarrassed that for the better part of fifty years, I took for granted the gift of the noble experiment that our Founding Fathers left us. I am ashamed and embarrassed that I never truly understood or appreciated the sacrifices made by my father and other servicemen and women or by those who gave the last full measure of devotion to preserve the freedom and liberty that I have enjoyed. While the assault on America, our freedom and liberty has been in the works for some time, I am ashamed and embarrassed that my generation may be the one that lets it all slip away and fails to meet its moral obligation to pass down to the next generation an America that is intact and secure.

You asked what it was that motivated me to get involved. In retrospect, it had clearly been building for years, but after the passage of the Patriot Act, the ever increasing bank bailouts of 2006, 2007, and 2008, the Henry Paulson, Ben Bernanke, and George W. Bush TARP two-step, and finally the $800+ billion dollar Obama stimulus, I had enough. I had been writing my representatives for some time, but I can remember standing in the bistro in the office where I work, and the TV was broadcasting

CNBC and I happened to catch the Rick Santelli rant. Tea Party stuck in my mind, and I Googled it a few days later and started finding hits and groups. Tax Day rallies were popping up all over the place and I joined the Philly Tea Party. I went to some of the organizing rallies, and I organized a group of co-workers and neighbors to join me in the pouring rain in Philly on 4/15/09. From there, Glenn Beck called for a national rally on 9/12, and the 912 organizations began forming. I joined the Lehighton 912 group, and as a motorcycle rider, I came across the Sons of Liberty Riders just before the 9/12/09 event in DC.

I checked out their web site, and I was the 13th member to join. Today, we are nationwide with more than 4,000 members, and we continue to grow. We work with all the other grassroot organizations to bring a unique present to the many rallies that we have attended. Our mission is education and our focus is on the Constitution. We accept all patriots, and our belief is that all of the challenges facing America today can be resolved by following the Constitution and reverting to the core principles and values that made America great. As I said earlier, the challenge is immense. We have been asleep at the wheel for so long that we are teetering on the edge of the precipice. I get depressed, angry, frustrated, and I have frequently questioned whether or not I am up to the task, but I just cannot and will not give up. I have to hold true to my principles and value, and I have to look at myself in the mirror. I rely on my fellow brother and sister patriots to pick me up. For that support, I will be eternally grateful. I think that Adrian Murray said it best. We must continually rededicate ourselves and just as those who came before us be willing to pledge our lives, our fortunes, and our sacred honor for this great quest.

Kyle Kieliszewski

I was first involved when I heard polls were showing Scott Brown was close to defeating Coakley for the Massachusetts Senate race. I was hooked that day! While starting to follow the election, I wanted to be involved and share the excitement. This is when I did some further research on the Tea Party, and started a group in Wisconsin. If you don't know why Scott Brown winning was exciting to me, you are not playing on the same field most Americans are! Since my involvement, I have fielded calls from reporters, interested citizens and others. I also changed my groups name to the Wisconsin Minutemen, because that's what a lot of us represent. We are not hard-core extremist, but rather concerned citizens that can mobilize on short notice when needed to help spread the word. We are also merely helping spread the word of who's running, what they stand for, and what it will mean to the average citizen. Wisconsin has formed a coalition of group leaders that have united in order to steer the parties at time. Not run or lead, but steer. It's a lot easier to get a meeting with a legislator if you have the backing of the group(s) vs. your own specific group.

Media rumors are false about the Tea Party getting weaker. *The Tea Party is getting stronger.* At a national level there are conference calls, radio programs, "war rooms" for group leaders only, etc.

Laura Long

About a year and a half ago my sister (Julie Griffin), who is very familiar with Meet-Up, formed a conservative group and invited the members to a restaurant to watch the Glenn Beck show on 9/12/2008. The response was overwhelming—we filled the restaurant. We knew that there were many more conservatives than we had imagined. It was then that I asked my sister if she minded if I took over the group. I am a mother of four kids. I have a very supportive husband and a full time job. My children are seven, eleven, twelve, and fifteen. So you can imagine that my time is limited. Even so, I felt compelled to become active, and so it began.

I started by inviting members of our group (Triangle Conservatives Unite!) to dinner/chats where we would invite local politicians to come speak. We would have about fifteen to twenty-five people show up at these meetings. Then I was able to speak at a Tea Party and our membership began to grow. People in the community found us online and the group became more active. Our calendar lists all conservative events in the area—from rallies to tea parties, from protests to dinner chats. KTMs (kitchen table meet-ups) began to form as more members became politically active. We started hosting the Tea Parties ourselves, and we headed to DC on 9/12/2009—what a fantastic day, surrounded by patriots! We have been to DC a number of times since then. It is frustrating to make the effort only to find out the legislators are not really listening to us. A perfect example of this is health care—the protest was huge and was not covered well by the media.

At our Tea Party on Tax Day 2010 we had around 2,000 people come out. It was a wonderful day and we were so happy to see Raleigh come to life! With elections coming up in the fall we are very busy planning our next Tea Party and some Get Out the Vote events. It is a very exciting time to be a conservative and I love learning about our history, our Founding Fathers and the formation of our Republic. The best thing about the Tea Party movement is the way it has inspired American citizens to discover how their country and government came to be, how fortunate and how blessed we are, how perfect the government our forefathers established is and how lucky we are to live in this great country.

Mary Kneupper

I was following the news on different programs and realized what Obama was doing—our government being run by socialists and not just him but others in the White House—and what I heard was so far left that I realized I must become involved to keep our country sovereign. Most importantly, for my granddaughters—I want them to have the freedom that I have always enjoyed.

One thing I have experienced personally is a decrease in the amount Medicare pays for certain procedures but an increase in our premiums, plus no cost of living adjustments for this year and following years. Well, I really didn't know how to go about doing something. Then one day I was talking to my brother about everything going on and he commented that we needed a Tea Party. I had heard of the Tea Party but didn't really know what they were about.

I had signed up for a lecture in Odessa, TX on the Constitution which was being hosted by the Odessa Tea Party. What I learned and really understood at the point was what our Founding Fathers had envisioned—a government of the people, by the people, for the people.

I came home and decided to organize a Tea Party because I wanted our community to be informed so that they could make informed decisions. At each meeting I proposed to have different topic for discussion. Starting with the Constitution, the Bill of Rights, cap and trade, immigration, health care reform and the list could just go on.

I then contacted the Odessa Tea Party and asked for their help in organizing one in Girvin, TX. We set a date and they came and answered questions and taught me how to hold the meetings. I had a wonderful turnout of thirty-one local ranchers, farmers, and even oilfield workers. I want to just take a minute to tell you about Girvin, TX. Nobody actually lives in Girvin now but in my dad's time it was the largest cattle shipping yard for these parts. All that is left of old Girvin is the one room schoolhouse and that is where we hold all our meetings, where we go to vote and sometimes just to get together.

I am a very patriotic person and believe the people should govern themselves. I have studied more on the Constitution, Bill of Rights, and Citizen's Rule plus several other publications. I also belong to the Heritage Foundation, Act for American and MRC and MOMs.

My two biggest concerns are the health care reform bill and immigration laws. I am totally against any government involvement in the health care field. I am for immigration laws that will punish any individual that is not a citizen of the United States by sending them back to their homes.

Arming ourselves with knowledge and gaining wisdom is the only way that we can take back our country. I remain committed to my goal of educating this community to the best of my ability. I pray daily that God will protect this great country of ours and give us guidance, knowledge and wisdom to do this. Pray for our leaders.

Loretta S. Wakefield

My involvement with the Tea Party movement is based on many things, but grew mostly from an interest in politics, pride in my country and respect for my father. I grew up as a military child. My father was a career veteran who began his military career in the US Navy, but switched to the US Air Force after marrying my mom (Norfolk, Virginia could be a scary place for a fifteen-year-old bride while her husband was out to sea.). My father served in WWII while in the Navy, having lied about his age so he could enter the military, and later, in the Air Force, served two tours in Korea during that conflict. There was a wall in our home filled with the many awards and medals my father received during his twenty-three years of service to this great nation. My parents were married fifty-eight years when my father passed away. During my growing up years, we lived in various places across the US and most of those assignments we lived in base housing. As a child on a military base I was sur-

rounded daily by the "military lifestyle"—troop forma-
tions marching along, families crying because Daddy was
deploying, families smiling because Daddy was coming home
and families packing their belongings because Daddy was being
transferred to yet another base. There were many rules that surrounded living on a military base back then, and there were
many rules in my home as well. I was taught to follow the rules.
One of the rules I was taught to follow involved a daily practice
on military bases. Every morning at the beginning of the work
day, and every afternoon at the close of the day, the loudspeakers would crackle and every man, woman and child would stop
and stand still. Traffic would stop and people would get out and
stand by their vehicles as the first notes of either Reveille or
Taps began to play. It was followed by the National Anthem, at
which time men not in uniform would remove their
hat, everyone would stand at attention with their hand over their
heart, and those in uniform would come to attention and salute.
There was no movement until the last note of the National Anthem had played and the loudspeakers crackled again before they
were silenced. That image in my mind remains one of my most
favored memories, and today, if I am on a military base and have
the honor of seeing this practice carried out, my heart still swells
with pride as tears come to my eyes.

I grew up witnessing the sacrifices being made by American
families across this country. I grew up learning respect for our
flag and pride in our country. I grew up knowing that some
things were bigger than ourselves.

As my father grew ill in his later years and I returned to my parents home to help care for him, we discussed his desires for his
funeral when he passed away. He was a Christian man, so he
knew his soul would rest with God, but there was one request
that he needed my assurance of. When the time came, he wanted
to be laid to rest during a full military funeral. Because of the
strain being put on our military due to the ongoing Iraq and Afghanistan war, the military base near our home had limited Honor

Guards available for funeral details and not everyone was guaranteed a full detail. It simply depended on when the need arose. My father had served his nation well, and I promised to fulfill that last request.

It was with a broken heart, but also a great sense of pride, that I watched a full detail of young men and women from Maxwell-Gunter Honor Guard lay my father to rest on a hot evening in July, 2005. This veteran had loved his God, his family and his country, and he had shown that to me throughout his lifetime and instilled in me that same emotion.

In 2009, as I watched our country turning away from the very principles and values I was raised to believe, I felt a need to speak up, to be heard. Although I had been actively involved in politics for a very long time, I knew there should be yet another way to make the voices of We the People heard. It was then that I became aware of the first Tea Party activities. As I listened to news reports about this new movement forming across our nation I had such a strong desire to become part of it. When I heard about the first Tax Day Tea Party being held in Wetumpka, Alabama that year, I made plans to attend with my sign in hand. It was an inspiring day, a day that gave me *real* hope for the future of America. My involvement grew in the following months. I participated in various rallies locally and around our state. I began helping with events and did more of the "background work" in this movement. On 9/12/09 I was part of the throngs of people who gathered in Washington, DC to show our unity, to be visible to the very government that was quickly spinning out of control. It was an amazing day, a day no one would have thought possible just a few short months before, a day that filled me with a pride so great I could not contain it and it often spilled over in my tears. Americans had awakened, they were engaged in a united effort and were no longer sitting idly by and watching America change before our eyes. We wanted the administration to know we were God-fearing, Constitution-loving patriots who stood together for one cause ... to take our country back. I thanked my heavenly father that day and shed tears as I thought of my earthly father. He would have been so proud of me ... and every person who stood with me that day because we loved our country. The country established by our Founding Fathers and blessed and protected by an Almighty God. My father instilled that love of country in me ... and the Tea Party movement was my way to fight for the very country my father had given so much to.

It has been more than a year since I attended my first Tea Party gathering. I am now the president of our local Tea Party group and am doing everything I can to help save our Republic because I believe she is in real danger of being lost. As I make plans to attend the 9/12 event in DC this year ... I ask my heavenly father for strength to do what I need to do to carry the message of the Tea Party movement to others and to help make a difference for our country. And I smile as I thank my earthly father for teaching me this love of country that makes me so proud to be part of the voices of We the People.

God Bless America ... "One nation, under God, indivisible, with liberty and justice for all."

Jim Bratten

I have only recently (last two years) engaged in activism, via organizing and facilitating Tea Parties, but have been a conservative most of my adult life.

Looking back, forty years or so, I was more "liberal" (less conservative?) than my parents, as was the case for many who graduated high school and entered college in 1966. My realization about what was being perpetrated upon my beloved country occurred around the close of the Vietnam conflict (I served in the US Navy from 1969 to 1973, finishing my last two years of college in 1975). That's when I began to read and research extensively—constantly testing what I was told against what I actually discovered—and I found that I was a conservative and there were absolutes.

That was 1980. I joined The Heritage Foundation, a conservative think tank, and became a member of the Conservative Book Club, building a comprehensive library of conservative thought and principle that continues to this day.

I read everything that I could ingest: from Burke and Locke, the founders, de Tocqueville, through Hayek, von Mises, Buckley, Chesterton, Churchill, to Reagan, Sowell and others. I carry a copy of the Declaration of Independence and the US Constitution in my car, and pray daily for the restoration of my country.

When President George W. Bush began losing his compass bearings and began moving left in 2003, I began to listen even more intently to talk radio and abandoned any hope for the future of a truly free press in this country. The evidence of the 2008 elections solidified my fears. I started writing my local newspapers and calling in to talk shows to voice my concerns for the direction in which my country and the American culture were being steadily pushed.

Along the way, my occupation moved my family from Minneapolis to Annapolis, then to Detroit, then to Pittsburgh, and finally to Evansville. I became deeply concerned with the apparent progressive takeover of our constitutional Republic. I joined and contributed to dozens of conservative groups across the nation in the process.

My retirement from Chrysler LLC in November 2008 allowed me the opportunity to become an activist—to do whatever I could to expose the progressives' plans, to speak, write and, finally, in early 2009, to demonstrate in the form of Tea Party rallies and other activities.

This action wasn't "elective"—it was a simple necessity. My wife and I joined a local Tea Party group in Evansville in late March 2009, and I quickly became a co-organizer, speaking at several Tea Party rallies, assisting in planning town hall meetings and petition drives and culminating in my wife's organization of a motor coach trip (full bus) to the US capital for the Taxpayers March on Washington on September 12, 2009 (I guess I dragged her into this...).

Shortly after the DC trip, I was invited by Americans for Prosperity to speak at a panel discussion on grassroots organizing during their third annual "Restoring the American Dream Summit" in Arlington, VA.

In late May, 2009 I had joined Tea Party Patriots as a local coordinator and a member of the National Leadership Council, and still participate in webinar conferences with other coordinators across the nation every Monday night. I travel when I can to other Tea Party groups to offer ideas, experience and encouragement.

Finally, this past January I accepted the invitation to serve on the board of directors of an independent conservative think tank here in Indiana. I now spend what time I have (after a full-time job I began at the end of last December) between the Indiana group, Tea Party Patriots, Americans for Prosperity, and The Heritage Foundation, assisting as I am able to restore the Founders' intent for our exceptional country and salvaging the remnants of the Constitution that is being shredded daily before our eyes.

As Ronald Reagan, Bill Bennett and others have described it—"America, the last best hope." It's up to us, now, to assure our children and grandchildren that they will inherit it intact.

It was given lovingly to us by countless sacrifices of our countrymen over 234 years. It's our heritage and must be passed on, for "without a heritage, every generation starts over" (to quote The Heritage Foundation).

Now you know why I'm doing this, why I'm involved in the Tea Party Movement, and how I arrived at this action. I really don't have a choice; I have a wife and son and they have a God-given right to individual freedom and liberty.

I am an American patriot and this is my country.

Jim Chiodo

At age sixty-five, I grew up watching black and white TV with Godfrey, Ed Sullivan and American Bandstand. I was even on the show a couple times (the girls looked older on TV). As a school kid, I touched the Liberty Bell, walked the halls of Congress at Independence Hall and the battlefields of Valley Forge. These were all relatively close by my home in the suburbs of Philly.

In the '60s, I never smoked weed or joined in any protests. I did wear the "costume" (flowery shirt, bell bottoms and had mutton chop sideburns) because I looked good in them. A number of my school friends never came back from Vietnam and I saw any protests as disrespect. When I saw those burning our flag, it singed my soul.

Through most of my life with the exception of a few traffic tickets, I was a straight arrow, voting mostly Republican. I endured the Carter years with double-digit inflation but never got involved in politics. My career and family were both doing nicely. I reached upper management and saw the prosperity born of the Reagan years. I also saw firsthand how business growth created jobs. Although not in an ownership position, I personally hired dozens and promoted others. It was a good feeling to see this growth and the impact it had on families.

After downsizing, my life took a turn. Going from a six-figure income to $10 an hour in a home improvement store was a shock. It gave me a glimpse of those with a different outlook on life. My feet didn't like walking on a concrete floor and it was a blow to my ego being told to retrieve carts from the parking lot by a pimply faced "manager." Still, this income paid my bills and I was glad for it. I took pleasure in helping customers with my extensive do-it-yourself skills. Although my career had been in computers and management, my dad taught me how to fix anything and this self-reliance defined who I was.

In this retail world, I encountered downsized men and women like myself and young people. Some of the youth were actually trying to work their way up. The rest were usually found hiding from work in the back room or calling in sick. In a sea of NASCAR racing fans, I was out of place with my sailboat magazines. Mostly, I saw people drifting through life and critical of any one with a corporate mentality. There was disdain for "the man" and any representation of corporate America. Banks were greedy and mean because they wouldn't provide a loan. No one seemed to care about their future. Even living paycheck to paycheck didn't preclude purchase of unnecessary items and partying even at the risk of missing rent or car payments. "I'll just let the bank take back my car" was the most ridiculous thing I heard.

I moved on from retail and into selling to the building industry just in time to see the housing bubble burst. Again, I was fortunate to be at an age where my obligations were minimal, my children grown and my wants limited. I didn't understand the real reason for the economic collapse and along with it most of my 401K going down the drain, but I started paying more attention to politics and didn't like what I saw. I didn't like the immoral example set by Clinton but the excess spending by Bush was worse although I am happy to say he did keep us safe after 9/11.

The election cycle of 2007 caught my attention and I ate up every bit of information. It scared me that Hillary might be back in the White House but on the other side of the table from Bill. From what I learned of Obama, the actual words from his mouth were beyond belief. When he was elected, I hoped that his pledge to end corruption was not an empty promise. I was wrong but never believed it could get as bad as it did. With each new onslaught of this out-of-control government, I am thinking it can't get any worse. Each day, I realize again I was wrong.

After the TARP and bailouts, I was shaken and started watching cable TV to learn what was really going on. Hearing of something called "We Surround Them," I met with several others of like mind but that group lost interest. Actively searching online for something called a "Tea Party," I met with some people in a city about one hour drive from me. My first Tea Party was in our state capital in Lansing. I remember the good feeling being among 8,000+ people who shared a similar feeling, trying to reverse the course towards socialism.

Reality struck in the next day when I saw no accounts of the 700+ Tea Parties across the country. Then, as little bits of the Tea Parties came out, I saw a media demeaning and viciously attacking me and the millions of others who share a Tea Party mentality. At that point, I jumped in with both feet, driving one hour each way to meetings. Discussions of a July 4th Tea Party came up and I found myself on the planning committee, increasing my one hour drives to two or sometimes three a week. At the July 4th rally, I sang the National Anthem and tried to stay on key but the tears streaming down my face made this difficult. More composed, I was able to take a turn at the podium comparing Thomas Paine's "Common Sense" sentiment with our plight today.

Again, following the rally, there was a news blackout. I continued to participate with the Tea Party group, and saw the numbers swell from initial dozen or so to several hundred. As September approached, we saw continued media demeaning of us. An optimistic belief spread that if hundreds of thousands gathered in Washington DC on 9/12, it could not go unnoticed.

My visit to DC along with an estimated 1.5 million others was the most awe-inspiring thing I have ever done. I could not get onto the capital grounds because there were too many others. From a vantage point outside the circle drive, the National Anthem could be heard. The singer (much more capable than I) deliberately paused between stanzas. Your could hear a pin drop during these pauses and my face became wet again.

Driving home to another news blackout and disparaging remarks about the Tea Party by the president, speaker and the media was the turning point. There could not have been a better marketing tool for the Tea Parties than these negatives directed at the millions of ordinary citizens.

My own efforts turned to organizing a group closer to my home. Today, we meet regularly with sixty to seventy in attendance. An outgrowth of our meetings, made possible by several local sponsors, is a weekly radio show which I host. The show is a small version of a larger audience live talk show and features guests for interviews and discussions.

The town hall meeting, health care protests and an energized populace made their feelings known. Still this didn't deter the president and a willing Congress to rubberstamp his agenda and still the will of the people is ignored. A realization has set in that the only way to reverse this will be the elections.

As a 527, our Tea Party cannot support any candidate. However, an offshoot called ICAUCUS, born in Utah prior to the 2007 primaries, resulted in replacement of a long term Republican incumbent named Jason Chavetz. This organization has now spread to all fifty states and hopes to seek out and actively support like minded conservatives to replace not just the Democrats but the RINOs who don't represent the true conservative nature of voters.

In our area, we have endorsed both a candidate for the US Congress and several other state offices. In addition to meetings and the radio program, my efforts and many others turn to the actual work of campaigning for endorsed candidates. In some cases we are up against long odds. My district is probably one of the strongest Republican areas of Michigan. There is no doubt a Republican will be chosen. The question is whether than candidate will truly represent the goals of smaller government, fiscal responsibility and adherence to the actual meaning found in the Constitution. It's hot, it's humid and I don't relish walking and knocking on doors to help the candidates we have endorsed. However, I shudder to think what will happen to our country if these efforts aren't taken nationwide.

Jim Isbell

OK, that's a fair question. How did a seventy-four-year-old retiree with nothing to gain and everything to lose get involved in the Tea Party movement?

To begin with, I was raised by wolves. Well, not exactly. But when I was eighteen months old a coyote cub came up from the canyon into the yard, and sat down beside me as I played on a blanket and my mother was in the house. That coyote became my pet and was with me for the next fourteen years.

Politically, I learned from Berry Goldwater. I had been flying under the radar since 1964 when I campaigned for Berry Goldwater door-to-door and watched the Democratic Party repeat lies and distortions about him in order to discredit him. Their claim was that if I voted for Barry Goldwater, we would get bogged down in a war in Vietnam. They claimed Barry would create conditions for an atomic war, and even ran ads with a little girl and an atomic explosion in the background. Apparently they were right. I voted for Barry Goldwater and we got bogged down in a war in Vietnam *and* North Korea and Iran has or will soon have atomic weapons.

It doesn't seem to matter that Barry Goldwater *lost*!

After Goldwater lost I was so discouraged by the politics that could vilify such a fine, upstanding patriot that I just decided to fly under the radar as long as what was happening didn't seem to bother my lifestyle. I was just twenty-eight years old so I wasn't thinking about my children and my grandchildren and my great grandchildren. But now I have two children, ten grandchildren and one great grandchild. Strangely, it all seems more important now.

For the next forty-five years I stayed out of sight and just paid my taxes, voted and let the world go by. Hell, I didn't expect to live past the age of fifty-five anyway because my father died of a massive heart attack at that age. I figured it was in my genes. But in 2009 at the age of seventy-three I realized that my genes were better than his and I might live a lot longer *and* things were going to hell in a hand basket under the current administration.

Realizing that I might be around to pay for this spending binge, this censorship of the Internet, this banning of books, this takeover of industry, this open borders for all no matter who they are, this assault on the First, Second and Tenth Amendments. I decided it was time I did something. The straw that broke the camel's back was when the property taxes in our town went up by 300% in the 2009 recession. The excuse was that "We need the money to run the county in this recession." Well, hell, I need the money to run my household, but there is no one below me that I can tax. So I have to cut back. But the county wasn't cutting back!

So, I organized the first Ingleside-On-The-Bay Tea Party on July 4th, 2009. In a town of an average population of 350, we had an attendance of 125 people to hear six local politicians speak. We threw tea into the bay (and immediately retrieved it before the EPA could bring suit). And we turned back the tax appraisals!

Less than a year later we held the second Tea Party on the 17th of April 2010. Our income taxes had increased under the current administration. Same location, a bit bigger crowd, five bands on stage and twelve politicians and a crowd of 250 ... that's more than the town turns out on a major election!

Then, three months later, on the 3rd of July 2010, we held the biggest one yet. A rolling Tea Party we organized in and started in Corpus Christi, TX and ended at the Ingleside-On-The-Bay Tea Party. We filled the park with 500+ spectators and twenty-one speakers (Democrats, Independents, Libertarians and Republicans), headlined by the Texas State Railroad Commissioner (R), Elizabeth Ames Jones and State Representative Todd Hunter (R). Four hours of music from the stage was followed by a fireworks display, with food and drink vendors throughout the afternoon and evening. It was a resounding success.

Why am I still involved? Well because we have to turn around this trend and regain control of our country and of the mainstream media who are stifling free speech by refusing to present the opposition view. In all three Tea Parties, it was not until this last one that the Tea Party was recognized on the 10 o'clock news ... after it happened, even though they had the press release several days before. They refuse to run our press releases and won't cover our events. This last one was too big for them to ignore completely.

Our group believes in free speech so we include *all* parties and ideologies. We feel that a fool will show that on stage and do more for our cause than banning him/her from the stage would do. We are now looking forward to our next Tea Party on the 16th of October 2010.

TEA PARTY LEADERS

Joey Gallgher

I would say my story began in the 2008 primaries, my sophomore year in high school. I didn't really like McCain so I turned to Obama. I researched Obama and at first glance everything sounded great but then I researched more and realized this guy was crazy!

Being from the Chicago area, people were treating him as if he was a godsend. I spoke out against him then but then I found myself with no candidate to support. I researched more and found my guy: Ron Paul. He, unlike all the other candidates, believed in America and the Constitution. I wasn't too deep into politics when Obama won the election but when the health care debate came around that's when I stepped up. I read the Constitution for the first time at age seventeen and I read Glenn Beck's *Arguing With Idiots*. I would get in arguments with fellow classmates and I would be out numbered but I would always hold my ground. Many thought it was up to the federal government to save us but I knew the answer was in the Constitution. One day I even wore a shirt to my Obama-loving government teacher's class that read "NObamacare." She asked me why I was against it and I simply said I was a capitalist (which really stunned her). Since then I have spent countless hours researching (so does every teenager, right?) the current American political system. I'm confident that I could hold my own against anyone in a political debate.

Jonathon Hill

As the oldest of six raised and educated at home by Christian parents, I was exposed at an early age to David Barton, a historian and founder of Wallbuilders (wallbuilders.org). From him, we learned the truth about how our nation was founded on biblical principles. Our parents taught us that we had the duty before God to be good citizens, to pray for our leaders, and to vote carefully.

I vividly remember hearing Mr. Barton talk about how powerful a phone call to a legislator can be. Just picking up the phone or writing a letter can have a powerful impact, especially at the state and local levels. So we did. We found some e-mail newsletters that kept us informed and started calling.

My parents always voted, and we anxiously watched the results come in after the 2000 presidential election. I was too young to vote, but looked forward to being able to cast my first vote in 2004 for George W. Bush, Senator Jim DeMint, and Governor Mark Sanford.

By the time 2007 rolled around, we began hearing a familiar name—Mike Huckabee. We'd heard of him through our home-school organization which had worked with him while he was governor of Arkansas, and a few years before we had picked up a copy of *Character Makes A Difference*, which was collecting dust on our bookshelf.

So, of course, we pulled the book off the shelf and read it to find out what sort of guy this Huckabee was. To say that we were inspired is an understatement. As providence would have it, we found out that he would be in the area only a couple weeks after we finished the book, and hearing him sealed our decision to work heart and soul for a candidate who, for the first time, truly was a man we felt represented us and would do what is right for our nation, no matter what it cost him.

In the fall of 2007, I found out that a friend with whom I hadn't spoken in years was an active grassroots coordinator in Missouri, so I contacted him. He helped me set up a group online for Huckabee supporters in my area and encouraged me along. I scrounged around and did my best to be helpful, but I was in over my eyeballs and rather overwhelmed by it all.

I put together several grassroots phone banks, and when the campaign finally got around to putting up a local office, I and some of my siblings worked the entire week before the SC Primary helping to coordinate volunteers and make those annoying get-out-the-vote phone calls.

We were heartbroken when he didn't win, but even more by who did—John McCain. And just when we thought all was lost, here came Sarah Palin! Well, needless to say, we worked with our local Republican Party that November. In addition, my Mom and sister were poll managers that year, and I did some poll watching for the first time. By that time, I was just about willing to do whatever I was needed to do, even though I really didn't know how, but I kept plugging along anyway because I had to do my duty. The challenges kept me depending on God, and He truly was faithful to help me.

November of 2008 came and went, and to our dismay Barack Obama was elected by many who couldn't even tell you who he was or why they were voting for him. Yet, Obama (and Bush) gave the USA a reality check, and the Tea Party movement was underway.

My sister heard an amazing story of how Keli Carender in Seattle (of all places) got so sick and tired of doing nothing that she organized a protest that attracted hundreds. We heard a few weeks later of a protest organized in Greenville, SC which drew 2,000 people after only a week of planning. We sensed that a something unusual was happening, that a sleeping giant was awakening, and that we needed to be a part of it.

So in April of 2009, after no one else stepped forward, I took the bull by the horns and organized a "Taxed Enough Already" protest in our town. Folks who had never picketed a day in their life were out in force, young and old alike. They said they were scared, that you can't spend your way out of debt, and that they were doing this for their children and grandchildren.

What a beautiful sight that was!

Here in SC, we just finished with the 2010 primary election, for the most part with good results, despite the fact that only one in four registered voters exercised their civic duty (and that was a record turnout!).

It is my grief that many people today are too busy pursuing the American dream to look around and see that the real American dream—freedom—is vanishing. I hope and pray that they will wake up, stop whining, and get to work before it is too late.

As for me? Give me liberty or give me death, and may God have mercy on our land!

Joshua Carter

Growing up in an educator's household I have always been taught what a privilege it is to have the education that is offered in this country. This is an ideal that I have carried with me my whole young life, but it has never had more meaning than now...

I have always been a reader. Activism and volunteer work are some other passions that I have slowly developed a love for over time. During my junior and senior years of high school I was on three separate hurricane relief trips to Biloxi, Mississippi in the devastating wake of Hurricane Katrina. These trips opened my eyes to see not only the struggles and pain of our own citizens here in the United States, but also the incompetence of our federal government in handling a crisis within our borders.

My senior year of high school I began a student-run activism group to combat the budget cuts in our school district. These cuts would eliminate elementary music programs, gifted and talented programs, and they would trim virtually every other department in the building. This was not going to be a simple one year solution but an annual event. The goal for our group was not only to raise awareness among the student body, but to educate them about the issue and to get them involved in some

344

way with the political movement to reverse the legislation that was bringing down our schools.

In a short time after our group swelled to over 100 members, we had networked with other students across the state and formed the Wisconsin Student's Coalition with groups that were in the same boat as our organization. We passed out flyers at parades, held presentations about the subject and hosted a legislative forum where all but two legislators declined our invitation. But as students we also had a duty to school, and before long exam week was upon us. We could not keep up the group full time and it never reached its full potential. The cuts ended up passing and future generations will never be able to enjoy music as my friends and I had been able to.

Though the organization did not go as far as I had hoped, through the experience I was able to gain insight into the political world of our legislators and was very displeased to see that both parties were heavily entrenched in their own politics and were willing to sacrifice the benefits of a community in the interest of staying in their offices.

Only a couple years later, Barack Obama was elected as President of the United States of America. On my campus I was amazed at how viral Obama's message was with the youth—nothing but change and optimism was on the lips of my fellow students and I almost bought into it. If we can say nothing else for Barack Obama, he ran one smooth campaign.

However, after doing some research I realized that he stood for virtually nothing I stood for and what's more, my fellow students, when asked about his policies and voting records, had virtually no knowledge of what the man stood for. They had derived their opinions from the sound bites that had been spoon-fed to us from mainstream media. This ignorance was appalling to me. I began to realize that the people of the United States have forfeited educated and informed voting decisions and instead have supported flashy smiles and fancily worded speeches, even if the politics behind them make no sense.

I have become involved in the Tea Party in the interest of educating others about the dangers of a government that is oversized and excessively wasteful. I hope to encourage others to look past the sound bites and the poster-boy smiles and to deeply scrutinize the men and women we put into office. Our federal government today is a far cry from what the founders of this country had intended and it will take dedicated citizens to take the power back from the special interests and the bureaucrats and to restore it to where it rightfully belongs: with the people.

Jeff Luecke

I was basically politically inactive before the 2008 election. My single issue was the Second Amendment. I contacted my senators and congressman regularly regarding protecting my gun rights.

During the Bush administration I was plenty perturbed with out-of-control spending and federal government overreach into states' rights. Medicare Part D and No Child Left Behind raised red flags but I guess I believed if President Bush kept us safe I was okay with whatever he and the Republicans were doing. As the presidential campaign progressed in late 2007 and early 2008, and we ended up with John McCain and Barack Obama, I became ever more fearful for our future.

Then came TARP and President George W. Bush stating he was abandoning free market principles to save the free market. This sent a shiver up my spine and I thought, "Let the failures fail!" Once Obama was inaugurated and TARP turned into deadbeat homeowner bailouts, and the federal government took over GM and Chrysler, and the new president gave the UAW preference over secured stockholders, I knew we were in for a dismal four years.

After that came President Obama's so-called stimulus package and his omnibus spending bill with 9,000+ earmarks. I was going crazy! In February of 2009 I, like many Americans, saw on YouTube the CNBC financial reporter, Rick Santelli, ranting on the floor of the Chicago Board of Trade about the government's bailouts and calling for a "Tea Party" in Chicago.

After poking around on the Internet learning more about the Tea Parties popping up all over the country, on April 15, 2009 I decided I would do that same. I found Tea Party Patriots' web site, registered my event and waited. Within a few days I was contacted by a local woman named Carol Ross who felt as I did— we had to do something. We corresponded via e-mail to set up our tax day Tea Party. We chose a venue, secured permits, arranged speakers and hoped people would show up.

We were joined by two others, Michael Heeren and (at the time) fifteen-year-old Joe Schueller. Michael was a great addition with many local contacts who supplied a PA system, balloons, helium, and much more. Joe was our link to young people and understood what massive debt would do to his generation and beyond. We actually held two Tea Parties on April 15, 2009. One was at noon and the other later in the afternoon. We were shocked to see 200+ people attend these rallies.

I emceed and spoke at both events. Michael ran the PA system and music. We had four to five speakers who talked about everything from the Constitution to health care to bailouts and the road to socialism. Yes, even then we saw the handwriting on the wall.

Since that first Tea Party we've been meeting and growing and educating ourselves and others as best we can. We held a Tea Party on the Fourth of July (2009) and another on Tax Day 2010. We held our own town hall meeting in September of 2009 to discuss health care, illegal immigration, government overreach and other issues. We've protested on the streets of Dubuque against government-run health care and illegal immigration.

We've started our "Patriot's Classroom" education series which covers many different topics and allows for open discussion between our members. We've all been paying close attention to the fools in Washington, contacting them on all the big issues (health care, spending, illegal immigration, bailouts, cap and trade, etc.)

I personally believe that with our current two party system, tea partiers must infiltrate and assume control of the Republican Party. Toward that end a number of our members attended the off-year Iowa caucuses and became delegates to our county, district and state GOP conventions.

We invited candidates to our meetings to see who, if anyone, we could back in the mid-term elections. We decide to endorse candidates who most closely aligned with the Tea Party core values of a return to constitutionally limited government, fiscal responsibility (cutting spending, taxes and regulations) and free markets.

I hope that going forward the Dubuque Tea Party will grow, learn and become more influential in the political process to affect change *back* to our founding principles recorded in the Declaration of Independence, the US Constitution and the Bill of Rights.

Kate Robertson

First, I believe Sarah Palin was the spark that woke me up. So I'd have to say that if it weren't for Sarah Palin coming onto the scene in our country, I would never have had the courage or inspiration to begin a Tea Party. Also, I believe without some supernatural guidance from God, I would never have put one foot in front of the other!

348

My husband Greg and I were building our house. Sometime in late February or early March 2009, our friend Sean was helping us pour concrete. At lunchtime we talked politics ... Christianity ... out-of-control government spending ... Sarah Palin ... Rick Santelli ... and the Tea Parties being organized across the country.

Within a few days, after hearing something on the radio, Sean and I both almost said in unison: "Silver City needs a Tea Party!" At first we were kind of joking about it, because we live in a town (we thought) that had few conservatives. Neither of us had ever done anything like this before—Sean worked in construction, and I had been a secretary. But the idea became stronger. We talked to people that were interested, but they were too busy working, raising their children, or had health issues that kept them from getting involved. I was basically free, because I was helping my husband build our house, and he was my "boss," so I could have time off to work on this project! The more Sean and I talked about it, the more we thought "How could we NOT do this?" And "If not us, who?" I felt I couldn't live with myself if I didn't at least try!

There were many sleepless nights. The main tax issue for me was that I didn't want our tax money to fund abortions. Other haunting thoughts kept running through my mind—our young men fought and died for our freedom, and I saw that freedom slipping away. They gave up their entire lives so we could live in a free country—and now we were letting what they fought for be trampled on? Who was standing up and remembering them? Wasn't there something we could do? We could at least *try* to have a Tea Party ... and create a platform for people who normally stay quiet to speak out.

It was not smooth sailing—there were plenty of discouraging events and plenty of naysayers, but there was also an inner urging that kept prodding me along, not allowing me to give up, saying, "just do it!" (Maybe the Holy Spirit?) I say that because it is *not* in my nature, and has never been in my nature, to be an activist or lead a group—but something just rose up within me when I looked around and witnessed the apathy among the people. They agreed that our country was heading in the wrong direction, but believed it was too late—that there was nothing we could do about it! I wanted to shout from the rooftops that we *could* do something and we *could* make a difference!

Many people in town scoffed at the idea of a Tea Party, and said we wouldn't have anyone show up, but we said, "Even if it's just the two of us standing on the street corner, we're going to do it!" Many more joined our effort to organize for the 15th. We hoped for about 50 people on April 15th, and ended up with over 650 in attendance!

Our initial intention was just to have one Tax Day Tea Party Event—and then we thought it would be over! From April 15, 2009 on, it's hard to recall all the details. This past year has been a whirlwind. We didn't realize that it would take on a life of its own, and people would start saying, "What will we do next?" I found myself in the midst of a large group of people, looking to me for direction—and I am *not* a leader (maybe just a community agitator?) If you are familiar with the movie "Being There" (starring Peter Sellers) that's what happened to me! Anyway, thank God that other excellent individuals with much more knowledge than me stepped up and helped lead the group. We ended up having weekly meetings, event after event, and we lived and breathed the Tea Party 24/7 from that point until the present!

The incredible thing is that we were basically all strangers coming together for a common cause. It didn't matter what background we came from, what political party, or the color of our skin, we were united in a common cause—a concern that our country was heading in the wrong direction, and we needed to pull together, to stand up before it was too late.

One thing I must add is that at the end of our April 15th event, I typed up all the comments from our scroll and sent them to our representatives and to President Obama. Typing them up was a very emotional experience for me—reading all the various heart-felt comments from local citizens. *That* is the reason that to this day, I just can't quit being involved in the Tea Party ... it's knowing we are helping to give the people a voice ... and if I ever get discouraged, all I need to do is re-read those comments from "We the People."

Kirk Groenig

I became really concerned in November 2008 with presidential elections as well as the overwhelming debt we as a country be-gan piling up. I stayed on the sidelines, read more and more and with the passing of TARP ($700 billion) I exploded! No more! With my children on their own, my wife and I were happy, en-joying life more, and had a new home but I could see I wouldn't be happy if I just sat and did nothing. Our country needed people to say—I'm madder than hell and hot going to take it no more!

On March 5, 2009, I investigated how to get permits for event and called into local radio stations, announcing I was planning first Tea Party for "Remember Us We the People." The date was planned for April 11, 2009 and a second one on April 15, 2009. People stepped up and helped organize the event and we pro-moted it on radio, TV and newspapers. We continue to have many events—so far, over fifteen. Our organization has a full board, web site and almost 1,000 members, with connections to over seventeen grassroots organizations in Washington State alone and with Tea Party Patriots nationally.

Stop ignoring us!

All we have to say: "Restore America's Greatness!"

"We hold these Truths to be self-evident, that all men are created equal, that they are endowed by their creator with certain aliena-ble rights, which among them are Life, Liberty and the Pursuit of Happiness" (From the Declaration of Independence)

God Bless America!

Larry Doran

I joined the United States Air Force not necessarily out of a driv-ing patriotism, but because the selective service draft was still in force at the time. At five-eight and 125 pounds, I wasn't really interested in slogging through mud, carrying a seventy-pound pack and rifle.

I scored very high on I.Q. and aptitude tests and was offered the chance to go to Yale University. For a young man from my background, that was an impossible dream. I jumped at the chance, not even caring what my field of study would be.

My new assignment was to become proficient with the Mandarin Chinese language as a member of the Office of Special Services, the precursor to the C.I.A. I was granted a top-secret security clearance, and became acutely aware of the need for intelligence gathering and covert operations as a means to protect America's national security. This was my motivation to become a true pa-triot. I took my oath of service very seriously and still do. The oath I took did *not* end with the phrase, "until I am discharged from the Air Force"!

I reentered civilian life in 1964 and was not at all politically ac-tive. In fact, I really thought all those sign-toting radicals were just kids using it as an excuse to get attention, and miserably failing in their attempt to prove how grown-up they were. I stre-nuously avoided conversations about politics and religion.

I married, got a good job, and raised three children. We wanted desperately to make their lives easier than our own. We've since found that we deprived them of many of the life lessons we learned that made us more mature, responsible, and reliable adults. Don't misconstrue that statement—I love my children very much. But because we didn't try to forge their character to fit our mold, they were taught values in school that we didn't necessarily appreciate. We attributed that to "changing times" and felt that they'd outgrow it and come to understand once they grew up. Hindsight proves that we should have been much more involved and aware of their schooling and the indoctrination that was being applied even then.

They've all grown and have families of their own now, and have blessed us with eight grandchildren.

I remember seeing the old MovieTone newsreels of Stalin, Hitler and Mussolini. I recall seeing the horrifying footage of Auschwitz being liberated. I saw Kruschev pound his shoe on the table at the United Nations, telling America that we would be defeated without firing a shot.

Still, I was sure "they" would never allow that to happen. I was confident that "they" would defend us to the death. I knew "they" would protect our cherished American Republic and that no one on earth would ever be able to bring America down. So I left it all up to "them."

When Ronald Reagan was president, I felt more American pride than I had ever felt before. He made sure that everyone here and abroad knew that there was something very different about America, something very strong, something very unique and special. And everyone knew that all of us Americans knew it too, and were defiantly proud of that difference.

Since then, I've seen Bill Clinton embarrass us all by defiling the office of our president. His lack of repentance and his belief that he is now the world's best-known "stud" makes me want to throw up. His disregard for the office and for America itself approaches treason in my view.

Liberal institutions of higher learning have given us politicians like Harry Reid, Nancy Pelosi, Barney Frank, and of course Barack Hussein Obama. Increasingly astonished and outraged at their actions, with arrogance and disdain for anyone that opposed them and their liberal socialist agenda, I found myself inwardly shouting, "Somebody, please *do* something!"

I began to watch and listen more intently, still not believing that I was witnessing the intentional destruction of capitalism, the Constitution, and our Republic itself. I read the Declaration of Independence, the Constitution and the Bill of Rights ... and the massive health care bill!

I was astounded at how many of our God-given rights, as defined in the Constitution, had been perverted or completely reversed without authority. I became aware of the myriad of "rights" demanded by screaming welfare-state supporters that simply were not granted or promised, and in fact do not exist.

I watched eminent domain laws become tools for government takeover. Are you aware that if the government deems that a new hotel would better serve the community than your residence, you can now be forced to surrender your home for that purpose? The fact that your great-grandfather homesteaded that land, and that your family lived and died there for generations, is not considered "pertinent" to those proceedings.

Stimulus payments to political friends in opposition to any sense of fiscal responsibility, trillions of dollars of taxpayer money unaccounted for, refusal to protect Americans at our Southern border, and total incompetence at resolving the total destruction of our shores along the Gulf Coast—these are all unbelievable acts taken by our current government.

Are these acts of stupidity or incompetence? I don't believe they are. I believe they are deliberate acts, as described by Saul Alinsky, to bring America down and see what happens.

The federal government's refusal to allow Americans to defend themselves at our Southern border, and in fact threatening to sue Arizona because they were derelict in their duty to manage immigration, is simply incredible and unacceptable.

The federal government's refusal to allow our Gulf Coast neighbors to defend their shores against the black tide that resulted from their refusal to allow drilling in 500 feet of water, thus forcing wells to drill in 5,000 feet of water with no history or proven ability to manage a failure of any wells that deep, is another travesty.

If the federal government refuses to protect Americans as they are sworn to do in their solemn oath of office, then I say, *"Get out of the way!"*

Cap and tax, the assault on our First and Second Amendments, and many other actions not widely publicized have irritated and frightened me. I'm deeply concerned about the future of America, and that of my children and grandchildren.

I am infuriated by the arrogant tone that I personally received when I contacted our congressman, Ben Nelson, the author of the "Cornhusker Kickback." It became painfully obvious that he still does not understand why conservative Nebraskans became so angry at him for selling his vote on health care, when all he did was get us a great deal!

When 1.5 million Tea Party demonstrators descended on Washington DC to air their grievances, they were met with disdain. Obama said they "amused" him. They were summarily dismissed, and I actually heard someone say it was no big deal;

they claimed they could get more folks to show up for a Tupperware convention!

Am I fed up? Yes! So when I heard that someone locally was starting a Tea Party organization, I became interested. I was surprised to discover that it is not a new political party trying to take on the Democrats and Republicans. I was even more surprised to discover it was made up of Republicans, Democrats, Libertarians and others, who simply want the government to become fiscally responsible, limit its activities to those defined by our Constitution, and let businesses *do* business rather than go out of business.

I decided I had to get on board. Of course, some of my personal beliefs regarding social and moral issues go even farther, but the Tea Party folks believe that if we can restore our constitutional Republic form of government, many of those issues will also be resolved.

Each of our high-level government officials is required by the Constitution to swear to an oath before being officially recognized as such; interestingly, not one of those oaths have a disclaimer indicating that the oath is only good for thirty days or until they leave office or until they decide to do otherwise. It is a solemn oath, intended to be a lifetime commitment.

I swore an oath of military service. I intend to keep it.

To remind our president, vice president, Congress and Supreme Court of their sworn oaths and the commitments they require, I submit the following. It is my fervent hope and prayer that they will somehow recognize the seriousness of their responsibility to keep them ... soon!

Oaths of Office

Federal Officials:

Each president recites the following oath in accordance with Article II, Section I of the US Constitution:

"I do solemnly swear (or affirm) that I will faithfully execute the office of President of the United States, and will to the best of my ability, *preserve, protect and defend the Constitution of the United States.*" [italics mine]

Each Congressman recites the following oath in accordance with Article 6 of the US Constitution:

"I do solemnly swear (or affirm) that I will *support and defend the Constitution* of the United States against all enemies, foreign and domestic; that I will bear true faith and allegiance to the same; that I take this obligation freely, without any mental reservation or purpose of evasion; and that I will well and faithfully discharge the duties of the office on which I am about to enter: *So help me God.*" [italics mine]

Each Supreme Court Justice takes the following oath in accordance with Title 28, Chapter I, Part 453 of the United States Code:

"I, [NAME], do solemnly swear (or affirm) that I will administer justice without respect to persons, and do equal right to the poor and to the rich, and that I will faithfully and impartially discharge and perform all the duties incumbent upon me as [TITLE] *under the Constitution* and laws of the United States. *So help me God.*" [italics mine]

Active, Reserve and Veterans of the United States of America:

Oath of Enlistment in the Armed Forces, except the National Guard (Army or Air):

"I, *(NAME)*, do solemnly swear (or affirm) that I will *support and defend the Constitution of the United States against all enemies, foreign and domestic*; that I will bear true faith and allegiance to the same; and that I will obey the orders of the President of the United States and the orders of the officers appointed over me, according to regulations and the Uniform Code of Military Justice. *So help me God.*" [italics mine]

Oath of enlistment in the National Guard (Army or Air):

"I, *(NAME)*, do solemnly swear (or affirm) that I will *support and defend the Constitution of the United States* and the State of *(STATE NAME)* against all enemies, foreign and domestic; that I will bear true faith and allegiance to the same; and that I will obey the orders of the President of the United States and the Governor of *(STATE NAME)* and the orders of the officers appointed over me, according to law and regulations. *So help me God.*" [italics mine]

Lesley Hollywood

The United States of America is quickly losing everything that makes it so great: freedom and liberty through the action of democracy. Those who are in positions of power, in both political parties, have forgotten the people who employ them—and we are losing our Republic one voter at a time.

The amount of unconstitutional legislation being quietly pushed by the Democratic majorities in the federal and state branches of government is nothing short of astonishing. But this is not new—the Republican Party wasn't much better when they held the majorities.

Although the Tea Party movement has been at times ridiculed, ignored and mislabeled, there is still something incredibly pure about it. And amazingly, with purity comes power. This movement manages to connect with mainstream America, a position both political parties have strived to obtain for decades. The Tea Party is a peaceful uprising of mainstream Americans, giving mainstream America a voice.

When I step outside of my Tea Party role, I actually watch American Idol, Dancing with the Stars, and I've even seen the Twilight movies. I enjoy spending time with my husband and my daughters. With my sisters, my parents, and my grandparents—I even have a few non-political friends!

My vocabulary includes curse words and I've been known to drink one too many margaritas on occasion. I like to shop, snowboard and take my daughters to the lake. I'm really just your average, mainstream, American mom, who's married to your average, mainstream, American dad. But even while living this simply complicated American life, I constantly worry for the future of my children. Not only do we live in a country full of mind-boggling crime and dangerous temptations, we also live under the constant abuse of our federal government. Our children are being assaulted by today's corruption, destroying their country like a cancer.

The only means of established protection our future generations have is the United States Constitution. This one single document, which each of our elected officials has or will swear to uphold, should have prevented the theft of our childrens' futures. But instead our Constitution was tossed to the wayside and along with it, the average American voter. This document, our country's supreme law, should have prevented government from gaining the power it has today.

But while attempting to help our children blossom into perfect little adults, destined for greatness, our minds became distracted and our eyes diverted. We quit doing our duty as Americans. We assumed "someone" was watching out for us. But no one was. It was this revelation that it took for something to snap inside of me. I could no longer do nothing.

The Tea Party was in its infancy when I first got involved. It was in a constant state of semi-organized chaos. The underground communication networks went viral, with the flow of information moving at breakneck speed.

The media ignored us, the Left ignored us, the Right ignored us. Outside of its own underground networks the Tea Party did not exist—but that didn't matter to us.

For those leading the Tea Party, this was not about fame or fortune or power or control. It was about the futures of our children, the future of our beloved country.

The media did not have to drool over an angry town hall meeting in order for that town hall meeting to have occurred, for the lawmakers who were present to have heard the voices of those present. The political parties in Congress did not have to acknowledge the receipt of millions of telephone calls, e-mails and handwritten letters for the outrage of Americans to ring clear. There was no way to muffle the sound as America stood up—we would not be quiet anymore.

When the Tea Party didn't go away, the voices didn't quiet, and the movement grew—others finally took notice. Some thought we were to become a new political party, shrugging off our abilities to gain influence. Others ridiculed the movement, calling it racist and uneducated. Many assumed it would be swallowed up by the Republican Party as we became labeled "the radical right."

Pundits would analyze the movement from the outside, rarely able to agree on what was happening on the inside. I always found it humorous that no one would come inside the movement and talk to those who were heavily involved before forming opinions. Well, they were all wrong. The Tea Party is the epitome of an organic grassroots movement, so de-centralized some may consider it a fault. It consists of people like me, your average moms and dads, businessmen and laborers, the unemployed and the overworked, the young and trendy, the old and traditional.

It is the common ground of a deep concern each and every one of us feels for our country—whether it be the crippling debt, the looming deficit, the expanding nanny state that resembles socialism to a frightening degree, or just the corrupt politicians who are stealing our liberties overnight. It is the emotion that drives us forward, into the unknown of a political system riddled with crooks. We have no choice but to try. The goal? To leave the children of the future with the same great country, full of opportunity, that we were at one time fortunate enough to inherit.

But the beauty and power of the movement lies within its chameleon walls. A movement so pure and disorganized is momentarily immune to corruption. This perfect storm of an uprising of a brilliant new political movement coupled with the staggering debt our country faces that has created the phenomenon now known as the Tea Party movement. A movement whose groups nationwide rarely resemble one another, function fully on a local level, and are so decentralized, it makes it nearly impossible to stop it, or even slow it down.

I am proud to be a member of the Tea Party, and look forward to where the future takes us.

Lyleann McCellan-Thee

My wish is that there was something magnificent or miraculous or awe-inspiring to tell you about my involvement in the Tea Party movement, but truth is I am so everyday ordinary it's not even funny. Looking back, I am surprised myself that I got in on the ground floor of our San Angelo Tea Party but am so very glad I did. I have always been a voter but admittedly not always a well educated one. For the most part I would cast my vote in an election, and then go on about my business. I didn't do much to follow actions of my elected officials other than listen to mainstream media reporting, and I sure had no idea at that time just how little I was being told! I actually stumbled across Rush Limbaugh on the radio one day and was amazed at what I heard. Before then, I didn't even know who Rush was. I discovered the AM channel was full of such programs and tuned in to hear what other talk show hosts had to say. In February 2009 I again "stumbled," this time on to an American Family Radio talk show station. The commentators were discussing Tea Parties being held across the country to protest federal government actions, and a web site was given for more information. At that time several such events had been held in a few larger cities, and now "the second wave" was being planned for April 15th. Upon visiting the web site I saw there was no Tea Party in the San Angelo area and thought that was strange. We are a city of 100,000 mostly conservative citizens, and I knew many were unhappy with the TARP bill passed under President Bush's watch and now President Obama's apologizing for America all over the place, not to mention taxes in general. Plus, by this time I am a grandmother of a precious little one-year-old boy, who thanks to recent government spending is already $30,000 in debt and hasn't yet earned a dime! Just what is this country going to look like when he comes of age? We San Angelo-ans needed an opportunity to participate and let our voices be heard. Without thinking any further I filled in my contact information and sent it off, not really knowing what to expect.

It was probably not an hour later my phone started ringing and it rang the rest of the day. People from the area saw my name listed as willing to organize a Tea Party, and they wanted to be involved. We set a date and time for our first meeting, and we planned a Tea Party for San Angelo for April 15th! Again, none of us knew really what we were doing, and we sure didn't know what to expect. But I tell you, when I arrived at our rally site that day and saw the crowd already gathering, I knew then something of historic proportion was happening all across the country, and I was proud we were participating. It really was an emotional moment. There was that feeling of knowing you were not alone, that you weren't imagining things. People did care and were concerned about freedom and liberty, our very way of life. Law enforcement officials on site estimated the crowd to be between 1,300 and 1,500 people!

This group that came together and now is known as the San Angelo Tea Party, Inc. is made up of everyday citizens just like me, concerned about the direction our country is headed and wanting to do something about it. We now have a board of directors, and I have the honor of serving as president. The passion, commitment and drive present in our organization is inspiring, and I am so blessed to be a part. It hasn't been easy. We have experienced some growing pains, had some heated disagreements, and been accused of not doing enough or of doing the wrong things. That is frustrating.

One of the first decisions that had to be made was what we wanted to achieve as an organization. Holding rallies and venting serves a purpose, but we knew from the beginning those alone wouldn't bring about the return of limited government and fiscal responsibility. After many discussions and debates, we chose education of our area citizens to be our focus rather than endorsing and campaigning for any particular political party or candidate. Apathy and ill-informed potential voters are issues we feel we can better address. Every meeting we have first-time attendees, and often this is not what they want to hear. They do not understand why we are not more into campaign mode. I explain it simply by saying our Founding Fathers knew if the citizens of a constitutional Republic were not well versed in the rights and responsibilities of living under such a government, they would not live under it for long.

This is another benefit I have derived from this endeavor—a re-acquaintance with my country's truly amazing history. Our Founding Fathers were divinely inspired, of that I am convinced. How could anyone even remotely familiar with our beginnings deny the significant impact Christianity had? The wisdom of our Founding Fathers remains unparalleled today, and it saddens me as I learn more about how far we have strayed from their vision for America. However, I have seen the determination of everyday citizens to be heard, to turn the tide and take this country back to sanity! The Tax Payers March on DC on September 12th was ill-reported by the media, but I can tell you there was close to 1,000,000 people there, if not more. Now that was a sight to behold!

We Americans do not need, nor do we want, to be wards of our government. We are waking up to the fact that we have been negligent in our duties as citizens of this great country to be informed and active in the political process, at all levels of government. It is exciting to see people stepping forward to read and track pending legislation, challenge elected officials in town halls, be involved in precinct and state conventions, conduct voter drives, run for office, show up at tax rate hearings and ask questions, and so much more. David Barton, an amazing historian, has reported people are actually spending money to buy books about American History! All this gives me such hope and optimism for tomorrow.

Thank you for the opportunity to present my Tea Party story, and best wishes to you with your book. I do believe there are many stories still to be written by countless Tea Partiers. Perhaps you will be able to compile several volumes through the years, as I believe the Tea Party movement will remain active, continuing its work to return our country back to foundational principles of limited government and fiscal responsibility.

TEA PARTY LEADERS

Ray Rayome

I think I became politically aware in my freshman year of high school in 1973. Two things contributed to this. I realized that I was quickly approaching the mandatory draft age, even though the Vietnam conflict was winding down but had not yet concluded. And our Student Council was in a vicious battle with the current Superintendent of Schools (1973 Hilton, NY).

The war and street riots of the turbulent '60s were fresh in my memory. I witnessed the country on the verge of tearing itself apart until the Nixon administration settled on getting the nation out of that hellhole.

But I played a small part in supporting our student government in challenging what appeared to be an unaccountable tyrannical administrator, and ultimately having him *removed*. Students. Kids, really. I was deeply impressed, but not really sold. Only because following graduation I did eleven years on active duty in the US Navy Seabees. To defend the Constitution you end up forfeiting some rights. And I had to learn to keep quiet.

My travel overseas impressed upon me the very manner by which the US was perceived. What struck me most was the sheer magnitude of poverty I encountered. The socialist and Islamic countries I visited put a dent in me. The memory I take away most was throngs of poor children in Egypt clambering to touch the stars on the back of our dress jumpers for good luck. For them, America was hope, freedom and prosperity. I've learned to never take my country for granted ever since.

The cause for the recent involvement started the moment the national media starting touting an unknown Senator from Illinois as the next *Messiah*. A political savior? Are you kidding me? First off, who is this clown? And secondly, age and experience has always taught me never surrender your trust to an elected official. I decided to pore into his background. What I discovered alarmed me greatly. The first anxiety fell squarely on the questions and subsequent lawsuits regarding his claims of being born in Hawaii. Followed by his radical associations, dangerous friends, empty rhetoric and scant record of his public and personal background. An engineer I worked with in Seattle asked me, "Is it because he's black that you don't like him?" I told him, "No. From the surface I find him both naïve and dangerous." And mentioned I would gladly vote for Colin Powell or Condoleezza Rice. His fishing trip to snatch an admission of "white guilt" from me resulted in no such luck.

Being a pronounced student of history, specifically American history, the word *progressive* kept creeping up into the political conversation. The progressives were radical socialists and communists during the '20s and '30s. And then to change the perception by which the nation identified them, they re-packaged themselves as *liberals*. Ironic how they are now reversing this label once again. Same wolf, different fleece.

But what struck me most of all was Obama/Soetoro's connection to radical Islam. I spent eight years teaching counter-terrorism in the military. This man's ties were profoundly disturbing, especially since Islam is unwavering in the destruction of the West, worldwide domination and the slaughter of infidels. Several of my friends are counted among their victims.

After returning to Colorado, an additional two actions beset me again. One was my realization that Obama was not a natural born citizen. This led me to volunteering myself to the lawsuit brought by Orly Taitz. Each state has two active or retired military veterans to act as plaintiffs in the case. I am subject to lifelong recall, as well as a Lt. Colonel on active duty in the USAF. Although the lawsuits continue to be deliberately bogged down in the court system (You may recall Obama privately met with the US Supreme Court prior to the inauguration—a move both unethical and illegal since he is a defendant in a pending case before that body), I believe the GOP is waiting for January

2011 to regain majority in the House to seek impeachment proceedings. Regardless, the World Net Daily people have approved my request for a "Where's the Birth Certificate?" billboard on behalf of the Wyobraska Tea Party. We look to take possession and install it sometime next week. Look for us in the news!

My wife (Daughters of the American Revolution Loveland Regent) mentioned a local group forming that was trying to address the expansion of the federal branch, the usurpations of our laws, and the inability of our elected officials to act for the Constituents they were elected to faithfully represent. This organization was "Liberty on the Rocks," formed by Amanda Teresi from Denver.

Although this group brought together people of like-minded persuasion, they generally lacked organization. But shortly thereafter, Glenn Beck launched his 912 campaign. Taking a cue from the larger Colorado Springs, Colorado 912 organization, we launched our own group in Loveland, which has had marked success. While were able to identify and assign group leaders watchdogging government areas of concern (i.e. health care, immigration, taxes, pending local, state and federal statues and Social Security), our Tea Party folks developed their own core organization, planned events, coordinated the activities, and then invited everyone to participate.

As you had mentioned on the telephone, the original Tea Party was a direct protest against the intolerable acts passed by the British Parliament and sanctioned by the king. Years of lawful and legal petitions to the crown by his loyal subjects were rejected. The Colonies were looked more upon as a commercial venture to be squeezed, regardless of the cash-strapped treasure the citizens of the Americas had spent in the previous conflicts with French and Indian uprisings. They felt no less English, and deserving of their ancient freedoms and rights. A precedent was set, but those settlers had always been left to their own devices.

To establish law, civil discourse and commerce where none were to be found. Nature and circumstances had created a new culture.

But consider this; The Tea Party supported Sarah Palin in the general election—not the GOP. The Tea Party conducted rallies, protests on local street corners and petitioned elected officials— not the GOP. The Tea Party placed 3 million law-abiding citizens on the Mall in Washington, DC regarding the health care bill—not the GOP.

But more importantly, it gave me an outlet to present and instruct a new breed of citizen lessons that we have long forgotten. That America is an *idea*. That our country comprises of fifty separate nation-states voluntarily bound together for the pursuit of our common goals and promotion of our national character. And that this character is the foundation upon which the Constitution claimed that the government shall be subservient to the governed. That our laws were expressly devised to restrict and inhibit the power of the administrations of men created solely to serve the people. And that the blessings of freedom and justice may be secured.

That ended January 20th 2009. We are now threatened by a Federal Branch that is:
- Prescribing our education
- Mandating our health care
- Nationalizing large segments of the private sector, like the banking and the automotive industries
- Propagating our dependence on foreign oil
- Ignoring the societal dangers of illegal immigration
- Perpetuating the culturally destructive influence of the welfare state

And in doing so, they have:
- Expanded the central government's power over the states
- Violated our Constitution
- Actively sought to suspend our inalienable rights
- Perverted both our laws and legislative process

- Seized private industry and destabilized our private sector
- Abused our currency and mortgaged our future to foreign powers
- Undermined our national defense, rejected our allies and prostrated themselves before our avowed enemies
- Acted to subvert our sovereignty and imperil our culture

My main organizational theme and focus, now, has been to use my public speaking ability and organizational sense to whip up public knowledge and interest in reasserting the primacy of the Tenth Amendment. This effort has put me into contact with others across the country, permitting me to consult with several towns in Texas. As well as helping a new group form in Florida.

But why I am doing this? Simple. America's laws and rights cannot defend themselves. They are neither Right nor Left. And the Tea Party offers independently thinking citizens to band together to defy the conventional notions of narrow-minded party affiliations, and strive to recapture the spirit and essence of the miracle brought forth by the intellect, courage and sacrifices by our forefathers. A force and character that for over 230 years has defiantly opposed tyranny, championed the weak, took a stand to defend both freedom and justice, and prevailed as the symbol towards the grand potential of individual human endeavor.

America doesn't need heroes—it demands them. So it then becomes, as it has always been, our responsibility to defend ourselves. To stand resolute where others cannot. To challenge the encroachment of tyranny, and against all who seek to trespass against us. And to encourage each citizen to join with me. In some small measure or in some small way, to be the first and last word in securing and protecting the people's liberties.

TEA PARTY – THE AWAKENING

Marion and Tom Bower

Our story is really very short. Last June 2009, my husband and I, along with my cousin and his wife attended the encore performance of Glenn Beck's Common Sense tour at a Maumee theater. Wow, I had listened to Glenn on the radio and we had attended two of his Toledo Shows. We left the theater that night realizing that we could no longer sit on our hands. The four of us decided that we would put on a 4th of July rally. We found a local parking lot that we were allowed to use and began trying to find *help*. Boy did we need it.

We purchased fifty copies of Glenn Beck's *Common Sense* to give away. That morning about 9 a.m. we towed our large flat bed trailer, a large flagpole, fifty copies of Common Sense, a portable speaker and what we hoped was our "common sense" to the parking lot. We had many tell us we were tilting windmills. At 10 a.m. we had about 200 people waiting to register and another 250 people waiting for the program to start. It was estimated that we had between 450 and 500 fellow patriots join us that morning. It was an amazing day with so many people thanking us for giving them a forum and a chance to speak up and out. They and we knew we were not alone in this—many felt the same as we did and were scared about what was happening to our country and our freedom.

Many of those that helped on the 4th stepped up again when we decided to have a local rally on 9-12. Wow—we decided to have this one at the local private airport. It was billed as a Fly-In, Drive-In Tea Party. I think it was the only one in the country that day. We had placed flyers around town, notified radio and TV and also newspapers. We decided it was a Tea Party, so we gave away Iced Tea and Hot Dogs. We also gave away pocket Constitutions and "Don't Tread On Us" bumper stickers. It was evident that when we ran out of parking we had a huge event on our hands. The estimated crowd was about 2,000 people. For a community of 17,000, that was more than we ever expected. The

370

owner of the airport, Rex Damschroder, took a plane up and did some aerial pictures of the event. We did have three planes fly in for the event. As with the July 4th event, this event also had no need for cleanup afterwards. We knew with the July 4th event that there was no paper or litter anywhere, but with this much larger event we were shocked that there was nothing to clean up. What great people conservative patriots are!

After that event, many of those helping decided that we needed to formally organize our group. In October of '09 we held our first formal meeting and discussed what we wanted to be and how we wanted to get there. Our mission statement says it all— "Through education, we will reclaim the vision for America that our Founding Fathers sacrificed to leave us as an inheritance."

We ordered more of the pocket Constitutions and to date have distributed about 2,000 to local schools and about another 2,000 at parades and rally events. In January we started two book studies on *The 5000 Year Leap*. That is the book to really put what our founders wanted in your face. Boy, are we off the road they laid for us. We have purchased about 200 copies of *The 5000 Year Leap* for sale at rallies and events as well as for the use of our members.

In October we hosted a movie showing of *Not Evil, Just Wrong* at the Clyde High School Auditorium. The Clyde School system had accepted 750 copies of the pocket Constitution for use in their 5th grade, middle school and high school government classes. We donated $350 from the proceeds of the movie to their American History and Government programs. So much of the money going to schools today is earmarked for math, science and the arts, with very little of extra funding going into such an important part of the education of our youth. Scott Nossaman, the middle school history teacher, is amazing, devoting so much time and effort into really making the Constitution and our Founding Fathers real to his students.

We have also purchased "Don't Tread On Us" flags and bumper stickers. It is so gratifying to drive around the area and see our flags flying and bumper stickers on vehicles in the area. People are no longer afraid to stand up and be counted. They know they are not alone.

On August 28, we will have two buses going from our area to the Glenn Beck 8-28 rally. Everyone on the trip is excited about the opportunity to meet with others that are likeminded.

My husband and I have a small business and thank goodness we do business with other small businessmen in the country. It is amazing to me that when we have people stop in to our office, they are thanking us for getting involved and trying to make a difference. When we got into this, the local newspaper asked why we were doing it. It did not take me long to answer that question: "We are doing this for our grandchildren!" They are not responsible for what the previous generations have done to this wonderful country, but boy are they going to have to pay for it. Our meetings always start out with prayer and end with the Doxology. We need to acknowledge and thank God for his continued blessings on this country and hopefully he will help guide the Tea Party movement around this country to turn our country around and soon. It is essential that we continue in a peaceful manner to bring light to what is going on in the dark recesses of our government and its leaders. We just recently ordered signs for our July 3rd rally (We are encouraging everyone attending to "Go to church tomorrow and pray for our nation"). The signs say "In God We Trust," "Pray for America," "II Chronicles 7:14," and our web site. Between "In God We Trust" and "Pray for America" is an American flag. We hope to see these up all over around our area.

We are not a large group, but we have many in our group that are very committed to trying to do everything they can to make our country what it was supposed to be. It is evident we need to turn back to God in this nation. Last night in our book study, I was amazed that five charts on the video showed the changes in America since the removal of prayer in our schools. SAT scores dropped dramatically and illegitimacy rates, divorce/single family homes, sexually transmitted diseases and crime went through the roof. This all happened since the '60s. What have we done to our nation and our people since our country has turned from God? God help us even if we do not deserve it.

Mary Wright

Becoming a member of the Tea Party was a fairly easy step for me. I grew up during the 1940s and patriotism was as much a part of my life as church and school. We saved string, gathered foil from gum wrappings, saved newspapers, emptied tin cans by removing their lids and mashing them flat, and prided ourselves on being able to take a few pennies to school to donate to the Red Cross. We had a flag in our window showing my daddy was serving in the Army. We bought savings bonds regularly. We were Americans and proud of it.

Like many Americans, I have always been interested in politics, though I have not been actively engaged. I have never missed voting in an election. Two years ago, I was adamantly opposed to Barack Hussein Obama and let family and friends know about it. That was not enough to keep him from being elected. As the past year and a half have unfolded, I have become more disenchanted with the ways things are going and have found myself wanting changes. My television does not display national news. I no longer subscribe to magazines like *Newsweek* or *Time.* I feel that Sean Hannity, Rush Limbaugh, Glenn Beck and Mark Levin are personal friends of mine!

Over a year ago, my daughter began working with the Richmond (VA) Tea Party. She has regaled me with stories of her activities and their work. She was a part of the 9/11 march last year and was in DC again last spring to protest the health care bill passage. She has been my anchor in the past year.

When the health care bill passed last spring, I called her crying. I couldn't stand the thought of what I could perceive was going to happen. Where was my America? Where were the freedoms and the rights I thought I had? I called my daughter that night, crying. I told her how depressed I was and how upset I was. I told her how alone I felt. Turning the tables on me, she said, "Mother, stop it. Get up out of that chair and go find some people who think like you do and want what you want. Start a Tea Party."

That night I called my brother who is a doctor here in town and talked to him. We agreed to go to a meeting of a local Tea Party. On the night of the meeting, his wife, his secretary and her husband Fred, and I went to our first Tea Party meeting. Three people were in attendance. The gathering was more like a support group than an action group. We left disappointed and still desirous of action. The next day, I contacted that group on Facebook and asked them to meet with us to discuss things. We never heard from them.

My daughter was here on April 15 because her father has terminal cancer. She talked me into going to the courthouse for the April 15 Tea Party. It was exhilarating. My brother had done some ads on the radio about showing up to register our discontent and about 250 people were there. That night, my brother, his wife, my daughter and I met to discuss Tea Parties and how to form one. Julie, my daughter, gave us great direction. We called in about five to eight other people we knew of and began making plans. After that meeting, Fred and I looked at each other and said, "We can do this."

We scheduled our first organizational meeting of the Wabash Valley Tea Party for May 25. We advertised on the radio and put out signs. About 200 people showed up. On June 15 we had a potluck meeting scheduled. In spite of a terrific storm that rolled through the area that evening, we had over 250 people present. Our roll now numbers over 400. We expect to reach 1,000 by election time. Congressional candidates are contacting us to speak to our members. The word is getting out. We did it! It has grown unbelievably fast. The word has spread and people from all over the Wabash Valley are responding. They want something to hold onto. They too want to know they are not alone. I have done what my daughter told me: I got up out of that chair and found some people who think like I do and want what I want. I started a Tea Party—with a little help from my brother!

It is difficult to say how many people have told me how mad they are and how much they want change. In a recent newsletter to members, I quoted Abraham Lincoln's Gettysburg Address:

> We are engaged in a great civil war, testing whether that nation or any nation so conceived and so dedicated, can long endure ... The world will little note, nor long remember what we say here, but it can never forget what they did here. It is for us the living, rather, to be dedicated here to the unfinished work which they who fought here have thus far so nobly advanced. It is rather for us to be here dedicated to the great task remaining before us— that from these honored dead we take increased devotion to that cause for which they gave the last full measure of devotion—that we here highly resolve that these dead shall not have died in vain—that this nation, under God, shall have a new birth of freedom—and that government of the people, by the people, for the people, shall not perish from the earth.

This is the job of the Tea Party—we must restore government of the people, by the people, for the people shall not perish from the earth. I am so proud that I made the decision to be a Tea Partier. See you in DC!

Michael Openshaw

I am a fifty-six-year-old database developer living in Plano, Texas. My family consist of my wife Catherine (Shin-Ning Ai),

375

my son Alan who just finished at UT Austin, and my "daughter" (in all but blood) <u>Winnifred Nazziwa</u> in Uganda.

Politically, I am a co-founder of the North Texas Tea Party, a highly active group in Collin County and beyond, encompassing many northern suburbs of Dallas. Our group was founded as a spinoff of the Dallas Tea Party, as we wanted the option of actively working for candidates and started with about a dozen. Our meetings normally field over 100 and we have 2,500 on our mailing list.

My story is a bit unusual in the Tea Party, in that I grew up in politics, working in grassroots campaigns in Kansas for Bob Dole and Barry Goldwater, staying active in the Reagan campaign of '76 and '80 and even serving a stint as Denton County GOP chairman (as a dirt-poor graduate student) in 1982. I moved away from politics toward the late '80s, as the people we used to call the Rockefeller Republicans took control of the Party machinery and came to the conclusion that the grassroots weren't all that important (and I started a family). I returned to politics at the start of Iraq War when it was obvious the press wasn't even trying for honest reporting. I read blogs like Michael Yon and Iraq the Model. I started my own blogs (<u>Datatroll</u> and my charity site Mzungu Mike). I kept my efforts online until Support the Troops rally started up and began attending some of those. Then came the fiscal insanity of the bank bailouts, the election cycle and the election of someone determined to drive us at warp speed into national bankruptcy. Our Baby Boomer generation and the generation that followed—through short-sightedness and self-centeredness—are responsible for this impending disaster and we have to fix it for the generations to follow.

I went looking for some way to act and attended my first Tea Party rally on April 15th, 2009, and immediately realized that a group was forming that was founded *only* on constitutional governance and fiscal responsibility. I became quite active, joined in founding the North Texas Tea Party, and helped formulate the concepts that drive the group, including the "Tea Approval" process for candidates and issues that proved pretty successfully at the state and county level. We also were effective at putting together rallies and counter-rallies on the health care issue, normally crushing turnouts of groups like MoveOn by ten to one.

I have since stepped away from leadership, allowing others to take effective control (I am a run-and-gun concept guy and have personal issues—including an upcoming charity trip to Africa in the fall and my son's impending brain surgery—that take up a fair amount of my time for now). The Tea Party group is not about any one individual; it is one of the finest and most unique political groups I've ever served with.

Monica Boyer

As I sat down to take on the task of writing the story of how our lives changed forever just a little over a year ago, I was confident that it would be an easy task. I excitedly agreed to take on the task. However, when I picked up my pen, I realized the reality of what I had just agreed to do. This was not going to be easy. Not only was I going to have trouble seeing the page through the tears, but I realized how in just one year, we have already carved out a piece of history. It takes my breath away. For the past thirteen years I had been busy doing what every other mom was doing. I was building my home business as a licensed home daycare provider, raising my four children, supporting my husband in his job, voting Republican and going to church. I was doing my part; building my own little corner of the American Dream. I was for the most part oblivious to what was going on in the political world. Everything seemed rosy. Life was good.

I started to see hints that trouble was on the horizon when I saw a heavy-handed government begin to over-regulate my industry and indoctrinate the children. I began to see warning lights go off, but there was no one to help. I had to learn about how government works just to survive as a business owner. I knew at that point my life had to change, but I had no idea how much. If I would have known what was just ahead, I would have *run away*!

After President Barack Obama was elected, things went from bad to worse. Parents could no longer afford to keep their children in my daycare, and so inevitably I had to close the doors. As I was doing laundry one evening, I turned on the television watched the Glenn Beck program. I will *never ever* forget that moment as long as I live. As I listened to Glenn, I felt the laundry slip from my hands, and tears began to fall down my face. He was talking about America and what was ahead for us if we did not find some way to wake people up. I remember just sitting on the floor and feeling like the weight of the world had just been lifted from my shoulders. Then ten tons were placed on my back. I looked at my four children. They were all sitting on the floor with me, silent as mice. I looked at each one of them ... looked deep into their eyes, and I knew right then that I had to do something. I didn't know what, but I had to do something. I could not let this president or this administration steal their future on my watch. I honestly don't think I slept for two days after that.

Finally, I did what I always do when I face an obstacle. I got on my knees and prayed. "Lord," I said, "I have no idea what you are up to. I am just a mom, I have nothing to give. No education, no political experience. The only thing I have is this mama bear inside of me that will protect these children with my last breath." I prayed earnestly for wisdom and direction and strength to do whatever I would have to do.

For the next few days, I fasted and prayed. I called our local Republican Party here in my town to see if there was anything I could do. The doors were pretty closed. They did not seem to think there was a problem. I think they even tried to sell me tickets for their next fundraiser!

My frustration continued to build. By complete accident, I happened to find out two of my friends from high school were beginning to feel the same way I was. We started to talk about our feelings of helplessness, but we still didn't know what we could do. March 12, 2009, was a day I will never forget. A few families gathered in a home to watch a special edition of the Glenn Beck program where the strategy was laid out. The battle lines were drawn, and we committed ourselves to educate and to begin the process of taking back our nation. It was a family deal. All the children were with us as we laughed and cried together. We were ashamed. Ashamed that we had not educated ourselves, ashamed that we had let this happen. I honestly admit that I had never read the Constitution before. That television show changed the course of history for our town. The people of this group became the core of the Tea Party, and then the core of Silent No More. The real leaders emerged from this meeting. We did not know what to do, but we knew we were not alone.

Then we heard about the Tea Parties. They were happening all over the country. People just like us were *doing* something. I had little "what if" ideas here and there, but I thought, "Surely someone else will have one here in our county. Surely someone has already thought of it." And I waited.

Time passed and there was nothing. I was beginning to grow increasingly restless as I watched the news each day. One morning I read the story of Esther in the Bible. This woman was fearless (Or seemed fearless). She was close to her God. She knew the danger of going to the king, but it didn't matter "for such a time as this." In fact she even said, "If I die, I die." That's courage! Pushing aside her fear, she went to the King, and saved her people from the harm that was about to befall them. That was the last straw for me. I picked up the phone and called my two friends. I said, "Guys, I can't sit at home anymore. What if *we* put together a Tea Party for our county? Do you think anyone would come?" We had no idea, but decided to try anyway. So on April 8th, with just one week, we began planning the first Kosciusko County Tea Party. We said, "Wouldn't it be great if we had twenty people show up?" We were so nervous. We counted our family members. If each of us had five or six family members show up that we would look like a success! We had flyers made and contacted the local newspaper. We were lucky enough to get a front-page article! We talked to everyone who would listen. We prayed and prayed and prayed.

April 15th came. The event was to be held at 6 p.m. Imagine our surprise as people started rolling in at 4:30! They brought signs, trailers, flags and kids. They covered the lawn of the courthouse. I remember standing on the steps looking up to the sky and breathing a thank you to God. That day our lives changed forever. 1,300 people came out!

I looked out across the sea of faces into the eyes of America. I saw tears, joy, and relief. I saw them realize for the first time that they too were not alone. It was the most moving experience of my life.

We continued to meet in homes learning about the Constitution, reading about our founders, and also meeting to pray for the country. One night, a group of eight of us sat around a kitchen table and decided that we could never go away, that we must continue to meet. It wasn't enough for us to meet once in a while with signs and cheers to excitement. We needed to actually change our country. We as a people had let this mess happen to our nation and we needed to fix it, starting with our own way of life. We were now responsible. We could never again be silent. A new name and new group was formed around that table: Kosciusko Silent No More.

Some of our earliest meetings were focused on what exactly we wanted to be about. What was our purpose? Were we still part of the Tea Party movement or something completely new? Should we join a coalition of other groups, or stand by ourselves? Could we take donations? Would we support candidates? Would we meet weekly, monthly? What would we do at the meetings? Do we have a president? A board? Was it possible for a group such as ours to make real lasting changes in the political realm? Would anyone listen to us?

It took several months of meetings to realize that we wouldn't have most of those answers for a while. We had to just do what we could and trust in God that the rest would come. And it did. Needs arose, and people stepped in to fill those needs, becoming the core board of our group. Funds were necessary to continue our projects, and funds were provided, always just enough to pull it off. It was a miracle. Actually, several miracles on an on-going basis.

The first need we had as a group was an American flag. We felt it was important to pledge our allegiance at every meeting. A man stood up and took his hat off and said, "Let's get this group a flag!" We passed the hat, and at the next meeting, our group had a flag!

Things began to move quickly for our group. Within a month we were placed under the microscope of media outlets, newspapers, and the public eye. We found ourselves having to be ready to give an account for what we believed at the drop of a hat! Two major events stick out in my mind, the first one being our Senatorial Candidate Debate. This debate was held for five of the Indiana Senatorial Candidates that were going to de-seat (at the time) liberal Evan Bayh (since them, Mr. Bayh has turned in his retirement papers). All five candidates agreed to this debate. This debate caught the attention of the national media! It was almost breathtaking to see the Fox News truck roll into town. Several times throughout the event, I just looked up to heaven and said, "Lord, why did you pick us to do this? Why are you using a small town in the state of Indiana to make a difference? The answer came to me after the debate (which was a *huge* success) was over. The Lord said, "Because you are willing." And that we are. We have no idea where this group is going, but we know our hands are open and we are willing to go where He sends us.

The second event that sticks out in my mind was held after the 2nd successful Tea Party in Warsaw. It was called One Nation Back to God. This event gripped my heart. The board of Kosciusko Silent No More realizes that we are nothing without our Savior ... our Creator. We have realized that without Him, we might as well stay home and play checkers. I believe this is what sets our group apart. Each board member sincerely believes that we must put him first ... we must give *Him* the glory for what He has done with this group. In fact we have a separate portion of the group *only* dedicated to prayer and intercession. The One Nation Back to God seminar was strictly for this reason. We brought in Reverend C.L. Bryant, Pastor John B. Lowe, Micah Clark from the American Association of Indiana, and Dave Koontz the Right to Life director in Kosciusko County. These men put it on the line for about 250 people. We had twenty-seven pastors from the surrounding areas come! There was not one person that left wondering what they should be doing. People left with a *new* mission, and a *new* purpose. *Churches began taking this idea and throwing away the fear of losing their 501(c)3 status.* It was an event of a lifetime!

I could give story after story about how God is using a tiny group of Americans—of Indiana Hoosiers—to make a difference. Their hearts are pure; they are moms and dads who have never done anything political in their life. They have jobs, kids and lives that they have put on hold to fight this battle of socialism and anti-Americanism. We have hit many hurdles, and have faced sadness as we had to plow through the agony of losing a congressman to an adulterous affair. This time when Fox News came into town, there was no excitement. There was sadness, and need to pick up our shoelaces, and get back to work electing the man that we felt could represent the 3rd district and not his own interests. After a strategic process, we immediately endorsed the candidate that most closely aligned with our values, and began the procedure to place him on the ballot. With the help of surrounding Tea Parties, he won. The Tea Party was able to flex our political muscle and see victory! This journey has truly been a miracle in the cornfields of Indiana. My life has been forever changed. History is being written for our children. I will never forget the time the governor's office told me, "Monica, we have given you everything you have asked for; we have worked with you, when you will quit asking? I paused and tears came to my eyes. I said, "Please let the governor know I will stop asking when I can look into my four beautiful children's eyes and with every fiber of my being tell them 'I did everything I could to protect you and give you the freedom that my grandfather fought so hard to give me.' That is when I will stop asking."

We continue to meet every 1st and 3rd Tuesday of each month. We are learning how to get involved locally and work within the two party system. We are learning that without the foundation, and the groundwork like the local precincts, that the national work will not be accomplished. It is the grunt work that will change history, not speeches or fame. This week I wrote an article for our local newspaper as a guest columnist. It explains our mission for Kosciusko silent No More and why we do what we do.

Ronald Wilcox

It was the spring of '08 which set me on my path to conservative activism. I was running one of the top-rated high-line automobile dealerships in New England. I was in charge of our certified pre-owned division and was selling and financing fifty to sixty cars a month. At fifty-nine years old I had spent most of my life working on straight commission and was finally seeing the rewards of my efforts. At the rate I was earning I figured I could retire at sixty-two. I always lived within my means because in this brutal industry you could lose your job at any moment for any reason. My workdays were ten to twelve hours and I rarely had two days off in a row. I was earning a good six figure income, driving exotic expensive automobiles and finally starting to relax with the knowledge that my future was bright and I was living the American Dream.

As we moved into the summer of '08, the politics started to heat up as November elections started to be the focus of the press. Day after day the papers promoted how bad the economy was and how under Republican leadership we were headed toward economic disaster. We were not seeing this in Connecticut but attitudes were starting to change. People were starting to believe this—they were being hammered in the media as part of Democratic campaign strategy. It was working. Though overall sales were up 24%, things were slowing down. As fall approached, everything tightened up. Banks became stricter, customers more cautious, and car values started to fall. We relied on vehicles coming off lease and we would be required by our manufacturer to purchase these vehicles and certify them. What was happening was their residual values fell dramatically and now much of our inventory we owned above market value. My commission checks were getting smaller and smaller and my workload was increasing.

When the elections took place, it was like someone came and closed the spigot. We went from crowded showroom to some days without a customer. As one of the top paid managers and on in my years, I could see the writing on the wall.

In January of '09 I was laid off for lack of work. I filed for unemployment and started my job search. As a top executive in the auto industry, I relied on my network of contacts whenever I felt like a change or for general information. Whenever there was movement in Connecticut I would be aware of this. What I found was that many of my contacts were also out of work or barely hanging on. Connecticut had lost $1/3^{rd}$ of their car dealerships and those still in business were cutting back. At sixty I was competing with forty and fifty year olds for the few positions that surfaced.

I found myself watching the news all day while combing the Internet looking for employment. What I discovered was that I wasn't getting the news! The newspapers weren't reporting what was really going on, nor was the local TV news. During the election I found myself watching more and more Fox News. And after watching Fox, MSNBC, and CNN, I realized I was learning things on Fox that never appeared on the other stations, particularly when it came to commentary. This angered me. What really amazed me was the $787 billion dollar stimulus bill which nobody bothered about or had time to read. Watching bailouts particularly for GM just ignited my anger.

I started to hear and see this thing called the Tea Party and learned that they were having a Tax Day rally in New Haven, CT. As a conservative I am not really one who likes to protest, but something drew me to New Haven. I knew virtually every bill and everything that was going on in Washington and felt this powerless frustration that I later found out was shared by millions. Our elected officials could care less what we thought, wanted or needed. They were career people and their only loyalty was to their party and keeping their jobs. When I arrived in New Haven I was amazed. There were hundreds of people, most in my age group. They were orderly, knowledgeable and deeply concerned. The main theme was that the government needed to honor people's rights as defined in the Constitution. Many people carried the Constitution with them. They announced an open microphone and I felt compelled to speak. I was the second speaker and I was able to rally and ignite the crowd merely by relaying the facts as they were unfolding. After I spoke I was approached by many people shaking my hand, hugging me, thanking me, asking me to run for office and requesting my e-mail address. I was deeply moved by this out pouring of support. I merely vocalized the frustration that everyone was feeling.

Time went by, I keep watching the news, I stayed in touch by e-mail with some of the people I met, kept looking and hoping for employment opportunities which did not exist.

We now had the health care bill before us and my fear of its passing required I do something. I saw what was in the stimulus bill and could only imagine what the health care bill contained. There were Town Hall meetings set up in my district and our congressman was holding a series of them. I attended one in Danbury and confronted him directly. I wanted to know how he could sign a $787 billion dollar bill without reading it. There was no way anyone could have read it based on the number of pages and the time allotted. Had anyone who ever worked in the private sector ever sign anything even remotely similar without reading it they would be immediately fired! He spent an hour or more answering complaints and requests that he not sign the health care bill. There was not one person who actually supported this bill. It was mostly outcries against it and pleas not to sign. I thought with this kind of opposition our congressman would listen to the people and vote against it. The next day I picked up the newspaper and read a quote from our congressman. *He stated that the people at the Town Hall meeting were overwhelmingly in support of this bill!*

That did it for me. Of all the things that were happening I would have to say this was the one incident that forced me to get involved. To have our congressman totally ignore his constituents and then openly and blatantly lie about it was the final straw. I called him numerous times but never got a call back. When the health care bill passed, he sent me a letter stating this was the most debated, most transparent bill ever passed. I guess he didn't hear Nancy Pelosi say, "You will know what's in the bill once we pass it." I also called our attorney general numerous times to ask him to join other states in filing suit to block this but as with my congressman never got a call back.

Since that time I joined the Tea Party movement. I helped in Tax Day 2010 bring some twenty-nine candidates to speak at a major Tea Party Tax Day event. I built relationships with many of these candidates and currently work with and support their campaigns. I have joined my local RTC and work with many other conservative groups. I attend every event I can, including our Republican State Convention. My primary goal is one of education; to provide conservative Americans with as much information regarding pending bills and legislation as possible so that they are actively involved and can have a voice in their government. The Tea Party movement and our groups provide them with the means to stay engaged and have a presence in the political arena. I do this as I continue to seek employment with hopes that someday the opportunities that once existed for everyone will be restored and that we will return to the conservative core values which made our country great.

Susan H. Forrister

When I first heard the words "too big to fail" spoken by then-president George W. Bush, I felt in my gut that we were headed down a path that would lead this country to ruin. Having the government bail out banks meant, of course, that the American people had to foot the bill. Then when both presidential candidates came out in support of this travesty, I began to lose all hope.

My frustration and anger only escalated as the Obama administration took shape and exactly what he meant by "fundamental change" became apparent. It made no difference that I did not vote for him; he was my president. But it became clear from the beginning that he represented a direction for this country that I was adamantly opposed to. He and his administration stood arrogantly before the cameras and proclaimed that this was what the people wanted: government-run health care, government-controlled energy, government-run banks and automakers, more government. I began to scream at my television. I felt completely disenfranchised. Alone. I felt that I just had to let them know that not *all* Americans wanted this. That me and my family were completely and utterly against bailouts, piling on insurmountable debt that our children and grandchildren could not meet; regulation of our energy, the media, and guns; and bigger government.

Then came April 15, 2009. That's the day I went to my first Tea Party in Atlanta. There I found fellow Americans carrying signs that expressed *my* anger, *my* frustration. Thousands of us stood as one against this takeover of our nation. Once again I had hope. I was not alone.

I left there with a pocket copy of our Constitution, and reacquainted myself with the grand old document—and a new awareness of all our liberties that had been steadily eroded over the years by our government. I also carried a fire in my soul and determined to start a Tea Party group in my county. I had no clue how to begin, but I surfed the Internet and landed on Americans for Prosperity and Virginia Galloway. With her help, I called the very first meeting of the Haralson County T.E.A. Party Patriots (Taxed Enough Already) and we held our own Tea Party that June. My husband and I attended the march on Washington on September 12, 2009. We volunteered at other Tea Parties, and I had the opportunity to work at this year's Atlanta Tax Day Tea Party—one year to the day when I first had my eyes truly opened to the Power of the People. Our little group is having our 2nd annual Tea Party this July 17th. I fully expect a crowd at least double that of last year.

The fight continues, and it will continue even after November. Even after the Presidential election in 2012, should the Lord let this old world go on. For once awakened, We the People can never again allow ourselves to fall asleep on the watch. We must be vigilant. We must stand firm and true. And we must never forget how easily our liberty and our country can be taken away.

TEA PARTY LEADERS

Pam Stout

I was born in 1943 in Bradford, England. My parents were forced to start working at the age of thirteen without what they considered a good education. They decided to move to the United States so that my sister and I would have better opportunities and escape the class barriers prevalent in England. In 1954, they received our visas and on June 4th we set sail for America.

I started college with the goal of becoming a teaching missionary. However, I met my husband and dropped out of school to be married. I returned to college and continued my studies in Home Economics. I completed my degree and decided to work in the social services arena. Initially, I worked with families of critically or chronically ill children. I helped them to obtain the care that their children needed. I wasn't well compensated and decided to look for a better paying position.

I was hired by a Housing Authority and became a Family Self-Sufficiency (FSS) Specialist. FSS was a program designed by Jack Kemp when he was the head of Housing and Urban Development Department. The program was charged with assisting families to become free of welfare and financially able to afford housing in the private sector. Individuals were to receive all the services needed to become self-sufficient.

Eventually, I became the Supervisor of Resident Services for the Public Housing program. It was my responsibility to oversee all social services provided to residents of public housing. I administered the FSS and Drug Elimination programs. During this time I was frustrated both by the waste of money that I saw and the lack of motivation in many residents. Procurement didn't seem to understand that it was my money they were wasting. The housing programs didn't help most residents. They accepted the assistance but suffered a diminished sense of self-worth.

TEA PARTY – THE AWAKENING

In 2001, I became ill and retired. I decided to move closer to my family and bought a house in Northern Idaho. I loved the beauty and the animals that were to become a part of my life. I was content with my life and yet I still had nagging concerns about the social programs that were costing our nation so much. I realized that these programs were reducing an individual's ability to become self-sufficient due to a lack of belief in self. We were also spending money that our nation could not afford.

I didn't act on my concerns until 2008, after several conversations with my children, especially my daughter. They agreed that we, as a nation, were heading for financial disaster. My daughter started stocking her pantry and purchasing items that would allow her to survive a future financial collapse. It was hard to ignore the failing financial security of America.

I was appalled by the first financial bailout and the election of President Obama. I had heard the spreading-the-wealth rhetoric and read about his socialistic background. I had seen the cost to Europe of all their social programs. My family and friends felt the ill effects of national health care and high taxes.

When the Tea Party movement started I was thrilled to finally be able to work towards saving our nation. I put my name on every web site that was available and decided to become an integral part of the movement. I attended two Tea Parties on April 15, 2009. Here in Sandpoint we met and organized a group that would continue the battle to return our nation to its founding principles. I was elected president and coordinated the efforts of a large group of concerned citizens.

Last September, my husband I attended the march in Washington, DC. It was one of the most moving experiences of my life. We met so many Americans that shared our concerns. They were willing to sacrifice time and money to return common sense, Judeo-Christian values and our Constitutional precepts to our nation.

Since that time I have continued to support the Tea Party movement. We have held monthly meetings and several Tea Parties. We have joined with other liberty minded organizations to educate the public on many issues.

In March I was asked to appear on the David Letterman show. It was a real thrill to be able to present my views on a liberal show. I even got a few laughs. I will continue to work to regain stability and common sense to America. We have a foundation that we need to return to. I chose to become an American and I will defend her with all my being.

Ralph Kraus

A lifelong Republican active in Republican campaigns, I became disenchanted with the GOP Party in recent years, when it seemingly turned away from conservative principles. I was particularly disenchanted with the party after the 2004 presidential election, when I noticed the face of the party became not conservatives but moderate RINOs.

The moderation of the ideals of Reagan, especially fiscal responsibility and homeland security, caused me to question where the party was headed. In early 2009, I became interested in the Tea Party movement mainly because it was anchored in traditional conservative principles. I eventually became a founding member and then the current head of the Erie County Tea Party Group, called "Patriots Unite," which has grown from 8 members to over 300 in just nine months.

The attraction of the Tea Party movement was its dedication to the Constitution and the Founding Fathers. The founders were opponents of tyranny, believers in natural law—that all human rights come from God—and that a too powerful central government was a threat to liberty. Central to the movement's belief is that our government is no longer responsive to the people and has indeed become the threat that our founders warned of. It has become the enemy of liberty.

The mission of Patriots Unite, and the overall movement, is to take our country back to its founding, starting at the local level. We are nonpartisan conservatives, who believe that both parties have failed us and that they need to be changed. We are doing this through education, local political activism, precinct organizing, recruitment, evaluation and support of like-minded candidates. We are committed to a true grassroots bottom-up movement to restore our government to "We The People," as our founders intended.

Randy McLendon

I became involved in the Tea Party movement at its very beginning, which I would pin at April 2009. Though I have been a conservative, both theologically and politically, my entire adult life, my political involvement had been limited to voting and occasionally making a political contribution and writing a letter to a congressman. However, my concern about our economy and particularly about candidate Obama caused me to pay closer attention this time around.

Once Obama was elected, it quickly became obvious he was going to be just what we feared, or worse. I think the turning point for me was when President Obama early in 2009 presented his budget which projected a $10 trillion deficit over ten years. Republicans were incensed, which provided some sense of relief that maybe things could be controlled. Well, when these incensed Republicans came up with their alternate budget which "only" had a $6 trillion deficit, that put me over the edge. I thought that we didn't have anyone in Washington really looking out for our interests, at least no one with the common sense we needed. That is when the phrase "Tea Party" began to be bandied about and I began to look for what was happening locally.

I live in a small beach town on the Gulf coast of Florida, Englewood, which is half in Sarasota County and half in Charlotte County. I Googled "Tea Party" in Englewood and found nothing—no contact information or anything going on. I decided at that point to put my name down as a contact point. I did see that in the neighboring town in Sarasota County—Venice—there was an April 15 Tea Party rally listed with a contact name of Patricia Rule and her e-mail address. I e-mailed Patricia and said that I wanted to be involved. Since I had been a pastor of a church for many years back in Georgia, I had experience in public speaking. I told her that if she could not find any well-known Venice personalities to speak I would help out to keep from having a rally with no speaker at all. Within a short time I got a call from Patricia and I became the speaker at the first Tax Day Tea Party Rally in Venice in 2009.

FYI—Patricia Rule had never done anything like this before either. She is a grandmother who was concerned about the future her grandchildren were going to have if we kept going in the financial direction we were headed. She had just "had enough" and decided she had to do something too, so she just stepped out and listed her name as a contact in Venice and decided to have a rally on the 15th.

So, Patricia, her husband Ken and I met to plan the first rally. It went well and we had over 600 people gather at the Gazebo in the park in downtown Venice. One of the attendees invited me to speak at a home meeting shortly thereafter.

Since I had put my name on several web sites as a contact point for Englewood, I began to receive an occasional phone call or e-mail. I began collecting contact information and had a few dozen names. People started asking me what we were going to do in Englewood. As we got closer to September, a few wondered if we were going to be going to the 9/12 rally in Washington. I put them in touch with some people who were planning a trip, but I couldn't go and most could not. So I decided we would invite people to my house on 9/12/09 to watch the TV coverage of the rally. We had twenty-three strangers come together for the first time. They wanted to know when we were going to meet again. We rented a room at the local sports complex on a Tuesday night in November and had eighty-eight people show up. They wanted to continue, so we met again in December (2nd Tuesday evening) and had a doctor speak about the health care issue and had 175 show up. We decided to continue meeting once a month on the 2nd Tuesday.

The purpose of the meeting was to provide a regular time and place to introduce new people to the movement and keep motivated and informed. We have grown and have new people at each meeting.

We have a web site—takingourcountryback.net—and have different committees working. We have strategy sessions, sign waving rallies, regular e-mails and whatever we can think to do to advance the cause of Taking Our Country Back.

Few people in our group have ever been involved politically and we are learning as we go along. We have people going to the 9/12 rally and the Restoring Honor rally on 8/28 in Washington. We are going to have a float in our local parade on Labor Day. We are also joining other local Tea Party groups for a large "30 Days to Freedom" rally at our local spring-training stadium on October 2.

A Couple of Seventy-Year-Olds!

It's strange how something as ordinary as reading the morning paper can be a life-changing event. That's the way it was for my husband, Claude, and me (Sunny). There it was, a full-page ad by someone who was obviously as concerned as I about the direction our great country was heading.

Claude and I both had the feeling that the progressive liberals had taken over both our national parties the last several years. We believed that America was in a politically Left spiral that was turning tighter and tighter and heading toward a disastrous implosion. Judicially, the US Constitution had been replaced mostly by case law and was held in low esteem from the Supreme Court down. The Executive Branch has been running roughshod over the other branches by the use of executive orders, which bypassed the checks and balances, and the House and Senate have both been in utter chaos. We had seen the promise of the conservative revolution of '94 fall far short of its potential.

The ad appealed to those of us willing to sacrifice an evening of TV to meet with like-minded folks on the County Courthouse steps at 6:30 p.m., on Thursday, and voice our concerns. For a small town like Aiken, SC, we were surprised to see over 150 there with us. About fifteen of us spoke from the podium and the message was universal: The government was completely out of control. It was trying to make a law out of a 2,000+ health care bill that no one had read. They had already spent over a trillion dollars on TARP and stimulus bills that they hadn't read and were promising more to come. We have to rise up and stop this nonsense.

It was announced that a bus was leaving from Columbia, SC, for Washington, DC the next evening to protest the health care bill. Six of us decided to go.   The bus left at 11 p.m. and drove all night. We got to the capital at about 9 a.m. and went straight to the Mall. There were already over 2,000 there and it wasn't starting till 1 p.m. News helicopters were overhead reporting the attendance as about 2,000. They never changed the number even though by 1 p.m. we had nearly filled two lawn sections which each hold about 40,000. We estimated there were well over 50,000 there. Typically, the AP reported "several hundred." While boisterous and loud, we were a well-behaved bunch of concerned citizens. I think we knew more about what the health care bill had in it than the average congressman. Obviously all out energy was for naught, because the bill passed and is now history.

At about 5:30 we loaded back onto the bus and rode all night back to Columbia, SC. Claude and I talked a great deal about this experience on the way back and decided that we needed to get involved on the local level. The six of us met two days later and decided to form "We the People, Aiken." Our goals were to vet candidates for local, state and national office and to monitor local issues. Of course we wanted more members, but felt that the list we had made of the people that showed up on the courthouse steps would help us grow.

First, We the People, Aiken decided to oppose a $236 million school bond issue referendum which we found out was backed by a billionaire national developer. They had the big bucks and a national organization called "Yes for Kids" pushing for passage. We had nothing but energy and the knowledge that this was going to negatively impact our community financially for years to come. Our research showed that the schools they wanted to tear down and rebuild had been rated in the 90th percentile and above by both teachers and parents the year before. The "Yes for Kids" message was that these same schools were virtually ghettos and unfit for human habitation.

With barely three weeks to go to the special election we sprung into action. We designed and printed flyers on our home computers, we wrote to the editor, we called in to radio talk shows. The Aiken Standard newspaper and the Chamber of Commerce were strongly backing the bond issue. We found out that the chamber was holding a *special meeting* to sell it to their membership the next day. Interestingly, they would not allow any opposition to the issue to be voiced. Claude and I decided to picket the meeting with handmade signs. The Chamber President asked a police lieutenant, attending the meeting, to go out and stop us from "harassing" the members. He very nicely informed us that we had every right to be there but that we didn't have a picketing permit. We volunteered to set aside the signs. He, because of department policy, had to call for backup and two squad cars showed with four officers. There we were, with little seventy-year-old blond me surrounded by four handsome young officers! Claude took pictures. This made the Augusta Chronicle, pictures and all.

We the People, Aiken was able to scrape together about $5,000 to oppose their huge, slick, multimedia campaign with full page ads, TV, very expensive slick mailers and newspaper editorials. The bond issue went down by a 71% to 29% margin. They were in shock. "Yes for Kids" had never been defeated by so large a margin.

Simultaneously with the "Vote No" campaign, Claude and I took on the job of gathering information about and inviting candidates to meet with us prior to the upcoming primary election. We also went to a Columbia Tea Party meeting to get a feel for how they were running their program. We found out about the Club for Growth and the South Carolina Club for Growth, which have a very comprehensive rating system on the conservative voting records (or lack thereof) of national and state legislators respectively. This is no easy task in South Carolina because the legislative bodies did not record their votes on bills (through new legislation sponsored by Nikki Haley and the state house now does publicly record its votes but the Senate still does not).

The SC Club for Growth rated Nikki Haley at the very top of conservative state legislators and she was one of four running for governor and the only female. She wasn't even on the radar, poll-wise, and had virtually no money. Because of her SC Club for Growth rating and the Columbia, SC Tea Party backing, we invited her to our home for a coffee and she was quick to accept. We then invited everyone we knew, handed out flyers in the neighborhood and listed it in the "Upcoming Events" in the Aiken Standard. Over forty showed up to our home and we were all blown away with Nikki's presentation. This girl had spunk and intelligence. She told us that money was a problem for her campaign and that they couldn't even afford to give away yard signs. She had just gotten the first Haley yard signs and would sell them for $5 each to help fund her campaign. We loved the idea and most bought them. Within weeks she started to rise in the polls. The Tea Party's got behind her statewide. The Aiken County Republican Party sponsored a debate between the governor candidates and we saw a phenomenon developing. When the debate was over, virtually no one went up to talk to anyone but Nikki. She had thirty people lined up to meet her and the others stood there with no one to talk to. My husband said, "Look out, something is going on here." Was he ever right—she rose in the polls to the top and then Sarah Palin endorsed her and she jumped to a twenty-point lead. She almost won the primary without a runoff, getting 49.5% of the vote. In the runoff she won with a 66% to 33% margin.

We also invited Jeff Duncan, another A+ rated, Club for Growth South Carolina State legislator and a candidate for the US House, to a coffee at about the same time. Once again we had about forty show up and once again we were blown away with his presentation, intelligence and knowledge of the issues that counted. He is the Tea Party dream candidate. His opponents were either very low on the Club for Growth scale or had no legislative experience at all. We got Foursquare behind him and became his unofficial Aiken County campaign managers. Again the Republican Party sponsored a debate for the US House candidates, all six of them. After the debate the 200 attendees voted Jeff the clear winner with 49% of the vote. The local candidate, Dr. Voshavski got 19% and the other four split the balance. Jeff came in second in the primary to Richard Cash, and we had two weeks to make up the difference. My husband put a 4' x 8' sign on a trailer with flags, etc. and towed it everywhere. Jeff and Richard Cash were about even in most of the district and Aiken had to be the place to make the difference. We put out nearly 200 yard signs but opponent's team pulled them as fast as we put them up. We refused to stoop to their level and left his alone. We organized a letter-to-the-editor campaign and swamped the paper with support for Jeff. We had a float and a truck in the Memorial Day parade with Jeff walking and shaking hands. We had him call into local talk shows and meet with small community mayors. We had home meetings. The campaign was sending out very effective mailers and doing robo calling. The results were interesting—Jeff narrowly lost in most of the district but won in Aiken County by a 70% to 30% margin and ended up winning the runoff by 51% to 49% district-wide.

Finally, we, in a brainstorming session, decided to organize a last minute debate, in Aiken, on the Sunday before the runoff election. We decided it would be an ice cream social, and we would invite *all* the runoff candidates to be in one place at one time. This had not been accomplished anywhere in the state, let alone little old Aiken. Jane Page Thompson and Claude split up the list and began inviting the candidates. We only had a week to pull this off. Right away we realized that it was Fathers Day … *oops*!

Not to worry, we'll do it anyway. Surprisingly, we were getting commitments. By Wednesday we had eight of ten agreeing to attend, including Nikki Haley, who by now was a national personality and appearing on national news almost daily. Claude invited Congressman Joe Wilson to host and moderate the event (he wasn't in a runoff) and he agreed. His son Alan Wilson was in a runoff for State Attorney General. We weren't sure we could get anyone to come out on a hot Sunday afternoon let alone Father's Day. Finally, Nikki Haley's opponent, Gresham Barrett, agreed to come and we had nine out of ten. It was a smashing success and we had over 400 attend. Everything went like clockwork. *The Republican Party leaders were shocked that this was put together in just eight days.*

The bottom line is that this all proves that even a couple of seventy year olds can, with the willingness to step up and do something rather than just wringing their hands, have a substantial effect on the outcome of our country's future. We are now the couple to go to, if you want something accomplished in Aiken County. Just last week Senator Jim DeMint's office asked us to organize a meeting for him next month. Our cell phone rings and Governor Sanford's office wants to ask us about what's going on in Aiken. That is what the Tea Party movement is all about.

After evaluating our We the People/Tea Party involvement over the last ninety days we have decided to direct our efforts through the local Republican Party but continue supporting the Tea Party wherever possible. We want to help in our small way to pull the Republican Party back to its roots and away from the progressive/liberal direction it has been taking. The party has steadily moved left, always saying we need to be closer to the center. Their philosophy is that if the party can somehow capture the independent vote by looking more like Progressive Democrats, we will win. This is totally wrong thinking. It has never worked and will never work. The left leaners always say, "We just haven't gone far enough left. If we can just become a little more like the Democrats, we will win the independent vote." We know better: the John McCain, Lindsey Graham (he is our next target) style is a loser. Americans are a right-of-center society and when given a right-wing choice they will vote Republican. History has proven this.

The last ninety days have been quite remarkable for us and the future promises more of the same. It's not only fun but quite fulfilling. Like I said, one never knows what an ordinary thing like opening the paper in the morning might bring. Who knows what the future holds for us. Whatever it is, we're ready and willing and able.

Steve Edwards

My "awakening" probably started in late summer 2007 when I became increasingly aware of disturbing news bites coming out of Washington, DC. Something was just not right. I had always been sort of lukewarm when it came to politics. As long as the politicians did their job and left me alone, I was happy. The problem was, lately, they were not leaving me alone.

I am a die-hard college football fan, University of Nebraska Cornhuskers, *Go Big Red*! Maybe it was the lackluster season they were having, though probably not, since I have watched them through thick and thin for the last forty years, but I started noticing things in the news I had never heard before. Things like "mortgage collapse," "derivatives," "bailouts," etc. I started tuning out football, a little, and watching more news programs to see how these changes may affect me. Half of the network newscasts seemed to be focused on celebrities and the latest Hollywood gossip, which I have never cared much about, so I started shopping around for news outlets that covered the stories in which I was interested.

That's when I stumbled upon Fox News channel. They seemed to give me the in-depth news coverage I craved. It wasn't long before I became aware of some of the commentators on Fox News, especially Glenn Beck. Glenn Beck was covering stories that I never heard or read in any other media. I was getting angry at my employees, the politicians, for allowing these blatant boondoggles in government and federal agencies to occur without so much as a protest from the halls of Congress. I was getting tired of throwing things at the TV about the same time that my pregnant twenty-two-year-old daughter and her husband had to move back in with us, victims of the recession.

On March 13th, 2008, Glenn Beck offered a program that promised to show me, and the thousands of others like me, a way back to the life I had known for the first sixty years of my existence. I became enamored of the 9 Principles and 12 Values he espoused on that program, and vowed, right then and there, that my daughter and granddaughter (we knew early on the baby was a girl) would have the same chances to pursue the American Dream that I had had. I didn't want my granddaughter coming to me in twenty years asking, "Grandpa, where were you when our freedoms were taken?"

I started the Yakima 912 Project that day, along with thirty-three other frustrated patriots, at the Abby's Pizza Parlor in Yakima. Various affiliations with similar groups in the Yakima area have now produced a mailing list of over 250 members, and that number is growing daily from the ridiculous abuses of power by the president, the House and the Senate, and the midterm elections loom.

Sandy Toth

I am sixty-six years old, in a wheelchair, and I started a Tea Party group because of Communism.

My grandparents came from eastern European countries, and became naturalized citizens. When I was little, we had relatives behind the Iron Curtain. I remember large duffle-bag-sized packages being sent to Hungary every year to family. We had to wash the new clothing and wrinkle everything to make it look used. Shoes had to be worn and scuffed. If it looked new, our family there would have to pay duties on the merchandise. Letters were very carefully worded to say nothing against the communists. Letters going either way were read and censored, or might never arrive at all. I remember my grandfather ranting about FDR and the betrayal at Yalta; it was something he regularly discussed.

After the Hungarian Revolution of 1956, many refugees came to our area, and we heard more about the life there: not being able to travel from one town to another without checking in with authorities in each place, mandatory ID papers, going to church was discouraged (Note: since the Iron Curtain went down, there has been a great resurgence of religion. One church in Budapest has 10,000 – 15,000 attendees every Sunday).

Fast forward many years of my life, and because I was disabled and more housebound, I started watching more news. I followed the 2008 candidates closely and Mr. Obama frightened me. I believed his political philosophy would lead toward socialism and communism. Then President Bush had TARP passed, next beginnings of the auto bailouts. All this was against the system that our country was based upon.

What finally absolutely enraged me was the stimulus bill, the American Recovery and Reinvestment Act, not only for the deficit spending, but also for the provisions in the bill mandating everyone's medical records in a federal database, comparative effectiveness research, and bureaucrats who could control our health care. I started calling senators before the final debate on the bill asking why these provisions were not covered in the debate.

When the bill passed, I started looking for ways to fight what was happening. I could see our freedoms and liberties disappearing. The radical agenda was moving more rapidly than I had anticipated. In March of 2009 I had not heard of any Tea Party movement in Columbus, and I decided to be the founder of one; I started learning how to be an organizer.

I will continue to be an activist as long as I can. We are losing more and more freedoms. Our representatives ignore us as their constituents. Deficit spending is absolutely horrendous. We the people must take our country back.

TEA PARTY – THE AWAKENING

Sandy Staats

In 2008, after my father's death, I began to study the develop-ments on national news about the upcoming election. I felt sure at that time that Barack Obama would not win the Democratic nomination, on account of his being inexperienced and with his extreme views. I was sure that Hillary would win the primaries. In 2008, I was shocked when he won the primaries. I was never that crazy about John McCain, but immediately took interest in his running mate, Sarah Palin.

I'm ashamed to say that before then, I had never voted. I regis-tered to vote as a nonpartisan voter, and began to watch Fox News, and to do extensive research on political agendas. In March of 2009, I had been excitedly watching the development of the Tea Party movement. I searched the Internet to find out if a Tax Day Tea Party was being scheduled for our area. By the end of March, nobody had stepped up yet to form a Tea Party locally. I did find a small group in Williamstown, WV, and be-gan attending meetings in March.

Then one day, on March 31, 2009, I had waited long enough, and signed up on the Tea Party Day web site to organize a local Tea Party rally. As I clicked the link, I looked at my husband and said, "I just got myself into something."

Within days, I received calls from many, many local residents offering assistance. At that time, I had just begun to realize what I had gotten myself into. With two weeks to prepare, it was sink or swim for me, as I had no idea what I was doing. On April 15th, at noon, I began to realize the scope of the task before me. It was pouring down rain and 600 residents showed up with um-brellas and chairs to see the first-ever Parkersburg, WV Tax Day Tea Party Rally. I was overwhelmed with the support.

I am not, nor have I ever been, a good public speaker. In college speech classes I earned great grades but was always petrified to speak in front of even a small audience. As I approached the stage to speak, I was half expecting to pass out. However, since our Tea Party group had been based on our beliefs in God, I believe He had a hand in everything I was doing. I made my speech, very amateurish, but without nervousness or fear. This surprised me, and I became just a little more confident each time I spoke.

After the rally was such a success, I decided to form our own group in Parkersburg. Being inexperienced, I have learned much through the past year, through trial and error. We still have monthly meetings and have had several rallies, picnics, etc. I talked to other Tea Party leaders for guidance, and have received much support locally. West Virginia Tea Parties have been given the credit for unseating the twenty-eight year incumbent, Alan Mollohan, who voted against West Virginians on many important bills. The funniest moment I can recall was when our group had a retirement party for Alan Mollohan before he lost in the primaries. I was tipped off that he was speaking at the Rotary Club at Blennerhassett Hotel. A local, blinded Vietnam veteran, David Huffman, who is an attorney, has assisted us financially.

David bought a huge cake for Mollohan's retirement. We had balloons, signs and megaphones, and rallied beside the hotel for two hours. After the crowd had left, a volunteer, Angie and I were cleaning up, when we were approached by Mr. Mollohan. He talked to us, ate a piece of cake, and I filmed the whole exchange and put it on YouTube. A week later he lost the seat!

I can never say the Tea Party has been easy. I have run into many obstacles, personality conflicts, and election woes, but it has always, and continues to be an inspiring and rewarding task. I continue to learn new things every day. I have met many wonderful people and I will *never* regret my involvement!

TEA PARTY – THE AWAKENING

Dr. Dan Eichenbaum

I believe that our country is in dire straits. In fact, we are on the edge of a financial abyss. Our federal government is controlled by an administration that believes deficits don't matter. They think that we can continue to borrow, print and spend our way to prosperity. We all know that deficits and debts do matter. We cannot continue sacrificing our children's and our grandchildren's futures by mortgaging tomorrow to pay for today.

In 1787, the founders gave us the Constitution, a document that forever changed the relationship between man and government. They believed in Natural Law—that each of us is born into freedom and that the proper role of government is to protect and secure the rights of life, liberty and property, not amend, abridge or restrict them. In addition, these rights are God-given and are not derived from any government.

Protected by these Constitutional guarantees, America became the land of opportunity for millions of legal immigrants who came because they believed that hard work and perseverance would lead to prosperity. The American Experiment, characterized by limited government and unlimited opportunity, has produced the greatest improvement in the human condition in the history of mankind. About 100 years ago, my grandparents were legal immigrants to this county. They came with nothing but the desire to live the American Dream. They enrolled in night school to learn English, went to work, and gladly became part of the great melting pot of our society, not to become hyphenated Americans, but to become just Americans. They sacrificed not only for their own future, but for their children's future, and for generations to follow.

Today, I stand for and live by the values that my parents and grandparents instilled in me as a child—always tell the truth, take responsibility for your actions, obey The Golden Rule, love God, and respect the sanctity of all life. The Ten Commandments, God's ultimate moral code, transcends any specific religion and applies to each of us. These are the very same Judeo-Christian values, the undeniable and absolute foundation of our country, that my wife Rhonda and I taught our own children to guide them toward successful lives.

The American way of life is under siege by progressive liberals who seek to replace individual rights with collective rights, property rights with so-called social justice, and American culture and history with radical multiculturalism. In the past eighteen months, we the people have begun to find our voice. Out of frustration and anger, a true grassroots movement is rising up all around our nation, growing larger and louder each day, demanding an end to business as usual and an end to the oligarchy in Washington.

After months of yelling at the TV, watching the progressive agenda ruin our country and our children's futures, the meaning of Edmund Burke's quote ("All that is necessary for evil to triumph is for good men to do nothing") had become obvious and compelling.

On April 15, 2009, my wife, daughter and I attended the Tax Day Tea Party protest in Atlanta, GA, expecting to join with only a few hundred other protesters. Instead, we became energized by over 20,000 patriots! We returned to our home in Murphy, NC, and, with a small group of local activists, founded, funded, and activated the Cherokee County 912 Project group. Membership grew to over 600 people in just a few months.

I went on to stand up for election to Congress 2010 in NC District 11 as the Tea Party candidate, finishing second in a six-man primary. So that my children and grandchildren may know freedom, I will continue to fight until the Constitution is restored as the law of the land.

TEA PARTY – THE AWAKENING

There is strength in numbers and members of the grassroots movement are mad as hell. We are not going to take it anymore, and, most importantly, we will vote.

Al Teal

When you asked me what provoked me to stand up and become a Tea Party organizer, so many reasons flood my mind but the one that broke the camel's back for me was in April 2009 when I read the DHS report on Right Wing Extremists ... how dare my government label the American citizens and veterans as potential terrorists just because the people disagree with the government on any issue, when *that is our right* to do so!

Bailouts and unread stimulus bills written by leftist organizations and forced down our throats. A bait and switch presidential campaign that took *everybody* by surprise. Well. I found a group of other Americans patriots that felt the same way and they were going to make a stand. I decided they would not stand alone. My wife Melody, our friend Becky and I piled into our little Chevrolet s10 and off we went to our first ever protest. None of us had ever done this before in our lives and we were joking about how we had to make sure we had bail money at home just in case. About forty folks showed up for that first rally and one moment that sticks out in my mind above all others was when a young teenage girl showed up with a puzzled look on her face and a two part question: "Are you allowed to do this? Isn't it against the law to protest the government?" I remember telling her *yes* we are allowed and that it is the right and the duty of every American to stand up and question their government's actions. She smiled and wandered off into the crowd. It hit me ... why does she not know this? What has happened in America?

Well, over a dozen rallies are behind us now and more are yet to come. We have rallied with the Tea Party Express twice and will do so again. Our Gadsden Flag was on the streets in the march on Washington on 9/12 and at our state capitol and in our home town. It will fly until we have *restored* the Republic and returned our government back into the confines of our Constitution. I took an oath "To preserve, protect and defend the Constitution of the United States of America against all enemies both foreign and domestic." I meant it! That makes me and all the others who stand up, Sons and Daughters of Liberty, Guardians of the Republic! Once we have restored our honor we will fade away into the background but we leave a warning behind to all tyrants: *"Nemo me impune lacesset,"* i.e. "No one will provoke me with impunity."

God bless the Constitution of The United States of America and all who defend her.

Robert Cressionnie

In 1987, some twenty-three years ago in Birmingham, Alabama, a young woman in her mid-thirties, slightly overweight and wearing glasses, appeared at my door. She explained that she was working to correct some of the wrongs in our society and government. Reflecting back on the experience, I realize now that she was well trained in the subtle tactics of playing on one's limited knowledge, ego, and human nature to ultimately extract contributions from cooperative dupes. I admit I was one—"was" being the operative term. She began by probing for hot button topics to ascertaining the level of my knowledge about current affairs. At the time, I was more concerned with working and restarting my life after a recent divorce than I was with politics and current affairs, so her task was made fairly easy. She used my limited knowledge of political affairs and a natural compassion toward others to extract twenty-five dollars, which I could ill-afford at the time, for the Rainbow Coalition. I had no idea that I was contributing money to an organization that actually promotes the leftist communitarian goals threatening the very lifestyle I was working toward.

Sometime around 1990 or 1991 I was given a copy of G. Edward Griffin's *Fearful Master*—an in-depth examination of the United Nations. Shortly after it, I acquired a copy of James Perloff's *Shadows of Power*. These two books opened the door to a world of perspective that I was unaware even existed. I was not satisfied to view these two books as conclusive and began to research and study past and current events, all the while looking for facts and perspectives unheard of in the mainstream media or public and private educational systems. I must say that my discoveries were shocking and fully supported the findings of both well researched and thoroughly documented books.

Unlearning the conditioning of a lifetime is perhaps the greatest hurdle I faced in coming to have a reasonable understanding and a realistic perspective toward the global sociopolitical system. We are taught as children even under the guise of diversity and multiculturalism to operate in a somewhat naïve micro-world, considering each interaction as a singular event with limited and finite consequences and reactions. The forces that operate in our sociopolitical system operate on a macro level far beyond the constrained view of mainstream Americans.

In the twenty years I have spent gathering information and knowledge in these areas, I have been careful to maintain a healthy level of curiosity, skepticism, and a document-it-before-you-believe-it attitude. This strategy has helped me avoid much time-wasting on tangential issues that so many are diverted into. Issues like the tax resistor movement, religious neutralism, conspiracy theories, wild speculation, secret societies, anti-Semitism, and a host of other energy- and time-wasting activities that serve to sap the energy from individuals and groups and to further obfuscate and understanding of the forces at work in this nation and the world. This wasted energy can better be spent seeking the restoration of limited constitutional government and thus an end to the unchecked corruption we see running rampant throughout our government on every level where the inherent checks and balances have been destroyed or sidestepped.

The Internet has proved to be a double-edged sword. While being a valuable tool with a huge amount of information readily available and at the same time a mire of rumor, rhetoric, urban legend, misinformation and unreliable sources that one must wade through to the reach the facts. E-mail has proven to be the same. I can't begin to count the number or urgent e-mails I've received from friends citing some catastrophe in the making only to find out after a simple search that the e-mail is a hoax or the event is long past or never took place. Like all tools, one must first learn to use it properly and safely.

In 1991 I was approached by a gentleman with the John Birch Society. I agreed to consider the organization and to evaluate the information they presented. During that research period, I was warned numerous times that the organization was everything from a subversive cult wishing to overthrow the government to an anti-Semitic and racist alternative to the Klan. I researched the history of the organization and its founder, studied their literature and articles, and visited with longtime members who gave me access to publications dating back to the '50s. For balance, I read numerous negative articles and commentary and followed up on the accusations of those articles. I could not find a single damning accusation based on fact or documentation. Most accusations were baseless and founded on the opinion of those subscribing to philosophies other than American ideals. Many accusations were found to be based on some off-handed comment or the actions of a single member. The results of my research on the John Birch Society prompted me to not only join but to lead a local chapter for many years now.

During my years as a chapter leader with the JBS I've learned that most people, while receptive to the philosophies of limited constitutional government, are too busy just trying to work, make a living, maintain a home, and care for their families and thus have little time to devote to issues for which there is no quick and easy fixes. The betrayal of Main Street America by both the Democrat and the Republican parties has further sapped the energy from us through terrible economic, domestic, and foreign policy such that most Americans don't understand exactly what's happening, don't have time to build that understanding, and certainly don't know how to fix the problems. Most have trusted their elected officials to focus on and fix those problems and ultimately have gotten the shaft in nearly every situation. One can count the legislation beneficial for working people on one hand while the subsidies for non-productivity, bailouts for too-large-to-fail corporations, foreign aid programs, unfair and damaging trade agreements, and other taxing legislation are too numerous and far reaching for most minds to grasp.

The one lesson I've taken to heart, as we all should, is that there is no quick fix to any of the issues facing this nation.

We have not gone to bed last night and awoken this morning to find all of these problems. It has been a long, slow and incremental process that has allowed the Gramscian philosophy of communitarianism to inundate our society and Keynesian economics to destroy the fiscal responsibility of our nation. It will be a long slow battle for the restoration of logic and common sense to this nation.

We as individuals have a sphere of influence, sometimes narrow and sometimes far-reaching. It is beyond practicality to know the full extent and impact that we truly have. Acceptance of that unknown and a belief in the principles of God-given rights and of limited government instituted to secure those rights has driven me for the last twenty years. I was fortunate in learning early on that extended debates with dyed-in-the-wool leftists would accomplish little other than burning up some time and energy. Over the years I have learned to bring the discussion down to the root principle and exclude the emotional rhetoric and personal attacks favored by the Left and those who simply don't know the principles upon which their argument rests, if it, in fact, rests upon any principle at all. There are many opinions that are passed off as principle when in reality they are nothing more than emotion-based desires with no real-world workable applications. It's easy to talk about, for instance, economic equality as a principle when in reality it's nothing more than a utopian desire with no possible practical application when the human element is factored in.

Shortly before the Tea Party movement came into full swing, several of us were already in the process or organizing a county level group to work for a more restrained fiscal policy in the county as well as property rights, the elimination of property tax on a primary residence, and other issues that affect the well being of individuals. Prior to the national spotlight focusing on the Tea Party movement, the apathy encountered among the public and unwillingness on the part of most to get involved in things they don't understand gave the appearance that it would be difficult to find the membership needed to have a significant impact with a county-level organization.

Mike Armstong, a good friend of mine, called together a meeting including those forming the county-level group, with the suggestion that we form a Tea Party group. There were sixteen individuals at the initial meeting; some were Republicans, some unaffiliated, and some were Democrats. Each was asked to think about forming this group and making a commitment to do their part.

At the second meeting we settled on the name—Tar River Tea Party. The Tar River flows through eastern North Carolina and ultimately empties into the Atlantic Ocean. We decided that the group should reach out to multiple counties and cities rather than localizing itself to a single town or county. At the second meeting we also established the basic principles for the organization so that it could stay on track and would be more effective in the long run. There are only a couple requirements for membership—we ask that prospective members familiarize themselves with the principles of the organization and commit to certain standards of behavior of our members.

The national Tea Party movement has formed for no single reason; there is no single motivating event that catapulted masses of people into this movement. Some were motivated by the socialistic ramblings of our current administration, some because they see the Tea Party as an alternative to the Republican and Democrat parties, and still others because they see problems in this nation that are not being addressed by the current political system. As with any movement there are those whose motivations are not consistent with the character of the movement; unfortunately, those individuals and groups should not be considered representative of the movement and yet often receive the focus of the media in what appear to be attempts to reflect isolated behavior and actions upon the entirety of the movement.

The wave of the Tea Party movement is still rising and has yet to crest. This fact is reason for many national groups including political parties to vie for control and centralization of the movement. Currently the movement is decentralized and very grassroots. One chapter can be destroyed or co-opted and the others continue on virtually unaffected. If, however, the movement is consolidated under a state-level or national-level leadership, it can be controlled or damaged in its entirety. The power of the Tea Party movement is in its uncontrollability and unpredictability. Once that is brought under control it will be rendered an impotent and mortally wounded entity that will wither into nothing more than a fund-raising do-nothing voting block that is as predictable as both the Democrat and Republican parties.

Once the Tea Party wave crests, many will assume the same apathetic attitude that a party is back in control and has our backs. This will be the wave crashing into the beach and receding back into the ocean. I shudder to think how many times I've heard the comments about our problems being solved at the next election.

I much prefer the slogan that the next election is only the beginning.

An understanding of this wave cycle and the impending crash into the sand is why I want to gather from the Tea Party movement a substantial group of those who understand or want to understand the nature of this battle. After twenty years, I'm not looking for an end to this battle; *I'm in this fight for life* and I'm finding others now stirred to action and willing to make that same commitment. So far we are off to a great start!

Robert Kilmarx

While I have always been somewhat involved in the governmental process, I was a typical American and only exercised my privilege/duty to vote at least in national elections. Then after sending these representatives to office I usually went back to my life and did not play any active role in holding these individuals accountable to me and my interests. My interest in current events was sporadic and I was not the news junkie as I am now. My life took a change on September 11, 2001. When this nation was so heinously attacked by Islamic radicals I came into awareness that this nation is in great peril. Since that infamous day I have remained fixated on news and events and my interest in government and the historical foundations of government has grown greatly.

As for my involvement in the Tea Party movement, I witnessed the birth of the movement in early 2009. My wife Tami was the first to become involved after attending the April 15th rally in Nashville where 10,000 citizens came together to protest this radical administration and its tax and spend agenda. I likewise started to become involved in late April after attending a similar rally in Jackson, TN. Tami and I both joined the local Tea Party Nation organization and began the process of networking and educating ourselves on our country's historic founding and the principals that molded our republic. The social network scene on

TPN was a great vehicle for us early on to get to know people and expand our knowledge. Tami and I used the forum and started blogging and becoming more active in the organization. This eventually led to us to become members of the advisory board as well as event organizers for the organization. As organizers we blossomed in that we found something that together we enjoyed doing and worked well as a team. We put together several great events and worked tirelessly tracking legislation, organizing protests, and working to expand the membership of TPN.

In August of 2009, we set out to create a unifying networking organization for Tea Party groups and individual concerned citizens so they can communicate and network together. We launched Tea Party Cooperative in September and set out to strengthen the movement by providing a place for Tea Party organizations to all link together and communicate and coordinate activities. We also launched a companion web site resource to provide a place to aggregate and convey information.

We organized the "Freedom Train" in September and caravanned to DC for the 9/12 March On DC. This was a profound event that had a tremendous impact on us both. So many good people of all ages amassed in DC for the largest most peaceful event I have ever bore witness to.

In October we launched the Tennessee Town Hall on our interactive web site. This was an effort to expand on the town hall meetings that were being conducted across the nation. The Town Hall was the nation's first online, ongoing, interactive town hall. Every two weeks we posted a question to the state's congressional candidates as well as gubernatorial candidates. The candidates were then able to answer the questions at their leisure and the membership of the cooperative could pose follow up questions or comments. Although fairly active at first, this initiative gradually died out during the grueling campaign season with so much being asked of the candidates.

It was around November that we reconnected with a couple of individuals who also worked with TPN and we began discussions on how to expand on some sort of unity organization for the Tea Party groups throughout Tennessee. This was to be more of a formal organization that would provide a more powerful voice for Tea Party groups across the state. And so the Tennessee Tea Party Coalition was born.

For the next couple of months we worked hard on building this coalition by contacting all of the Tea Party organizations in the state and putting together a formal structure for the group. Through an ongoing process of weekly conference calls and document sharing we drafted a formal document outlining the coalition with its purpose, vision and values, strategic objectives, platform, as well as our structure and by-laws. With that we convened the first Coalition Caucus meeting in February of 2010 with more than fifty organizers from forty-three Tea Party organizations in attendance. The caucus meeting was a daylong meeting conducted under parliamentary procedure. At the end of the grueling day we did emerge with a coalition and elected the initial steering committee.

Once again, we began to refocus our attention on yet another new endeavor. As we are both active members in our church family and devout Christians, we wanted to build a faith-based activism network. I had come to realize the core of all of the ills of our society can be traced back to the rise of progressivism and the decline in the moral fabric of the family and society. What we have today is a spiritual battle that has manifested itself in the political realm. It was about this same time that Glenn Beck did a show on the history of the Christian church and its important role in our country's founding. He mentioned how it was the colonial pastors who were instrumental in turning the war around. General Washington was suffering numerous defeats in the early days of the war for our independence when he asked an influential pastor to assist and muster the locals into a fighting

417

force. This man was John Peter Muhlenberg, and he issued the call one Sunday morning during his service and 300 members of his congregation joined the cause. These pastors became known as the Black Robe Regiment, and it is in their spirit that we formed our new initiative also called the Black Robe Regiment.
We have created both a resource/study site as well as social networks for the Black Robe Regiment and have been continuously growing this group. We have reached out to patriot pastors around the nation and they are stepping up and speaking out. We have also become very active in our local elections and have participated in numerous vetting forums and debates. This has led us to endorse several candidates for Congress, governor, as well as local leaders. Tami is currently working on a couple of campaigns in addition to her daily work as a nurse. We have also picked up the mantle of leadership for the Tennessee Tea Party as its current president and leaders have suffered stress, burnout and life's struggles. So we are rebuilding a web site and working towards organizing several great events to reinvigorate this organization.

Where this all takes us God only knows. I do know that we will never again let our guard down and neglect to hold accountable those who *we* select to represent us in office. We will continue to work on awakening the church and moving Christians to take more of an active role in the body politic and the social sphere. It is my deepest prayer that the 2010 elections will see a rebirth of conservative leadership for our nation. We must bring the limited balance of powers that the founders designed back into balance.

As for advice on how to organize and grow a group or movement I can only suggest to keep it real. Always lead with integrity and honesty and never get caught up in the power and influence that may come as your group grows. Always check back on the core reasons of why you became involved and keep that fire as your base. The main thing that I would stress is that you must allow others in and to be a part of the endeavor and always remember that we are all governed by but one leader, our Lord Jesus Christ.

May God bless you, and may God bless the Unites States of America.

Ron Parks

I have been a registered Republican my whole life; however, I had voted for more conservative Democrats in certain races, like the one Lindsey Graham was in. I was a primary voter, election year voter, off-year voter—I voted! At fifty-three years of age I have seen and lived through the Ross Perot attempt at buying the presidency. I was a Texan at the time, having been born in Dallas Texas. I watched the 1993 Republicans swarm into office with their Contract with America ... and I witnessed their ineffective results as they failed to carry through. And then, most recent was a president from Texas who was my governor, and his lame attempt at relating to American conservatives who understood, if nothing else, what it looked like when the economy was tanking; what it looked like to have an opportunity to get a real conservative into the Supreme Court; what it looked like to be bullied into believing that a near trillion-dollar bailout with non-existent monies was a good and saving thing. Then finally, to watch a little known man from nowhere get elected into the office of president with the media's power of persuasion. A man with a questionable past, who as I understand would have been unable to have garnered security clearance to have visited a number of places within the government, and now they would answer to him.

I had listened to Rush, Hannity, and Beck for a long time. They had kept me informed and focused on many issues. Beck had been stepping out there for some time leading up to and prior to the 2008 elections. His show had begun placing an urgency within me regarding our country's path. I received many e-mails from different associations where I responded with e-mails, phone calls, or faxes as urged. One of those e-mails asked if I agreed with Rick Santelli's now famous rant and if I would be willing to join forces with other like minded people to form a Tea Party in my area. Absolutely! I responded. I was tired of standing by brooding, doing nothing other than my American right of voting, which didn't seem to be getting it done. Sure, I would attend a Tea Party! I filled out the web questionaire and went on with my busy life.

Later the next week, while working at a construction site, my wife called me and said she received a call from someone who was directed to me as the leader of the Tea Party in the Charleston, SC area. She asked me if I knew what she was talking about and I responded, "I don't have a clue." Then it hit me—this must have something to do with that "thing" I signed up for!

I took her name and number and called her on my way home from work that evening. She was so excited to get my call and even more excited that there was a Tea Party in her area that she would be able to attend. She wanted more information and for me to take her name so as soon as that info became available I could contact her. I didn't want to discourage her so I more or less told her it was in the infant stages and I would keep her posted as to the progress.

It is now late February 2009, so I went online looking for other Tea Party info and perhaps others in our area who may be further ahead of me. I soon realized there were April 15th Tax Day Tea Parties being planned across the country. Wow! That didn't give a newbie much time. I soon found another guy who was waiting on a group of Young Republicans to come up with plans that he had intentions of joining. However, there were many contingencies and I realized that if decisions weren't made quickly and we didn't move out immediately, we would not be able to give this event the credibility and attention that it deserved. I told him that I was moving forward with the creation of a web site, with or without him and a few others he was talking with—time was of the essence. He called me the following day and said to count him in. At fifty-three years of age I created a web site and began organizing a Tea Party for the first time, while working a day job in High-end Residential Construction and keeping my farm and family duties up at home in Moncks Corner, South Carolina.

Within two months of planning and organizing we had close to 7,000 people attend our first Tea Party in Charleston, South Carolina on April 15, 2009. It was a beautiful thing.

Justin Holland

I was 'tea party' before the tea party movement. In my early years, my politically active Grandmother, a strict disciplinarian, instilled the values of individual freedom and responsibility, and the perils of big socialist government. After watching me spend time enthralled reading sport magazines and the sports sections of newspapers, one day she handed me a book, "The Conscience of a Conservative", by Barry Goldwater, to read. Once I read the book, my political philosophy and I how I felt about my country had taken shape.

Proud to be a Viet Nam Veteran, and when I joined the US Navy in the 1966, I took the oath to defend the Constitution ("...support and defend the Constitution of the United States against all enemies, foreign and domestic;..."). That is something that lasts a lifetime and doesn't just go away as soon as you leave the service.

As a young sailor stationed in California, I began to follow Ronald Reagan when he first ran for Governor of California. His political philosophy and view of the world fit my political leaning more than any other politician before or since. Voting for him in his first gubernatorial primary and six times subsequently (Governor twice, 1976 Republican Presidential primary, 1980 Presidential primary, and President twice), I have perhaps voted for him as much as anyone.

TEA PARTY – THE AWAKENING

After my service during the turbulent Viet Nam era, my entire career was spent in designing, researching, analyzing, developing systems intended to defend our country. From working during the Reagan era Cold War years on systems, such as non-strategic nuclear forces, for the United States to prevail and deter the Soviet threat to missile defense systems making ballistic missile threats impotent, people need to realize the fight for our country is not just about Tea Party stuff.

The whole idea that started the Tea Party movement in the first place is that we need to get the federal government back in line with what their role is: limited government (and the promotion of STATES' rights), strong national defense, fiscal responsibility... Those of us who taken the oath to defend against all enemies, foreign and domestic, have seen the usurpation of the Constitution by our leaders in federal government. We have seen over the last forty-five years the erosion of our rights and freedoms, a **gift** our founding fathers gave us -- the Constitution.

This erosion, as we know it, gained momentum during the "Great Society" and "equal rights" movement during the presidency of Lyndon Johnson. This period of time brought us much of the government-sponsored and funded medical care (Medicare, Medicaid, etc) and "equal rights" programs (EEOC, ERA, etc) that are being built upon today with a vengeance to continue our country down a fast-paced race to socialism, and then to communism/totalitarianism. I firmly believe our current federal government and its way of operating are "domestic enemies" to our historical Constitutional Republic form of government.

The country I believe in and fought for is being driven in a direction that is completely opposite. From the Health Care bill, which was imposed on the American people through dictatorial methods, to bailouts using crony capitalistic politics, to imposing on America hidden agendas, such as Cap and Trade, Financial Reform, Net Neutrality, Labor Union bailouts, we can see the government elitists and their enablers are leading America down the path of a Totalitarian society using methods every socialistic dictatorship has used in history. This is not the country I believe in and I have fought for or I want to see left for posterity. If the socialists succeed, the United States will not be the society that is the last hope for mankind. In my heart I know the vast majority of American people have these same sentiments, and it is my hope that people get involved in whatever movement - be it Tea Party or whatever - that will restore our Government back to what it should be, as embodied in the **Gift** of our Founding Fathers.

The Tea Party movement must move from being reactive to a proactive movement with a stated, coherent, well-articulated, well-thought-out vision of where we want the country to be. The Tea Party movement must devise a political process to achieve this vision, and identify those leaders who can best help achieve this vision.

In summary, it is important to realize that we did not get to where we are – a society on the fast road to socialism – overnight. This has been a cultivated effort that has been in motion for many years and has allowed the Federal Government to take a little more of our freedoms at every opportunity. The solution will not appear overnight either. However, it is imperative that all US citizens who have been instilled with values such as self-discipline and accepting responsibility for one's actions and the desire to continue to live the American way of life provided to us by our Founding Fathers MUST work together through whatever means we can to return our country's government back to one based on the US Constitution. We have to accept the responsibility to make our fellow Americans who have become complacent and content to accept continuous handouts from our Government aware of where that philosophy is leading us.

Movements, such as the Tea Party movement, must allow the education of the American voting public to be a benefit of involvement in a movement. However, the most important, immediate responsibilities of these movements are to research, vet, and recommend candidates believed to be the best candidates for their desired office. Educating the public as to the basic principles of our Government as laid out in the Constitution is a noble cause, but providing well-researched recommendations to help the public make informed decisions in electing the best candidates to return us to this way of governing is a more critical immediate goal.

Regino Valle III

I am 57 years old, married for 40 years, father of two and a grandfather of five. As a young man I joined the military and swore an oath to defend and protect our Constitution. I took the oath seriously, unlike many of our politicians. I grew up with the cold war, I never in my wildest dreams imagined having such a government as we have today. We have been asleep for too long, we must get involved in order to save our constitution, for our children and grandchildren. This is not the free America, I grew up in. Sadly, many of our younger generations, don't even realize what they have lost. I decided over a year ago, that I had to get involved. I joined the tea party group, 912ers and We Texans. My wife and I took part in the rally against the Obama healthcare bill, also a rally in Austin, Texas urging our Governor to take a stand for Texas. Prior to this I have never been politically involved, other than going to the polls on election day

Lisa Nancollas

My story actually starts in 2000. During that year, I had two near-death experiences which profoundly influenced my outlook on life, especially regarding health care!

The first experience involving health care policies, a doctor and two nationally prominent politicians, spurred my skepticism and disapproval of our government. These prominent individuals

succeeded in repeatedly getting away with blatantly and fla-
grantly unacceptable behavior. As many people say, "follow the
money. If it looks like a pig, then it is a pig. If it stinks, then it
stinks for a reason!" The behavior of these people infuriated me.
I couldn't believe they could get away with this! What is the
world coming to? Have we lost our values?

I believe in the values which my parents instilled in me: working
hard, treating people with kindness and believing in God. So
what was I supposed do? Do nothing anything about it because I
signed a confidentiality agreement?

I am not that stupid! I may not be able to talk in detail about this
scandal, but I still have the right to vote and contest laws which
strip us of our freedoms.   So, as the years went on, I became
more involved in politics. I joined my local Republican Party,
became Judge of Elections for my township and I ran for County
Commissioner. I did not win the County Commissioner race.
But I did learn a lot about local politics. It is just as repugnant as
DC politics. I wasn't going to let losing the County Commissioner race dissuade me from reaching my goal. I just had to
think outside the box.

What could I do to make me feel comfortable about the future of
the US? I didn't know it at the time, but gradually I realized
from talking to other people in my town, on the internet and
people in other states, that many people felt similar to me. Many
expressed their disappointment in our government, were
ashamed of many of their political leaders for their foul behavior
and irresponsible spending, and were disheartened to see the
United States becoming a nanny state.

 It wasn't until I watched Glenn Beck that I realized that I was
not alone, although I still did not know how to voice my concerns. I loved watching Glenn Beck; he said everything I wanted
to say. Finally, I was starting to feel vindicated. However, I still
felt that I needed to get involved, to help preserve America.

In 2000, my husband, Paul, and I took a trip to Mount Everest. This is the other near death experience involving politics and healthcare which ignited my political activism.

We went to climb to the Everest Base Camp, delivering eye medicine to the clinics in Everest. During our climb, I contracted severe gastroenteritis. This started when we were in a remote region in Sagarmatha National Park, at high altitude. I knew I needed to be evacuated from Everest. But, how was that going to happen? There was no phone and no electricity available that far up the mountain. When we initially arranged this trip, we were told that there was a remote possibility that we might never return home. Needless to say, that was on my mind as I was vomiting in front my fellow climbers! My husband and our guide tried desperately to make contact with others Sherpas below us on the mountain by radio to ask them to relay the message that they had a woman who needed to be evacuated by helicopter from the mountain as soon as possible. I saw the look on their faces. They weren't sure they would be successful contacting an evacuation helicopter pilot. Our guide sent several Sherpas down the mountain to personally relay the message in case the radio communications did not go through. Thus far, our Sherpas had been very reliable. In fact, they had been great to us, so I held out hope that I would be evacuated soon. My hope was deflated when I realized that helicopters and other planes could only fly into the Everest region in the morning, due to the fact that the airport in nearby Lukla had no radar. The chances of any helicopter arriving for me anytime soon were slim. In the meantime, there was nothing anyone could do for me except watch me vomit. The friends that I made on this trip were very comforting to me, but I saw the worry in their eyes. I was worried too. The helicopter didn't arrive until the next day, and there was no nurse, no IVs, no intubation kit and no external defibrillator on this helicopter; just my husband, me and the pilot! As we took off, the pilot turned around to my husband and said "I can't save you if you're dying, but I can take your body back to Kathmandu." I was shocked! My husband and I didn't say much on our flight to Lukla to refuel. Finally, after an hour of refueling we took off for Kathmandu where the hospital was located. Instead of landing on the hospital roof, the helicopter landed on the runway. I got out of the helicopter and collapsed onto the runway. The most embarrassing part of this was the fact that there were three men standing on the runway who watched me collapse, but they did not render any assistance. I later learned that, because of cultural mores, these men could not touch me or comfort me.

I subsequently realized that my husband had disappeared. As I was overcome with paroxysms of nausea, I didn't worry that he was gone. I continued to lie on the runway, hoping that a plane would not run me over. Thank God there were no arriving flights at this time. Eventually, my husband returned to the airport in a jeep with four armed guards. I was told that the King of Nepal had given his "OK" for my trip out of the airport and to the hospital.

After this prolonged delay, I could have been dead. Could you see liberals in the US screaming that they should be able to go straight to the hospital to receive immediate healthcare? I could not envision people having to ask Obama if they could receive healthcare. Unfortunately, however, the US is moving more in that direction. We now have many more regulations on "medically necessary" treatments than we ever had before, and our "King" Obama gets to decide your outcome just as the King of Nepal decided my outcome. The only difference is that in Nepal, I was a US citizen, so I received better treatment than the average Nepalese citizen.

I was loaded into the back of a jeep with my husband and our four armed guards. We drove off the runway and were stopped by two gunmen. After a protracted discussion, which was unintelligible to me, we were allowed to proceed. I hoped that I was finally on my way to the hospital. But no; I was taken to a clinic instead!

The clinic doctor told me that he had nothing in his clinic that could help me. He said that I needed to go to a "rich" American hospital in Nepal. At this point, I was very surprised to hear that there was an American hospital in Nepal. The doctor said that we should take a cab to the hospital, because ambulances were not safe. I did't ask what he meant by that.

At long last, I arrived at the Emergency Room of the "rich" American hospital. I could not sit or lie down because there were no beds or chairs. Instead, patients were required to stand while they were evaluated by the nurse and doctor   I didn't know what to do at this point. As a registered nurse, I immediately noticed that the nurse had blood caked in her fingernails. There must have been days of dried blood on her hands. I saw her go to the sink and wipe her hands on paper towels.   I noticed that she didn't use water. She turned to us and said in her best English, "no water".   I asked about gloves. She said "no gloves". At that point, both my husband and I wanted to get the hell out of there! And this facility was considered to be the "rich" American hospital. I was afraid to think what other hospitals were like in this country.

These and other trips I made to other countries make me thankful to live in the USA. But I am very concerned that we are rapidly moving in the direction of socialism. I don't want to live like citizens of Nepal or Austria, who are afraid of being turned into government officials if they are too outspoken.

My father, grandfather, uncles and other brave military men and women have made great sacrifices for world freedom, so it is my goal to do what I can to continue this fight at home.

Last year I attended my first 9-12 rally in Washington, DC. I met some great people from Lewistown, PA on the bus to DC. After attending this rally, my friend, Joann Tate, who was on that bus trip, called the women from Lewistown together for meeting at

Bing's Dinner. It was there, that five of us (Lisa Nancollas, Joann Tate, Damaris Reinhardt, Pauline Yoder and Marilyn Yale) first started the Mifflin County 9-12 Project. Over the past year, our group has grown to over 200 members. Our plans are to continue to make our voices heard. And we pray to God for the strength to continue the fight for democracy and self-determination.

****

Epilogue

The call for ceaseless vigilance of protecting our liberties…has been answered.

Contrary to our culture today, especially in the media, where solutions are expected to be implemented immediately, the Tea Party Movement realizes that the November 2010 election is merely a 'battle' in the revolutionary war of political reform. That the best that can be hoped for during this election is to install a 'tourniquet'.

As with the Tea Partiers of the 1770s, this movement is a life time commitment, the tipping point has been reached.

The Patriots are awake.

New Patriot Publishing will be releasing *Bill of Reform* in December, 2010.

A book that does not pit Republicans against Democrats, it exposes decades of a run-away Federal Government.

Problems, yes, however, the solutions are surprisingly refreshing and offer Patriots a clear path to restoring our former Glory!

In Liberty,

Bring Back the Glory!

Brent Morehouse

www.newpatriotpublishing.com